THE FREUD FILES

How did psychoanalysis attain its prominent cultural position? How did it eclipse rival psychologies and psychotherapies, such that it became natural to bracket Freud with Copernicus and Darwin? Why did Freud 'triumph' to such a degree that we hardly remember his rivals? This book reconstructs the early controversies around psychoanalysis, and shows that rather than demonstrating its superiority, Freud and his followers rescripted history. This legend-making was not an incidental addition to psychoanalytic theory but formed its core. Letting the primary material speak for itself, this history demonstrates the extraordinary apparatus by which this would-be science of psychoanalysis installed itself in contemporary societies. Beyond psychoanalysis, it opens up the history of the constitution of the modern psychological sciences and psychotherapies, how they furnished the ideas which we have of ourselves, and how these became solidified into indisputable 'facts'.

MIKKEL BORCH-JACOBSEN is Professor of French and Comparative Literature at the University of Washington. He is the author of highly influential books on the theory and history of psychoanalysis, and co-author of the best-selling *Le livre noir de la psychanalyse* (*The Black Book of Psychoanalysis*).

SONU SHAMDASANI is Philemon Professor of Jung History at the Centre for the History of Psychological Disciplines at University College London, and is widely regarded as the leading Jung historian at work today. His numerous books have been translated into many languages, and his most recent edited work, C. G. Jung's *The Red Book. Liber Novus* (2009), was awarded the Heritage Award from the New York Book Show for the best book in the last twenty-five years.

Books by both authors have been recipients of the Gradiva Award from the National Association for the Advancement of Psychoanalysis.

The Freud Files: An Inquiry into the History of Psychoanalysis

Mikkel Borch-Jacobsen
and
Sonu Shamdasani

CAMBRIDGE
UNIVERSITY PRESS

CAMBRIDGE UNIVERSITY PRESS
Cambridge, New York, Melbourne, Madrid, Cape Town,
Singapore, São Paulo, Delhi, Tokyo, Mexico City

Cambridge University Press
The Edinburgh Building, Cambridge CB2 8RU, UK

Published in the United States of America by Cambridge University Press, New York

www.cambridge.org
Information on this title: www.cambridge.org/9780521729789

First published 2012

Printed in the United Kingdom at the University Press, Cambridge

A catalogue record for this publication is available from the British Library

Library of Congress Cataloguing in Publication data
Borch-Jacobsen, Mikkel.
The Freud files : an inquiry into the history of psychoanalysis / Mikkel Borch-Jacobsen
and Sonu Shamdasani.
    p.   cm.
Includes bibliographical references and index.
ISBN 978-0-521-72978-9 (pbk.)
1. Psychoanalysis – History.   2. Freud, Sigmund, 1856–1939.   I. Shamdasani, Sonu,
1962–   II. Title.
BF173.B68127   2012
150.19′5209–dc23

                                                                                    2011020724

ISBN 978-0-521-50990-9 Hardback
ISBN 978-0-521-72978-9 Paperback

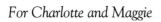
For Charlotte and Maggie

Contents

Acknowledgements

This book began in 1993 as an inquiry into Freud historians and their work. We had become aware of the upheavals that had affected Freud studies since the 1970s, which were completely transforming how one understood psychoanalysis and its origins. Intrigued by the new histories of the Freudian movement, we decided to interview the key players to gather their testimonies in a collective volume. These interviews were transcribed and annotated (we reproduce a few excerpts in the following), but the volume itself remained unfinished, for in the meantime our investigation had changed.[1] Quite quickly, it became apparent that it was not possible to situate ourselves with the neutrality and ironic detachment that we had initially adopted. The stakes were too high, and too much remained to be researched and verified before one could attempt to pass judgment on the endless controversies around psychoanalysis. Instead of describing them from the outside, we became drawn in, and here put forward our own contribution to the history of the Freudian movement.

This book is the product of this engagement, but also an attempt to regain, through historical reflection, some of the distance that we at first maintained towards our object of study. We wanted to study the history of the history of psychoanalysis and to understand better the basic issues of this fascinating and conflictual field – fascinating because of the conflict. We wanted, in the end, to draw consequences from historical criticism for the understanding of this strange movement. For any reckoning with the status of psychology, psychiatry and psychotherapy in today's societies at some point requires coming to terms with Freud and his legacy.

We would like to thank all those who accompanied us in this task and above all the historians who agreed to be interviewed. Many became friends (when they were not already) and guides in the minefields of Freud studies: Ernst Falzeder, Didier Gille, Han Israëls, Mark S. Micale, Karin Obholzer, Paul Roazen, François Roustang, Élisabeth Roudinesco, Richard Skues,

Anthony Stadlen, Isabelle Stengers, Frank J. Sulloway, Peter J. Swales. Many others deserve our gratitude for their help, hospitality, advice, support and criticisms: Vincent Barras, Bill Bynum, Henry Cohen, Frederick Crews, Todd Dufresne, Jacques Gasser, Angela Graf-Nold, Henri Grivois, Malcolm 'Mac' Macmillan, Patrick Mahony, George Makari, Michael Neve, Enrique Pardo, Eugene Taylor, Marvin W. Kranz, Fernando Vidal, Juliette Vieljeux and Tom Wallace. We also thank those in the public and private archives that we worked in for their assistance. We would like to thank Philippe Pignarre, editor and friend, for his immediate interest in the project and valuable advice during the final stages of its composition. At Cambridge University Press, we would like to thank Andy Peart for taking on the project, and Hetty Marx for her patience with the endless delays.

The French edition of this work appeared from Éditions du Seuil in 2006. This edition has been revised and rewritten. We would like to thank John Peck for his editorial suggestions and Kelly S. Walsh for providing draft translations of chapter 3, and sections of chapters 2 and 4. His work on chapter 3 was made possible by a grant from the Graduate School of the University of Washington, which is gratefully acknowledged.

Citations from Anna Freud are reproduced with the authorisation of the heirs of Anna Freud © 2000 the estate of Anna Freud, by arrangement with Mark Patterson and Associates. Translations of citations from French and German are our own. In some places, translations from the Standard Edition of Freud's works have been modified. Responsibility for views expressed here is our own.

Introduction: the past of an illusion

> The history of the World, I said already, was the Biography of Great Men.
>
> Carlyle (1959 [1841]), 251

Vienna, 1916. Freud decided to canonise himself. In front of the audience which had come to hear the eighteenth of his *Introductory Lectures on Psychoanalysis*, given at the University of Vienna, the founder of psychoanalysis undertook to indicate his place in the history of humanity.

Sigmund Freud: But in thus emphasizing the unconscious in mental life we have conjured up the most evil spirits of criticism against psycho-analysis. Do not be surprised at this, and do not suppose that the resistance to us rests only on the understandable difficulty of the unconscious or the relative inaccessibility of the experiences which provide evidence of it. Its source, I think, lies deeper. In the course of centuries the naive self-love of men has had to submit to two major blows at the hands of science. The first was when they learnt that our earth was not the center of the universe but only a tiny fragment of a cosmic system of scarcely imaginable vastness. This is associated in our minds with the name of Copernicus, though something similar had already been asserted by Alexandrian science. The second blow fell when biological research destroyed man's supposedly privileged place in creation and proved his descent from the animal kingdom and his ineradicable animal nature. This revaluation has been accomplished in our days by Darwin, Wallace and their predecessors, though not without the most violent contemporary opposition. But human megalomania will have suffered its third and most wounding blow from the psychological research of the present time which seeks to prove to the ego that it is not even master in its own house, but must be content itself with scanty information of what is going on unconsciously in its mind. We psycho-analysts were not the first and not the only ones to utter this call to introspection; but it seems to be our fate to give it its most forcible expression and to support it with empirical material which affects every individual. Hence arises the general revolt against our science, the disregard of all considerations of academic civility and the releasing of the opposition from every restraint of impartial logic.[1]

Copernicus, Darwin, Freud: this genealogy of the de-centred man of modernity is by now so familiar to us that we no longer note its profoundly arbitrary character. This is not because one should necessarily be offended by the evident immodesty of the historical tableau presented by Freud. After all, Kant was not especially humble when he spoke of effecting a 'Copernican revolution' in philosophy,[2] and Darwin did not hesitate to predict that his theory would provoke a 'considerable revolution'[3] in natural history. As Bernard I. Cohen and Roy Porter[4] have shown, the motif of the 'revolutions' effected by Copernicus, Galileo and Newton is a commonplace in the history of science since Fontenelle and the encyclopédistes, and Freud was certainly not the first, nor will he be the last, to recycle it to his advantage. However, he was by no means the only figure in psychology to do this, which immediately relativises his version of the evolution of the sciences. At the end of the nineteenth century, there was a veritable plethora of candidates vying for the title of the Darwin, Galileo or Newton of psychology. But how did Freud's audience, and indeed so many others, come to believe in Freud's entitlement, rather than that of one of his rivals?

Waiting for Darwin

According to Freud, the originality of psychoanalysis lay in the fact that it had accomplished in psychology the same type of scientific revolution which Copernicus and Darwin had effected in cosmology and biology. However, this ambition was one shared by many psychologists at the end of the nineteenth century, from Wundt to Brentano, from Ebbinghaus to William James.

> **Franz Brentano:** We must strive to achieve here what mathematics, physics, chemistry and physiology have already accomplished ... a nucleus of generally recognized truth to which, through the combined efforts of many forces, new crystals will adhere on all sides. In place of *psychologies* we must seek to create a *psychology*.[5]

From all sides, it was maintained that psychology had to separate itself from theology, philosophy, literature and other disciplines to take its rightful place in the orchestra of the sciences. Armchair speculation would give way to the rigours of the laboratory. When the Swiss psychologist Théodore Flournoy obtained his chair in psychology, he insisted that it be placed in the faculty of sciences.

> **Théodore Flournoy:** In placing this chair in the faculty of sciences, rather than in that of letters where all the courses of philosophy are found, the Genevan government has implicitly recognized (perhaps without knowing it) the existence of psychology as a particular science, independent of all philosophical systems, with the same claims as physics, botany, astronomy ... As for knowing up to what point contemporary psychology does justice to this declaration of the majority, and has truly succeeded in freeing itself from all metaphysical tutelage of any colour, that is another question. For here not less than elsewhere the idea should not be confounded with reality.[6]

Taken together, Brentano's imperative and Flournoy's reservations depict the 'will to science' (Isabelle Stengers)[7] which historically presided over the setting up of the new discipline. 'Scientific' psychology didn't emerge as the fruit of a lucky discovery, a fortuitous invention, or by some ill-defined process of natural development. It was *desired* by its various promoters, and imagined on the model of the natural sciences. It was envisaged that psychology would complete the scientific revolution through applying the scientific method to all aspects of human life. Until then, knowledge of Man had been scattered between the stories of myth and religion, the speculations of philosophy, the maxims of morality, and the intuitions of art and literature. Psychology would replace these incomplete and partial knowledges by a true science of Man, with laws as universal as physics and methods as certain as those of chemistry.

> **Freud:** The intellect and mind are objects for scientific research in exactly the same way as any non-human things. Psycho-analysis has a special right to speak for the scientific *Weltanschauung* at this point … Its special contribution to science lies precisely in having extended research to the mental field. And, incidentally, without such a psychology science would be very incomplete.[8]

From the very beginning, the 'new psychology' presented itself as an 'imitation' of the natural sciences (a sort of scientific version of the 'imitation of the Ancients'). The philosopher Alasdair McIntyre remarked, 'pre-Newtonian physicists had … the advantage over contemporary experimental psychologists that they did not know that they were waiting for Newton'.[9] By contrast, the new self-styled psychologists inevitably *simulated* the science to come. The most perspicacious asked whether psychology would ever obtain the heights of its models.

> **William James to James Sully, 8 July 1890:** It seems to me that psychology is like physics before Galileo's time – not a single elementary law yet caught glimpse of. A great chance for some future psychologue to make a name greater than Newton's; but who then will read the books of this generation? Not many I trow.[10]
>
> **James, 1890:** When, then, we talk of 'psychology as a natural science' we must not assume that means a sort of psychology that stands at last on a solid ground … it is indeed strange to hear people talk

triumphantly of 'the New Psychology' and write 'Histories of Psychology', when into the real elements and forces which the word covers not the first glimpse of clear insight exists . . . This is no science, it is only the hope of science . . . But at present psychology is in the condition of physics before Galileo and the laws of motion, of chemistry before Lavoisier and the notion that mass is preserved in all reactions. The Galileo and the Lavoisier of psychology will be famous men indeed when they come, as come they some day surely will.[11]

For James, psychology was only the 'hope of a science', the preparatory work for its Galileo and Newton, who were yet to come. The Berlin psychologist William Stern was of a similar view. In 1900, in an article to salute the new century, he drew up a largely negative balance sheet of the new discipline. One was far from the unity sought by figures such as Brentano. Aside from an empirical tendency and the use of experimental methods, he saw little in the way of common features. There were many laboratories with researchers working on special problems, together with many textbooks, but they were all characterised by a pervasive particularism. The psychological map of the day, Stern wrote, was as colourful and chequered as that of Germany in the epoch of small states.

> **William Stern:** [Psychologists] often speak different languages, and the portraits that they draw up of the psyche are painted with so many different colours and with so many differently accented special strokes that it often becomes difficult to recognize the identity of the represented object . . . In short: there are many new psychologies, but not yet the new psychology.[12]

Already by the turn of the century, there was little consensus in psychology. Thus, for psychologists, the task became one not only of distinguishing the new psychology from what had gone before, but of forwarding their own claims to form the one scientific psychology, over that of their colleagues. Rhetorical analogies to scientific heroes readily lent themselves to such a situation. A number of figures suggested candidates for the role of the new Galileo or Newton of psychology. Théodore Flournoy placed the laurel on Frederic Myers, one of the founders of psychical research.

> **Flournoy:** Nothing permits one to foresee the end that the future reserves to the spiritist doctrine of Myers. If future discoveries will come to confirm his thesis of the empirically verified intervention of the discarnate in the physical or psychological frame of our phenomenal world, then his name will be inscribed in the golden book of the great initiators, and join those of Copernicus and Darwin; he will complete the triad of geniuses having most profoundly revolutionized scientific thought in the cosmological, biological, psychological order.[13]

For Flournoy, who had by then read and reviewed Freud's *Interpretation of Dreams*, the founding genius of psychology wasn't Freud, but Myers. Likewise, Stanley Hall stated in 1909 that 'the present psychological situation calls out for a new Darwin of the mind'.[14] In 1912, Arnold Gesell proclaimed it was Hall himself who was the 'Darwin of psychology'.[15] Hall later recalled that this 'gave me more inner satisfaction than any compliment ever paid me by the most perfervid friend'.[16] Others nominated Freud.

> **C. G. Jung:** Freud could be refuted only by one who has made repeated use of the psychoanalytic method and who really investigates as Freud does ... He who does not or cannot do this should not pronounce judgment on Freud, else he acts like those notorious men of science who disdained to look through Galileo's telescope.[17]

> **Eugen Bleuler to Freud, 19 October 1910:** One compares [your work] with that of Darwin, Copernicus and Semmelweis. I believe too that for psychology your discoveries are equally fundamental as the theories of those men are for other branches of science, no matter whether or not one evaluates the advancements in psychology as highly as those in other sciences.[18]

> **David Eder:** The work of Freud in psychology has been compared by one of his disciples to that of Darwin in psychology.[19]

The disciple in question was Ernest Jones, who flattered himself with having been the first to have accorded Freud the title of 'Darwin of the mind' in his *Papers on Psycho-Analysis* of 1913.[20] In 1918, in the course of a debate with the psychologists William Rivers and Maurice Nicoll, the latter representing Jung, Jones expanded upon this analogy.

> **Ernest Jones:** The contrast between this [Jung's] view and Freud's is just the same as that between the positions adopted by Drummond and Wallace, on the one hand, and Darwin and Huxley on the other, regarding the origin of the mind and soul – a matter which in the scientific world was decided half a century ago.[21]

> **Frank J. Sulloway:** Jones saw himself in relation to Freud as T. H. Huxley – 'Darwin's bulldog' – had stood to the embattled Darwin a half century earlier.[22]

Thus one sees that the question of who posterity would view as being the founding genius of psychology was hotly debated at precisely the same time when Freud nominated himself. This self-canonisation, which has been taken as self-evident, immediately loses its authority, and appears for what it was: a peremptory attempt by Freud and his followers to act as if posterity had already unilaterally settled the debates between psychoanalysis and other psychologies in their favour, and discarded any other claimants to this position. Some figures vigorously protested.

> **William McDougall:** The only authority we have for accepting this [the theory of the social bond presented by Freud in his *Group Psychology*] as the necessary and sole permissible line of speculation, for regarding our explanation of social phenomena as necessarily confined within the limits of the sexual libido, is the authority of Professor Freud and his devoted disciples. I, for one, shall continue to try to avoid the spell of the primal horde-father and to use what intellect I have, untrammelled by arbitrary limitations.[23]

> **Alfred Hoche:** To top it all, the [Freudians'] dogmatic arrogance leads them to compare Freud's role with the historical position of Kepler, Copernicus and Semmelweis, and are compelled, according to a comical reasoning, to find the proof in the fact that they all had to battle the resistance of their contemporaries.[24]

Wilhelm Weygandt: Freud's teaching has been compared with the puerperal fever theory of Semmelweiss, which was initially ridiculed and then brilliantly recognised. If we certainly also revolt against this, it would still be cruel to compare Freud with Hahnemann, the founder of homeopathy. It is perhaps closer to think of Franz Joseph Gall, whose theories, despite some striking points of view and findings, fell into rejection immediately due to their uncritical exaggeration and utilisation, including good and bad components.[25]

Freud: I was either compared to Columbus, Darwin and Kepler, or abused as a general paralytic.[26]

Adolf Wohlgemuth: Freud–Darwin! You may as well couple the name of Mr. Potts, of the *Eatonswill Gazette*, with that of Shakespeare or Goethe ... Both Copernicus' and Darwin's work was violently attacked and herein may be some resemblance to Freud's, but yet what a sea of difference! Who were the attackers of Copernicus and Darwin? The Church, whose vested interests were endangered. Astronomers, as far as they dared in those dark days and were not Church dignitaries, or teachers at clerical universities, received the work of Copernicus and his successors with admiration. Biologists and geologists were almost unanimously enthusiastic about Darwin's work. The chief objectors ... to Freud's theories, I say, are psychologists *vom Fach* [professional psychologists], that is exactly those people who stand to Freud's work in the same relation as the astronomers to Copernicus, and the biologists and geologists to Darwin's work, and who hailed it with joy and admiration.[27]

So why should we have faith in Freud, rather than in his rivals? Because Freud 'triumphed' to such a degree that we hardly remember names such as Stern, Flournoy, Hall, Myers or McDougall? Because the 'scientific revolution' effected by this new Copernicus banished them to the realms of pseudo-science? This would be to invoke precisely what one is attempting to explain. This would amount to begging the question, conceding everything to the 'victor', whereas we would like to know precisely how he won and why. Was it because Freud's competitors were finally forced to concede defeat? Because a consensus emerged around his theories, despite the 'violent oppositions' and the 'resistance to psychoanalysis' that he alleged? Or was it, quite simply, because he managed to make everyone forget the controversy itself, and even the existence of many of his rivals?

> **Freud:** Neither speculative philosophy, nor descriptive psychology, nor what is called experimental psychology . . . as they are taught in our Universities, is in a position to tell you anything serviceable of the relation between the body and the mind or to provide you with the key to an understanding of possible disturbances of the mental functions.[28]

> **Freud:** The theory of psychic life could not be developed, because it was inhibited by a single essential misunderstanding. What does it comprise to-day, as it is taught at college? Apart from those valuable discoveries in the physiology of the senses, a number of classifications and definitions of our mental processes which, thanks to linguistic usage, have become the common property of every educated person. That is clearly not enough to give a view of our psychic life.[29]

'Make the past into a tabula rasa', chanted the French revolutionaries. It is in the nature of revolutions to do away with opponents, whether it be with the swipe of the guillotine or with epistemic breaks, and to rewrite history from the moment of 'year 1' of the new scientific or political order. Freud's parable of the 'three blows' provides a marvellous illustration of this purging of history, right down to its transcription. Indeed, this edifying story has its own interesting genealogy, which is passed over in silence by Freud. As Paul-Laurent Assoun has shown in his *Introduction to Freudian Epistemology*,[30] before being taken up by psychologists, the comparison of humiliations produced by the Copernican and Darwinian revolutions comes from the well-known Darwinian propagandist Ernst Haeckel, who popularised it in several of his works.

> **Ernst Haeckel:** The two great fundamental errors are asserted in [the Mosaic hypothesis of creation], namely, first, the *geocentric* error that the earth is the fixed central point of the whole universe, round which the sun, moon, and stars move; and secondly the *anthropocentric* error, that man is the premeditated aim of the creation of the earth, for whose

service alone the rest of nature is said to have been created. The former of these errors was demolished by Copernicus' System of the Universe in the beginning of the 16th century, the latter by Lamarck's Doctrine of Descent in the beginning of the 19th century.[31]

Haeckel: Just as the *geocentric conception* of the universe – namely, the false opinion that the earth was the centre of the universe, and that all its other portions revolved around the earth – was overthrown by the system of the universe established by Copernicus and his followers, so the *anthropocentric conception* of the universe – the vain delusion that Man is the centre of terrestrial nature, and that its whole aim is merely to serve him – is overthrown by the application (attempted long since by Lamarck) of the theory of descent to Man.[32]

Haeckel: In the same way that Copernicus (1543) gave the mortal blow to the geocentric dogma founded on the Bible, Darwin (1859) did the same to the anthropocentric dogma intimately connected to the first.[33]

This 'genealogical schema' (Assoun) appears to have circulated freely in scientific circles, to the point where it was taken up without attribution by Thomas Huxley,[34] and by the physiologist Emil Du Bois-Reymond in a talk given in 1883 under the title 'Darwin and Copernicus'. This talk caused a sensation, and immediately made Du Bois-Reymond one of the favourite targets of the anti-Darwinians.

Emil Du Bois-Reymond: Hardly had I been presented by Haeckel as an adversary of Darwin, I suddenly passed in the eyes of the reactionary organs and the clerics as the most distinguished defender in Germany of the Darwinian doctrine and they formed a circle around me to throw at me rantings full of furious hatred.[35]

Haeckel did not appreciate his position being usurped in such a manner.

Haeckel: Fifteen years ago I myself developed the comparison of Darwin and Copernicus, and showed the merit of these two heroes who had destroyed anthropocentricism and geocentrism, in my lecture, *Über die Entstehung und den Stammbaum des Menschengeschlechts* [On the development and family tree of the human race].[36]

Haeckel: Darwin became the Copernicus of the organic world, just as I had already expressed in 1868, and as E. Du Bois-Reymond did fifteen years later, repeating my statement.[37]

Seeing Haeckel's sensitivity to questions of intellectual priority, it is not difficult to imagine what would have been his response to Freud's lecture. The latter did not content himself, like Huxley or Du Bois-Reymond, with comparing Darwin to Copernicus. He took over the reasoning and even the terms of Haeckel, simply adding a third stage, which Flournoy had already done before him: after the critique of geocentrism, of anthropocentrism, that of egocentrism – with no mention of Haeckel or Flournoy, both of whom he read. Even within psychoanalysis, some were struck by the audacity of Freud's claims.

Karl Abraham to Freud, 18 March 1917: The other paper, which you sent me in proof ['A difficulty in the path of psycho-analysis' in which Freud took up the theme of the three blows] gave me special pleasure, not only because of its train of thought but particularly as a personal document . . . Judging from the most recent paper, you might after all be tempted to come to this furthest north-eastern corner of Germany, if I tell you that your colleague Copernicus lived in Allenstein for many years.[38]

Freud to Abraham, 25 March 1917: You are right to point out that the enumeration in my last paper is bound to create the impression that I claim my place alongside Copernicus and Darwin. However, I did not want to relinquish an interesting idea just because of that semblance, and therefore at any rate put Schopenhauer in the foreground.[39]

Here we see a commonplace presented as an 'interesting idea' which had simply occurred to Freud, who elides the history of this analogy. The manner in which these debates have been forgotten, leaving Freud as the sole claimant to the prize, is emblematic of the effects of the Freudian legend.

The Lancet, 11 June 1938: His [Freud's] teachings have in their time aroused controversy more acute and antagonism more bitter than any since the days of Darwin. Now, in his old age, there are few psychologists of any school who do not admit their debt to him. Some of the conceptions he formulated clearly for the first time have crept into current philosophy against the stream of wilful incredulity which he himself recognised as man's natural reaction to unbearable truth.[40]

Stephen Jay Gould: [A]s Freud observed, our relationship with science must be paradoxical because we are forced to pay an almost intolerable price for each major gain in knowledge and power – the psychological cost of progressive dethronement from the center of things, and increasing marginality in an uncaring universe. Thus physics and astronomy relegated our world to a corner of the cosmos, and biology shifted our status from a simulacrum of God to a naked, upright ape.[41]

'The powerful, ineradicable Freud legend'[42]

The fable of the three blows provides a good example of what the historians Henri Ellenberger and Frank Sulloway have called 'the Freudian legend'. One sees here nearly all of the key elements of the master narrative woven by Freud and his followers: the peremptory declaration of the revolutionary and epochal character of psychoanalysis, the description of the ferocious hostility and irrational 'resistances' which it gave rise to, the insistence on the 'moral courage'[43] which was required to overcome them, the obliteration of rival theories, relegated to a prehistory of the psychoanalytic science, and a lack of acknowledgement of debts and borrowings.

Legenda is a story meant to be repeated mechanically, almost unknowingly, like the lives of the saints that were daily recited at matins in the convents of the Middle Ages. Just as the removal of these *legendae* from history facilitated their vast transcultural diffusion, so the legendary de-historicisation of psychoanalysis has allowed it to adapt to all sorts of contexts which on the face of it ought to have been inhospitable to it, and to constantly reinvent itself in a brand-new guise.

Each has his own version of the legend – positivist, existentialist, hermeneutic, Freudo-Marxist, narrativist, cognitivist, structuralist, deconstructivist and now even neuroscientific. These versions are as different as can be, but they have this in common: they all celebrate the exceptionalism of psychoanalysis, removed from context, history and verification. The longevity of psychoanalysis is not incidentally bound up with the manner in which the Freud legend continues to expand and adapt itself to changing intellectual and cultural milieux. In this sense, it is not simply a question of reducing the Freud legend to a fixed narrative, which would simply require a point-by-point refutation, as Sulloway attempted.[44] Rather, the legend has an open structure, capable at any moment of integrating new elements and discarding others whilst maintaining its underlying form, which remains recognisable. The elements can change, particular theories or conceptions of Freud can be abandoned or remodelled to the point where they become completely unrecognisable, but the legend survives.

> **James Strachey:** Though it may flatter our vanity to declare that Freud was a human being of a kind like our own, that satisfaction can easily be carried too far. There must have been something very extraordinary in the man who was the first able to recognize a whole field of mental facts which had hitherto been excluded from normal consciousness, the man who first interpreted dreams, who first accepted the facts of infantile sexuality, who first made the distinction between the primary and secondary processes of thinking – the man who first made the unconscious mind real to us.[45]

> **Strachey:** [Freud's self-analysis,] like Galileo's telescope, opened the way to a new chapter in human knowledge.[46]

> **Jones:** Future generations of psychologists will assuredly wish to know what manner of man it was who, after two thousand of years of vain endeavour had gone by, succeeded in fulfilling the Delphic injunction: know thyself . . . Few, if any, have been able to go as far as he did on the path of self-knowledge and self-mastery – even with the aid of the pioneer torch he provided with his methods and previous exploration,

and even with the invaluable assistance of years of daily personal work with expert mentors. How one man alone could have broken all this new ground, and overcome all difficulties unaided, must ever remain a cause for wonder. It was the nearest to a miracle that human means can compass, one that surely surpasses even the loftiest intellectual achievements in mathematics and pure science. Copernicus and Darwin dared much in facing the unwelcome truths of outer reality, but to face those of inner reality costs something that only the rarest of mortals would unaided be able to give ... It would not be a great exaggeration if we summed up in one phrase Freud's contribution to knowledge: he discovered the Unconscious.[47]

Joseph Schwartz: [The development of the analytic hour by Breuer and Freud was] analogous to Galileo's use of the telescope to explore previously unknown structures in the night sky. Freud and Breuer were the first to permit the human subject to speak for him/herself ... For the first time, a space had been created where the meanings of subjective experience could be purposefully sought until they were found.[48]

Ilse Grubrich-Simitis: It can be asserted with some justification that the book [Breuer and Freud's *Studies on Hysteria*] so to speak ushered in the century of psychotherapy.[49]

Jacques Lacan: I have come here [in Vienna] – not unfittingly, I think – to evoke the fact that this chosen city will remain, this time forever more, associated with a revolution in knowledge of Copernican proportions. I am referring to the fact that Vienna is the eternal site of Freud's discovery and that, owing to this discovery, the veritable center of human beings is no longer at the place ascribed to it by an entire humanist tradition.[50]

Lacan: Indeed, Freud himself compared his discovery to the so-called Copernican revolution, emphasizing that what was at stake was once again the place man assigns himself at the center of a universe. Is the place that I occupy as subject of the signifier concentric or eccentric in relation to the place I occupy as subject of the signified? That is the question.[51]

Paul Ricoeur: In an essay written in 1917 Freud speaks of psychoanalysis as a wound and humiliation to narcissism analogous to the discoveries of Copernicus and Darwin when in their own way they decentered the world and life with respect to the claims of consciousness. Psychoanalysis decenters in the same way the constitution of the world of fantasy with respect to consciousness.[52]

Thomas S. Kuhn: In the nineteenth century, Darwin's theory of evolution raised similar extrascientific questions. In our own century, Einstein's relativity theories and Freud's psychoanalytic theories provide centers for controversies from which may emerge further radical reorientations of western thought. Freud himself emphasised the parallel effects of Copernicus' discovery that the earth was merely a planet and his own discovery that the unconscious controlled much of human behaviour ... we are the intellectual heirs of men like Copernicus and Darwin. Our fundamental thought processes have been reshaped by them, just as the thought of our children will have been reshaped by the work of Einstein and Freud.[53]

That even a philosopher of science of the caliber of Kuhn repeats the Freud–Copernicus comparison illustrates the extraordinary cultural success of the Freudian legend – in other words, of psychoanalysis itself. Psychoanalysis attempted to impose itself in the twentieth century as *the* only psychological theory worthy of the name and *the* only psychotherapy capable of theorising its own practice. In many circles, calling into question the existence of the unconscious, the Oedipus complex or infantile sexuality could provoke the same response as to creationists or members of the Flat Earth Society. In such locations, psychoanalysis became indisputable and incontrovertible. It was 'blackboxed', to use the language of sociologists of science, that is to say, it was accepted as a given that it would be simply futile to question.[54] The Freud legend and its acceptance are the expression of this successful blackboxing, of this supposed victory of psychoanalysis over rival theories. Better still, they are this blackboxing itself, which protects the contents of the black box from inquiry. Indeed, why would one want to reopen it? Why would one want, for example, to stir up the old controversies that accompanied the elaboration of Freudian theory, when everyone knows it triumphed once and for all over the 'resistances to psychoanalysis', just as Copernicus and Darwin won out over the irrational prejudices that prevented man from seeing the truth?

Harold P. Blum and Bernard L. Pacella: At this time, Freud's initial propositions, first findings and landmark case reports are no longer vital for the validation of psychoanalytic formulation . . . Freud is part of our culture, our way of comprehending personality development and disorder. All rational psychotherapy is based upon psychoanalytic principles. Psychoanalysis provides a fundamental mode of exploring and understanding art and literature, biography and history, etc. Concepts of repression, regression, denial, projection, and 'Freudian slip' have become part of our language.[55]

Opening the black box

The success of the theory is explained by its truth, and its truth in turn is legitimated by its success. What we have here is an example of what the sociologist of science David Bloor[56] calls an 'asymmetrical' explanation, that is, one that argues from the victory in a scientific controversy to beat the vanquished hollow and refuses to listen to their arguments. Who would give a 'symmetric' attention to points of view which have already been condemned by the tribunal of history?

It is precisely this which historians, critics and scholars of psycho-analysis have been attempting for several decades now. They have been reopening the black box of psychoanalysis, and have attempted to understand *how* psychoanalysis triumphed over its adversaries, *how* for many it succeeded in establishing itself as the science of the psyche, without awarding the title in advance. Despite decades of relativising and contextual studies, the history of science today still continues to be dominated by the study of the prestigious hard sciences, which have comparatively secure societal positions. The contestations of psychoanalysis provide a unique window onto how certain ideas about the mind and human relations came to be regarded as established knowledge, and formed the received ideas of several generations.

Good historical practice is characterised by close attention to contexts, the eschewal of hindsight and all forms of presentism. In this regard, contemporary historians are necessarily in conflict with 'Whig history', that is to say, history written from the perspective of the victor. This is particularly critical in the history of science, where there is always a strong temptation to read the past from the perspective of the current state of scientific research, conceived as the progressive unveiling of an essentially atemporal truth of nature. For quite a while, the history of science was written by scientists, with all the partiality which this supposes, or by philosophers attempting to award retrospectively the title of scientificity to the victors. Thus it is essential that historians resist this epistemocentrism to be able finally to speak *historically* of the sciences, at the risk of colliding with the certitudes of scientists themselves, or rather, with scientism. From this perspective, Bloor's 'principle of symmetry' is nothing but the application to the sciences of a methodological principle which is common in good historical practice.[57]

One finds the same problem and the same evolution in the history of psychoanalysis. This was started by Freud himself in 1914, in the heat of the dissensions and controversies which threatened to shipwreck the movement, and with obvious polemical intent. It was subsequently taken up by followers and fellow travellers such as Fritz Wittels, Siegfried Bernfeld, Ernest Jones, Marthe Robert, Max Schur, Ola Anderson and, closer to us, figures such as Peter Gay, Élisabeth Roudinesco and Joseph Schwartz. Whatever the respective merits and the sometimes considerable erudition of their works, it is not unfair to remark that their historiography remains profoundly Freudian, and does not put into question the general schema of the narrative proposed by the founder, even when their research forces them to abandon or revise this or that element of the legend. Even though these revisions have accumulated over the course of the years, they have too often been treated as simple retouchings of detail which do not modify the basic legend, and not as invitations to reconsider Freudian theory. On the contrary, the validity of the latter continues to be presupposed, even when it is contradicted by history. Thus one had to wait for historians who were independent of psychoanalytic institutions for Freudian theory to be envisaged for the first time as a problematic construction, in need of explication, rather than an intangible a priori.

Admittedly, the Freudian legend had been criticised before, sometimes ferociously. Freud's adversaries at the time did not fail to stress the inaccuracy and tendentiousness of his historical self-presentations,[58] and there were a number of alternative histories of psychology and psychotherapy, such as Pierre Janet's admirable three-volume *Psychological Medications*.[59] But such rival versions by psychologists in their turn defended particular theoretical positions, and, at the end of the day, were no less partisan and asymmetric than Freud's.[60] Only historians not party to a particular psychological school could attempt to give non-partisan accounts of these controversies, without prejudging the results and the respective validity of the theories in question.

The first who set out to correct this situation was the historian of dynamic psychiatry Henri Ellenberger.

Henri Ellenberger: In Switzerland I knew two pioneers of psychoanalysis: the clergyman Oskar Pfister, a long-time friend of Freud, and Alphonse Maeder, who had been closely linked to the history of psychoanalysis. Both of these men told me of many events that they had either fathered or witnessed. Later, when Ernest Jones published his official biography of Freud, I was struck by the disparity with the two pioneers' accounts ... In the second volume of his biography, there is a famous chapter enumerating the so-called persecutions that befell certain psychoanalysts. I drew up a list of the incidents, and checked each one of them with primary sources. Among the cases on which I was able to gather dependable information, I found 80 percent of Jones' facts to be either completely false or greatly exaggerated.[61]

Instructed by this episode, Ellenberger realised that Jones' biography was not an isolated occurrence, and that it illustrated, in a much more general fashion, the striking absence of a history of psychiatry worthy of the name. Written by the protagonists themselves, the history of psychiatry was often only a string of personal anecdotes and partisan rumours designed to promote this school or that theory. (Ellenberger gave the example of the legend constructed around Pinel by his disciples and elevated to the rank of the founding narrative of psychiatry.[62])

To remedy this situation, Ellenberger followed several simple methodological rules which he enumerated at the beginning of his monumental work of 1970, *The Discovery of the Unconscious. The History and Evolution of Dynamic Psychiatry*. On the one hand, never take anything as given; verify everything (even if Rorschach's sister swears that his eyes are blue, ask for his passport). Always use original documents and, whenever possible, first-hand witnesses; read texts in their original language; identify the patients in this observation or that case history; establish the facts through mercilessly separating them from interpretations, rumours and legends; on the other hand, resist the theoreticism and spontaneous iatrocentrism of psychiatrists by replacing their theories in their multiple biographical, professional, intellectual, economic, social and political contexts, and by taking account of the role played in their elaboration by the patients themselves.[63]

From this perspective, demythologising critique, which is the aspect which one most often recalls of Ellenberger's work, cannot be separated from the symmetrical gesture of contextualisation, insofar as it is the nature of psychiatric legends to efface historical contexts. In his unpublished notes on the problem of psychiatric legends, Ellenberger repeatedly stressed the link between these two aspects of his work.

> **Ellenberger:** The legend becomes the property of a closed group, of a school, a family (Nietzsche), of a corporation and a family (Pinel). A closed school (cf. the Epicurians). Continual selection of documents: destruction, guarding, diffusion. Role of publishers, editors, readers.

Later, relative deformations, through the change of perspective, through the disappearance of the context, which render the works of the author unintelligible.[64]

Ellenberger noted that the Freudian legend, which is clearly the major target of *The Discovery of the Unconscious*, essentially turns around two themes: that of the *solitary* hero surmounting the obstacles placed across his route by malicious adversaries and that of the absolute *originality* of the founder – two ways of negating the friendships, the networks, influences, legacies, readings and intellectual debts – in short, everything which would link Freud to his historical epoch. Ellenberger's book, with its 932 pages and 2,611 footnotes, is by itself a striking demonstration of the absurdity of this presentation of psychoanalysis. Ellenberger unearthed a century and a half of researches conducted by hundreds of magnetisers, hypnotisers, philosophers, novelists, psychologists and psychiatrists, without which psychoanalysis would have been unthinkable. And for good measure, he flanked his chapter on Freud by three others dedicated to his great rivals, Janet (placed first), Jung and Adler, so as to stress that this history of dynamic psychiatry neither commenced nor terminated with psychoanalysis, contrary to what the contemporaneous teleologically inclined histories of Gregory Zilboorg, Dieter Wyss or Ilza Veith contended.[65]

> **Ellenberger:** The current legend . . . attributes to Freud much of what belongs, notably, to Herbart, Fechner, Nietzsche, Meynert, Benedikt, and Janet, and overlooks the work of previous explorers of the unconscious, dreams, and sexual pathology. Much of what is credited to Freud was diffuse current lore, and his role was to crystallize these ideas and give them an original shape.[66]

It is clear from the unpublished notebooks left by him after his death that in the course of his research Ellenberger became extremely critical with regard to psychoanalysis – more so than one would suspect from his published writings.

> **Ellenberger:** Psychoanalysis, is it a science? It does not meet the criteria (unified science, defined domain and methodology). It corresponds to the traits of a philosophical sect (closed organisation, highly personal initiation, a doctrine which is changeable but defined by its official adoption, cult and legend of the founder).[67]

One finds this same project of contextualising psychoanalysis in the work of Frank Sulloway, the second historian after Ellenberger to have radically changed the manner in which we perceive psychoanalysis. Freud claimed to be a new Darwin, a 'Darwin of the mind'. Sulloway proposed to take this slogan as literally as possible. In his book with an Ellenbergian subtitle, *Freud, Biologist of the Mind. Beyond the Psychoanalytic Legend*,[68] he showed in a very convincing manner how the principal 'discoveries' were actually deeply rooted in the biological hypotheses and speculations of his Darwinian era. Behind libido, infantile sexuality, polymorphous perversity, erotogenous zones, bisexuality, regression, primary repression, the murder of the primary father, originary fantasies and the death drive, Sulloway unearthed the forgotten 'sexual theories' of Krafft-Ebing, Albert Moll and Havelock Ellis, Haeckel's vast biogenetic frescoes, Wilhelm Fliess and Darwin's speculations on biorhythms, or again the theory of the transmission of acquired characteristics of Lamarck. In so doing, Sulloway intellectually rehabilitated Freud's friend, confidant and collaborator Wilhelm Fliess, generally presented in Freud biographies as a dangerous paranoiac and crank with grandiose and extravagant theories. Not only were Fliess' theories perfectly plausible in the context of the biogenetic speculations then in vogue, but they were favourably received by a not inconsiderable number of his contemporaries (beginning with Breuer). Thus there is no need, as some have proposed, to imagine an irrational transference on the part of Freud towards his friend to explain how he could have chosen him as a privileged interlocuter for so many years: they simply shared the same colleagues, the same ideas and the same readings.

> Sulloway: I am not saying that Fliess was a great scientist, I'm just saying that what he was doing was reasonably plausible and radical at the same time, and therefore appealed to Freud's own radical sensibilities. Obviously, Freud and Fliess intellectually stimulated each other a great deal and to discover that this relationship could be placed in a nineteenth century context in which it all made sense and took on respectability was a very fun thing to do in terms of the research involved.[69]

Just as with Ellenberger, Sulloway's historical contextualisation clashes head on with the Freudian legend and notably with the idea that psychoanalysis was born when Freud abandoned the neuro-physiological and biological theories of his time to the benefit of a purely psychological science, founded on clinical observation and the self-analysis of its founder.

> Sulloway: How is it possible, in a self analysis, not to be conditioned by all the scientific knowledge, reading and diverse evidence that you have gathered from half a dozen other disciplines? How could you prevent those relevant sources of information from steering your self analysis in a certain direction? If you begin to read in the literature that the infant is much more sexually spontaneous than you had ever thought, how could you not probe that issue in your own self analysis? So it shouldn't come as a big surprise if you then uncover a memory of having seen your mother naked at age two. If every book you are reading is telling you that and you then discover it in your own life, well, big news! It is obvious, not even profound.
>
> The self analysis has been made into a causal agent of Freud's originality in traditional Freud scholarship, but that simply is not true. It is like an uncontrolled experiment: things that are going on in self analysis get credited for all of Freud's intellectual changes, but those things themselves are coming in from somewhere else. The self analysis is one of the great legendary stories in the history of science and although Freud himself really didn't spawn that aspect of the myth, he did nothing to prevent it from spreading.[70]

For Sulloway, the 'legend of the hero' (following Joseph Campbell)[71] elaborated by Freud and his disciples essentially served two purposes.

On the one hand, through presenting the image of an isolated Freud, it allowed one to assert the radicality of the new science of the mind whilst clandestinely recuperating the contributions of Darwin, Haeckel, Fliess, Krafft-Ebing, the sexologists, and other figures. On the other hand, and more profoundly, it effectively protected psychoanalysis against the vicissitudes of scientific research. Once transmuted into psychological discoveries, the evolutionary hypotheses which underlay psychoanalytic theory could be maintained in spite of everything, even when they were refuted in their original fields. Deracinated, psychoanalysis became a discipline apart, cordoned off and protected from the refutation of some of its founding presuppositions.

> **Freud:** My position, no doubt, is made more difficult by the present attitude of biological science, which refuses to hear of the inheritance of acquired characteristics by succeeding generations. I must, however, in all modesty confess that nevertheless I cannot do without this factor in biological evolution.[72]

Following Sulloway, the Freudian legend is not an anecdotal or propagandist supplement to psychoanalytic theory (which it remains to some extent for Ellenberger). On the contrary, it is the theory itself. Questioning the Freudian legend leads to questioning the status of psychoanalysis itself. Ellenberger, with Swiss prudence, characterised psychoanalysis as a half-science ('demi-science').[73] Sulloway, on the other hand, does not hesitate to describe psychoanalysis as a pseudo-science immunised against criticism by a very efficient propaganda machine and by historical disinformation.

> **Sulloway:** Since I wrote this book on Freud, I have come to see psychoanalysis as something of a tragedy, as a discipline that evolved from a very promising science into a very disappointing pseudo-science ... When I began the book, I approached Freud as most people do, as one of the great minds of the twentieth century, somebody on a par with Copernicus and Darwin, as he himself indicated. But the more I looked into the development of psychoanalysis, the more I discovered that it was based on outmoded 19th century assumptions that were

clearly refuted by the rediscovery of Mendel's laws in genetics, by the refutation of Lamarckian theory in evolutionary biology and by the discarding of the various sort of Helmholtzian physiological assumptions that were crucial to Freud's thinking about hysteria. So when I got to the end of this book, I found myself somewhat reluctantly having to admit that Freud was not the great discoverer I – and others – had thought. I became in spite of myself a critic not only of psychoanalytic theory, but also of what I increasingly saw as the act of construction of a historical legend to prevent this view of Freud from being widely understood.[74]

Freud wars

The appearance of works by Ellenberger and Sulloway was followed by a veritable avalanche of 'revisionist' works,[75] each more critical than the last of the Freudian legend. Whilst, in the main, the works of Ellenberger and Sulloway were focused on intellectual history, Paul Roazen launched a social history of the psychoanalytic movement, through conducting oral histories, not unlike the anthropologists of science, who have attempted to study and distinguish what scientists actually do in contrast to their public statements about their work. Roazen's interviewees presented recollections of Freud which were radically discrepant from the image of Freud prepared by his biographer-disciple, Ernest Jones. Likewise, Peter Swales embarked upon a vast and meticulous archival investigation, only partially published, which reconstructed Freud's social and intellectual world in turn of the century Vienna, and presented a comprehensive account of the origins of psychoanalysis which was completely at variance with the Freudian legend. The philosopher Frank Cioffi showed how the key episode of the 'seduction theory', proposed in public and then abandoned in private by Freud between 1896 and 1897, did not unfold according to Freud's subsequent accounts, effectively deconstructing the official version of the discovery of the Oedipus complex and unconscious infantile sexual fantasies.[76]

Such studies have shown to what extent Freud's 'observations' and case histories were at times selective, tendentious and even dishonest. Freud, one learns, did not hesitate to modify or to conceal this or that biographical element to fit his theory,[77] to take liberties with chronology[78] and translation,[79] to present self-analytical accounts as objective cases supposedly interpreted through brilliant detective work,[80] or to present imaginary therapeutic results whilst proclaiming the therapeutic superiority of psychoanalysis to other forms of psychotherapy. For example, there is no evidence that 'Anna O.' was ever cured by Breuer,[81] any more than 'Emmy von N.',[82] 'Cäcilie M.',[83] 'Elisabeth von R.'[84] or the 'Wolf Man'[85] were by Freud. Other patients, passed over in silence or mentioned anonymously, were hardly better off after their analyses, such as Emma Eckstein,[86] Elise Gomperz,[87] Elfriede Hirschfeld,[88] Anna Freud,[89] 'A. B.'[90] or the unfortunate Horace Frink.[91] Conversely, some scholars have conjectured that 'Katharina' and 'Dora' may never have been ill in the first place.[92]

The most immediate effect of this new Freud scholarship has been to reopen the controversy around psychoanalysis, which the domination of the Freudian legend in certain quarters had frozen for more than half a century. The unconscious, infantile sexuality, the Oedipus complex, repression, transference, all these notions which had been taken for granted became hot topics which were bitterly disputed. The 'Freud wars' raged. Journal covers were titled 'Is Freud dead?'[93] Works were published with titles such as *Why Freud Was Wrong*,[94] *The Freud Case. The Birth of Psychoanalysis from the Lie*,[95] *Despatches from the Freud Wars*[96] or again *The Black Book of Psychoanalysis*,[97] and articles on Freud in magazines regularly sparked off an avalanche of indignant letters of protestation from the adversarial camp, followed by responses.[98]

Freudians resorted to dusting off the old arguments which had once worked so well (the pathologisation of adversaries, the imputation of 'resistance to psychoanalysis', of puritanism, of antisemitism) and they invented new ones, which were better adapted to the new situation: claims to the so-called 'progress' of psychoanalysis since Freud to render all criticism out of date, critiques of the supposed 'scientism' and 'positivistic credulity' of Freud historians, without forgetting the unanswerable retort: 'The never-ending backlash against Freud confirms the potency of his theories.'[99]

> **Janet Malcolm:** Roazen's book [*Brother Animal*] is trivial and slight. Its scholarship, like that of many other works of pop history, does not hold up under any sort of close scrutiny.[100]

> **Kurt Eissler:** When Roazen writes . . . then I find myself forced to refer the reader to Freud's comments on Daniel Paul Schreber's self-revelations.[101]

> **René Major (concerning Mikkel Borch-Jacobsen):** If he sticks to the archive and believes that it has no exteriority which permits it to be read or stops it from being 'anarchived' itself, he is prey to spasmodic convulsions worthy of Grand Mal. The Grand Mal of the archive. This illness is also of a sexual nature.[102]

> **Yosef Hayim Yerushalmi:** The offensives against psychoanalysis have become confounded with attacks against the personal integrity of Freud which have attained a degree of defamation without precedent.[103]

As for the new historians, they denounced Freudian dominance of the media, the press campaigns waged against dissidents, and the restriction of Freudian archives. How did it come about that so many documents deposited in public institutions such as the Library of Congress in Washington were officially inaccessible to researchers, and some documents until 2113 (or now indefinitely)? And why were these access restrictions, implacably applied when it came to independent researchers, suddenly lifted when it came to insiders of the psychoanalytic movement?

In 1994, a large international exhibition under the auspices of the Freud Archives and the Library of Congress in Washington was announced. None of the new Freud scholars figured in the organising committee. In protest, forty-two of them (including the authors of this book) sent an open letter to the Library of Congress to express their wish that the exhibition reflect 'the present state of Freud research' and requested that someone representing their views be added to the organising committee.[104] The request was not considered. Then, for apparently completely independent reasons, the Library of Congress announced that the exhibition would be postponed to enable the organisers to raise the necessary funds. This inflamed the controversy. The letter, which would otherwise have sunk without a trace, was taken to be responsible for the postponement. The organisers attributed the Library of Congress' decision to the petitioners' political and media pressure and protested, claiming that they were defending 'freedom of expression'. The news was immediately reported in the international press: once more, Freud was the butt of censure! A counter-petition was organised in France by Élisabeth Roudinesco and Philippe Garnier. This gathered together more than 180 signatures, some of them prestigious, to denounce the 'blackmail to fear', the 'puritan manifestations', the 'witch hunt' and the 'dictatorship of several intellectuals turned into inquisitors'. The so-called inquisitors retorted by a press release, read by practically no one, in which they protested against the manipulation of the media by their adversaries.[105] At that point, the Library of Congress announced that the organisers had found the necessary funds to mount the exhibition and that it could take place as initially intended. In the meantime, the latest Freud war had taken place.[106] Once more, historians and critics had been misrepresented and slandered, and the media manipulated to present a heroic image of an embattled revolutionary science of psychoanalysis.[107]

This book is about the Freud wars, old and new. It reopens the controversies which surrounded the inception of psychoanalysis and shows what we may learn from them about the fate of a once fashionable would-be science. It is striking to see the extent to which contemporary polemics around psychoanalysis repeat, in a quasi-somnambular manner, those which took place at the beginning of the century. It is well known that, from 1906, Freud's theories were the subject of a fierce international controversy, in which the leading contemporary figures of psychiatry and psychology participated: Pierre Janet, Emil Kraepelin, William Stern, Eugen Bleuler, Gustav Aschaffenburg, Alfred Hoche, Morton Prince and many others. What is less known is the fact that this controversy came to a close with the defeat of psychoanalysis at the congress of the German psychiatric association, held in Breslau in 1913, where speaker after speaker rose up to denounce psychoanalysis in an unequivocal manner. The reason for this 'induced amnesia' is the fact that Freud and his followers acted as if the controversy ended in their favour. The apologue of the three blows with which we began perfectly illustrates this: what is widely known about Freud's adversaries is that they were motivated by irrational resistances as well as sexual repression and that they were definitively relegated to the scrapheap of the prehistory of science, just like the adversaries of Darwin and Copernicus. Consequently, we know little of the objections which they addressed to psychoanalysis nor do we know how Freud surmounted them. As we shall see, this was for a good reason, as one may question whether they were ever surmounted. When one places Freud's 'victory' over his adversaries in its historical context, one sees that it was imaginary, and that it rests on a negative hallucination concerning the critiques of psychoanalysis.

We propose, therefore, to reopen the files of these critiques and old controversies, consigned for too long in the 'prepsychoanalytic' attic, and restage the debates. Once the dust has been shaken off them, these files prove to be strikingly at variance with received opinion, which explains why some of them were so carefully censured, or classed as 'top secret' by the guardians of the Freud archives. Given how hard to retrieve much of this material is, we have deliberately chosen to cite excerpts in extenso, letting the historical actors speak in their own voices and creating a polyphonic text, rather than filter through paraphrases. Taken together, they show a history which has very little in common with that which one finds in the works of Freud and his biographers, and which was taken at face value for so long. This history, as we shall see, demonstrates the extraordinary apparatus by which this would-be science of psychoanalysis installed itself in contemporary societies. Beyond psychoanalysis, it opens up the history of the constitution of the modern psychological sciences and psychotherapies, and how they furnished the ideas which we have of ourselves, and how these became solidified into incontrovertible 'facts'.

I

Privatising science

I find that one of the greatest bonds between us is our feeling for
science and for what science really means. I hardly think that Freud
always had a completely clear grasp of that.

Ernest Jones to Marie Bonaparte, 2 July 1954[1]

Why do the current controversies revolve around the *history* of
psychoanalysis and the manner in which it has been written? Why
such vehemence on both sides, why a 'war'? After all, the philosophical, epistemological and political critiques of psychoanalysis never
aroused such passion. Psychoanalysis was reproached by Karl Jaspers
for mixing up hermeneutic understanding (*Verstehen*) and the
explanation (*Erklären*) of the natural sciences, by Jean-Paul Sartre
for confounding repression and 'bad faith', by Ludwig Wittgenstein
for confusing causes and reasons, by Karl Popper for avoiding all
scientific falsification, by Adolf Grünbaum for proposing an episte-
mically inconsistent clinical validation and by Michel Foucault for
producing sexuality under the cover of unmasking it. None of this
affected psychoanalysts. Even the provocations and magnificent rhetorical violence of Gilles Deleuze and Felix Guattari's *Anti-Oedipus* did not
lead them to lose their composure. On the contrary, it is as if advocates
of psychoanalysis were not perturbed by these debates because they

30

legitimate their discipline, letting the adherents invariably escape unharmed, entrenched in the private sphere of the psychoanalytic clinic. The more Freud is debated, it is often said, the more it confirms his significance.

Why then such sudden susceptibility concerning historical details, some of which on first sight appear to be quite trivial? Why is it so important for psychoanalysts to maintain the version of events given by Freud and his authorised biographers? Is it simply a question of a dispute between experts, a controversy between historians such as we often see? Not in this case, because the dispute here is not simply one between factions of historians, or of ways of interpreting the historical record. More deeply, it pits historians against a radically dehistoricised version of psychoanalysis, disguised as a 'history of psychoanalysis'. From this perspective, similarities abound between the 'Freud wars' and the 'science wars', which rage elsewhere between historians, sociologists and anthropologists of science on the one side and scientistic ideologues on the other. In both cases, what is at stake is the historicisation, and correspondingly the relativisation, of 'facts', 'discoveries' and 'truths' ordinarily presented as atemporal and universal and shielded from the variations and contingencies of history (it is of little importance here whether psychoanalysis styles itself as a science or not, as it still nevertheless presents itself as a universal theory, a general ontology valid for all). These debates are not external to the science or the theory, because they bear on this demarcation itself: can one or should one separate the science or the theory from its history? To take up the famous Mertonian distinction, can one separate what is 'internal' from what is 'external'?[2] Can one, as Reichenbach would have it, trace a limit between the context of discovery (the anecdotal account of the emergence of concepts) and the context of justification (the properly scientific work of proof)? It is the refusal of these demarcations by the new historians of science and of psychoanalysis which has generated such scandal, because it puts into question the pretensions of this or that discipline to scientificity and to theoretical hegemony.

However, the comparison between the 'Freud wars' and the 'science wars' stops right here. Even if some scientists feel attacked in their most intimate convictions by the historicisation of science practised by 'science studies', those who are really threatened by this are rare. On the contrary, many scientists don't mind opening their notebooks and laboratories to historians and anthropologists when asked, and some do not hesitate to recognise how they are portrayed, even if they draw different conclusions from those of their observers.[3] This is a sign that they feel themselves sufficiently strong to bear the test of historical and anthropological inquiry. The same is not the case for psychoanalysis, where intrusions of historians into the Freudian 'laboratory' are generally perceived as unacceptable transgressions which should be denounced. For a discipline concerned with the past, psychoanalysis is strangely allergic to its own history, and for good reason: for it is precisely here that it is vulnerable.

> **Isabelle Stengers:** [Psychoanalytic circles] have tried – with great success up to now – to occupy the domain of the present indefinitely and stop historians from having access to documents and archives. Everything takes place as if what happened to Freud one hundred years ago is still so confidential and private that it justifies sequestering archives, censoring correspondences and obstructing the pursuits of historians doing their work. It is to be believed that the secrets of psychoanalysis are weightier than those of diplomacy or international history. One knows today that Churchill decided to let Coventry be bombed rather than reveal to the Germans that the British had deciphered their code. But one can still not have access to this or that correspondence with Freud which could inform us about this or that detail of his private life! It seems that there is something there that is too explosive for one to dream of divulging. This is perfectly absurd. In terms of what concerns me, I see here the sign that psychoanalysis has failed to adopt the normal regime of scientific production. In contrast to the sciences, psychoanalysis is vulnerable to its past.[4]

'Psychoanalysis is my creation'

The exact sense of this vulnerability remains to be understood. Is it simply a question of 'all too human' secrets of the founder's biography, which would simply be factors external to the theory? Freud, as his biographers invariably note, did not like biographers and did everything to make their task more difficult.[5] At least on two instances, in 1885 and in 1907, he destroyed most of his notes, intimate diaries and personal papers, veritable holocausts in which correspondences as precious for the comprehension of the origins of psychoanalysis as those with Bernheim, Breuer, Fliess, August Forel, Havelock Ellis and Leopold Löwenfeld probably perished. The same thing happened in 1938[6] and again in 1939,[7] and one knows that he would have destroyed his letters to Wilhelm Fliess were it not for the refusal of Marie Bonaparte, who had acquired this correspondence on the express condition that he could not regain possession of them.

> **Freud to Marie Bonaparte, 3 January 1937:** The matter of the correspondence with Fliess has affected me deeply … Our correspondence was the most intimate you can imagine. It would have been highly embarrassing to have it fall into the hands of strangers … I do not want any of them to become known to the so-called posterity.[8]

> **Diary of Marie Bonaparte, entry of 24 November 1937:** But when later, at the end of February or the beginning of March 1937, I saw [Freud] in Vienna and he told me he wanted the letters to be burned, I refused … One day he told me: 'I hope to convince you to destroy them.'[9]

> **Freud to Martha Bernays, 28 April 1885:** One intention as a matter of fact I have almost finished carrying out, an intention which a number of as yet unborn and unfortunate people will one day resent. Since you won't guess what kind of people I am referring to, I will tell you at once: they are my biographers. I have destroyed all my notes of the past fourteen years, as well as letters, scientific excerpts, and the manuscripts of my papers … As for the biographers, let them worry, we

have no desire to make it too easy for them. Each of them will be right in his opinion of 'The Development of the Hero', and I am already looking forward to seeing them go astray.[10]

Freud to his 'unsolicited biographer'[11] Fritz Wittels, 18 December 1923: Needless to say, I would never have desired or promoted such a book [Wittels (1924)]. It seems to me that the world has no claim on my person and that it will learn nothing from me so long as my case (for manifold reasons) cannot be made fully transparent.[12]

Fair enough, one could say. No one likes anyone rummaging around in their private life. Who would criticise Freud for wanting to resist the indiscrete curiosity of biographers and historians? With Freud, however, this reserve (this censure) was combined with a very active and highly public autobiographical writing, which, moreover, he merged with the presentation of the psychoanalytic theory itself. From this perspective, one cannot reduce Freud's manipulation of his biography to a simple private affair, without consequence for psychoanalysis. The presentation of the theory was intimately bound to the the founder's self-presentation, and what affects one inevitably affects the other.

Freud: *History.* – The best way of understanding psycho-analysis is still by tracing its origin and development.[13]

It was very early, from his first synoptic presentation of psychoanalysis, the 'Five lectures on psychoanalysis' presented at the Clark conference in 1909, that Freud started to present his doctrine in the form of an autobiographical narrative. Even if the first sentence attributed the paternity of psychoanalysis to Josef Breuer, the rest of the text retraced Freud's own evolution, from the abandonment of cathartic hypnosis up to the application of psychoanalysis to the problem of artistic creation, passing by the successive discoveries of repression, the meaning of dreams and infantile sexuality. This mode of autobiographical exposition was only accentuated in his 'History of the psychoanalytic movement' and the 'Short account of psychoanalysis', and culminated in his 'Autobiographical study', which had been requested by L. R. Grote for the fourth volume of his *Die Medizin der Gegenwart in Selbstdarstellungen* [Contemporary Medicine in Autobiography].

> **Freud:** I have already more than once published papers upon the same line as the present one, papers which, from the nature of the subject, have dealt more with personal considerations than is usual or than would otherwise have been necessary … Since I must not contradict myself and since I have no wish to repeat myself exactly, I must endeavour to construct a narrative in which subjective and objective attitudes, biographical and historical interests, are combined in a new proportion.[14]

But why, we may ask, does 'the nature of the subject' require such an emphasis on 'personal considerations'? We have become so used to this autobiographical presentation of psychoanalysis that we no longer notice the oddness of this statement. After all, why should there be any intrinsic link between psychoanalysis and Freud's person?

It is not so much the autobiographical form as such which is a problem, for Freud was not the first pioneer of psychology and of psychotherapy to have adopted it – one thinks of the memoirs of Wundt, Stanley Hall, August Forel, Emil Kraepelin, Albert Moll, Havelock Ellis and later Jung.[15] There was also, from the 1930s, a systematic collection of autobiographical accounts from the principal figures in psychology, such as Pierre Janet, William McDougall, James Mark Baldwin, J. B. Watson, William Stern, Edouard Claparède, Jean Piaget and Kurt Goldstein. One need only peruse the volumes of this monumental *History of Psychology in Autobiography*,[16] initially published under the editorship of Carl Murchison, to see that a number of the autobiographies of Freud's contemporaries were no less 'subjective', tendentious and lacunary than his.[17] That of Watson in particular cedes nothing to Freud in terms of aggressive invective.

> **John Broadus Watson:** The War played havoc with my work … I returned to Washington and was transferred to the Aviation Medical

Corps to work under Colonel Crabtree on oxygen deprivation. Did some work of an unsatisfactory nature, got into trouble because my own Corps asked me to write them, directly and not through military channels, what I thought of the famous 'Rotation Test.' I was nearly court-martialed for doing so. I was returned by Colonel Crabtree to Aviation with the notation 'that he be not allowed to serve his country in his scientific capacity, but he be sent to the line'; in other words, the wish was implied that I be killed speedily ... The whole army experience was a nightmare to me. Never have I seen such incompetence, such extravagance, such a group of overbearing, inferior men. Talk of putting a Negro in uniform![18]

However, none of Freud's contemporaries appear to have linked their theories to their own person, and for a good reason: that would have meant putting into doubt the objectivity of the theory, in making it an expression of the theorist's subjectivity.[19] By contrast, Freud never ceased to affirm the objective *and* subjective, universal *and* local character of psychoanalytic theory.

> **Freud:** No one need be surprised at the subjective character of the contribution I propose to make here to the history of the psycho-analytic movement, nor need anyone wonder at the part I play in it. For psycho-analysis is my creation ... I consider myself justified in maintaining that even to-day no one can know better than I do what psycho-analysis is, how it differs from other ways of investigating the life of the mind, and precisely what should be called psycho-analysis and what would better be described by some other name.[20]

> **Freud, regarding Jung and the Zurich school:** They are unwilling to give up their connection with psycho-analysis, as whose representatives they became known to the world, and prefer to give it out that psycho-analysis has changed. At the Munich Congress I found it necessary to clear up this confusion, and I did so by declaring that I did not recognize the innovations of the Swiss as legitimate continuations and further developments of the psycho-analysis that originated with me.[21]

Here, Freud inscribes psychoanalysis within a patrilineal descent: what is not of his lineage, what does not descend directly from him,

the father of psychoanalysis, should not bear the name of psychoanalysis. But if psychoanalysis is Freudian, this should by no means be
understood in the manner in which one speaks of 'Newtonian'
physics or 'Pasteurian' medicine. Whatever the historical role of
Newton or Pasteur in the theories which bear their name, their
subjectivity and personality do not play a role in the theories themselves or the debates and controversies to which they gave rise. That
it was Sir Isaac Newton or another who formulated the laws set forth
in *Principia* is not important to the physicist who proposes to test,
extend or contest them. The movement of the modern sciences, in as
much as they have put forward theories or general ontologies capable
of creating a universal consensus, is linked to what Merton called
scientific 'communism', i.e., the rejection of the idea of private
property in matters of knowledge. The critique of the argument
from authority, understood either in the rationalist perspective of
Descartes or in the empiricist perspective of Boyle, amounts to the
same thing: in each instance it is a matter of appealing to a 'clear and
distinct idea' or to a 'matter of fact' whose evidence is binding on
everyone and can be repeated by anyone, independently of the
personage of the scholar. For moderns, knowledge is only legitimate
when it is impersonal enough for everyone to agree about it, in other
words: when it belongs to no one in particular. As Steven Shapin has
noted, extending the works of Niklas Luhmann and Anthony
Giddens,[22] one of the most critical features of the 'scientific revolution' under way in the seventeenth century was the progressive
abandonment of the trust placed in the individual testimony of
persons judged to be of integrity and virtue in favour of neutral and
anonymous institutions, founded on mechanisms of transindividual
verification and self-regulation.

> **Steven Shapin:** Modernity guarantees knowledge not by reference to
> virtue but to expertise. When we give our trust to – 'have faith in' –
> modern systems of technology and knowledge, our faith is now widely
> said not to be in the moral character of the individuals concerned but

in the genuine expertise attributed to the institutions. The expertise of individuals is itself considered to be vouched for by the institutions from which they speak and which are the ultimate sources of that expertise.[23]

By contrast, Freud seems to return to a premodern position when he insists on the moral qualities which enabled him alone to reveal that which had remained hidden until then to all other mortals. Indeed, if the psychoanalytic 'nature of the subject' and Freud are so insepa-rable, then it is because it wasn't sufficient to stumble on the uncon-scious to 'discover' it. Courage and a staunch heart were necessary to be able to confront the somber truth of sexuality and the innumerable resistances which it aroused. Only a man without fear and above reproach could face such a daunting task, namely Freud.

> **Freud to Marie Bonaparte, 16 December 1927:** If you had known Breuer, he was a great mind, a mind quite superior to me. I had only one thing: courage to stand up against the majority, faith in myself.[24]

> **Freud:** I treated my discoveries as ordinary contributions to science and hoped they would be received in the same spirit. But . . . I under-stood that from now onwards I was one of those who have 'disturbed the sleep of the world,' as Hebbel says, and that I could not reckon upon objectivity and tolerance. Since, however, my conviction of the general accuracy of my observations and conclusions grew even stron-ger, and since neither my confidence in my own judgment nor my moral courage were precisely small, the outcome of the situation could not be in doubt.[25]

But this isn't all. Freud still had to surmount the *internal* resistances to the truth, otherwise he would never have been able to confront the external obstacles which he met with along the way. This is a central element in the story that Freud tells us, which explains why it was he alone who 'discovered' the unconscious. No one was capable of confronting the truth of unconscious without the aid of analysis. Consequently, the primal analyst had to have been a *self*-analyst. Freud, we are told, was the first in the history of humanity who analysed himself and it was thus that he could lift the repressions which prevented his predecessors and contemporaries, indeed all of humanity, from seeing the truth. In his 'History of the psychoanalytic movement', Freud claimed that it was thanks to the analysis of the dreams of his patients and his own that he found the courage to proceed despite the opprobrium which he was subject to.

> **Freud:** It was only my success in this direction that enabled me to persevere . . . Moreover, I soon saw the necessity of carrying out a self-analysis, and this I did with the help of a series of my own dreams which led me back through all the events of my childhood; and I am still of the opinion to-day that this kind of analysis may suffice for anyone who is a good dreamer and not too abnormal.[26]

The theory impeccably wraps around itself, explaining its own discovery. The indissoluble linkage which Freud established between his object and his own person now becomes clear: he himself was the 'royal road' to the unconscious. Henceforth, there would be no other route to it. In place of the ideal of a replication of an objective experience, independent of the experimenters, was substituted the mimetic emulation of the master, of the primal analyst who alone knew what others didn't. Psychoanalysis was indeed Freud's science.

The politics of self-analysis

Sándor Ferenczi to Freud, 17 March 1911: There has certainly never been any *intellectual* movement in which the *personality* of the discoverer has played such a great and indispensable role as yours has done in psychoanalysis.[27]

Harry K. Wells: Psychoanalysis proper is essentially the product of Freud's self-analysis.[28]

Ernst Kris: The first and perhaps most significant result of Freud's self-analysis was the step from seduction theory to full insight into the significance of infantile sexuality . . . In the summer and autumn of 1897 his self-analysis revealed the essential features of the Oedipus complex and enabled him to understand the nature of Hamlet's inhibition. Insight into the role of the erotogenic zones in the development of the libido followed.[29]

Ernest Jones: In the summer of 1897 . . . Freud undertook his most heroic feat – a psychoanalysis of his own unconscious . . . Yet the uniqueness of the feat remains. Once done it is done forever. For no one ever again can be the first to explore those depths . . . What indomitable courage, both intellectual and moral, must have been needed![30]

Eissler: Here we return to the enigma of Freud's personality . . . His findings had to be wrested in the face of his own extreme resistances – the self-analysis being comparable, in terms of the danger involved, to Benjamin Franklin's flying a kite in a thunderstorm in 1752, in order to investigate the laws of electricity. The next two persons who tried to repeat his experiments were both killed.[31]

The self-analysis, always described by Freud's biographers as heroic, unprecedented and superhuman, is at the core of the Freudian legend. It is therefore instructive to trace how and why it acquired this centrality. At the outset, there was nothing unique or original in practising self-analysis, conceived as introspective self-observation. Freud's self-analysis was only slowly and gradually elevated to the presently quasi-mythic place at the heart of the psychoanalytic movement.

Thomas Hobbes: Whosoever looketh into himself, and considereth what he doth, and when he does think, opine, reason, hope, feare, &c, and upon what grounds; he shall thereby read and know, what are the thoughts, and Passions of all men, upon like occasions.[32]

Immanuel Kant: The wish to play the spy upon one's self . . . is to reverse the natural order of cognitive powers . . . The desire for self-investigation is either already a disease of the mind (hypochondria) or will lead to such a disease and ultimately to the madhouse.[33]

Auguste Comte: The thinker cannot divide himself into two, of whom one reasons whilst the other observes him reason. The organ observed and the organ observing being, in this case, identical, how could observation take place? This pretended psychological method is then radically null and void.[34]

William James: Like most psychologists ... he makes of his personal peculiarities a rule.[35]

Placed back in the wide frame of psychology at the end of the nineteenth century and at the beginning of the twentieth, Freud's self-analysis is only a chapter in the history of introspection. It is important to recall that throughout the nineteenth century, despite the strictures against it expressed by figures such as Kant and Auguste Comte, introspection continued to be the main method of philosophical psychology. Initially, this hardly changed with the advent of the new 'scientific' psychology. Franz Brentano maintained that psychology, like any other natural science, had to be based on perception and experience, straightforwardly including self-perception in this.

Brentano: Above all, however, its source is to be found in the inner perception of our own mental phenomena.[36]

For the new psychology, inner experience appeared as the prize domain for exploration. Thus it was natural that psychologists would practise self-observation and self-experimentation (which was still used in medicine at this time). The identically titled works of Alfred Maury and Joseph Delbœuf, *Sleep and Dreams*,[37] are good examples of this introspective genre. At the same time, which seems strange to us today, the first 'subjects' of the new experimental psychology were the experimenters themselves – Fechner, Hering, Helmholtz and Ebbinghaus.[38] Even in Wundt's laboratory, where the experimenters also acted as subjects, the experimental procedures were essentially intended to render introspection more reliable and replicable, and in no respect to eliminate it. It was only later, with the famous debate on 'imageless thought', that introspection was gradually abandoned as a method in psychology, notably in favour of the third-person experimentation promoted by behaviourism, with its methodological rejection of all private mental states. From this perspective, Freud's decision at the end of the summer of 1897 to take himself as his investigative object was not exceptional in the context of the time. On the contrary, it was perfectly routine and predictable.

> **Freud to Wilhelm Fliess, 14 August 1897:** The chief patient I am preoccupied with is myself. My little hysteria, though greatly accentuated by my work, has resolved itself a little further . . . The analysis is more difficult than any other. It is, in fact, what paralyzes my psychic strength for describing and communicating what I have won so far. Still, I believe it must be done and is a necessary intermediary stage in my work.[39]

Taken in the narrow sense of systematic therapeutic analysis, centred on the recollection of childhood memories, the self-analysis appears to have been extremely brief, and, in Freud's own view, disappointing (a point rarely mentioned by his biographers). Actively pursued from the beginning of October 1897 (two weeks *after* the abandonment of the seduction theory),[40] it was finished six weeks later in a lucid assessment of failure.

> **Freud to Fliess, 14 November 1897:** My self-analysis remains interrupted. I have realized why I can analyze myself only with the knowledge obtained objectively (like an outsider). True self-analysis is impossible; otherwise there would be no [neurotic] illness. Since I am still contending with some kind of puzzle in my patients, this is bound to hold me up in my self-analysis as well.[41]

> **Freud to Fliess, 9 February 1898:** As for the rest, everything is still in a state of latency. My self-analysis is at rest in favor of the dream book.[42]

Taken in the larger sense of self-observation, however, the self-analysis began much earlier, with Freud's interpretation of his dreams which he routinely noted on waking,[43] and continued with his analysis of his childhood memories (the so-called screen memories), as well as forgettings, lapses and failed acts. It is in this sense that Freud mentions in *The Psychopathology of Everyday Life* that, at the age of 43, he began to be interested in 'what was left of my memory of my own childhood'.[44] This coupling of an analysis of one's dreams and childhood memories was not without precedent, as one already finds it in Delbœuf's *Sleep and Dreams*, where one of the major themes is the capacity of dreams to recall forgotten memories. In this regard, Delbœuf's analysis of the 'dream of lizards and of the *asplenium ruta muraria*'[45] seems to have served as the model of the analysis of the 'dream of Irma's injection in *The Interpretation of Dreams*'.[46] Further, as Andreas Mayer has justly noted,[47] this self-observation should also be situated in the continuation of the 'introspective hypnotism' practised at that time by figures such as August Forel, Eugen Bleuler[48] and Oskar Vogt, who had all published first-person accounts of the hypnotic state.[49] The idea of the introspective study of subliminal or unconscious psychic states was definitely in the air.

August Forel: The object of psychology is the study of so-called psychic functions of our brain by direct introspection … Those cerebral functions which do not fall into the ordinary field of attention of our consciousness in a waking state or its memories escape direct introspective psychology. But modern studies have made us increasingly aware that a large part of the cerebral functions called unconscious possess an introspective shimmering which we can surprise in certain circumstances and one designates this fact by the term 'subconscious,' a term which for good reason is being increasingly adopted.[50]

Freud: I have noticed in my psycho-analytical work that the whole frame of mind of a man who is reflecting is totally different from that of a man who is observing his own psychical processes … In both cases attention must be concentrated, but the man who is reflecting is also exercising his critical faculty … The self-observer on the other hand need only take the trouble to suppress his critical faculty. If he succeeds in doing that, innumerable ideas come into his consciousness of which he could otherwise never have got hold … What is in question, evidently, is the establishment of a psychical state which, in its distribution of psychical energy (that is, of mobile attention), bears some analogy to the state before falling asleep – and no doubt also to hypnosis.[51]

Freud himself did not seem to have accorded a special status to his self-analysis, at least at the beginning. In the first edition of *The Interpretation of Dreams*, as Peter Gay has noted, the term 'self-analysis' hardly signifies more than 'self-observation'.[52] Freud spoke of 'self-analyses' (in the plural) regarding his interpretation of his dreams, and he utilised the term to designate the ensemble of his work of self-inspection in *The Interpretation of Dreams*, which demonstrates that he did not understand it in the strict sense of analytic work upon oneself.

> **Freud:** Thus it comes about that I am led to my own dreams, which offer a copious and convenient material … No doubt I shall be met by doubts of the trustworthiness of 'self-analyses' of this kind … In my judgment the situation is in fact more favourable in the case of self-observation than in that of other people; at all events we may make the experiment and see how far self-analysis takes us with the interpretation of dreams.[53]

> **Freud:** [In] the dream about the strange task set me by old Brücke of making a dissection of my own pelvis … the dissection meant the self-analysis which I was carrying out, as it were, in the publication of this present book about dreams.[54]

Freud's self-analysis only gradually acquired the more technical – that is to say, properly *Freudian* – meaning that it now has in psychoanalytic vocabulary. Indeed, it was only in the preface of the second edition of *The Interpretation of Dreams* that Freud made the first public allusion to his psychoanalysis of himself.

> **Freud:** For this book has a further subjective significance for me personally – a significance which I only grasped after I had completed it. It was, I found, a portion of my own self-analysis, my reaction to my father's death – that is to say, to the most important event, the most poignant loss, of a man's life.[55]

Suddenly, the public learned that the book on dreams was only a fragment of a self-analysis, the full content of which was simultaneously withheld. This clearly completely resignified the work, as well as that on the psychopathology of everyday life. Behind the published, public science, there was now the private, secret 'science' of Freud. Behind the manifest content of the books on dreams and on the psychopathology of everyday life, there was also their latent, 'Oedipal' content. Psychoanalysis itself became a riddle, with only Freud possessing its key. Furthermore, the self-analysis not only furnished the esoteric meaning of psychoanalysis, it now emerged as something very different from other introspective practices, insofar as self-observation was merged with self-therapy. To observe oneself was no longer sufficient: one had to *cure oneself* of the blindness with regard to the unconscious, as Freud had done. The upshot of this was that not anyone could practise psychoanalysis – contrary to the case with hypnosis, suggestion, and other medical and psychological therapeutic techniques. To be a psychoanalyst, one had to cure oneself, or in other words, psychoanalyse oneself. In 1909, to the question of how one became a psychoanalyst, Freud replied: 'by studying one's own dreams'.[56] The following year, he noted that would-be psychoanalysts had to devote themselves to a self-analysis in order to overcome their resistances.

> **Freud:** Now that a considerable number of people are practising psycho-analysis and exchanging their observations with one another, we have noticed that no psycho-analyst goes further than his own complexes and internal resistances permit; and we consequently require that he shall begin his activity with a self-analysis[57] and continually carry it deeper while he is making his observations on his patients. Anyone who fails to produce results in a self-analysis of this kind may at once give up any idea of being able to treat patients by analysis.[58]

On the surface, nothing could be more democratic: anyone could – and should – repeat Freud's self-analysis. The problem was that this directive wasn't accompanied with any instructions, as no one except Freud himself knew what this self-analysis consisted in (one should bear in mind that his letters to Fliess were only published decades later). Consequently, what could be more natural than to turn to the expert on self-analysis to ask his advice? A number of figures duly did. Ernest Jones and Sándor Ferenczi, for example, sent detailed accounts of their self-analyses to Freud, who responded with interpretations, suggestions and directives. These mimetic 'self'-analyses could with much justice be regarded simply as analyses by correspondence. Furthermore, they were hardly examples of open-ended inquiry, as what was to be found was already known in advance, and scripted by psychoanalytic theory.

In other cases, however, the practice of self-analysis dangerously slipped out of Freud's control. Each analyst could appeal to the findings of their own self-analysis, thus resulting in a cacophony of divergent interpretations. There where Freud found Oedipus, others found Electra. Where he insisted on the paternal complex, others insisted on the maternal complex. Where he 'discovered' infantile sexuality, others discovered 'organ inferiority'. Where he saw the workings of the 'libido', others saw the 'aggressive drive'. It is not a coincidence that the epoch when Freud placed his trust in the practice of self-analysis was also that of the monumental disputes between Freud, Adler, Stekel and Jung. Insofar as the ultimate criterion for the validity of psychoanalytic interpretations was self-analysis, each could invoke his own to delegitimate the interpretations and theories of others and accuse them of projecting their own unanalysed complexes into their theories or of having succumbed to neurotic resistances. Nothing enabled one to settle the symmetric conflicts of interpretations which were tearing apart the psychoanalytic community.

> **Freud to Ernest Jones, 9 August 1911:** As for the internal dissension with Adler, it was likely to come and I have ripened the crisis. It is the revolt of an abnormal individual driven mad by ambition, his influence upon others depending on his strong terrorism and sadismus.[59]

> **Alfred Adler:** Freud had a bad time with my verbal remarks ... my gentle rejection: 'Standing in his shadow is no fun' – that is, being

blamed for all the inconsistencies of Freudianism simply because of cooperating in the psychology of neurosis. Without delay, he interpreted it as a confession of my rebellious vanity, so that he could deliver it up to the unsuspecting readers.[60]

Wilhelm Stekel: In one session that took place after Adler had seceded, [Freud] claimed that Adler suffered from paranoia. That was one of Freud's favorite diagnoses; he had applied it to another important friend of his from whom he had separated.[61] Immediately in his slavish choir, voices resounded which enthusiastically confirmed this ridiculous diagnosis.[62]

It was precisely to remedy this situation, which threatened to shatter the psychoanalytic movement, that Jung proposed in 1912 that every prospective analyst had to be analysed by another analyst – i.e., had to submit to a training analysis. This was quickly seconded by Freud in the same year.

Jung: There are analysts who believe that they can get along with a self-analysis. This is Münchhausen[63] psychology, and they will certainly remain stuck. They forget that one of the most important therapeutically effective factors is subjecting yourself to the objective judgment of another. As regards ourselves we remain blind, despite everything and everybody.[64]

Freud: It is not enough ... that [the physician] himself should be an approximately normal person. It may be insisted, rather, that he should have undergone a psycho-analytic purification and have become aware of those complexes of his own which would be apt to interfere with his grasp of what the patient tells him ... I count it as one of the many merits of the Zurich school of analysis that they have laid increased emphasis on this requirement, and have embodied it in the demand that everyone who wishes to carry out analyses on other people shall first himself undergo an analysis by someone with expert knowledge ... But anyone who has scorned to take the precaution of being analysed himself ... will easily fall into the temptation of projecting outwards some of the peculiarities of his own personality, which he has dimly perceived, into the field of science, as a theory having universal validity; he will bring the psycho-analytic method into discredit, and lead the inexperienced astray.[65]

It is important to realise that training analysis was a striking departure from current practices in medicine and psychiatry. Whilst self-experimentation was still common, it would have been unthinkable to require that a would-be practitioner of hypnosis undergo hypnosis, or a would-be surgeon undergo surgery. After attending the psycho-analytic congress in Weimar in 1911, James Jackson Putnam commented on this in a talk.

> **James Jackson Putnam:** Then I learned, to my surprise and interest, that a large part of these investigators had subjected themselves, more or less systematically, to the same sort of searching character-analysis to which their patients were being subjected at their hands. It is fast getting to be felt that an initiation of this sort is an indispensable condition of good work.[66]

In theory at least, training analysis was supposed to guarantee that the theories and interpretations of analysts were not deformed by their 'neurosis'. As we have seen, this had also been the aim of the self-analyses which had previously been undertaken. In practice, it guaranteed that everyone interpreted in a manner authorised by Freud or those of his disciples whom he had analysed. Henceforth, analysts would no longer be free to decide the meanings of their dreams by themselves. Better still, they were no longer free to decide whether they were neurotic or not, or even if they had been fully analysed. All of this would be determined by their analyst, in an infinite regress going back to Freud himself. Thus the 'psychoanalytic purification' coincided with an institutional purging and a herme-neutical standardisation. Gone was the anarchy of uncontrolled and uncontrollable self-analyses, and the infernal cycle of diagnoses and counter-diagnoses. The recapturing of the psychoanalytic movement had begun. From now on, Freud and his lieutenants would have the final word.

The decisive role of training analysis in the institutionalisation and propagation of the psychoanalytic movement has often been noted, as well as the rigidly hierarchical and centralised power relations between analysts which it set up.[67] It is less often noted that it was instituted as a response to an inescapable difficulty of psychoanalytic theory. Indeed, who could adjudicate the validity of psychoanalytic interpretations since the unconscious, by definition, gives no response to this question (being only accessible through being 'translated'[68] – that is to say interpreted)? And how could one arrive at a consensus in a case of disagreement? If a patient rejected an analyst's interpretations, the latter could always claim that he knew more because he had submitted to a personal analysis. But what if it was another analyst who objected to his interpretation? What if the patient refused the asymmetry of the analytic situation and set out to analyse the analyst? Whatever way one looks at the question, nothing authorises the analyst to declare that his interpretation is necessarily superior to that of his colleague or of his patient except the institutional arrangement which underwrote his interpretation. The vehicle of training analysis which Jung proposed was an institutional response to an aporia which could not be resolved on a theoretical level.

However, this 'solution' immediately raised another difficulty: what of Freud? If every analyst derived their authority from their training analysis, from where did Freud derive his? As long as psychoanalysts trained themselves through self-analysis, Freud's self-analysis did not pose any problems (on the contrary, it was regarded as the prototype). But now the rules of the game had changed, and the status of Freud's self-analysis was exposed. Who could guarantee that Freud's analysis had been complete? On the one hand, Jung's proposition enabled the closure of the controversy with Adler and Stekel, and on the other, it opened a new one, this time between Freud and himself. For how could Freud impose his interpretations on Jung if he had, by his own terms, not been analysed?

> **Jung to Jones, 15 November 1912:** Freud is convinced that I am thinking under the domination of a father complex against him and then all is complex-nonsense ... Against this insinuation I am

completely helpless . . . If Freud understands each attempt to think in a
new way about the problems of psychoanalysis as a personal resistance,
things become impossible.[69]

Jung to Freud, 3 December 1912: May I draw your attention to the
fact that you open *The Interpretation of Dreams* with the mournful
admission of your own neurosis – the dream of Irma's injection –
identification with the neurotic in need of treatment. Very significant.
Our analysis, you may remember, came to a stop with your remark that
you 'could not submit to analysis *without losing your authority*.' These
words are engraved on my memory as a symbol of everything to
come.[70]

Jones to Freud, 5 December 1912: I enclose a curious letter from
Jung . . . Did Brill tell you that he maintains that *you* have a severe
neurosis? Another beautiful projection.[71]

Jung to Freud, c. 11–14 December 1912: Even Adler's cronies do not
regard me as one of yours [*Ihrigen*, instead of *ihrigen*, 'theirs'].[72]

Freud to Jung, 16 December 1912: But are you 'objective' enough to
consider the following slip without anger? 'Even Adler's cronies do not
regard me as one of *yours*.'[73]

Jung to Freud, 18 December 1912: You go around sniffing out all the
symptomatic actions in your vicinity, thus reducing everyone to the
level of sons and daughters who blushingly admit the existence of their
faults. Meanwhile you remain on top as the father, sitting pretty. For
sheer obsequiousness nobody dares to pluck the prophet by the beard
and inquire for once what you would say to a patient with a tendency
to analyse the analyst instead of himself. You would certainly ask him:
'*Who's* got the neurosis?' . . .I am namely not in the least neurotic –
touch wood! I have namely *lege artis et tout humblement* let myself be
analysed, which has been very good for me. You know, of course, how
far a patient gets with self-analysis: *not* out of his neurosis – just like
you.[74]

Freud to Ferenczi, 23 December 1912: The embarrassing sensation of
the moment is the enclosed letter from Jung, which Rank and Sachs
also know about . . . I must say he is really impudent . . . With
deference to my neurosis, I hope I will master it all right. But he is
behaving like a florid fool and the brutal fellow that he is. The master

who analyzed him could only have been Fräulein Moltzer, and he is so foolish to be proud of this work of a woman with whom he is having an affair.[75]

Freud to Jones, 26 December 1912: As regards Jung he seems all out of his wits, he is behaving quite crazy ... I directed his attention to a certain *Verschreiben* [slip of the pen] in his letter ... It was after this that he broke loose furiously, proclaiming that he was not neurotic, having passed through a $\Psi\alpha$ treatment (with the Moltzer? I suppose, you may imagine what the treatment was), that I was the neurotic, I had spoiled Adler and Stekel, etc. ... It is the same mechanism and the identical reactions as in the Adler case.[76]

Ferenczi to Freud, 26 December 1912: Jung's behavior is uncommonly impudent. He forgets that it was *he* who demanded the 'analytic community' of students and treating students like patients ... *Mutual analysis* is nonsense, also an impossibility.[77] Everyone must be able to tolerate an authority over himself from whom he accepts analytic correction. You are probably the only one who can permit himself to do without an analyst ... despite all the deficiencies of self-analysis (which is certainly lengthier and more difficult than being analyzed), we have to expect of you the ability to keep your symptoms in check. If you had the strength to overcome in yourself, without a leader (*for the first time in the history of mankind*), the resistances which all humanity brings to bear on the results of analysis, then we must expect of you the strength to dispense with your lesser symptoms. – The facts speak decidedly in favor of this.

But what is valid for *you* is not valid for the rest of us. Jung has not achieved the same self-mastery as you. He got the results ready-made and accepted them lock, stock and barrel, without testing them out on himself. (I don't consider being analyzed by Fräulein Moltzer to be a fully adequate analysis.)[78]

Ferenczi, more lucidly than Freud, saw well that to reproach Jung in the manner in which he had reproached Freud would not serve anything. Since mutual analysis would not resolve the problem of conflicts of interpretation, Ferenczi proposed to re-establish the asymmetry (i.e., the principle of authority) through affirming the exceptional character of Freud's self-analysis. Instead of letting himself be drawn by Jung into a conflict of equals from which no one could escape unharmed, it was necessary to refuse the very terms of the debate and regain the 'meta' level. And what better way to do this than substituting a theory of the great man, of the singular and inimitable genius, for ordinary scientific and scholarly debate?

Just as the inauguration of training analysis was a means of institutionally resolving the hermeneutic conflicts inherent in psychoanalysis, the elevation of Freud's self-analysis to an exceptional status enabled him to escape from the problem of the symmetry introduced by training analysis – and from Freud's having to submit to analysis, and to the authority of someone else. For the institution of training analysis to work, there had to be one ultimate authority, who in turn could not be analysed. Thus Freud's self-analysis became the central pillar of psychoanalytic theory. Without it, psychoanalysis would collapse into a chaos of rival interpretations, with no means to adjudicate between them.

> **Lacan:** Now, it is quite certain, as everyone knows, that no psychoanalyst can claim to represent, in however slight a way, an absolute knowledge. That is why, in a sense, it can be said that if there is someone to whom one can apply there can be only one such person. This *one* was Freud, while he was still alive. The fact that Freud, on the subject of the unconscious, was legitimately the subject that one could presume to know, sets anything that had to do with the analytic relation, when it was initiated, by his patients, with him.[79]

Freud appears to have adopted Ferenczi's solution implicitly, even if a degree of modesty stopped him from presenting himself as brazenly as his disciple did. Hence his remark in 'On the history of the psychoanalytic movement', which is clearly a rejoinder to Jung:

> **Freud:** I am still of the opinion to-day that this kind of analysis may suffice for anyone who is a good dreamer and not too abnormal.[80]

The 'anyone' in question was himself. After the hiatus of the war, training analysis rapidly became the rule within the psychoanalytic movement. In 1919, Karl Abraham published an article in which he described self-analysis as a particular form of the resistance to psychoanalysis.

> **Abraham:** One element in such a 'self-analysis' is a narcissistic enjoy-
> ment of oneself; another is a revolt against the father. The unrestrained
> occupation with his own ego and the feeling of superiority already
> described offers the person's narcissism a rich store of pleasure. The
> necessity of being alone during the process brings it extraordinarily
> near to onanism and its equivalent, neurotic day-dreaming, both of
> which were earlier present to a marked degree in all the patients under
> consideration.[81]

At the Berlin Psychoanalytic Society, founded in 1920, Abraham, Hanns Sachs and Max Eitingon developed a standardised method of production of analysts through the triad of training analysis, supervision and seminars. This was soon emulated by all other psychoanalytic societies and also by other rival schools of psychotherapy. In 1925, at the psychoanalytic congress in Bad Homburg, a resolution was passed which formalised the necessity of a training analysis for all psychoanalytic candidates. Henceforth, to recall the previous epoch of self-analyses became bad taste. To Paul Schilder (who had not been analysed), Freud wrote in 1935 that those of the first psychoanalysts who had not been analysed 'were never proud of it'. As for himself, he added, 'one might perhaps assert the right to an exceptional position'.[82]

Thus we see that what was initially a short period of self-observation, which could in principle be replicated by anyone, became, through a series of disputes and crises, a literally extraordinary and unprecedented event, reserved for Freud alone. From now on, one could attribute anything to this exceptional event, as psychoanalysis itself was supposed to have arisen from it. It wasn't only the abandonment of the seduction theory or the discovery of the Oedipus complex and infantile sexuality that were attributed to it. At the end of his large volume on Freud's self-analysis, Didier Anzieu enumerated no less than 116 psychoanalytic notions or concepts which were elaborated by Freud in the course of his self-analysis, which he dated between 1895 and 1901.[83] Implicit in this is the notion that Freud's discoveries could only have been arrived at through the creation of a revolutionary new method of analysis which Freud was the first to use. Freud's self-analysis thus becomes the mythical origin of psychoanalysis, the historical event which places it outside history. Others, like Schur,[84] did not hesitate to identify psychoanalysis with Freud's interminable self-analysis (1895–1939). It followed that there couldn't be progress in psychoanalysis which was not a post-mortem deepening of the self-analysis of the founder (1895–). Every new development in psychoanalysis had to be backdated to the inaugural event itself. The mythification and the dehistoricisation of psychoanalysis were now complete.

The politics of replication

The heroic self-analysis never took place – or at least, it never took place in the manner in which it has been recounted. What transpired was a retrospective construction, aimed at immunising psychoanalysis from conflicts within it. It was a legend, but one with a very precise function: to silence opponents, to end the mutual diagnoses and to re-establish the asymmetry of interpretations in Freud's favour. To anyone who objected to the arbitrariness of his interpretations, he could now oppose his privileged, solitary and incomparable experience of the unconscious. Ultimately, the legend of Freud's self-analysis was a means to justify the argument from authority.

It is important to note that this legend was elaborated precisely when psychoanalysis left the domain of academic discussion to become a *Freudian* school of psychotherapy, and where disagreements were resolved simply by the exclusion of dissidents (after Adler, Stekel and Jung, there were Rank, Ferenczi and many others). The legend of the self-analysis corresponded to the privatisation of psychoanalytic science, which would henceforth be Freud's cause.

Freud often described the foundation of the International Psychoanalytic Association (IPA) as a necessary recourse, given the unanimous rejection of his theories by psychiatry and university psychology. However, the history of Freud's relations with his peers was actually much more complex. Far from psychoanalysis simply being excluded from institutions and academic exchanges, it deliberately withdrew from them, rather than attempting to create a consensus around its theories in an open manner. From this perspective, the ostracism of psychoanalysis is no less legendary than Freud's self-analysis. In fact, as we will see, the gradual privatisation of psychoanalysis was the mark of a failure to adapt to the normal regimes of scientific and scholarly discussion.

Initially, Freud did attempt to get his theories recognised by his peers. At the turn of the century, he had already gained a certain notoriety, but his theories were far from being at the centre of discussions between German-language psychiatrists (one of the reasons being that he was viewed as a neurologist without much psychiatric experience). As a Privatdozent, he was entitled to give lectures at the University of Vienna, but his audience was so small that he sometimes had trouble getting the minimum requirement of three attendees.[85] Those interested in psychoanalysis were generally either colleagues who became patients (such as Wilhelm Stekel) or patients who became colleagues (such as Emma Eckstein). Freud was clearly not faring well at promoting his theories. The situation changed somewhat in 1902. At the instigation of Stekel, he gathered together a group of doctors for weekly meetings. The other initial members were Alfred Adler, Max Kahane and Rudolf Reitler, soon followed by others. The proceedings were not harmonious.

> **Freud:** There were only two inauspicious circumstances which at last estranged me inwardly from the group. I could not succeed in establishing among its members the friendly relations that ought to obtain between men who are all engaged upon the same difficult work; nor

was I able to stifle the disputes about priority for which there were so many opportunities under these conditions of work in common.[86]

The structure of these discussions did not follow that of other psychological and psychiatric associations, as Fritz Wittels subsequently recalled.

> **Fritz Wittels:** Freud's design in the promotion of these gatherings was to have his own thoughts passed through the filter of other trained intelligences. It did not matter if the intelligences were mediocre. Indeed, he had little desire that these associates should be persons of strong individuality, that they should be critical and ambitious collaborators. The realm of psychoanalysis was his idea and his will, and he welcomed anyone who accepted his views. What he wanted was to look into a kaleidoscope lined with mirrors that would multiply the images he introduced into it.[87]

All this changed in 1904, when Eugen Bleuler, the director of the famous Burghölzli psychiatric hospital in Zurich, came into Freud's view.[88] That year, Bleuler reviewed Löwenfeld's *Psychical Obsessional Phenomena*,[89] which contained a chapter on Freud's and Janet's theories, and singled out Freud for praise.

> **Bleuler:** In his studies on hysteria and dreams, Freud has shown a part of a new world, and that is not all. Our consciousness sees only the puppets in its theatre; in the Freudian world, many of the strings which move the characters are shown.[90]

> **Freud to Fliess:** An absolutely stunning recognition of my point of view ... by an official psychiatrist, Bleuler, in Zurich. Just imagine, a full professor of psychiatry and my ††† studies of hysteria and the dream, which so far have been labelled disgusting![91]

This was not the first time that Bleuler had recommended Freud to the attention of his colleagues. In 1892, Bleuler had reviewed Freud's edition of Bernheim's *New Studies on Hypnosis, Suggestion and Psychotherapy* and praised Freud's translation.[92] In 1895, he wrote a positive review of Breuer and Freud's *Studies on Hysteria*, in which he nevertheless asked if their results weren't due to suggestion.[93]

Bleuler's interest in Freud's work was thus clearly linked to his interest in hypnosis and suggestive psychotherapy. This was no accident, for Bleuler had been a pupil of August Forel,[94] one of the great figures of European neurology and psychiatry and the promoter of a psycho-therapy of Bernheimian inspiration.

Forel, another important figure in this story, was also interested in Freud's work. In 1889, Freud started a correspondence with him, and wrote a very positive review of his book on hypnotism.[95] Forel recommended Freud to Bernheim when he went to Nancy, and invited him to the editorial committee of the *Zeitschrift für Hypnotismus*, a journal which he had founded in 1892 to draw together the Bernheimian movement.[96] He cited Freud in the second edition of his book on hypnotism among doctors who had taken up the issue of therapeutic suggestion following the work of the Nancy school.[97] A little later, he followed the works of Breuer and Freud with interest, going as far as introducing them to his American colleagues in a lecture he gave in 1899 at the celebration of the tenth anniversary of the founding of Clark University.[98] In 1903, he again cited favourably Freud's method of treatment, apparently not realising that the latter had given up cathartic hypnosis in the interim.[99]

> **Forel:** With hysterical people especially, regular mental disturbances can arise through suggestion and autosuggestion, and be cured only in the same way. Dr. Freud in Vienna has built up a whole doctrine and method of treatment based on the fact of such autosuggestions and the way they arouse the emotions. He calls a subconsciously preserved emotional affect ... *strangulated emotion* and with patients in whom it is present he tries by hypnotic suggestion to get back the memory of the original situation which produced the trouble in the first place, for often the patients themselves have forgotten it. Then by quieting suggestions he sets it aside. This undoubtedly succeeds in certain cases, but the mechanism is not always so simple. Every case is different, and we must individualise extraordinarily if we wish to get behind all the psychological conditions involved in such a trouble. But it is certain that if you gradually win the full confidence of such patients

you finally get back to the true cause of their disturbances and find out that the trouble really rests on suggestive effects of strong past emotions, particularly unpleasant emotions, which have established themselves chronically in the brain and continually disturb all its activities more or less.[100]

In 1898, Bleuler had succeeded Forel as director of the Burghölzli. The clinic proved to be the ideal terrain for psychoanalysis. Indeed, it is important to note that prior to the introduction of psychoanalysis at the Burghölzli, the practice of psychotherapy was already well established, together with the in-depth investigation of patients' histories, including the topic of sexuality. Forel had introduced there the use of hypnosis and suggestion and used them as techniques of experimentation, therapeutics and social control. However, in line with other hypnotic practitioners such as Bernheim, they had come to the view that whilst there were some benefits of the use of hypnosis and suggestion with psychotics, they had limited therapeutic value in this area. It is possible that one reason why Bleuler introduced psychoanalysis into the Burghölzli was to experiment with its potential therapeutic value with psychotics. The practice of psychoanalysis, in this sense, would simply have been seen as adding a few further variations to the existing repertoire of suggestive and hypnotic techniques. The institutional set-up at the Burghölzli permitted such an experimental utilisation.

In 1905, Bleuler and Freud commenced a correspondence, which lasted until 1914. Bleuler's letters to Freud are on open access at the Library of Congress, but aside from a few excerpts which have been cited, Freud's letters are not accessible.[101] On 9 October 1905, Bleuler wrote to Freud that he was convinced of the correctness of Freud's *The Interpretation of Dreams* as soon as he read it. However, he had trouble analysing his dreams, and so he wanted to send some to the master. Would Freud like to help him? Bleuler's self-analytical experiment directly followed from his self-investigation of hypnosis under Forel, and it was in keeping, more generally, with the use of introspection in psychology. It also followed the symmetric and dyadic practices prevalent at the Burghölzli. In *The Interpretation of Dreams*, Freud had asserted that the way to become a psychoanalyst was by interpreting one's dreams. Bleuler's request logically followed this recommendation: to master psychoanalysis, he would turn to Freud to learn how to analyse his dreams. Bleuler simply tried to replicate Freud's self-analysis.

Freud was more than happy – because this enabled him to consider his eminent colleague as a *patient*, introducing a dissymetry in their relation which had been absent in the symmetric rotations between subject and experimenter which Bleuler had been used to at the Burghölzli. When Bleuler's introspective judgments did not chime with Freudian theory, they were disqualified as resistances. Unsurprisingly, Bleuler vigorously protested.

> **Bleuler to Freud:** I am not aware of a struggle in your sense against the theory. I can also find no grounds for such a struggle in me.[102]

On 28 November 1905, Bleuler narrated to Freud how he had had diarrhoea at night from time to time, since puberty. He had long had a presentiment that this was connected to sexuality, but did not know how. The prospect for Freud was tantalising. Through Bleuler's interest, psychoanalysis had found a crucial beachhead from which to launch itself on the German-language psychiatric world. All he had to do was to get Bleuler to assent to his interpretations (and hope for some alleviation in his bowel movements).

> **Freud to Bleuler, 30 January 1906:** I am confident that we will soon conquer psychiatry.[103]

Unfortunately, Bleuler's intestines remained resistant to Freud's interpretations.

> **Ernst Falzeder:** One major factor for Bleuler's eventual decision not to fully endorse psychoanalytic theory, and to leave the psychoanalytic movement, was that . . . this *experimentum crucis* failed . . . Freud largely fostered this kind of negative reaction himself (that he soon came to regard as an offspring of resistance) by making exaggerated claims as to the simplicity and self-evidence of his healing-cum-research method.[104]

In the meantime, other experiments were taking place at the Burghölzli in the field of experimental psychopathology on associations. These were inscribed in a more general tendency to utilise the methods of the new scientific psychology in psychiatry. The psychiatrist Gustav Aschaffenburg, a student of Wundt, had applied the latter's work on verbal associations to psychopathological research. This drew the interest of the Burghölzli psychiatrists, notably Jung and Franz Riklin. It was hoped that the association experiment could provide a quick and reliable means of differential diagnosis. Despite grand promissory claims in print by Bleuler, this project was an abject failure. Experimenters failed to differentiate sexes, let alone make fine diagnostic discrimina-tions. Jung and Riklin salvaged the operation by linking failures to respond and failed reaction times to Freud's account of repression. The stimulus words, they claimed, could be regarded as indicators of affec-tively stressed complexes.

The linkage was fateful. Jung claimed that psychoanalysis was a difficult art, and that what was lacking was a basic framework. This could be provided by the association experiment, which could facil-itate and shorten psychoanalysis.[105] However, what was described as psychoanalysis strictly along Freud's lines included hypnosis and the recollection of traumatic sexual memories, from the time of the *Studies on Hysteria* and the defunct seduction theory. Visibly, news of changes in Freud's theories were slow to reach the Burghölzli. Jung, together with Forel and most contemporaries, did not realise that Freud's method had radically changed – and for good reason, since Freud had not clearly indicated his rupture with Breuer and his abandonment of the seduction theory.[106]

> **Jung:** At last in one of the latest sessions, came the narration of an event which in every respect had the significance of Freud's youth trauma.[107]

In paper after paper, the Burghölzli researches replicated Freud's abandoned theories. Association experiments, followed by abreac-tion, were throwing up a series of childhood sexual traumas. In other words, the Burghölzli psychiatrists were replicating and providing proof for theories which Freud had already abandoned. The situation was paradoxical. Freud had finally found an echo in mainstream psychiatry, but it was for theories which he had given up. Scientific replication, which was supposedly the source of reliable consensus, had led to the uncontrollable proliferation of simulacras. Freud, as one sees in his first exchanges with Jung and Abraham, had a delicate damage limitation exercise on his hands.

At any rate, Bleuler and Jung's advocacy of Freud (and before them, that of Forel) brought psychoanalysis far greater visibility in German-language psychiatry. The Burghölzli became the hotbed of psychoanalysis, and foreign visitors, such as Ernest Jones, Sándor Ferenczi and Abraham Brill, streamed to it, as it was the only institution where one could learn how to practise psychoanalysis. Psychoanalysis was treated not as a separate discipline, requiring specific training or authorisation to practise, but as an auxiliary technique in medicine and psychiatry. Visitors to the Burghölzli were able to hear lectures on the subject, attend staff meetings where patients were subjected to analytical questioning, and have some sessions of analysis with figures such as Jung, Riklin and Maeder. The Burghölzli utilised an open model of instruction, similar to the one that Bernheim had established at Nancy for the teaching of hypnosis.

Furthermore, Jung and Riklin's reformulation of the association experiment into a tool for clinical experimentation appeared to present psychoanalysis in a contemporary experimental manner. It was publicly demonstrable, complete with statistics, measurements down to the millisecond and sophisticated laboratory equipment such as the pneumograph. The association experiment had thus all the paraphernalia and trappings that were being increasingly taken as the hallmarks of science in psychology. Compared with this, Freud's sole apparatus of the couch seemed a relic of the hypnotic era. If one wanted to find out about psychoanalysis, the first destination of choice was therefore not Vienna, but Zurich. This brought several

problems with it, at least from Freud's point of view. Indeed, it
fostered a situation in which a growing number of psychiatrists started
getting interested in psychoanalysis without being in direct contact
with him. In addition, and more worryingly, if psychoanalysis could
easily be practised and tested, it could also as easily be disproven.

When a theory achieves greater visibility, it inevitably attracts
discussion and contradiction. From 1906 onward, a series of debates
about psychoanalysis took place in psychiatric congresses, which
lasted until 1913. It is striking that, despite invitations, Freud himself
did not take part. Aloof disengagement and deputised representation
were to be Freud's style. He delegated the task of defending his
theories to his followers and, withdrawing behind a haughty silence,
which his contemporaries viewed as a refusal of debate.

> **Jung, 29 August 1953:** He never risked himself in a congress and never
> defended his cause in public! ... This always made him afraid!
> America was the first and only time! ... He was too touchy![108]

May 1906, Baden-Baden: a congress of the South West German
Neurologists and Psychiatrists. Gustav Aschaffenburg, Professor of
Psychiatry at Cologne and former student of Wilhelm Wundt, presented
a paper on the 'Relations of sexual life to the development of nervous
and mental illnesses'. After considering the work of Leopold Löwenfeld
and Willy Hellpach, Aschaffenburg turned his attention to Freud.
Löwenfeld had noted that at the present time, since Freud alone was
the master of the psychoanalytic method, there was no way to test his
results. Aschaffenburg maintained, on the contrary, that this could be
done through the association experiment. Referring to Jung's recent
work, he argued that psychoanalysis was not fundamentally different
from the association experiment, and a consideration of the latter demonstrated that Freud interpolated a sexual meaning into harmless processes. Against this explanation Aschaffenburg acknowledged that one
had to consider the objection that patients confirmed Freud's interpretations. Daily experience showed that patients often expressed foolish

explanations for events and accepted them from others. The power of influence – particularly when Freud himself was convinced of the correctness of his conceptions and that his patients were hysterics – was enough to explain why this happened.

> **Gustav Aschaffenburg:** Freud lets the person whom he examines associate freely and this continues until, from time to time, he thinks that he has discovered a precise index, and then he draws his patient's attention to this and gets him to associate further starting from this new point of departure. But most patients who go to see Freud already know in advance where he wants to go and this thought immediately evokes complexes of representations connected to the sexual life ... But if the sexual trauma always appears with him as the final result of his psychoanalyses, there is in my view only one possible explanation: that Freud as much as his patients is a victim of an *auto-suggestion*.[109]

Thus an objective evalution of the analytic procedure was quite possible. Aschaffenburg's evaluation was resoundingly negative.

> **Aschaffenburg:** Freud's method is incorrect for most cases, dubious for many, and unnecessary for all.[110]

Freud did not reply to Aschaffenburg's critique. Instead, it was answered in print by Jung. Jung began by writing that he was replying to Aschaffenburg's 'very moderate and careful criticism' so as not to throw out the baby with the bath water. His line of defence was quite simple. First, he modified Freud's 'principles' 'with the understanding of the author' to the statement that an indefinitely large number of cases of hysteria stem from sexual roots.[111] Secondly, he argued that the only way to disprove this was to use Freud's method. If he wanted to substantiate his criticisms of arbitrary interpretation and auto-suggestion, this was all Aschaffenburg had to do.

> **Jung:** As soon as Aschaffenburg meets these requirements, that is to say, publishes psychanalyses with totally different results, we will have faith in his criticism, and then the discussion of Freud's theory can be opened.[112]

Jung's reply appeared in the *Müncher medizinische Wochenschrift* in October. The following month, there was a meeting of the South West German Psychiatrists in Tübingen. Two Swiss psychiatrists and former students of Forel, Ludwig Frank and Dumeng Bezzola, spoke on the analysis of psychotraumatic symptoms. Their interest in Breuer and Freud's cathartic method had been encouraged by Forel and his close collaborator Oskar Vogt.[113] Frank continued to develop it. Encouraged in this by Forel and Vogt, they both shared an interest in Breuer and Freud's cathartic method, which Frank had continued to develop under the name psychanalysis (*Psychanalyse*). Frank's presentation was induced by Aschaffenburg's critique at the congress in Baden-Baden, to which he objected, just like Jung, that only those who had practised psychanalysis were entitled to pass judgment on it. Based on his own experience, Frank presented a series of cases which, he claimed, demonstrated the effectiveness of the original Breuer–Freud method.

The support which Bezzola and Frank could provide Freud and the Burghölzli team was sizeable, since they could call on Forel and had numerous emulators in Forel's school (Karl Graeter, R. Loÿ, Charles de Montet, Philipp Stein, W. Warda,[114] etc.). Here were psychiatrists from across Europe who were replicating psychoanalysis and producing independent confirmations of it – exactly what was needed, in principle, to create a consensus around Freud's theories. However, the problem was that the psychanalysis of which Frank spoke was no less dissimilar to Freud's method than Jung and Riklin's first association experiments.

Above all, it was a psychoanalysis without the 'o'. Freud's first use of the word psychoanalysis was in a paper published in French in the *Revue neurologique*.[115] His French neologism, *psychoanalyse*, appears to have been directly modelled on the word psychotherapy.

> **Freud:** I owe my results to a new method of psychoanalysis [*d'une nouvelle méthode de psychoanalyse*], Josef Breuer's exploratory procedure ... By means of that procedure – this is not the place to

describe it – hysterical symptoms are traced back to their origin, which is always found in some event of the subject's sexual life appropriate for the production of a distressing emotion.[116]

Curiously, Freud provided no definition, justification or extended description of the term, but simply retroactively applied it to what he had been content to describe in the previous year as a method of psychotherapy. Pierre Janet was later to complain that Freud had simply appropriated his work and that his psychoanalysis was nothing but a copycat name for his own psychological analysis (*analyse psychologique*).

> **Pierre Janet:** They [Breuer and Freud] spoke of psychoanalysis where I had spoken of psychological analysis. They invented the name complex, whereas I had used the term psychological system . . . They spoke of catharsis where I had spoken of the dissociation of fixed ideas or of moral disinfection. The names differed, but the essential ideas I had put forward . . . were accepted without modification.[117]

Thus, for Janet, psychoanalysis was nothing but a copycat name for his own psychological analysis. Forel and his students, on the other hand, noted that Freud's term was a barbarism which indicated an ignorance concerning the correct formation of words from Greek roots.[118]

> **Dumeng Bezzola to Jung, 1 May 1907:** One speaks of psychoanalysis, as if the apostrophising was not as appropriate as with other compounds. Who says psychoiatry, psychoasthenia, etc.?[119]

> **Forel:** I write 'psychanalysis' like Bezzola, Frank and Bleuler, and not 'psychoanalysis' as Freud does, according to the rational and euphonic derivation of the word. On this subject, Bezzola remarks for good reason that one writes 'psychiatry' and not 'psychoiatry'.[120]

In addition, this psychanalysis relieved of its 'o' was a *Breuerian* psychanalysis. Frank and Bezzola reproached Freud for having abandoned the essential element of the cathartic method – hypnosis – without a convincing explanation. Hence, Frank recommended a type of hypnoanalysis combining interpretation and the induction of a hypnoid state. (Thus, before Lacan's return to Freud, there had already been a return to Breuer in the history of psychoanalysis.)

> **Ludwig Frank:** The original Breuer–Freud method which Freud later abandoned was analysis under hypnosis. I use this method most often and have studied it in the course of the years and it appears to me to be valuable.[121]

Bezzola likewise proposed a 'modification of the Breuer–Freud procedure', which he called 'psychosynthesis'. He placed the patient in a relaxed position with closed eyes and, instead of Freudian associations, collected direct sensory impressions. In this regard, he found Jung's association complexes of great heuristic value. Introductory hypnosis as well as Freud's procedure of interpretation was unnecessary, since the self-observation of neurotic sensations could by itself bring about the experience corresponding to the hypnoid state.

> **Bezzola to Jung, 1 May 1907:** Like psychoanalysis, it is another modification of the Breuerian method. The principle of healing (discovered by Breuer) remains the same.[122]

Finally, just like Breuer, Frank and Bezzola refused to follow Freud in his unilateral insistence on sexuality, however enlarged.

> **Frank:** Freud has abandoned this method [the cathartic method] since many years. It is very much to be regretted that he has not given the grounds for this. His new method of treatment through interpretation and the limitless enlargement of his concept of sexuality have provoked in the discussion such a violent opposition to everything promoted and accomplished by Freud that there is a danger that also Breuer's method of treatment and valuable developments by Freud [an allusion to the pressure method described by Freud in the *Studies on Hysteria*] will become forgotten and overlooked ... It seems to me that Freud no longer takes account in his method of interpretation, at least in a great number of cases, of the important role of the hypnoid state in their genesis, to which he himself had drawn attention.[123]

Frank also noted that he had found that he couldn't lead all cases back to a sexual cause, and he also thought that it wasn't necessary to look for one if the treatment was successful. Clearly, the psychanalysis and psychosynthesis that Frank and Bezzola advocated against Aschaffenburg were *rivals* to Freud's psychoanalysis. These new allies were in fact competitors.

In the discussion following Frank and Bezzola's presentations, the psychiatrist Alfred Hoche expressed his profound scepticism regarding Freud's new method.

> **Hoche**: Certainly there is much that is new and good in Freud's teaching of the psychoanalysis of hysteria; unfortunately the good is not new and the new is not good. That only good can come from medico-therapeutic effect of a deepened analysis of psychic phenomena and an intensive entering into the particular individuality of a single case, that for the patient to become clear about latent oppressing things and thus come to an expression where understanding is available, can be a relief, and even a solution. All this is not new. But the frequency with which the specifically sexual factor should play the main role according to Freud and others is not good. What have we then heard today? That doctors who have applied psychotherapy with interest and energy have succeeded in eliminating in a suggestive manner a series of subjectively tormenting conditions. That this is possible, we have known for a long time, but it does not need the label of a special method, which comes with the pretension of indicating something completely new. He who reads the Freudian 'Fragment of a hysteria-analysis' without prejudice will only put it down shaking his head. For my part, I must confess that it is for me wholly incomprehensible how anyone can take the train of thought produced there seriously. Still less do I understand it, if we – those present – are reproached that we are not at all in a position to be spoken with as long as we have not likewise utilized this 'method'. Such a reproach misfires, since we take the whole presupposition to be invalid. It therefore borders on comic relief when the opposition to Freudian ideas is set in parallel with the resistance of contemporaries to Copernican views, as happened in private discussions.[124]

In response, Jung, who was also present, reiterated Frank's (and his own) view that one could not assert that Freud was wrong without having employed psychanalysis. To this, the psychiatrist Max Isserlin replied that he had attempted to replicate Jung's experiments, and whilst he had confirmed Jung's thesis that emotionally stressed complexes led to lengthened reaction times, he had found no data which established a standardisation of these complexes in the sense of Freudian theory, i.e., sexual traumata. Finally, Robert Gaupp cautioned against Hoche's views as being too harsh. Whilst he was opposed to the exaggerations of the Freudian teaching, Bleuler and his school had the right to the unprejudiced verification of their experimentally established positions.

In the published version of his paper, Bezzola added an appendix in which he protested Hoche's complete identification of his views with Freud's theory of neurosis. He had not stressed his differences in his paper, he wrote, out of respect for the stimulation he had received from Breuer and Freud's *Studies on Hysteria*.

> **Bezzola:** Freud analyses symbolism and interprets it according to the causative experience. He constructs and suggests this. I let it be put together by the patient himself through primary sensations and movement impulses. I let it be directly experienced. With Freud the doctor works under the control of the patient, with me the patient works under the control of the doctor. With me the danger of false interpretation is excluded, because I avoid every suggestion, except those for relaxation.[125]

Bezzola couldn't have been clearer: Freud's psychoanalysis – with its false interpretations and suggestions – had been superceded by his own psychosynthesis. It is worth noting here that Freud was not the only figure at this time who claimed that he was not imposing on the patient: Bezzola was using against him precisely the same argument that he was using to distinguish his method from other psychotherapeutic techniques. Freud viewed the situation differently. At this stage, he found no need to differentiate psychoanalysis from psychosynthesis.

> **Freud to Jung, 7 April 1907:** Bezzola's work does not give me the impression of honesty ... The appended remarks spring from a very

hopeful personal cowardice. To deny that psychosynthesis is the same as psychoanalysis seems downright deceitful.[126]

Jung's relations with Bezzola soured. On 24 May, he described him to Freud as a 'small *and common* soul'.[127] Freud replied: 'I have no reason to regard Bezzola and Frank as belonging to us.'[128]

Frank and Bezzola's project, to dissociate themselves from Freud and to propose a non-Freudian psychanalysis or psychosynthesis, had the complete support of Forel. From the moment when he realised how far Freud had departed from his original method, Forel became very critical of him. Just like Aschaffenburg and Hoche, he was disturbed by the arbitrariness of Freud's interpretations, as well as by his increasing influence in Forel's former institution, the Burghölzli. As his correspondence between 1907 and 1910 shows, he urged his disciples to take strong positions against the Freudian deviation, so as to be able to separate the 'the true wheat from the chaff'.[129]

Forel to Frank, 15 November 1907: This Freud cult disgusts me, just as it disgusts Bezzola. I leave open the question if the famous discovery of Freud is really his and doesn't rather belong to Breuer, but it is certain that in Vienna, where people aren't prudish, Freud has a very bad reputation which is not unfounded ... It appears to me as if Bleuler is no longer the director of the Burghölzli, but Jung, and I am sorry.[130]

Forel to Bezzola, 22 November 1907: For that reason you do not need to join any Freud club, by any means. For me, Freud himself is highly unsympathetic, but I think you will achieve more in your position if you confront Frank peacefully and frankly and if you sometime fight a battle with the Freud fools, than if you make way for them.[131]

Forel to Bezzola, 21 September 1908: I have now a case in treatment (through hypnosis) that had been completely shattered through psychoanalysis of Freud & his school. The person became half crazy from outspoken 'sexual' interpretations of the most harmless things. I think there is a type of psychoanalysis that produces more complexes than it eliminates![132]

Bezzola to Forel, 22 August 1909: I hope to put the last touches to a more important publication sometime this January. The essential aim is to defend the sovereignty of the psychic against the foreign inter-pretations of its means of expression and to anticipate the objections of the Freudian school that I do not go the bottom of 'complexes'.[133]

Forel to Bezzola, 17 May 1910: It worries me that you haven't written your book about your experiences. This is an *urgent* necessity. The whole question is completely corrupted and discredited by Freud and his clique. It is high time that the reasonable and scientific psychana-lysts intervene with a serious and important work.[134]

Not content with anti-Freudian agitation in the background, Forel wrote to Breuer, whom he had known since his student days in Vienna, to ask him to indicate precisely 'which part of psychanalysis went back to him, what role he had in psychoanalysis'.[135] Breuer obliged. He himself was responsible for 'everything which directly followed from the case of Anna O.' – the theory of hypnoid states and non-abreacted affective representations, the notion of retention hys-teria and analytic therapy (Breuer first wrote 'psychanalytic'). Freud was responsible for the notions of conversion, defence neuroses, and the accent placed on defence to the detriment of hypnoid states (hardly 'to the benefit of his theory', Breuer added). To both of them belonged the emphasis on 'the prominent place assumed by sexual-ity'.[136] Thus Breuer did not hesitate to claim his part in the discovery of the role of sexuality in hysteria. At the same time, just as he had done in *Studies on Hysteria*, he stressed the asexual character of Anna O.

Breuer to Forel, 21 November 1907: The case of Anna O., which was the germinal cell of the whole of psychoanalysis, proves that a fairly severe case of hysteria can develop, flourish and be resolved without having a sexual basis.[137]

Forel immediately forwarded his letter to Bezzola, recommending him to 'read between the lines':[138] Breuer had stated that the analytic therapy directly derived from the case of Anna O. One could draw the conclusion that since this case lacked a 'sexual basis', true psych-analysis had nothing to do with the Freudians' sexuality and 'fabrica-tion of complexes'.[139]

> **Forel, 1908:** On the other hand, the psychanalytic method discovered by Breuer and Freud is very important, thanks to which one can eliminate the pathogenic effect of emotional traumas and the possi-bility that they continue to exercise devastating supplementary effects in the subconscious cerebral life through enabling them to be relived. However, on this point Freud has also made a unilateral construction and simply abandoned the foundation of suggestion and hypnosis, whereas in reality all these phenomena should be studied and under-stood in their harmonious interdependence. When one proceeds dif-ferently, as when one bores into the research of so-called complexes, one risks, in the numerous cases where these continually come to the surface, arriving at a noxious training of the brain, a fabrication of complexes which can be particularly disastrous in the case of sexual complexes.[140]

Discussions concerning psychoanalysis continued at the International Congress for Psychiatry, Neurology and Psychology in Amsterdam in September 1907. The controversy was becoming internationalised. Freud had initially been invited, along with Janet.

> **Freud to Jung, 14 April 1907:** When I was invited, Aschaffenburg was not to be the other speaker; two were mentioned, Janet and a native. Apparently a duel was planned between Janet and myself, but I detest gladiatorial fights in front of the noble rabble and cannot easily bring myself to put my findings to the vote of an indifferent crowd.[141]

If a Freud–Janet duel was not to be, owing to Freud's no-show, there was still another duel on offer.

> ***Monatschrift für Psychiatrie und Neurologie***: The *Jung–Aschaffenburg* duel was looked forward to with great anticipation by many German-speaking participants.[142]

The fifth session was on hysteria, and featured presentations by Janet, Aschaffenburg, Jung and Gerbrandus Jelgersma. Janet opened the session by presenting a résumé of his work on hysteria. Aschaffenburg followed, limiting himself to a discussion of Freud's method of free association and Jung's association experiments: why did Freud and his followers find sexual complexes so frequently? To answer this question, Aschaffenburg narrated a case of obsessional neurosis which he had treated to test the Freudian method. This was clearly a response to Jung's previous paper, and Aschaffenburg claimed that this case demonstrated how thoughts could be led in a certain direction.

> **Aschaffenburg:** The Freudian and Jungian method results in sexual representations, because it promotes the emergence of sexual representations through directing and often really forcing attention to the sexual sphere.[143]

Freud and Jung thus suggested the associations they claimed only to observe. His own researches had convinced Aschaffenburg that such an investigation was embarrassing and potentially harmful for the patient and that the success of the treatment did not surpass that of other harmless methods.

Aschaffenburg was followed by Jung, who opened by stressing that if he restricted himself to Freud, it was not out of disregard for the outstanding work of Charcot, Moebius, Strumpell, Janet, Sollier, Vogt, Binswanger, Krehl and Dubois (interestingly enough, this statement was cut when Jung republished the paper later the same year). The best way to understand Freud's work, Jung claimed, was through a historical overview.

> **Jung:** The theoretical presuppositions for the mental work of Freudian research lie above all else in the knowledge of Janetian experiments. Breuer and Freud's first formulation of the problem of hysteria starts from the facts of psychic dissociation and of unconscious psychic automatisms. A further presupposition so emphatically stressed by Binswanger among others is the aetiological significance of affects. Both these presuppositions together with the experiences drawn from the theory of suggestion result in the currently generally recognised view of hysteria as a psychogenic neurosis. Freud's research is directed

to finding by which means and in what manner the mechanism of the production of hysterical symptoms works.[144]

Jung proceeded to give an account of Freud's theoretical development. Jung referred throughout to psychanalysis, *sans* 'o'. Jung noted, admittedly, that the present psychanalytic method was much more complicated than the original cathartic method, and took two years of extensive practice to be able to use with any security.[145] But he also added that this brought it close to other contemporary methods.

> **Jung:** In this respect the new Freudian method has a great similarity with Dubois' method of education ... Bezzola's method of psychosynthesis on the other hand is a direct, very interesting further development of the Breuer–Freud cathartic method of abreaction. The theoretical basis of Freudian psychanalytic method, which has grown entirely through practical empiricism, is still covered in a deep darkness. Through my association research I think that I have at least made a few points accessible to experimental investigation, though all theoretical difficulties have still not yet been overcome.[146]

One can only presume that, on reading this, Freud may well have had second thoughts about deciding not to attend this congress. In Jung's history the basic presuppositions of his own research lay principally in Janet's work on dissociation and automatisms, coupled with the work of Otto Binswanger, suggestion theory (i.e., Bernheim and Forel) and the generally recognised notion of hysteria as a psychogenic neurosis. In addition, Freud's new method was linked with Dubois and placed alongside Bezzola's. Jung was clearly attempting to recruit allies and was casting his net as widely as possible. However, this had the effect of completely diluting the specificity of psychoanalysis as Freud understood it. What is worse, Jung suggested that the deep darkness which lay over the theoretical basis of Freud's method was being clarified through the light shed by Jung's own association experiments. Freud could not have failed to notice the similarities with Frank and Bezzola. Freud was in danger of becoming a bystander, a footnote in the history of the psychoanalytic movement.

Jung's paper ran over time and was cut short.

Ernest Jones: Unfortunately [Jung] made the mistake of not timing his paper and also of refusing to obey the chairman's repeated signal to finish. Ultimately he was compelled to, whereupon with a flushed angry face he strode out of the room. I remember the unfortunate impression his behaviour made on the impatient and already prejudiced audience, so there can be no doubt about the issue of the debate.[147]

In the discussion, the issue of the possibility of replication of Freud's results was raised once again. Otto Gross noted that the whole debate centred around the question of whether the Freudian method could be verified without a knowledge of the special Freudian technique. Frank repeated his and Jung's claim that those who had not practised the method themselves could not judge it. To this, Heilbronner replied that in his clinic in Utrecht his assistant Schnitzler had made experiments concerning the existence of affectively stressed complexes, and the results had been negative. The discussion was concluded by Pierre Janet, whose prior references to Freud in his works had so far been respectful. This was not to be the case this time.

Janet: The first work of Breuer and Freud on hysteria is to my mind an interesting contribution to the work of French doctors, who for fifteen years have analysed the mental states of hysterics by means of hypnotism or automatic writing. The French authors have shown certain interesting cases in which the fixed subconscious ideas played a great role. Breuer and Freud have shown similar cases, but they have immediately generalised and have declared that all hysteria is constituted by subconscious fixed ideas of this kind. In a second study they have noted problems of the genital sense in certain hysterics. This is perfectly exact: one notes fixed ideas of an erotic order with some hysterics, insufficiency of the sexual sense, or more or less light perversions of the genital instincts. This is incontestable and this has been described many times with a great depth of pathological analysis. But why generalise these true observations in a completely excessive manner, why declare that all hysteria consists in this genital perturbation of several patients?[148]

In other words, what was good in psychoanalysis was not new, and stemmed from Janet's own work. What was new was not good, and could safely be left to Freud.

Freud Inc.[149]

Psychoanalysis was not faring well in open debate at psychiatric congresses. If Bleuler and Jung's advocacy had put psychoanalysis on the map, there was the very real danger that it would now be publicly tested, disproven and discarded by leading psychiatrists. So a new plan of action took shape. On 30 November 1907, Jung informed Freud that a new arrival, Dr Jones from London, together with Jung's friends from Budapest[150] had suggested a congress of Freudian followers. On 30 January 1908, Jung informed Karl Abraham that he was not going to invite Bezzola, and asked Abraham to find more participants, 'provided that they are people with pro-Freudian interests. Please would you stress in each case the private nature of the project.'[151] The 'First Congress for Freudian Psychology', which took place at the end of April in Salzburg, was to be a secret admittance by invitation only event, with no criticism allowed. This *private* meeting, which set the tone for future psychoanalytic congresses across the world, represented a return to Freud's weekly meetings with his disciples in Vienna. Once again, Freud could see his ideas replicated by the kaleidoscope which Wittels referred to.

However, what Bleuler would later call the politics of the closed door did not entirely solve the situation; far from it. In accordance with a pattern which would be constantly repeated, the controversies which the Freudians attempted to evade externally soon resurfaced internally. Ultimately, there was little difference between the external debates and the internal dissensions.

Already at the first meeting at Salzburg, a conflict arose between Jung and Abraham, who had previously worked under Jung and Bleuler at the Burghölzli. Both presented papers on dementia praecox (which would soon be termed 'schizophrenia' by Bleuler), and whilst Abraham attempted to apply Freud's libido theory to its elucidation, Jung presented his view that the loss of reality in dementia praecox could not be explained on the basis of the libido theory, and indeed, that the condition could not be explained purely psycho-genically, and invoked an unknown toxin as a possible aetiological factor. Whilst Abraham did not mention his former superiors at the Burghölzli, aside from a few gestures of praise, Jung's paper was basically independent of Freud's work. Freud interpreted this doctrinal dispute betwen Jung and himself as a priority dispute between Abraham and Jung.

> **Ernst Falzeder:** The controversy between Abraham and Jung amounted to a 'war by proxies'. Both spoke not only for themselves, but also for Freud and Bleuler respectively and let us repeat that Abraham had himself been a member of the Burghölzli team … Freud had actively encouraged Abraham to present his paper and even assured him that it would not bring him into conflict with Jung … Thus it seems that Freud had brought about the very conflict he then deplored. He then tried to obfuscate that fact and to put the blame on Abraham and Jung. In the aftermath of the Congress, Freud reinterpreted the conflict as a *priority dispute between Abraham and Jung*; a conflict over the priority of being the first to solve the riddle of schizophrenia with the help of psychoanalysis. Simultaneously, however, Freud made it perfectly clear that the actual priority was with *himself.*[152]

This set the tone for how Freud would attempt to settle disputes within his movement, through arranging his followers in a hierarchical manner and asserting his authority. In reframing his horizontal conflict with Jung into one between his disciples, Freud was arrogating the right to intervene in the debate vertically, from a position of uncontested authority. This strategy furnished the model which Freud would follow in subsequent internal conflicts: each time one of his collaborators attempted to have an open discussion with him as between equals, as his psychiatric colleagues had attempted to do from the exterior, he reduced him to the status of a pupil, leaving him no choice but to toe the line or quit the movement and join the growing crowd of his critics. Hence, the boundary between the interior and the exterior of the movement was extremely fluid and was constantly being redrawn as a result of expulsions. The closed door began to resemble a revolving door.

At the same juncture, there were significant moves on the outside. In 1908, Forel published an article proposing the idea of a general association of psychotherapy.[153] Assessing the current state of the discipline, he noted the undesirable presence of all sorts of pseudo-therapists: 'Charlatans, magnetic healers, the New York Institute of Science, Lourdes miracle workers, Spas, Naturepaths and co.'.[154] By contrast, there were the anti-suggestive therapies of Lévy and Dubois, advocating persuasion and the will based on a confused dualist psychology. Then there was the psychanalytic method of Breuer and Freud, which represented a very important development. Unfortunately, Freud had developed his earlier studies in a unilateral manner, abitrarily discarding hypnosis and suggestion, instead of studying phenomena in their interdependence. Faced with this regrettable situation, Forel proposed to create a truly scientific international society of psychotherapy. He added that the aim of such a society was essentially to organise annual congresses which would draw together psychotherapists of all tendencies, without exclusions. In August 1909, Forel sent a circular letter to the main representatives of European psychotherapy, including Freud and Jung, to invite them to join the International Society of Medical Psychology and Psychotherapy, which he proposed to establish with Oskar Vogt and Ludwig Frank. Forel felt that the lack of coordination between the different orientations of psychotherapy was a critical problem. He wanted to create order in this 'tower of Babel'[155] by facilitating scientific exchanges and through establishing 'a clear international terminology, capable of being accepted in a general manner by different people'.[156]

Forel, circular of August 1909: On the one hand, psychotherapy is completely neglected by the faculties of medicine; on the other hand, it consists in individual attempts which are entirely dispersed, without links between them. In the congresses, one has rarely had the time to discuss the important questions which are brought in: hypnotism, suggestion, psychanalysis, in the measure insofar as these meetings are occupied with other subjects.[157]

Forel, first Congress of the International Society of Medical Psychology and Psychotherapy (7–8 August 1910):[158] Hypnotic suggestion (there is little difference if it is employed in the waking or sleeping state) and psychanalysis are psycho-therapeutic agents of the first order and have proved reliable. Yet today one is supremely unaware of them in the medical faculties, just as one ignores the true scientific psychology.[159]

Forel, official announcement of the foundation of the International Society of Medical Psychology and Psychotherapy: [Psychotherapy] thus comprises, above all, therapeutic suggestion, psychanalysis and analogous methods, based directly on a well-understood psychology . . . But scorned and neglected in general by the faculties of medicine, psychology and psychiatry have been studied above all by autodidacts who have formed special or local schools, such as at Paris, Nancy, Vienna, etc., schools which have each developed according to their special ideas, without contact with the others, without in-depth scientific discussions, without agreement on terms.

As a result of this situation, it seems to me that many things are highly necessary.

1   Obtain an international agreement to help the scientific discussions in the domain which occupies us – agreement on the facts and on the terms.

2   Unify neurological science and make it known in all its branches by the faculties of medicine.[160]

Freud and Jung had already left to attend the Clark Conference and to conquer America. They found Forel's circular on their return at the beginning of October. By that time, the Society had already been founded.[161] The formation of this society placed them in an unexpectedly awkward position. Forel proposed to draw together the diverse psychotherapies, without according a special status to psycho-analysis. Forel and Frank were taking the reins, under the banner of a true scientific psychology, and were offering Freud and Jung a back seat in the new organisation. After a long hesitation, Freud and Jung nevertheless decided to accept Forel's invitation in mid November, so as not to leave the field to their rivals.[162] The same month, at a professional meeting of Swiss psychiatrists, Forel and Jung made an alliance to isolate Constantin von Monakow, co-founder with Paul Dubois of a third association of psychotherapists, the Society of Neurologists.[163] In December, Forel sent Freud a dedicated copy of the eleventh edition of his book *Brain and Soul*.[164] More surprising yet, Freud briefly envisaged infiltrating the International Order for Ethics and Culture of Pastor Kneipp, an organisation in which Forel actively participated, before abandoning the idea on Jung's advice.[165]

> **Jung to Freud, 11 February 1910:** PsA makes me 'proud and discon-tent', I dont want to attach it to Forel, that hair-shirted John of the Locust, but would like to attach it with everything that was ever dynamic and alive … I shall submit this crucial question for PsA to the Nuremberg Congress.[166]

In the meantime, the idea of an International Association of Psychoanalysis had germinated, formally grouping together adherents to Freud's doctrine. The timing was clearly not accidental.

> **Freud to Ferenczi, 1 January 1910:** Incidentally, what do you think of a tighter organisation with formal rules and a small fee? Do you consider this advantageous? I also wrote Jung a couple of words about this.[167]

> **Ferenczi to Freud, 2 January 1910:** I find your suggestion (tighter organization) extremely useful. The acceptance of members, however, would be just as strictly managed as it is in the Vienna Society; that would be a way of keeping out undesirable elements.[168]

Meanwhile, discussions continued to rage concerning psychoanalysis. On 29 March, there was a heated debate on psychoanalysis at the

Medical Society in Hamburg, following a talk by Jan van Embden on the psychoneuroses. Embden launched an attack on psychoanalysis. He argued that the significant role which Freud attributed to sexuality had not been proven, and that the success of Freud's theory, like that of Dubois, rested on suggestion and education. He warned against referring patients to asylums where psychoanalysis was practised (in all likelihood, his main target was the Burghölzli). In the discussion, Trömner argued that the basic elements of Freud's theory of hysteria were fine (i.e., the conversion of non-abreacted affects), but that Freud had erected monstrous theories from Breuer's correct starting point. As for Freud's interpretations of dreams, he notes that they were nearly identical to those which had been proposed long ago by Scherner. Max Nonne noted that, following Emil Kraepelin and Theodore Ziehen, most German psychiatrists were critical of psychoanalysis. He argued that sexual traumas were actually common in childhood, but that they were not the causes of traumas in the Freudian sense. Like Embden, he stated that he would not let a patient in a sanatorium be treated in a Freudian manner.[169]

Shortly after the Hamburg discussion, the Freudians regrouped, and the creation of the International Psychoanalytic Association was formally announced at the Nuremberg Congress (30–31 March 1910). At Nuremberg, Ferenczi presented a rationale for the new organisation. Presenting a heroic account of Freud's struggle against opposition, he maintained that from the beginning psychoanalysts had been met with empty invective, and that hence 'we were thus, very much against our will, involved in a war'.[170]

> **Ferenczi:** New workers streamed into the new scientific field discovered by Freud just as they had streamed in the wake of Amerigo to the new continent discovered by Columbus, and they too had to, and still have to, conduct guerrilla warfare, just as the pioneers in the New World did.[171]

If Freud was Columbus, it followed that other psychologists and psychiatrists had to take the role of the American Indians. Ferenczi, waxing strategic, noted that this warfare waged by the psychoanalysts had not been successful thus far, because of the lack of central direction and the self-serving conduct of some psychoanalysts. The time had come to rectify this by forming a centralised organisation. This would have the advantage of segregating others who took an independent interest in psychoanalysis. Such 'friends', he claimed, were more dangerous than enemies. As an example he cited psycho-synthesis, without even mentioning Bezzola by name. Thus, for Ferenczi, the formation of the IPA was justified as much by the neccesity to defend against undesirable allies as by the need to rally the troups against the enemies. Later that same year, Freud echoed Ferenczi's reasoning.

> **Freud:** Neither I myself nor my friends and co-workers find it agreeable to claim a monopoly in this way in the use of a medical technique. But in face of the dangers to patients and to the cause of psycho-analysis which are inherent in the practice that is to be foreseen of a wild psycho-analysis, we have had no other choice. In the spring of 1910 we founded an International Psycho-Analytical Association, to which its members declare their adherence by the publication of their names, in order to be able to repudiate responsibility for what is done by those who do not belong to us and yet call their medical procedure psycho-analysis. For as a matter of fact wild analysts of this kind do more harm to the cause of psycho-analysis than to individual patients.[172]

By wild psychoanalysts, Freud evidently had figures such as Bezzola and Frank in mind.

In his 'History of the psychoanalytic movement', Freud justified the creation of the IPA by the necessity of drawing the ranks together, 'since official science had pronounced its solemn ban upon psycho-analysis'.[173] However, it is clear that the IPA was first and foremost a means of resisting psychoanalysis being swallowed up by the competition represented by Forel and his friends. As Freud explained to Bleuler in October of the same year, one of the 'reasons for organizing a society' was 'the need to present to the public genuine psychoanalysis and protect it from imitations (counterfeits) which would soon arise'.[174] We have become so used to considering psychoanalysis as *Freudian* that we do not even consider that there could have been non-Freudian psychanalysts. But this is a retrospective (asymmetric) illusion, which grants victory to the IPA over rival organisations. At the time, the strict identification of psychoanalysis with Freud was by no means self-evident. As we have seen, there was widespread debate concerning who could rightfully claim possession of *Breuer's* heritage. In this respect, the creation of the IPA was an attempt to gain the upper hand in the (symmetric) mimetic rivalry between the Freudians and the Forelians. Which one was to conquer the new continent of psychotherapy: psychanalysis according to Breuer, Forel and Frank, or psychoanalysis according to Freud and his followers? Without much exaggeration, one could say that before splitting into rival schools, the IPA itself was the product of a schism within the psych(o)analytic movement.

Around the same time, Frank published a book titled *Psychanalysis*,[175] in which he openly advocated return of psychanalysis to Breuer, critiquing the Freudian deviation. Unsurprisingly, Freud did not appreciate this.

> **Freud to Jung, 22 April 1910:** On the other hand it was with pure distaste that I read Frank's cowardly and abject book on psycho-analysis, in which he naturally accuses me of exaggerating the importance of sexuality and then proceeds to go me one better.[176]

Initially, however, the relations between the Forelians and the Freudians were not completely openly hostile. We have already seen signs of this fact.

Frank attended the Nuremberg Psychoanalytic Congress[177] (one can imagine what he would have made of Ferenczi's harangue) and Ernest Jones went to the first congress of Forel's society in Brussels in August 1910[178] (Freud himself had declined Vogt's invitation, as usual).[179] The appearance was that the Freudians were continuing to play the game of scientific exchanges. However, one incident at the time of the inauguration of the International Psychoanalytic Association revealed that this was not a scholarly society like others. The psychiatrist Max Isserlin, who had written a critical review of Jung's *The Psychology of Dementia Praecox*,[180] requested permission to attend the Nuremberg conference.

> **Jung to Freud, 2 March 1910:** I beg you to let me know *by return* whether we should allow such vermin to come to N. [Nuremberg]. Myself, I'd rather not have the bastard around, he might spoil one's appetite. But our *splendid isolation* must come to an end one day.[181]

> **Freud to Jung, 6 March 1910:** I too believe that our isolation must come to an end some day, and then we shall not have to hold separate congresses. But I think that day is still far off and that we can do with other guests than Isserlin.[182]

Isserlin was barred from attending. The incident shocked many, since such exclusive practices were unheard of in medicine and psychiatry at this time. Emil Kraepelin was furious.[183] It was in this context that Hoche, two months later, gave a paper to the congress of neurologists and psychiatrists of south-west Germany in Baden entitled 'A psychic epidemic among doctors'. His accusation was clear: the Freudians were behaving like a cult.

> **Hoche, 28 May 1910:** In a surprising manner, a great number of disciples, some clearly fanatical, have presented themselves to Freud and follow where he leads them. To speak of this as a Freudian school is in reality completely misplaced, as it is a question not of facts which are scientifically provable or demonstrable, but of articles of faith; in truth, if I leave aside a few more considered heads, it is a community of believers, a sort of sect, with all the characteristerics which go along with this ... To become a member of the sect isn't at all easy. This demands a long novitiate which is ideally terminated by the master himself. At the same time, not anyone can become a disciple, but only those who have faith. He who does not believe has no success, and with few exceptions, cannot speak. What is common with all the members of the sect is the high degree of veneration for the Master, which only perhaps finds its analogue in the personality cult of the circle of

Bayreuth [i.e., around Wagner] . . . The Freudian movement is in fact a return, under a modern form, of a *medicina magica*, a secret doctrine which can only be practised by qualified interpreters of signs.[184]

As for Bleuler, he was so taken aback by the Isserlin incident that he was reluctant to join the new association. Not content with having barred Isserlin from attending the congress, the Freudians had decided to restrict membership of the IPA to the faithful. Bleuler considered that such exclusionary tactics had no place in a scientific society, and he wrote a long letter to Freud on 13 October 1910 to try to persuade him to reverse this decision.[185] Diplomatic initiatives were launched to get Bleuler on board. Even dream analysis was enlisted in the cause. Jung wrote to Freud on why Bleuler hadn't joined:

Jung to Freud, 13 November 1910: The dream tells what the real reason [for Bleuler's resistance] is. It is not as he says, that Stekel is in the society; I am the one who is holding him back. He throws Isserlin in my face, obviously as a screen for his homosexual resistance.[186]

At the beginning of 1911, Bleuler finally relented. However, as we will see, this was not to last long. The revolving door started to turn.

Indeed, whilst these external conflicts were raging, they were compounded by internal conflicts at the very centre of the movement, between Freud and Alfred Adler, his most talented follower in Vienna. In the years following the Salzburg conference, rivalry and conflict between Freud's Viennese and Swiss followers had intensified, as Freud attempted to shift the seat of power to Zurich to forge an international movement. In 1910, Adler and Wilhelm Stekel became the editors of a newly formed journal, the *Zentralblatt für Psychoanalyse*, formed in part as a rival to the Swiss-dominated *Jahrbuch*. When the Vienna Psychoanalytic Society began to formalise itself, Adler was appointed its first president in 1910. Adler's own views increasingly diverged from Freud. In essence, they were as little of Freudian inspiration as Jung's ideas on dementia praecox or Bezzola's psychosynthetic procedures. Freud's response? Diagnosis.

Freud to Jung, 25 November 1910: My spirits are dampened by the irritation with Adler and Stekel, with whom it is very hard to get along. You know Stekel, he is having a manic period ... Adler is a very decent and intelligent man, but he is paranoid; in the Zentralblatt he puts so much stress on his almost unintelligible theories that the readers must be utterly confused ... He is always claiming priority, putting new names on everything, complaining that he is disappearing under my shadow, and forcing me into the unwelcome role of the aging despot who prevents young men from getting ahead.[187]

Freud to Jung, 3 December 1910: It is getting really bad with Adler. You see a resemblance to Bleuler; in me he awakens the memory of Fliess; but an octave lower. The same paranoia.[188]

With this simple step, his theories could be dismissed. For Freud, Adler's recent presentation 'suffers from paranoid vagueness'.[189]

Freud to Ferenczi, 16 December 1910: I have now overcome Fliess, which you were so curious about. Adler is a little Fliess *redivivus*, just as paranoid. Stekel, his appendage, is at least called Wilhelm.[190]

Freud to Jones, 26 February 1911: But [Adler] is of a morbid sensibility ... Adler's views were clever, but wrong and dangerous to the spreading of PsA, his motives and his behaviour are all throughout of neurotic nature.[191]

Ferenczi to Freud, 17 March 1911: You are not only the discoverer of new psychological facts but also the *physician* who treats us physicians. As such you have to bear the burdens of transference and resistance. It is, of course, unpleasant when you have to deal with incurable or not easily accessible physicians (e.g., an infantile perverse Stekel and a paranoid Adler).[192]

This pathologisation of dissent not only enabled the delegitimation of Adler's theoretical innovations, it also mitigated a predictable rejoinder by Freud's critics: 'even your own psycho-analysts don't agree with you!' Indeed, if Adler remained a psychoanalyst – and one with a prominent institutional position and in a powerful position with regard to psychoanalytic literature – Freud's defences against his critics would simply backfire. The simple rejoinder that the views of critics were nullified because they hadn't practised psychoanalysis now posed a serious problem when someone such as Adler, one of the founding members of Freud's Wednesday psychological society from 1902, presented views which in critical respects coincided with those of Freud's critics.

> **Freud to Jung, 3 December 1910**: The crux of the matter – and that is what really alarms me – is that he [Adler] minimizes the sexual drive and our opponents will soon be able to speak of an experienced psychoanalyst whose conclusions are radically different from ours.[193]

Adler's innovations opened the possibility of a proliferation of concurrent psychoanalyses, which was precisely what the founding of the IPA had attempted to stop. Thus simple theoretical disagreement would have been insufficient – it was necessary that Adler lose all credibility.

In January and February 1911, a series of four meetings was convened in Vienna to discuss the theoretical differences between Freud and Adler.

> **Stekel**: One Freudian after another got up and denounced, in well-prepared speeches, the new concepts of Adler. Even Freud himself read a paper against his pupil.[194]

> **Minutes of the Vienna Psychoanalytic Society, 1 February, 1911**: Personally, he [Freud] resented the fact that the author talked about the same things as he did, but without designating them by the same terms they already had, and without making any efforts to establish any relationship between his terms and the old ones . . . Adler's writings are not a continuation upward, nor are they a foundation underneath; they are something else entirely. This is not psychoanalysis . . . In thus denying the reality of the libido, Adler behaves exactly as the neurotic ego does.[195]

> **Stekel**: At the next meeting, Freud defended his behaviour toward Adler. He said, 'Adler isnt a normal man. His jealousy and ambition are morbid.'[196]

The pathologisation of opponents was now publicly meted out to Freud's own pupils. After these meetings, Adler and other associates resigned and formed a Society for Free Psychoanalytic Research, a pointed rejoinder to Freud's authoritarian tactics. Freud himself promptly took over the chairmanship of the Vienna society and denounced Adler's departure as a heresy.[197] In October of the same year, the Vienna Psychoanalytic Society forbade membership of both societies.

> **Adler, 1912**: The impulse for the founding of the 'Society for Free Psychoanalytic Research' came in June, 1911, from several members of the 'Vienna Psychoanalytic Society', that was under the direction of Professor Sigmund Freud. These members had occasions to point out that it was being undertaken to commit the members of the original Society scientifically to the entire range of Freud's assumptions and theories. For these members, such a development not only seemed difficult to reconcile with the fundamental principles of scientific research, but particularly dangerous with a science as young as psycho-analysis. In their opinion, it would further place in question the value of the results that had already been achieved if members of the Society were prematurely bound to certain formulas and thereby obliged to give up the possibility of undertaking research directed toward new solutions.[198]

It wasn't enough only to expel dissidents: others had to be barred from entering. One year after the Isserlin episode, Hans Maier, who had succeeded Jung at the Burghölzli, was excluded from attending the Zurich Psychoanalytic Society. Freud had previously asked Bleuler to break off his relations with the psychiatrists Alfred Hoche and Theodore Ziehen under the rationale that they were critical of psychoanalysis. After the Maier episode, Bleuler decided that he had had enough and left the IPA.[199]

> **Hans Maier to Alphonse Maeder, 25 October 1911**: What I had against the Association from the beginning was its organisation and its composition, from which I thought I foresaw that it would lead to a clique formation which I absolutely detest in the scientific field. I must

say that the events of the years which have passed since then have surpassed my fear by far, and I had never thought that an alteration of individual personalities and their whole attitude in scientific and professional matters could show itself in a short time in such a manner and in such strength, as had occurred.[200]

Bleuler to Freud, 27 November 1911: To my great regret I must yet again leave the psychanalytic association. In a polite but very definite way my secondary doctor, whom I had occasionally invited to the scientific meetings, was asked to come no more. To give the exact form: he was told he must either join or waive his appearance, after which he explained he could not join due to definite reasons.[201]

Freud to Jung, 30 November 1911: Maier in any case must go.[202]

Bleuler to Freud, 4 December 1911: The 'who is not for us, is against us', the 'all or nothing', is in my opinion necessary for religious communities and useful for political parties. For this reason I can understand the principle as such, but I consider it harmful for science … I recognize in science neither an open nor a closed door, but no door, no doorstep at all. For me, Maier's position is as valid or invalid as of anyone. You say he wanted only the advantages [of being a member], but wanted to make no sacrifice. I cannot understand what kind of sacrifice he should have made, except to sacrifice one part of his views. You would not demand this of anyone … I do not believe that the interest of the Association demands such exclusionary behaviour in any way whatsoever; I definitely believe the opposite. This is not a 'Weltanschauung'.[203]

Bleuler to Freud, 1 January 1912: If it were a scientific association in the same sense as other ones, nobody could have objected, and it would simply have been useful. But it is the *type* of association that is harmful. Rather than to strive to have many points of contact with the rest of science and other scientists, the Association isolated itself with barbed wires from the external world, which hurts both foe and friend … The psychoanalysts themselves have validated the malicious words of Hoche about sectarianism, which at that time was unjustified.[204]

It was now Forel's turn to weigh in. With the sixth edition of his book *Hypnotism*, he added a lengthy chapter on psychanalysis. The first paragraph rectified Freud's neologism. The second attributed the discovery to Breuer. After recalling that the roots of psychanalysis were to be found in Liébeault's theory of suggestion, he enumerated the authors who had developed the psychanalytic method: Freud, Vogt, Graeter, Frank, Bezzola, Du Montet, Loÿ, etc. One can imagine Freud's reaction to see himself cited as one continuer amongst others of Breuer's work. The rest of the chapter was a detailed critique of Freud and Jung's theories, accusing them of insisting in a unilateral manner on sexuality and for having abandoned the valuable resources of the cathartic method, hypnosis and auto-suggestion for an arbitrary and dogmatic system of interpretation.

> **Forel:** The discoverer of the psychanalytic method from the point of view of its psychological as well as therapeutic significance was Dr. Joseph [*sic*] Breuer of Vienna … We close this chapter by thanking Breuer above all, but also Freud, K. Graeter and Frank, as well as the other authors whom we have cited, for their fecund ideas. This thanks does not extend to the dangerous hypotheses and dogmas of the Freudian school, properly speaking.[205]

> **Freud to Ferenczi, 21 May 1911:** Forel has presented me with the 6th edition of his *Hypnotism*; but what is in there about ΨA is, regrettably, dim-witted and represents the decidedly not dim-witted biases of Frank and O. Vogt, whose services – I do not know what they are – he can't praise highly enough – they are puny Johnny-come-latelys, nothing more. His arguments, e.g., against sexuality, are really depressing for a man who has written a fat book about the sexual question.[206] It really put me out for once.[207]

Eight months later, the dispute between the two psych(o)analytic factions broke out in a series of exchanges in the *Neue Zürcher Zeitung*, the main Zurich newspaper. This important controversy, which was first reconstructed by Ellenberger,[208] has been passed over by Freudian historiography. It forms the first example of the numerous polemical Freud wars played out in newspapers and popular periodicals. The spark which gave rise to it was a highly critical talk on psychoanalysis by Dr Max Kesserling, a specialist in nervous disorders at the Kepler-Bund in Zurich. This was an anti-Haeckelian organisation dedicated to denouncing the use of science for atheist propaganda. It seems that the Kepler-Bund decided to discuss psycho-analysis after a review of Frank's book in the *Neue Zürcher Zeitung* which drew a materialist lesson from it. On 2 January, the *Neue Zürcher Zeitung* published a review which denounced Kesserling's talk and the Kepler-Bund. This led to an avalanche of letters by adepts and adversaries of psychoanalysis. The most acerbic attacks against psychoanalysis came from Franz Marti, who made fun of the sexual obsessions of the psychoanalysts with comical examples. Jung intervened to defend the honour of psychoanalysis. He critiqued Kesserling for having a debate on matters of medical research in front of a general public.[209] He accused Marti of not having a medical qualification and of behaving in an anti-scientific fashion through taking up the controversy in the newspapers. He also claimed that the psychoanalytic concept of sexuality was much more extended than the 'vulgar'[210] concept which its critics held. To this, Marti retorted that, in practice, psychoanalytic interpreta-tions always went back to the so-called vulgar meaning.

> **Jung to Freud, 23 January 1912:** We have been victims of 'black-mail'[211] by the newspapers and were reviled although no names were named. I have even consulted a good lawyer with a possible view to bringing libel action. But there is little prospect of success because the attack was indirect. I have therefore confined myself to a public protest by the International PsA Association, Zürich branch; it will appear shortly in the press.[212]

On 25 January, it was Forel's turn to enter the debate, defending psychanalysis. He accused Kesserling and Marti of confounding the true psychanalysis of Breuer and Frank with the psychoanalytic devi-ation of Freud and Jung.

> **Forel:** It is deeply to be regretted that such a fruitful and thoroughly correct theory such as Breuer's cathartic theory should come into

miscredit through the onesidedly sexual and endless digression of the
Freudian school. From the side of the Freudian school, much too much
exegesis, interpretation of dreams, and belleletristic studies of literary
antiquity have been brought in, and thus the scientific method has
been abandoned. In public the matter has then become dilettantish
playing around.[213]

Kesserling and Marti replied by implicitly assimilating Forel to the
Freudians. On 1 February, Forel replied that whilst they had good
reason to critique the Freudian school, this should not lead one to
condemn psychanalysis as such – which wasn't Freudian, but Breuerian.

> **Forel:** I must consequently clearly state that serious researchers
> entirely share with Mr. F[ranz] M[arti] his condemnation of the uni-
> lateral character of the Freudian school: its sexual church outside
> of which there is no salvation, infantile sexuality, its Talmudic-
> theological interpretations and so on ... What Mr. F. M. does not
> say is that next to the sectarian, sexual and further derailments of the
> international psychoanalytic movement, there is another psychanaly-
> sis without o, which applies itself honestly, parallel to the study of
> the theory of suggestion (hypnotism) and psychotherapy, to separate
> the true scientific kernel from the researches of Breuer and Freud, to
> deepen them thanks to a quiet and serious study, and to make them
> useful for the therapy of nervous disorders.[214]

The letter was followed by a short response from Marti thanking Forel
for his clarification, and declaring that the discussion was closed, to
everyone's satisfaction. Thanks to Forel's move, Jung was isolated on
the sidelines, and he himself was taking hold of a psychanalysis purged
of its Freudian excesses.

> **Ludwig Binswanger to Freud, 5 March 1912:** In the Zurich press
> campaign, it was Forel who annoyed me most with his underhand
> conduct.[215]

Stuck between Freud and his colleagues (between the inside and the
outside), Jung's position became more and more untenable. As we
have seen, it was in the same year that conflict between Freud and

Jung broke out into the open.[216] This was potentially disastrous. Freud was not only on the point of losing his most precious ally, who had led the war of which Ferenczi spoke (and taken the blows in his place), but also the whole Zurich school, and with it the hope of internationalising the psychoanalytic movement and colonising psychiatry. Psychoanalysis was in danger of returning to becoming a local, Viennese affair. Furthermore, after Adler, Jung was the second psychoanalyst who was putting forward positions which increasingly resembled those of Freud's critics.

> **Freud to James Jackson Putnam, 20 August 1912:** After the disgraceful defection of Adler, a gifted thinker but a malicious paranoiac, I am now in trouble with our friend, Jung, who apparently has not outgrown his own neurosis.[217]

> **Freud to Putnam, 1 January 1913:** For me it seems like a déjà vu experience. Everything I encounter in the objections of these half-analysts I had already met in the objections of the non-analysts.[218]

These matters came to a head at the psychiatric congress in Breslau in 1913, which can be seen to have been the last great battle of the first Freud wars.[219] The organisers had arranged a session on the importance of psychoanalysis, with Bleuler and Hoche due to speak. It was clear from the outset that Freud's adversaries were determined to launch a final assault on his psychoanalysis. Before the congress Hoche had sent round a circular letter to colleagues seeking information concerning unsuccessful treatments by psychoanalysis. In an attempt at pre-emptive damage control, the Freudians published Hoche's circular in the *Internationale Zeitschrift für Psychoanalyse*.

> **Freud to Jung, 3 March 1913:** Hoche's circular letter has come into our hands. Maeder is going to send it to you for publication in the Internat. Zeit.[220]

> ***Internationale Zeitschrift für ärztliche Psychoanalyse*, 1913:**
> *An Opponent of Psychoanalysis*

We believe we are fulfilling a duty, if in this position we hang below this circular from Prof. Hoche in Freiburg.

Freiburg I. B., 1 February 1913. Dear esteemed colleague! I have taken on with Bleuler the report *On the value of psychoanalysis* for the annual meeting of the German Association for Psychiatry (in May in Breslau). It would be of great value to me and to others to gain a reliable judgement of the manner and extent of the damages caused by psychoanalytic procedures to patients. I ask you for the courtesy, if you have such factual material at your disposal, to communicate it to me in a form suitable for yourself. (I do not have in mind precise figures nor detailed individual case histories.) The use I intend will be without indication of names and will occur in such a way that it will in no way anticipate possible comments or discussion on your part. I know from my own experience how disagreeable such a survey will feel, but to my regret I see no other way of obtaining this important material. With the expression of my friendly thanks, I am, yours truly, Hoche.[221]

Hoche, presentation at Breslau, 1913: The editors of this journal have apparently already become so foreign to the medical manner that they do not know that it is very frequently sought to measure the dangerousness of particular therapeutic interventions, for example, narcosis and so on, through statistical methods.[222]

On the surface, it appeared as if Bleuler was going to defend psychoanalysis, in the by now well-established tradition of congress duels. However, to judge by a letter from Sweasey Powers to Smith Ely Jelliffe, written immediately after the congress, the truth was somewhat different. Lurking behind the scenes was none other than Emil Kraepelin. As he expressed it, the object of the congress was to give Bleuler an opportunity of renouncing Freud.

Sweasey Powers to Smith Ely Jelliffe, 25 May 1913: [Kraepelin] asked me if I did not realize that all of the members and that is to say all of the prominent psychiatricians in Germany were against it. I then said that I hoped to hear some scientific facts brought against it. He then said that was not the purpose of bringing up the discussion. The purpose was to give Bleuler the opportunity to publicly back-slide from the Freud-school as his name was considered to have had a great influence in keeping the Freud theories alive. The purpose was also to place the German psychiatricians on record as being against the Freud theories.[223]

Bleuler began his 'Critique of Freudian theory' by articulating his subjective standpoint.

> **Bleuler:** My critique is in this respect a subjective one: I judge Freud's theories in the first instance through my own experience.[224]

Bleuler could not have been clearer: far from being external, his critique was based on the results of his self-analysis, but also of his course of analysis by correspondence with Freud. Bleuler noted that his 1911 paper on psychanalysis had stressed the positive side;[225] this one would represent the negative, with the advantage of further experience. Bleuler's tactic was to identify and single out each aspect of Freud's theories, and those of some of his followers, and to indicate what he accepted and what he rejected, in a meticulous and detailed fashion. Such an itemised view was precisely what Freud was militating against. Bleuler's paper represented the most detailed examination of psychoanalytic concepts which had yet been undertaken.

Hoche began his paper by stating that he had studied the psychoanalytic literature and that he too had analysed his own dreams according to the Freudian interpretations (according to Freud's statement at the Clark conference in 1909, this would be sufficient to make him a psychoanalyst). Considered from a theoretical perspective, Freud's theory was one of the many possible philosophies of the unconscious, and as such, made assertions which superceded any possible experience.

> **Hoche:** On the dark stage of the unconscious, the theory can let whatever it wants happen.[226]

Being unverifiable, psychoanalytic interpretations were thus completely arbitrary. In this respect, the study of the literary products of the sect enabled a specific methodology to be identified.

Hoche: One of the most important means with which the results
are reached and secured is the confusion of the possibility of thinking
of a connection with the proof of one, the confusion of the finding
of the analogy between different processes with the proof of their
identity, the confusion of the emergence of an idea with established
knowledge.[227]

As Hoche saw it, this was advanced through apodictic and dogmatic
assertions, rash assertions and the abdication of generally convincing
proofs. Given the sect-character of the movement, these had a suggestive effect on the believers.

Hoche: What occurs to one person today will on the next day already
become a proven fact and be used as the basis for further inferences.[228]

This peculiar social psychology of the movement was augmented
by Freud's studious avoidance of general congresses and the holding of private congresses. Referring to Wilhelm Stekel's greetings
for the Weimar psychoanalytic congress, Hoche noted sarcasti-
cally that his characterisation of the movement as a sect three
years ago had in a certain sense been accepted by the Freudians
themselves.

Stekel, 1911: We all have the need to feel that we do not stand alone,
and that we belong to a large school, whose disciples are spread over
the whole Earth. Each single one of us stands against a world of
opponents, and must assert himself against the scorn and mockery of
the opponent ... We know that the future is ours. One cannot work and
create alone without the acknowledging resonance of fellow men. One
must build up one's faith from the faith of others. This is the deep
meaning of the psychoanalytic congresses, which have become for us
a matter of heart ... On this day of celebration we feel that we are
brothers of an Order which requires a sacrifice from each individual in
service of the generality.[229]

The sect-character of the movement was reflected in the schisms, and
Hoche took it as a fortunate sign that the best minds were leaving the
movement.

By reproaching psychoanalysis with having returned to a private form of knowledge, Hoche did not know how correct he was. In 1912, Ernest Jones had already proposed the formation of a secret committee to Freud, charged with defending the purity of Freudian doctrine against heretical deviations.

> **Jones to Freud, 30 July 1912:** [A] small group of men could be thoroughly analysed by you, so that they could represent the pure theory unadulterated by personal complexes, and thus build an unofficial inner circle in the *Verein* and serve as centres where others (beginners) could come and learn the work.[230]

> **Freud to Jones, 1 August 1912:** What took hold of my imagination almost immediately is your idea of a secret council composed of the best and most trustworthy among our men to take care of the further development of Ψα.[231]

> **Jones to Freud, 7 August 1912:** The idea of a united small body, designed, like the Paladins of Charlemagne, to guard the kingdom and policy of their master, was a product of my own romanticism.[232]

> **Jones, 1955:** There would be only one definite obligation undertaken among us: namely, that if anyone wished to depart from any of the fundamental tenets of psychoanalytical theory, e.g., the conception of repression, of the unconscious, of infantile sexuality, etc., he would promise not to do so publicly before first discussing his views with the rest.[233]

To each of his Paladins, Freud gave a golden ring.

Hoche's main attention was directed to psychoanalytic therapy. He viewed it as 'essentially an old suggestive technique in a new pseudo-scientific guise'. It was not surprising that hysterics were receptive to it, as this was the case with all new methods which surrounded themselves with mysteries. The believing doctor and patient were both under the suggestive effect of the same circle of ideas. Another category of patients was those in conditions where spontaneous remissions were common, such as neurasthenia and depression. But above all, Hoche contested that psychoanalytic therapy was without dangers. Basing himself on the results of his survey, he presented a series of cases where psychoanalysis has purportedly done more harm than good. He concluded that Freudians trumpeted their successes whilst passing over their failures in silence.

> **Hoche:** In very many cases, psychoanalytic therapy is a direct damage to the patient.[234]

The only remaining interest of psychoanalysis lay in the cultural and historical field. In the discussion, one after the other, the leading lights of German psychiatry – Kraepelin, Stransky, Weygandt, Liepmann, Forster, Kohnstamm – and of psychology, in the figure of William Stern, got up to condemn Freud and his pretensions to originality.

> **Kraepelin:** Munich rejects Freud's psychoanalysis ... The good in it is not new, and essentially stems from Janet. Kr. stresses how much harm has already been caused by this method and energetically warns against its use.[235]

> **Wilhelm Weygandt:** For historical correctness, it should be noted that it is above all Breuer, who, following French authors such as Janet, laid the basis of the most solid elements of psychoanalysis, whilst Freud now reaps the rewards.[236]

> **O. Kohnstamm:** Honesty requires one to note that this method of psychanalysis had already been practised by P. Janet. Then Breuer–Freud and Oskar Vogt followed around the same time, and *last but not least* L. Frank.[237]

> **William Stern:** Psychoanalysts, who regularly reproach their adversaries on their professional ignorance, also work in this domain [the psychology of childhood] as complete dilettantes; scientific research on infants either does not exist for them or is submitted to all sorts of interpretive modifications until it can be connected to their conceptual system.[238]

> **Erwin Stransky:** The systematic ignorance of the works of other researchers and the systematic refusal of opening themselves to the criticisms is one of the distinctive traits of psychoanalytic

obedience ... The most fatal error [of Freudian theory] resides in the interpretive mania without restraint and in the confusion between interpretation and proof.[239]

Only Stegmann stood up to defend the Freudian cause. In conclusion, Bleuler indicated that there was much which was correct in what Hoche had said, to which he could subscribe. He maintained that there was much that was good and much that was false in psychoanalysis. The difference between them was that he wanted to maintain and purify what was good in it. None the less Hoche directly held Bleuler, whom he described as the figurehead of the sect, with his scientific reputation, directly responsible for the spread of psychoanalysis. He expressed his sympathy for Bleuler for being excluded from the movement. According to Eitingon, Hoche requested that Bleuler give up his protectorate of the psychoanalytic movement. Breslau was an overwhelming defeat for the movment. Freud's dream of conquering psychiatry lay in ruins, and psychoanalysis was almost unanimously rejected by the profession.

> **Freud to Abraham, 23 May 1913:** Breslau was bad. According to Eitingon, who was there, Bleuler behaved most unpleasantly ... Only Stegmann was present from our side ... Hoche did get the laughter on his side.[240]

Following the conference, Bleuler's paper was critiqued by Ferenczi, who attempted to pathologise Bleuler.

> **Ferenczi:** There is nothing left but to assume that the founder of the concept of ambivalence is himself ambivalent with regard to psychoanalysis.[241]

However, this could not hide the gravity of the situation. The public defeat at Breslau only intensified the conflict with Zurich. The whole psychoanalytic movement was in danger of escaping from Freud's control, as Jung was the head of the IPA. After having been rejected outside, Freud now risked being rejected inside. The correspondences between Freud, Jones, Abraham and Ferenczi, only published in their entirety over the last few years, show that Freud was fully aware of this danger and sought to take evasive action. Should he dissolve the IPA and form a new organisation? Or should he resign before being ejected by Jung? None of these solutions appeared to be viable. There were not enough numbers to impose the dissolution of the IPA on the Zurich contingent. As for leaving the IPA, one could imagine the pleasure that it would give to Forel, Bleuler, Kraepelin, Hoche, Frank, Bezzola and their colleagues to see Freud leave his own organisation.

> **Jones to Freud, 25 April 1913:** I am deeply impressed by the success of Jung's campaign, for he appeals to formidable prejudices. It is, in my opinion, the most critical period that Ψα will ever have to go through, and we formed the [Secret] committee not at all too early.[242]

> **Freud to Ferenczi, 8 May 1913:** According to reports from Jones we have bad things to expect from Jung and should brace ourselves for the collapse of the organization at the Congress. Of course, everything that strives to get away from our truths has public approval in its favor. It is quite possible that they will really bury us this time, after they have so often sung a dirge for us in vain.[243]

> **Jones to Freud, 4 November 1913:** *Vereinigung.* I am in favour of dissolving, as you all are, but I do not understand the urgency of acting at once until we can correspond with one another . . . Ferenczi says that a dissolution is better than our being forced to resign.[244]

> **Ferenczi to Freud, 8 November 1913:** After Jones' and Abraham's explanations, I don't think we can bring about the dissolution of the International Association. Nothing remains but a collective resignation of those members of all groups who are with you. An International Psychoanalytic Association from which you, Abraham, Jones, all Viennese and Budapesters, Brill (perhaps Putnam) have resigned – with Jung at the head – won't count for much. You must immediately set in motion the founding of the new Association.[245]

Freud to Jones, 22 November 1913: We know J.'s position is a very strong one, our only hope is still he will ruin it himself.[246]

In response to this situation, Freud decided to stake his all. Abraham, Jones, Ferenczi and Eitington were directed to publish conjoint attacks against Jung, in a carefully orchestrated campaign. Freud himself turned to writing his 'bomb', the 'History of the psychoanalytic movement'. From the opening lines, it was quite clear that one was no longer dealing with even a pretence of open scientific discussion. As we have seen, Freud peremptorily declared that he alone was authorised to decide what was psychoanalysis, his creation. This argument from authority was clearly a response to the proliferation of Breuerian, Forelian, Adlerian and Jungian deviations. The vehemence with which Freud denounced Breuer, Jung, Adler and official science indicated his failure to resolve the question on the theoretical level, to persuade his colleagues of his definition of psychoanalysis. The extraordinary polemical tone of Freud's 'History' reflects this defeat. Giving up all pretension at objectivity, Freud accused his adversaries of shameful motives, duplicity, incompetence, mental pathology, and in the case of Jung, racism.

Freud to Ferenczi, 24 April 1914: Jung's surprising resignation has made our task much easier ... Perhaps he has succumbed to the salvo in the *Zeitschrift*, and the bomb in the *Jahrbuch* is coming too late.[247]

Freud to Abraham, 25 June 1914: So the bombshell has now burst, we shall soon discover with what effect. I think we shall have to allow the victims 2 to 3 weeks' time to collect themselves and react.[248]

Confronted by this, the Zurich group decided to leave Freud with his psychoanalysis, and resigned en masse – which is precisely what Freud wanted to achieve. Just as Adler had done before them, they justified their decision through referring to the incompatibility between Freud's attitude and the freedom of scientific research.

Minutes of the Zurich Psychoanalytic Society, 10 July 1914: Freud's demonstration published in the Yearbook of Ψa ('On the history of the Ψα movement') is in an unequivocal manner bound to the authority of the theory of one individual. The Zurich branch considers this standpoint to be incompatible with the principle of free research.[249]

In terms of posterity, Freud's strategy was a masterstroke. In the absence of prominent alternative accounts by Adler and Jung, Freud's so-called 'History' became a founding document of the psychoanalytic movement and the basis of its official history, subsequently elaborated in numerous articles, books and biographies. Freud had managed to snatch victory out of defeat, passing in silence over embarrassing episodes (Forel, the Breslau congress), and transforming disagreements concerning psychoanalysis into irrational resistances. It is no exaggeration to say that without this tendentious rescripting of history, psychoanalysis would not have been able to propagate itself and attain the prominence which it had in the twentieth century.

It is important to note that this victory was the reverse of its failure to attain widespread assent through open discussion and debate, and came at the cost of the complete privatisation of the science of psychoanalysis under the sole possession of Freud, and of its separation from the prevailing norms of the academic world. Between 1905 and 1914, Freud had sought to internationalise the psychoanalytic movement through seeking allies, initially through Bleuler and Jung. Henceforth, psychoanalysis came to be propagated from the interior, through producing more psychoanalysts in the form of patients turned into disciples. In this regard, the success which psychoanalysis came to have was due not to its capacity to convince its opponents (who remained sceptical), but to the unique form of transmission which it inaugurated.

It was not without reason that Hoche compared this mode of transmission to a sectarian proselytising. However, it was combined with a remarkable modernism, perfectly adapted to the market economy in the burgeoning area of private-practice psychotherapy. One had to pay significant amounts to have access to Freud's secret art (in contrast to the open form of transmission practised by Bernheimian hypnotic and suggestive psychotherapy). But it was also possible in turn to recoup this expenditure, as the practice gave one an independent livelihood. Separated from the university and the school of medicine (Freud formally stopped teaching in 1917), psychoanalysis became a private enterprise, recruiting clients (and hence potential followers) in an unregulated market, independent of all university or governmental authority. Psychoanalysis effectively became Freud's firm, organised like an international company based on franchises. All sorts of subsidiaries could be formed across the world, on the condition that they faithfully reproduced the proprietary mode for forming analysts.

> **Thomas Szasz:** To Freud, psychoanalysis was like an invention, which the inventor could patent, thus restricting the rights of others in its use. Thus, Freud insisted that psychoanalysis was to be dispensed only in accordance with his specifications. But he went even further: he declared that only he, and no one else, could change or modify the original formula ... Here is his explanation, in his own words, of his objection to Adler: 'I wish merely to show that these theories controvert the fundamental principles of analysis (and on what points they controvert them) and for that reason they should not be known by the name of analysis.'[250] So the issue was not whether Adler was right or wrong, but what should be called psychoanalysis. It was as if Freud had patented Coca Cola. He did not really care whether Pepsi Cola or Royal Cola or Crown Cola were better. He merely wanted to make sure that only his products carried the original label.[251]

From this perspective, it was no longer the content of a theory which was important, but the fact it was sanctioned by Freud and his official representatives. The unity of the psychoanalytic movement was not really maintained by a joint allegiance to a body of doctrine (we have seen that it never really consistently had one) or to a research methodology, but solely by reference to the Freud label, maintained by a feudal structure of authority. Freud did not hesitate, after the first Freud wars, to appropriate silently many of the theoretical innovations which he had so violently denounced when they were initially proposed. After Adler's departure, Freud incorporated aspects of his theories under the banner of psychoanalysis, and the same thing happened with others. As Ellenberger notes, Freud took over Adler's conceptions of an autonomous aggressive drive, of the confluence and displacement of the drives and the internalisation of external demands.

> **Ellenberger:** The shift of psychoanalysis to ego psychology was to a great extent an adaptation of former Adlerian concepts.[252]

> **Stekel**: Everything I discovered was considered common property or was attributed to Freud. I could give countless examples of that.[253]

> **Stekel:** Freud later adopted some of my discoveries without mentioning my name. Even the fact that in my first edition I had defined anxiety as the reaction of the *life instinct* against the upsurge of the *death instinct* was not mentioned in his later books, and many people believe that the death instinct is Freud's discovery.[254]

> **Jung, 1957**: [Freud] later started to work on concepts that were no longer Freudian in the original sense ... He found himself constrained to take my line, but this he could not admit to himself.[255]

> **Freud to Ferenczi, 8 February 1910:** I have a decidedly obliging intellect and am very much inclined toward plagiarism.[256]

This tacit recuperation of the theories of dissidents or of external critics became one of the most striking traits of the psychoanalytic movement, and it demonstrates that what was at stake in the formidable disputes between Freud and his adversaries was not the intrinsic value of particular ideas, but of who could lay claim to them. A particular conception was not psychoanalysis when it was put forward by Adler, Stekel or Jung, but it could become one when it was advanced by Freud. As Szasz noted, psychoanalysis had become a trademark.

The immaculate conception

The privatisation of analytic theory is particularly marked in the 'History of the psychoanalytic movement'. Freud justified the subjective character of his narrative through the necessity of reaffirming his monopoly over psychoanalysis – his science – against the claims of his rivals.

> **Freud:** No one need be surprised at the subjective character of the contribution I propose to make here to the history of the psychoanalytic movement, nor need anyone wonder at the part I play in it. For psycho-analysis is my creation … I consider myself justified in maintaining that even to-day no one can know better than I do what psycho-analysis is, how it differs from other ways of investigating the life of the mind, and precisely what should be called psycho-analysis and what would better be described by some other name. In thus repudiating what seems to me a cool act of usurpation, I am indirectly informing the readers of this Jahrbuch of the events that have led to the changes in its editorship and format.[257]

Consequently, the first section of the work was dedicated to establishing Freud's claim over his invention in a quasi-obsessional manner. Going back over what he had said five years earlier at the Clark conference, Freud now denied Breuer any role in the conception of psychoanalysis, properly speaking. He recounted, publicly for the first time, how Breuer had reacted when faced with the 'untoward event' of Anna O.'s sexuality.

> **Freud:** It will be remembered that Breuer said of his famous first patient that the element of sexuality was astonishingly undeveloped in her and had contributed nothing to the very rich clinical picture of the case … Now I have strong reasons for suspecting that after all her symptoms had been relieved Breuer must have discovered from further indications the sexual motivation of this transference, but that the universal nature of this unexpected phenomenon escaped him, with the result that, as though confronted by an *untoward event*, he broke off all further investigation. He never said this to me in so many words, but

he told me enough at different times to justify this conjecture of what happened.[258]

Translation: Through cowardice, Breuer had recoiled where Freud had the courage to continue. In the same spirit, Freud recounted how Breuer, Jean-Martin Charcot and Rudolf Chrobak had made cryptic remarks in passing concerning the role of sexuality in the neuroses.

> **Freud:** These three men had all communicated to me a piece of knowledge which, strictly speaking, they themselves did not possess. Two of them later denied having done so when I reminded them of the fact; the third (the great Charcot) would probably have done the same if it had been granted me to see him again.[259]

Translation: No one before Freud had established an explicit link between sexuality and the neuroses. Better still, when he presented his views on the sexual aetiology of the neuroses, his colleagues (notably Krafft-Ebing, but also Breuer) unanimously rejected them.

> **Freud:** But the silence which my communications met with, the void which formed itself about me, the hints that were conveyed to me, gradually made me realize that assertions on the part played by sexuality in the aetiology of the neuroses cannot count upon meeting with the same kind of treatment as other communications ... Meanwhile, like Robinson Crusoe, I settled down as comfortably as possible on my desert island. When I look back to those lonely years, away from the pressures and confusions of to-day, it seems like a glorious heroic age. My *splendid isolation* was not without its advantages and charms. I did not have to read any publications, nor listen to any ill-informed opponents; I was not subject to influence from any quarter; there was nothing to hustle me ... Meanwhile my writings were not reviewed in the medical journals, or, if as an exception they were reviewed, they were dismissed with expressions of scornful or pitying superiority.[260]

> **Freud:** For more than ten years after my separation from Breuer I had no followers. I was completely isolated. In Vienna I was shunned; abroad no notice was taken of me. My *Interpretation of Dreams*, published in 1900, was scarcely reviewed in the technical journals.[261]

Isolated, rejected, misunderstood, Freud owed nothing to anyone. Besides, he didn't even read what others wrote.

> **Freud:** The theory of repression quite certainly came to me independently of any other source; I know of no outside impression which might have suggested it to me, and for a long time I imagined it to be entirely original, until Otto Rank showed us a passage in Schopenhauer's *World as Will and Idea* in which the philosopher seeks to give an explanation of insanity. What he says there ... coincides with my concept of repression so completely that once again I owe the chance of making a discovery to my not being well-read ... In later years I have denied myself the very great pleasure of reading the works of Nietzsche, with the deliberate object of not being hampered in working out the impressions received in psycho-analysis by any sort of anticipatory ideas.[262]

> **Freud:** I read Schopenhauer very late in my life. Nietzsche, another philosopher whose guesses and intuitions often agree in the most astonishing way with the laborious findings of psycho-analysis, was for a long time avoided by me on that very account; I was less concerned with the question of priority than with keeping my mind unembarrassed.[263]

> **Freud:** I do not know of any outside influence which drew my interest to them or inspired me with any helpful expectations ... I have held fast to the habit of always studying things themselves before looking for information about them in books, and therefore I was able to establish the symbolism of dreams for myself before I was led to it by Scherner's work on the subject ...[264] Later on I found again the essential characteristic and most important part of my dream theory – the derivation of dream-distortion from an internal conflict, a kind of inner dishonesty – in ... the famous engineer J. Popper, who published his *Phantasien eines Realisten* [Fantasies of a Realist][265] under the name of Lynkeus.[266]

This enumeration of the claims to theoretical virginity could simply appear to be vain or pretentious, but it actually served a precise goal: to affirm Freud's exclusive rights over his creation. If Freud started from zero, if he submitted to no outside influence, if he made his discoveries in complete isolation and even despite his colleagues, psychoanalysis belonged to him alone, like a patented invention. Thus he could do what he liked with it, decide who could utilise it, denounce unauthorised copies and piracy. The aim of Freud's history was to establish this autocratic political authority through affirming the absolute originality of the theory.

The problem is that this history is a fable, a scientific fairytale. As numerous Freud scholars have shown, there is hardly a single element of this narrative that holds up under careful scrutiny. The 'splendid isolation', for example? Freud was never as isolated as he subsequently claimed in the years following the publication of *Studies on Hysteria*. On the contrary, this work gave him a certain local and international notoriety, and the Breuer–Freud method was frequently discussed and practised by those interested in psychotherapeutics, as we have seen.

Janet, 1894: We are happy that Breuer and Freud have recently verified our already ancient interpretation of fixed ideas in hysterics.[267]

William James, 1902: In the wonderful explorations by Binet, Janet, Breuer, Freud, Mason, Prince, and others, of the subliminal consciousness of patients with hysteria, we have revealed to us whole systems of underground life, in the shape of memories of a painful sort which lead a parasitic experience, buried outside of the primary fields of consciousness.[268]

Havelock Ellis, 1898: I agree with Breuer and Freud, the distinguished Viennese investigators of hysteria, who seem to me to have thrown more light on its psychic characters than any other recent investigators, that the sexual needs of the hysterical are just as individual and various as those of normal women, but that they suffer from them more largely through a moral struggle with their own instincts and the attempt to put them into the background of consciousness.[269]

Ellis, 1898: Charcot had established the psychic character of [hysteria] ... The nature and mechanism of this psychic process he had left wholly unexplained. This step was left to others, in part to Charcot's successor, Janet, and in a very large measure, I am inclined to think, to the Viennese investigators, Breuer and Freud, and by taking it they have, I venture to say, not only made the first really important contribution to our knowledge of hysteria since Charcot's investigations, but have opened the way to the only field in which the study of hysteria can now perhaps be fruitful . . . The investigations of Breuer and Freud . . . have further served to show that hysteria may be definitely regarded as, in very many cases at least, a manifestation of the sexual emotions and their lesions, in other words, as a transformation of auto-erotism.[270]

Bleuler, 1896 (regarding *Studies on Hysteria*): In any event, the fact that this book gives a completely new way of tackling the manner in which the psychism functions is one of the most important additions of these last years to the field of normal or pathological psychology.[271]

Moreover, Freud was respected and professionally supported by important figures such as Kraft-Ebbing and Hermann Nothnagel, who backed up his candidacy for the post of *professor extraordinarius* (*after* he had made public his claims on the sexual aetiology of the neuroses). He had a close intellectual collaboration with Wilhelm Fliess, to the point where Freud proposed that the latter co-sign the work which became *The Three Essays on the Theory of Sexuality*,[272] and he corresponded with eminent figures such as Havelock Ellis and Leopold Löwenfeld.[273] He rapidly gained disciples (even if they ultimately didn't remain so) – Felix Gattel and the future winner of the Nobel prize for medicine, Robert Bárány, in 1897–8, Hermann Swoboda in 1900, Stekel in 1901, Adler, Kahane and Reitler in 1902.[274] The initial reviews of his books were neither as rare nor as negative as he later claimed.[275]

Freud was by no means the first to interest himself in sexuality and its relations with the neuroses. The connection between neurasthenia and masturbation, which formed an essential part of his theory of the actual neuroses, directly followed from George Beard's *Sexual Neurasthenia*,[276] and one finds it in many figures in medicine at that time, such as Krafft-Ebing, Löwenfeld, Erb, Strümpel, Peyer or Breuer.[277] Furthermore, whilst Charcot, following Briquet, had rejected the ancient uterine theory of hysteria,[278] hysteria continued to be associated with female sexuality by many practitioners, including Breuer.[279]

> **H. B. Donkin:** Among the activities artificially repressed in girls, it must be recognized that the sexual play an important part and, indeed, the frequent evidence given of dammed up sexual emotions ... have led many to regard unsatisfied sexual desire as one of the leading causes of hysteria ... forced abstinence from the gratification of any of the inherent and primitive desires must have untoward results.[280]

> **F. A. King:** [Hysteria] occurs most often in single women, or rather in those, whether single or married, whose sexual wants remain ungratified. 'It is sometimes cured by marriage' ('Watson's Practice,' p. 455) ... 'Carter on Hysteria' (pp. 35, 36) observes: 'The sexual passion is more concerned than any other single emotion, and perhaps as much as all others put together, in the production of the hysteric paroxysm.'[281]

> **J. Michell Clarke (concerning _Studies on Hysteria_):** It is interesting to note a return, in part at least, to the old theory of the origin of hysteria in sexual disorders, especially as the tendency of late years has been to attach very much less importance to them.[282]

> **Alfred Binet and Théodore Simon:** [Freud and Breuer] have been led to take up again the old idea that hysteria merits its name, when one takes the uterus as a starting point; it is one of the most singular backward moves that one knows of.[283]

> **Konrad Alt:** Many hysterics had suffered severely from the prejudice of their relatives that hysteria can only arise on a sexual foundation. This widely spread prejudice we German neurologists have taken endless trouble to destroy. Now if the Freudian opinion concerning the genesis of hysteria should gain ground the poor hysterics will again be condemned as before. This retrograde step would do the greatest harm.[284]

> **Breuer:** I do not think I am exaggerating when I assert that _the great majority of severe neuroses in women have their origin in the marriage bed_ ... It is perhaps worth while insisting again and again that the

sexual factor is by far the most important and the most productive of pathological results. The unsophisticated observations of our predecessors, the residue of which is preserved in the term hysteria, came nearer the truth than the more recent view which puts sexuality almost last, in order to save the patients from moral reproaches.[285]

Breuer to Fliess, 16 October 1895: As regards the sexual basis of the disease, my examination of Selma B. has been serious and thorough. She says that she sometimes masturbated as a child of about 10 or 12 years of age, and presumably thereafter. She can say nothing about duration or intensity, but since at the age of 16 or 17 she experienced a severe neurasthenic condition it may be assumed that both were considerable. Though she may quite easily have been one of those people for whom a little harm produces serious consequences.[286]

Breuer: A third objection [to Freud's theories] concerns the overvaluation of sexuality. One can perhaps say in this connection that, to be sure, not every symptom of hysteria is sexual, but that the original root of the same probably is. Neurasthenia is certainly an illness that is sexual in root.[287]

Contrary to what Freud claimed, Breuer's disagreement with his young colleague after the publication of *Studies on Hysteria* was not to do with the role of sexuality in the neuroses, but only with what seemed to him to be an excessively exclusive claim concerning the role of sexuality in hysteria and neurasthenia.[288] The ideas of the libido, infantile sexuality, erogenous zones and bisexuality to which Freud turned after his abandonment of his seduction theory were all part of the Darwinian heritage which he shared with his sexological colleagues, and notably with Fliess (whom Freud systematically omitted from his historical accounts).[289]

Sanford Bell: The emotion of sex-love ... does not make its appearance for the first time at the period of adolescence, as has been thought ...The unprejudiced mind in observing these manifestations in hundreds of couples of children cannot escape referring them to sex origin.[290]

In short, if one resituates Freud's theories on sexuality in their context, one sees that they were neither as revolutionary nor as scandalous as he claimed.

Likewise, it is difficult to imagine that Freud's interest in dreams owed nothing to the voluminous psychological literature on the subject by figures such as Scherner, Hervey de Saint-Denys, Maury, Strümpell, Wundt, Volkelt, Hildebrandt or Delbœuf (selectively cited by him in the first chapter of *The Interpretation of Dreams*) or by Charcot, Janet and Krafft-Ebing (strangely passed over in silence).[291] To claim as Freud did in his autobiographical study that the science of his time had pronounced an 'excommunication'[292] on the subject of dreams is simply false. In this respect, one may well ask why he insisted so much on the fact that he arrived at the theory of dream symbolism[293] (which was absent from the first edition of *The Interpretation of Dreams*) independently of Scherner, when the latter anticipated other more important parts of his theory, such as dreams being the disguised fulfilment of sexual wishes. As Irving Massey and Stephen Kern have both noted, Freud, in his historical review of the literature on dreams, seems systematically to have avoided citing the passages in the works of his predecessors which came closest to his own theories.

Karl Albert Scherner: Sexual impulses that arise during sleep, and their representation in dreams, are totally indifferent to morality; the fantasy simply takes as its motif the sexual vitality that is given in the physical organism and presents it symbolically; the chastest virgin and the respectable matron, the priest who has renounced earthly things, and the philosopher, who grants to the sexual drive only the measure and purpose decreed by morality, are equally, willy-nilly, dreamers of sexual arousal.[294]

F. W. Hildebrandt: The dream provides us with such fine aperçus of self-knowledge, such instructive allusions to our weaknesses, such clarifying revelations of half unconscious dispositions of feelings and powers, that on awaking we are entitled to be astonished at the demon who with true hawk eyes has looked into the cards. But if it is so, what rational grounds could keep us from individual questions of self inquiry, and especially with the one great main question: who is the real master in our house?[295] The hints of dream life should certainly be heeded![296]

Similarly, whether Freud had actually read Schopenhauer – and there are many reasons for thinking that this was the case[297] – he most certainly would have been aware that the term and concept of repression played an important role in the work of his teacher Meynert, who had taken it from Herbart,[298] and that in his initial formulations, the psychic mechanism which this designated was very close to the dissociation of Charcot, Binet and Janet. As for his claims to have avoided reading Nietzsche, William McGrath established that it would have been nearly impossible for him not to have read him when he was a young student, and a member of the *Leseverein der deutschen Studenten Wiens*, a pan-Germanic reading group which avidly studied the works of Schopenhauer, Wagner and Nietzsche.[299] Besides, one learns from a letter to Fliess that Freud had 'acquired Nietzsche' (most probably the Naumann edition of Nietzsche's works which were being published then).[300]

> **Freud to Fliess, 1 February 1900:** I have just acquired Nietzsche, in whom I hope to find words for much that remains mute in me, but have not opened him yet. Too lazy for the time being.[301]

Far from being born through the presuppositionless chance encounter of Freud and the unconscious, psychoanalysis was the product of the intersection of multiple readings, debates and discussions. Even the bibliographies of his early works show that Freud was a voracious multilingual reader of the scientific and philosophical literature of his time, constantly on the look out for what was new in fields as diverse as evolutionary biology (Darwin, Haeckel), sexology (Krafft-Ebing, Moll, Ellis, Iwan Bloch, Magnus Hirschfeld), German neurology and cerebral anatomy (Wernicke, Meynert), British psychophysiology (Maudsley, Bain), French abnormal psychology (Taine, Ribot,

Binet, Janet), experimental and therapeutic hypnotism (Charcot, Bernheim, Delbœuf, Forel), the philosophy of the unconscious (von Hartmann), aesthetics (Lipps, Fischer), etc. Like many leading researchers, Freud keenly followed developments in related fields, mindful of priority vis-à-vis his colleagues and rivals, in the quest to establish the one true scientific psychology. In this regard, Jones' claim that Freud 'was never interested in questions of priority, which he found merely boring',[302] is clearly false. The renowned sociologist of science Robert K. Merton counted no less than 150 priority disputes in Freud's works, which on average comes out to over three per year – and this was before the major exchanges of correspondence had been published.[303]

> **Freud to Fliess, 29 November 1895:** Wernicke's pupils, Sachs and C. S. Freund, have produced a piece of nonsense on hysteria (on psychic paralyses),[304] which by the way is almost a plagiarism of my 'Considerations, etc.' in the *Archives de neurologie*.[305] Sachs's postulation of the constancy of psychic energy is more painful.[306]

> **Freud to Fliess, 14 November 1897:** I was able once before to tell you that it was a question of the abandonment of former sexual zones, and I was able to add that I had been pleased at coming across a similar idea in Moll. (Privately I concede priority in the idea to no one.)[307]

> **Minutes of the Vienna Psychoanalytic Society, 11 November 1908:** Strange as it may sound, infantile sexuality was really discovered by him – Freud; before that, no hint of it existed in the literature ... Moll gleaned the importance of infantile sexuality from the *Three Essays*, and then proceeded to write his book. For that reason, Moll's whole book is permeated by the desire to deny Freud's influence.[308]

> **Freud to Fliess, 10 March 1898:** I opened a recently published book by Janet, *Hystérie et idées fixes* [Hysteria and Fixed Ideas][309] with a pounding heart and put it aside again with my pulse calmed. He has no inkling of the key.[310]

> **Freud to Fliess, 31 August 1898:** I found the substance of my insight stated quite clearly in Lipps, perhaps rather more so than I would like.

'The seeker often finds more than he wished to find!' ... The correspondence [of our ideas] is close in details as well; perhaps the bifurcation from which my own new ideas can branch off will come later.[311]

Fliess to Freud, 20 July 1904: I have come across a book by Weininger, in the first biological part of which I find, to my consternation, a description of my ideas on bisexuality and the nature of sexual attraction consequent upon it – feminine men attract masculine women and vice versa. From a quotation in it I see that Weininger knew Swoboda – your pupil – (before the publication of his book), and I learned that the two men were *intimi*. I have no doubt that Weininger obtained knowledge of my ideas via you and misused someone else's property.[312]

Freud to Fliess, 27 July 1904: For me personally you have always (since 1901) been the author of the idea of bisexuality; I fear that in looking through the literature, you will find that many came at least close to you. The names I mentioned to you are in my manuscript [the *Three Essays on the Theory of Sexuality*];[313] I did not take books along with me, so I cannot give you more precise documentation. You will certainly find it in *Psychopathia sexualis* by Krafft-Ebing ... I can without feeling diminished admit that I have learned this or that from others. But I have never appropriated something belonging to others as my own ... So now, with regard to bisexuality, I also do not want to be in such a position vis-à-vis you ... On the other hand, there is so little of bisexuality or of other things I have borrowed from you in what I say, that I can do justice to your share in a few remarks ... P.S. Möbius has devoted a pamphlet, 'Sex and Immorality,' to Weininger's book ... He claims various ideas of Weininger as his own. It will certainly be of interest to you to look up which ones.[314]

To affirm the embeddedness of the genesis of Freud's work within the multiple intellectual networks and debates of his time is by no means to assert that he was a plagiarist or that there was nothing novel in his work – far from it. There is no denying the fact that Freud elaborated an original synthesis from the theories from which he drew, and it is precisely this which makes his work interesting. What Freud historians have contested is that psychoanalysis, unlike any other psychological theory, was born through a process of 'immaculate conception' (Peter Swales).[315] Far from emerging ready-made from what Freud called its prehistory,[316] it was embedded within historical and theoretical contexts, without which its emergence would be inexplicable and simply miraculous.

2

The interprefaction of dreams

Text for Psycho-analysts: 'Seek and ye shall find.' B Matt. vii. 7; Luke xi. 9.

Wohlgemuth (1923), 223

The 'history of psychoanalysis' which Freud and his followers recounted is by no means a history as generally understood. Rather it is an edifying fable, a scientific 'family romance', designed to negate the humble historical origins of psychoanalysis. How else can one understand why Freud devised such a mythic account, which could so easily be factually contradicted? Moreover, it is obvious that Freud would have been aware that many of his contemporaries would not have taken seriously his pretensions of originality. This was precisely what critics such as Hoche, Aschaffenburg, Forel and others stressed.

> **Hoche:** How is such a [psychoanalytic] movement possible? Without doubt a negative presupposition is the lack of a historical sense and philosophical training on the part of the followers able to be fanatical for the theory.[1]

> **Aschaffenburg:** When Freud strongly overestimates himself and the significance of his theory, and with sharp words presents the psychiatrists from whom he has much to learn, even concerning elementary

knowledge, as incapable, then one must regard him as having been spoilt by the blind admiration of his disciples.[2]

Forel: It does not occur to me to deny the great service of Freud and his particular school. Yet I must make two objections to him; first, that he ignores the works of his predecessors in a methodical manner, and second, that he presents all sorts of hypothetical things as facts ... According to Hitschmann's book, [*Freud's Theory of Neuroses*[3]] one would believe that Freud discovered the unconscious! We need only refer to the numerous works of modern psychology, as well as to Dessoir's more strictly defined concept of the 'underconscious' [*Unterbewussten*] ... to show how incorrect such a view is ... Freud would like to revolutionise the entire domain of psychology and psychopathology. As we have seen, he ignores his predecessors and those who do not agree with him with a sovereign silence.[4]

Vogt, International Congress of Medical Psychology and Psychotherapy, 7–8 August 1910: I object that a man like myself who has collected his own dreams since the age of sixteen and has investigated the problems under discussion here since 1894, that is, almost as long as Freud has done and longer than any of his disciples, should be refused the right to discuss these questions by any Freudian![5]

Morton Prince: But in the pursuit of these [psychoanalytic] researches there has been too great a disregard of large numbers of facts, of psychopathological data which have been accumulated by the patient investigations of other observers. It is much as if a bacteriologist had confined his studies to the investigation of a single bacillus and had neglected the great storehouse of knowledge acquired in the whole bacteriological field.[6]

Victor Haberman: Now why should Kraepelin, Ziehen, Hoche, Isserlin, Aschaffenburg, etc., men trained in psychology and psychiatry, men whose studies in association-psychology and in psychopathology (to say nothing of their neurological work) are familiar to every student in these fields, some of whose studies have become 'classical' and the fundamentals for subsequent work – why should these painstaking investigators be 'ignorant of' and 'have no feel for the subject'? Why should they be 'incompetent and unable to judge'? Why should it be that 'they have not mastered the theory,' these real masters of psychology and psychopathology! That they should not be able to comprehend and apprehend what these remarkable members of the Psychoanalytic Society have mastered with ease – some of them writing *ex cathedra* on the subject directly they were weaned to it – these wondrous wielders of the Deep Psychology, with their vast experience (whence derived?) and their profound learning in soul-analysis (whence acquired – all from the reading of Freudian literature?).[7]

Wohlgemuth: Almost complete ignorance is manifested everywhere [in Freud] of the literature and the results of modern psychology, of experimental method and of logic.[8]

In addition, most of the protagonists of Freud's accounts were still living (notably Breuer and Bertha Pappenheim), and hence there was the risk that they might publicly contradict him. How are we to understand, then, this rescripting of history?

To invoke Freud's 'megalomania' or 'desire for grandeur' (openly avowed in *The Interpretation of Dreams*) or his 'paranoia' (the myth of the hostile irrationality of his colleagues, the invocation of 'resistances to psychoanalysis', the pathologising of adversaries, etc.) is insufficient and comes down to utilising the same sort of reductive psychopathological interpretations which Freud liberally applied to others. What such explanations leave out of account is that Freud's histories were primarily directed towards a particular public: from 'The history of the psychoanalytic movement', Freud was principally preaching to the converted and was no longer preoccupied with the objections of his peers. The congresses leading up to Breslau had indicated that psychoanalysis was not going to get very far in open academic debate in psychiatric circles. Through the formation of the International Psychoanalytic Association, directed behind the scenes by the paladins of the Secret Committee, Freud now had the ideal vehicle to propagate his ideas. With its own societies, journals and publication house, the movement could spread with scant regard for the views of the medical, psychiatric and psychological professions. Henceforth, anyone who questioned Freud's version of events could simply be expelled from the movement. Protected from the world by his disciples, Freud could recreate his own reality and his own history, without fear of being contradicted. From this perspective, the legend of the isolated and persecuted scientist is less the expression of Freud's megalomania or mythomania, than the reflection of the institutional isolation of psychoanalysis. Conversely, the legend maintained the identity of the movement, portraying its mythic independence from and superiority over all other psychological and psychiatric theories. To view the legend simply as a means to satisfy Freud's ambition and narcissism or simply as a means to promote psychoanalysis in the competing psychological marketplace misses the intimate connections between the legend and psychoanalysis itself.

The immaculate induction

It is critical to grasp the significance of the Freudian rewriting of history and the de-historicisation to which it led. The Freudian legend wasn't simply a separate means of propagation or self-promotion added onto the theory. It was an integral part of it. Without the legend, the claim of psychoanalysis to scientific status would never have achieved the credibility that it did. We have already seen how the myth of Freud's self-analysis served to protect psychoanalysis from the conflict of interpretations which threatened it from within. Likewise, the legend of the immaculate conception of psychoanalysis played the role of epistemological immunisation against internal as well as external critiques. If Freud dedicated so many pages to establishing his originality and his presuppositionless theoretical virginity, it wasn't only because he was obsessed by questions of priority and intellectual propriety. It was pre-eminently because he wished to defend himself from the claim that he had imposed preconceived ideas onto clinical material, rather than having let himself be led by it. The myth of the immaculate conception of psychoanalysis enabled him to claim that he was free of all influence and that his observations were completely unprejudiced, free of any 'anticipatory ideas' which could contaminate the material. As we have seen, this was the main criticism which was constantly addressed to him by his critics. They claimed that psychoanalysis was an a priori system and that it applied a completely arbitrary interpretive framework on the material. To use the positive language which Freud shared with his detractors, it was a 'speculation' without an experiential basis.

> **Breuer:** If Freud's theories at first give the impression of being ingenious psychological theorems, linked to the facts, but essentially aprioristically constructed, then the speaker [Breuer] can insist that it is actually a matter of facts and interpretations that have grown out of observations.[9]

> **Freud to Fliess, 7 August 1901:** You take sides against me and tell me that the reader of thoughts merely reads his own thoughts into other people, which renders all my efforts valueless.[10]

> **Albert Moll:** The impression produced in my mind is that the theory of Freud ... suffices to account for the clinical histories, not that the clinical histories suffice to prove the truth of the theory. Freud endeavours to establish his theory by the aid of psycho-analysis.[11]

> **William James to Flournoy, 28 September 1909:** [Freud and his pupils] can't fail to throw light on human nature, but I confess that he made on me personally the impression of a man obsessed with fixed ideas. I can make nothing in my own case of his dream theories, and obviously 'symbolism' is a most dangerous method.[12]

> **Alfred Binet and Théodore Simon:** Here is what the method of psychoanalysis consists in. It is hardly anything other than a provoked confession, with the advantages and risks which are well known, if the authors did not accept as an article of faith that thanks to such an analysis, old and forgotten states could be authentically restored ... This is Freud's main hypothesis. It is a bold and very interesting hypothesis and is very amusing from a literary perspective. But as for us, we find it dangerous and useless. Dangerous, because none of this has been proved, and one risks taking a veritable fancy for an authentic restoration.[13]

> **Arthur Kronfeld:** [Freud] uses something as a means of proof which has already presupposed the correctness of what is to be proven ... But the

results of the psychoanalytic method are only correct according to the presupposition of the correctness and the validity of Freudian theory.[14]

Janet: What characterises this method [psychoanalysis] is symbolism. When it is useful to the theory, a mental event can always be considered as the symbol of another. The transformation of facts, thanks to all the methods of condensation, displacement, secondary elaboration and dramatisation can be enormous, and it results in the situation where a fact can signify whatever one wants ... It is a consequence of the confidence of the authors in a general principle posed at the outset as undiscussable that it is not a question of proving it by facts but of applying it to facts.[15]

Haberman: We have then in Freud's *unconscious*, to recapitulate, a metapsychological or mythopsychological subconscious, a conception remarkably interesting, but a vague hypothesis nevertheless, nowhere accepted by psychologists, built upon as yet undemonstrated fundamentals – and far removed from the path of factual science.[16]

Forel: What I reproach the Freudian school with is a systematic, rash generalisation and dogmatisation of certain observations which are correct in themselves, bound up with an interpretative projection of their fantasies onto the latter ... On the other hand, without exception one finds a tendency to turn the products of a fertile imagination into risky hypotheses, to dogmatise these fantasies and then to want to prop them through an almost talmudic exegesis, through constructions of all sorts of extreme hair-splitting (sometimes taken to absurdity), so that one becomes gradually led from the field of science into the field of sectarian theology.[17]

Kraepelin: Here we meet everywhere the characteristic fundamental features of the Freudian trend of investigation, the representation of arbitrary assumptions and conjectures as assured facts, which are used without hesitation for the building up of always new castles in the air ever towering higher, and the tendency to generalization beyond measure from single observations.[18]

Adolf Meyer: My attitude towards Freudianism is that of seeing in it a cult – an obsession by a formula useful and expressive of some facts commonly neglected, but still unheedful of the appeal to a frank acceptance of critical common-sense at its best in preference to a one-sided schema.[19]

Wohlgemuth: Nowhere in the whole of Freud's writings is there a shred of proof, only assertions, assertions of having proved something before, but which was never done, and mysterious reference to inaccessible and unpublished results of psycho-analyses.[20]

H. L. Hollingworth: In other words, the 'psychoanalogy' [term given by Hollingworth to psychoanalysis] is all in the explanation, in the theory of the analyst, not in the material of the case. This indeed is quite opposed to the assumptions and quite explicable without them.[21]

Joseph Jastrow: The time has come to make clear that the principles of psychoanalysis are not any such order of realities, but are conjectures, schemes, constructions of Freud's fertile imagination ... While following Freud's course in developing such concepts as complexes, libido, the unconscious, conversion, regression, identification, transference, sublimation, and a score of similar postulates, we must have constantly in mind that they are not 'discoveries' in the sense that Freud came upon them, with all the features and garbs which he describes, in the jungles of the land of the psyche, or that had Freud not entered upon his Columbian voyage, they would have been similarly reported by any other qualified observer entering the same terrain and underbrush of an unexplored mental continent. The *'discoveries' are hypotheses* – and they are nothing more.[22]

These critiques of the speculative arbitrariness of psychoanalytic methodology were regularly accompanied by warnings against its suggestive aspects, in the sense of Bernheim and the Nancy school. Freud, according to his peers, was not content to see his own theories in the minds of his patients, he also involuntarily suggested the responses he needed to support them. Hence, contrary to his claims, his 'observations' had no objective validity and the testimony of patients could not be invoked as the support of his theories. Moreover, from being impartial witnesses of therapeutic efficacy, the psychoanalytic method often transformed such patients into disciples, hence into active protagonists on one side of the controversy.

John Michell Clarke, concerning *Studies on Hysteria*: The necessity of bearing in mind, in studying hysterical patients, the great readiness with which they respond to suggestions, may be reiterated, as the weak point in the method of investigation may perhaps be found here. The danger being that in such confessions the patients would be liable to make statements in accordance with the slightest suggestion given to them, it might be quite unconsciously given to them, by the investigator.[23]

Robert Gaupp: Anyone who can give his questions a suggestive twist, whether done consciously or unconsciously, can obtain from susceptible patients any answer which fits into his system. That may be the reason why Freud's psychoanalyses abound in material which other researchers seek in vain.[24]

Forel: I claim that Freud greatly exaggerates this cause of nervous troubles [traumatic reminiscence] and above all in generalising it to cases where the patient remembers nothing, often suggesting to his patients all sorts of things which are more detrimental than useful, above all in the sexual domain.[25]

James Jackson Putnam: When the physician is fully imbued with the belief in the sexual origins of the patient's illness he must, by virtue of the closeness of this relationship, be in a position to impress his views, unconsciously, upon his patients and might easily draw from them an acquiescence and endorsement which would not in reality be as spontaneous as it seemed.[26]

Arthur Muthmann: With this process [abreaction] suggestive influences by the physician play a prominent part. A powerful suggestion which then acts auto-suggestively is especially the explanation respecting the method. The patient is informed that his illness is due to some forgotten experience. If this experience could be discovered, then his complaints would be cured. With a proper course of procedure the patient seizes at once the connection of resuscitating reminiscences with his illness, and, from its very inception, there is attached to this idea the suggestion that the respective symptoms will disappear.[27]

Hoche: The confirmation that the followers of the theory give for the 'discoveries' of complexes which have become unconscious are not surprising. The believing doctor and patient (or rather the female patient) are equally under the suggestive effect of an identical circle of ideas. The patients already certainly fully know what is expected of them ... Above all one sees that the eventual therapeutic effect finds its explanation without having to profess to the principles of Freudian theory; essentially ... it is the old suggestive technique in a new pseudoscientific guise.[28]

Moll: Moreover, I believe that the cures effected by Freud (as to the permanence of which, in view of the insufficiency of the published materials, no decisive opinion can as yet be given) are explicable in another way. A large proportion of the good results are certainly fully explicable as the results of suggestion. The patient's confidence in his physician, and the fact that the treatment requires much time and patience, are two such powerful factors of suggestion, that provisionally it is necessary to regard it as possible that suggestion explains the whole matter.[29]

Bernard Hart: The preconceptions of the analyst, the particular moments at which he sees fit to intervene in the patient's narrative, the emphasis which he directs to certain features of the narrative, the point at which he deems the flow of associations to have reached the significant element, all these are abundantly able to produce decided alterations in the subsequent functioning of the patient's mind.[30]

One sees that for many of Freud's critics, it was one and the same thing to criticise the arbitrariness of his theoretical hypotheses and to denounce the suggestive character of his technique. This was not accidental. By the 1890s, psychiatrists and psychologists were acutely aware of the demise of Charcot's theories through the criticism of the Nancy school, and of the ease with which one could take one's theories to be real through suggesting them to patients or to subjects of psychological experimentation. Despite (or rather because of) their positivism, they didn't trust many of the clinical 'confirmations' which Freud invoked in support of his theories. In the 1920s, the young Karl Popper recalled this whilst elaborating his famous critique of the non-falsifiable nature of psychoanalytic theory.

Karl Popper: Those 'clinical observations' which analysts naïvely believe confirm their theory cannot do this any more than the daily confirmations which astrologers find in their practice ... what kind of clinical responses would refute to the satisfaction of the analyst not merely a particular analytic diagnosis but psychoanalysis itself? ... Moreover, how much headway has been made in investigating the question of the extent to which the (conscious or unconscious) expectations and theories held by the analyst influence the 'clinical responses' of the patient? (To say nothing about the conscious attempts to influence the patient by proposing interpretations to him, etc.) Years ago I introduced the term *'Oedipus effect'* to describe the influence of a theory or expectation or prediction *upon the event which it predicts* or describes: it will be remembered that the causal chain leading to Oedipus' parricide was started by the oracle's prediction of this event. This is a characteristic and recurrent theme of such myths, but one which seems to have failed to attract the interest of the analysts, perhaps not accidentally.[31]

In psychology and psychiatry, heuristic hypotheses ('speculations') have a much more problematic status than in other fields, because of the role of human influence, that is, of what William Carpenter called 'expectant attention' or what Bernheim called 'suggestion'. In physics, chemistry and molecular biology, there is the possibility that an erroneous conjecture will eventually be corrected through experiment or calculation, even if this is far from being necessarily and automatically the case.[32] In these disciplines, as Andrew Pickering[33] cogently explains, the 'material agency' resists the hypotheses made about it, thus obliging the investigator to rectify them accordingly (this is what Pickering calls the 'dialectic of accommodation and resistance'). It is not the same in social psychology and psychopathology, where heuristic hypotheses are tested on 'human agencies' that are inevitably interested in the theories of which they are the object. In such cases, one can no longer count on the resistance of the experimental object, as human agency tends to accommodate itself to the experimental or therapeutic context. It was precisely this looping effect that Bernheim and Delbœuf recognised in hypnosis experiments under the heading of suggestion. Subjects accommodated experimenters, mirroring their explicit and implicit suggestions as well as their theoretical expectations. Meanwhile, experimenters were likewise affected by their subjects, and both were caught up in a field of reciprocal suggestions from which no external vantage point could be found.

> **Joseph Delbœuf:** Finally I give the explanation of the phenomena exhibited at the Salpêtrière: they are due to training and suggestion. The operator will have regarded the characteristics presented by his first subject to be essential for all individuals, rather than purely accidental. Unconsciously using suggestion he will have transformed them into habitual signs. He will be attached, without knowing it, to obtaining them with other subjects who will have produced them by imitation, and thus the master and his pupils, reciprocally influencing each other, will not cease to feed their error.[34]

> **Hippolyte Bernheim:** When one has seen how suggestible hysterics are, even during their fit, how much they easily realise the phenomena which one expects or that they have seen produced in others, one cannot stop oneself from thinking that imitation, working by auto-suggestion, plays a great role in the genesis of these manifestations . . . I thus believe that the grand hysteria which the Salpêtrière presents as classical, unfolding in clear and distinct phases like a chain hysteria, is cultivated hysteria.[35]

Bernheim and Delbœuf spoke of hysterical and hypnotic phenomena, but the implication of their analyses went far beyond the limited frame of therapeutic and experimental hypnotism, particularly as they reduced these to one effect among others of suggestion. The production of psychological artefacts which they highlighted in the hypnotic and psychotherapeutic relation was precisely what the hypnotic specialist Martin Orne rediscovered seventy years later at the centre of experimental psychology laboratories under the name of 'demand characteristics of the experiment'.[36] Orne showed how experimentation in psychology was inevitably affected by the reaction of its subjects. Far from being purely passive objects, the subjects are perfectly aware of being observed, they wonder what the experimenter wants to prove and do their best to validate what they take to be his hypotheses. This simple observation, which extends and generalises what Bernheim and Delbœuf had remarked concerning hypnotised subjects, hasn't ceased to haunt experimental social psychology. A multiplicity of procedures has been designed to allay this problem, without much success. Indeed, it is not simply a question of what had been called the 'personal equation' of the investigator,[37] nor even the inevitable distortion introduced by his or her subjectivity (the 'principle of indetermination' which characterises the human and social sciences, according to Georges Devereux).[38] More fundamentally, what is in play here is the degree to which psychological experimentation provokes real modifications in the behaviour and self-awareness of its subjects, insofar as they adapt to the theories and hypotheses applied to them, not unlike the manner in which the rat of the behaviourists or the drosophila of the geneticists adapts to laboratory conditions.[39] One could well say that the theory *produces* its 'object', not only in the Kantian sense of organising it conceptually, but much more literally, in the sense in which the subject of experimentation transforms itself to adapt to the theory. It is the 'Oedipus effect' which Popper described: the hypotheses of the psychologist provoke what they claim to describe or predict, transforming reality instead of merely reflecting it.

> **Wohlgemuth:** The Psycho-analyst in looking for 'complexes' is like an *agent provocateur*. He stirs up trouble where there was none before, and then says he discovered a plot.[40]

It was this subtle production (or rather, co-production) of psychological artefacts which Freud's peers saw when they spoke of 'suggestion' and 'auto-suggestion', rather than, as Freud claimed, direct suggestions of command, such as 'You will now sleep' or 'Your symptoms will disappear tomorrow.' Freud frequently protested that analysis was a non-directive method which had nothing to do with the crude hypnotic suggestion of its beginnings.

Freud: It is not only in the saving of labour that the method of free association has an advantage over the earlier method. It exposes the patient to the least possible amount of compulsion ... It guarantees to a great extent that no factor in the structure of the neurosis will be overlooked and that *nothing will be introduced into it by the expectations of the analyst.*[41]

Freud to Jung, 7 October 1906: For reasons of principle, but also because of his personal unpleasantness, I shall not answer Aschaffenburg's attack ... He is still taking up arms against the hypnotic method that was abandoned ten years ago.[42]

But Freud's peers, thanks to their familiarity with the work of the Nancy school, saw clearly that the replacement of direct hypnotic suggestion with the method of so-called free association by no means settled the problem of suggestion understood as creation of artefacts.

Forel: Since the introduction of the doctrine of suggestion one reads at the end of the praises of a large number of vaunted new remedies, 'Suggestion is excluded.' It is in just such cases that a purely suggestive action is most probable.[43]

Prince: I would point out, however, that the method employed by Freud in fact makes use of the principles of hypnosis; for the state of abstraction, in which the so-called free associations of the subject are obtained, is in *principle* hypnosis ... I say so-called free associations, because when the attention is concentrated on a particular theme the associations are determined by this fact. There is no such thing as free associations under these conditions.[44]

One could very well suggest without hypnosis, and it was for this reason that, in his psychotherapeutic practice, Bernheim dispensed with trance induction and turned towards suggestion in a waking state. Consequently nothing guaranteed the fact that Freud's method of free association would be any less suggestive than other psycho-therapeutic methods, or that his theories would be more objective than his master Charcot's.

Benjamin Logre: From the school of the Salpêtrière, so brilliant in so many respects, Freudianism retained, enriched and systematised, what was least fortunate: the culture of hysteria.[45]

Hart: A lengthy investigation of a patient's mind means that one is no longer examining at the end of the investigation the object one set out to observe, but an object which has progressively altered during the course of the investigation, and altered in a way which may have been largely determined by the investigation itself. This was the circumstance which vitiated absolutely and completely the painstaking conclusions drawn by Charcot and his school of the Salpêtrière. A perusal of the literature of double personality suggests strongly the existence of a similar vitiating factor ... It is not easy to avoid the conclusion that the method of psychoanalysis contains potential sources of distortion at least as great as those in the instances just mentioned.[46]

R. S. Woodworth: Psychological experimenters (as Messer and Koffka) have frequently observed that it is very difficult to secure a really free association ... It is rather strange that the Freudians ... should assume that the subject is really passive in the process of the analysis, and should omit to inquire what sort of tendency or control may be exerted on the movement of thought. If we ask ourselves this question, we notice that the psychoanalyst instructs his subject to be passive and uncritical, and to give expression to every thought that comes up, no matter how trivial or embarrassing it may be. The subject is warned time and time again that he must keep back nothing if he wishes the treatment to succeed. It is easy to see that such instructions tend to arouse a definite set of mind towards that which is private and embarrassing; and this easily suggests the sexual. Certainly one cannot be in the hands of a Freudian for long without becoming aware that sexual matters are of special interest and concern, and thus, if at all responsive, getting a strong mental set in that direction.[47]

Jastrow: The so-called 'free association' is not free, not completely, not convincingly so. It is altogether too prone to be guided by the analyst's attitude, questions, known views, personal relations to the analysee. The opportunities for suggestion are abundant; they intrude subtly, however much one is on one's guard. I do not refer to the cruder forms of suggestion in the same physician–patient relation which

deceived so astute a psychiatrist as Charcot in the 'discovery' of three
distinct hypnotic states … I do imply that the probing may readily
have a suggestive effect, if there is … an anticipatory theory behind it
and a knowledge on the part of the patients of what is expected of
them.[48]

Even the so-called 'resistances' of patients prove nothing, as how
could one exclude the possibility of 'resistance' as obliging (by 'transference love'), or as a form of trained behaviour, to conform to
theories of the analyst? From the 1880s onwards, it was quite common
to suggest to hypnotised patients not to remember something, or not
to respond to suggestions. Delbœuf, however, pointed out that the
hypnotic amnesia demonstrated by Bernheim was simply trained
behaviour. On what grounds, then, could one establish that the
situation was radically different in analysis?

> **Freud:** In every analytic treatment there arises, without the physician's
> agency, an intense emotional relationship between the patient and the
> analyst which is not to be accounted for by the actual situation. It can
> be of a positive or of a negative character and can vary between the
> extremes of a passionate, completely sensual love and the unbridled
> expression of an embittered defiance and hatred … We can easily
> recognize it as the same dynamic factor which the hypnotists have
> named 'suggestibility,' which is the agent of hypnotic *rapport* and
> whose incalculable behaviour led to difficulties with the cathartic
> method as well.[49]

As Aschaffenburg and Hoche argued, patients knew in advance what
was expected of them. Hence it would be no surprise if patients
exhibited all the manifestations of resistance or negative transference
as portrayed in psychoanalytic theory. For Freud, such manifestations
attested to the existence of an objective, non-dissimulating unconscious, as it resisted his suggestions and theoretical hypotheses.[50] But
in the eyes of his colleagues, this resistance to the theory could itself
be suggested by the theory. For such experienced hypnotic researchers
such as Forel, Moll and Janet, the contrast which Freud established

between the long and difficult 'working-through' of analysis and the deceptive facility of hypno-suggestive therapies was simply falla-cious.[51] Paradoxically, the insistence that psychoanalytic therapy did not operate by suggestion heightened its suggestive effects.

Jerome Frank: Viewed solely as methods of persuasion, evocative therapies may paradoxically heighten the therapist's incentive and ability to influence the patient through their stress on his neutrality and objectivity. This tempts him to induce the patient to express material that confirms his theories, because he can regard it as inde-pendent evidence for them; and the patient is induced to accept the therapist's formulations because he believes them to be his own.[52]

Freud: It is perfectly true that psycho-analysis, like other psychother-apeutic methods, employs the instrument of suggestion (or transfer-ence). But the difference is this: that in analysis it is not allowed to play the decisive part in determining the therapeutic results. It is used instead to induce the patient to perform a piece of psychical work – the overcoming of his transference resistances – which involves a permanent alteration in his mental economy.[53]

Freud: Besides all this I have another reproach to make against this method [the 'hypnotic procedure by suggestion'], namely, that it con-ceals from us all insight into the play of mental forces; it does not permit us, for example, to recognize the *resistance* with which the patient clings to his disease and thus even fights against his own recovery.[54]

Freud: In these hypnotic treatments the process of remembering took a very simple form. The patient put himself back into an earlier situation, which he seemed never to confuse with the present one . . . Under the new technique very little, and often nothing, is left of this delightfully smooth course of events . . . This working-through of the resistances may in practice turn out to be an arduous task for the subject of the analysis and a trial of patience for the analyst. Nevertheless it is a part of the work which effects the greatest changes in the patient and which distinguishes analytic treatment from any kind of suggestive influence.[55]

Freud: But you will now tell me that, no matter whether we call the motive force of our analysis transference or suggestion, there is a risk that the influencing of our patient may make the objective certainty of our findings doubtful. What is advantageous to our therapy is damaging to our researches. This is the objection that is most often raised against psycho-analysis, and it must be admitted that, though it is groundless, it cannot be rejected as unreasonable. If it were justified, psycho-analysis would be nothing more than a particularly well-disguised and particularly effective form of suggestive treatment and we should have to attach little weight to all that it tells us about what influences our lives, the dynamics of the mind or the unconscious. That is what our opponents believe; and in especial they think that we have 'talked' the patients into everything relating to the importance of sexual experiences – or even into those experiences themselves – after such notions have grown up in our own depraved imagination. These accusations are contradicted more easily by an appeal to experience than by the help of theory. Anyone who has himself carried out psycho-analyses will have been able to convince himself on countless occasions that it is impossible to make suggestions to a patient in that way ... After all, [the patient's] conflicts will only be successfully solved and his resistances overcome if the anticipatory ideas he is given tally with what is real in him. Whatever in the doctor's conjectures is inaccurate drops out in the course of the analysis; it has to be withdrawn and replaced by something more correct.[56]

This last argument, which Adolf Grünbaum has proposed to call the 'tally argument',[57] consists in postulating that 'psychic reality' resists the theory exactly like 'material reality'. Psychic reality, in other words, was objective, indifferent to the wishes, expectations and suppositions of psychologists or psychoanalysts. The patient could only be truly cured if the theory corresponded to reality, hence the cure provided a criterion to judge the validity of the analyst's interpretations and constructions.

Freud never accepted the idea that his theories could create or modify the phenomena which he described, as his peers objected. In his view, his theories were quite independent of the reality which they described. From an epistemological perspective, Freud was a classical positivist, for whom the fundamental basis of knowledge was observation – the perception and description of phenomena.

Like all good positivists, such as Ernst Mach, who seems to have been his principal reference in epistemological matters,[58] he firmly distinguished between observation and theory. In general, positivists were wary of theories, which brought with them the risk of mistaking the idea for the thing and tipping over into fruitless metaphysical speculation. Thus they attempted to delimit the sphere of theory, clearly demarcating it from observation. For the most part, they knew that science wasn't only a matter of inductive generalisation from observations, and that one could not avoid heuristic hypotheses. But they insisted that such hypotheses be perceived as such, i.e., as nothing other than theories. In a paradoxical and yet logical manner, the accent which positivists placed on observation often led to conventionalism or ludic theories: one could speculate, imagine and play with ideas, as long as it was clear that these were only ideas which could ultimately be corrected by experience. For positivists, concepts were disposable. As Mach explained, they were 'provisional fictions' which were necessary as one had to begin somewhere, but one shouldn't hesitate to dispense with them when one came up with better ones. For Freud, the 'basic concepts'[59] of his metapsychology were only 'fictions',[60] 'mythical entities',[61] 'speculative superstructure[s]',[62] 'scientific constructions'[63] or 'working hypothes[es]'[64] destined to be replaced if they came into conflict with observation.

> **Ernst Mach**: It lies in the nature of hypotheses to be changed in the course of enquiry, becoming adapted to new experiences or even dropped and replaced by a new one or simply by complete knowledge of the facts. Enquirers who keep this in mind will not be too timid in framing hypotheses: on the contrary, a measure of daring is quite beneficial. Huygens' wave hypothesis was not a perfect fit and its justification left much to be desired, causing not a little trouble even to much later followers; but had he dropped it, much of the ground would have been unprepared for Young and Fresnel who would probably have had to confine themselves to the preliminary run-up. The hypothesis of the emission was adapted little by little to the new

experiences ... Hence experience worked continually to transform and complete our representations, enabling a better fit with our hypotheses.[65]

Freud: We can only say: 'We must call the Witch to our help after all' [Goethe, *Faust*, I, 6] – the Witch Metapsychology. Without metapsychological speculation and theorizing – I had almost said 'phantasising' – we shall not get another step forward. Unfortunately, here as elsewhere, what our Witch reveals is neither very clear nor very detailed.[66]

Freud: It is perfectly legitimate to reject remorselessly theories which are contradicted by the very first steps in the analysis of observed facts, while yet being aware at the same time that the validity of one's own theory is only a provisional one. We need not feel greatly disturbed in judging our speculation upon the life and death instincts by the fact that so many bewildering and obscure processes occur in it – such as one instinct being driven out by another or an instinct turning from the ego to an object, and so on. This is merely due to our being obliged to operate with the scientific terms, that is to say with the figurative language, peculiar to psychology (or, more precisely, to depth psychology). We could not otherwise describe the processes in question at all, and indeed we could not have become aware of them.[67]

Mach: By elimination of what it is senseless to explore, what the special sciences can really explore emerges all the more clearly: the complex interdependence of the elements. While groups of such elements may be called things or bodies, it turns out that there are strictly speaking no isolated objects: they are only fictions for a preliminary enquiry, in which we consider strong and obvious links but neglect weaker and less noticeable ones. The same distinction of degree gives rise also to the opposition of world to ego: an isolated ego exists no more than an isolated object: both are provisional fictions of the same kind.[68]

Freud: The true beginning of scientific activity consists rather in describing phenomena and then in proceeding to group, classify and correlate them. Even at the stage of description it is not possible to avoid applying certain abstract ideas to the material in hand, ideas derived from somewhere or other but certainly not from the new observations alone. Such ideas which will later become the basic concepts of the science are still more indispensable as the material is further worked over. They must at first necessarily possess some degree of indefiniteness; there can be no question of any clear delimitation of their content. So long as they remain in this condition, we come to an understanding about their meaning by making repeated references to the material of observation from which they appear to have been derived, but upon which, in fact, they have been imposed. Thus, strictly speaking, they are in the nature of conventions – although everything depends on their not being arbitrarily chosen but determined by their having significant relations to the empirical material, relations that we seem to sense before we can clearly recognize and demonstrate them.[69]

Mach: However, for the scientist it is quite a secondary matter whether his ideas fit into some given philosophic system or not, so long as he can use them with profit as a starting point for research. For the scientist is not so fortunate as to possess unshakeable principles, he has been accustomed to regarding even his safest and best-founded views and principles as provisional and liable to modification through experience.[70]

Freud: *Psycho-analysis an Empirical Science.* – Psycho-analysis is not, like philosophies, a system starting out from a few sharply defined basic concepts, seeking to grasp the whole universe with the help of these and, once it is completed, having no room for fresh discoveries or better understanding. On the contrary, it keeps close to the facts in its field of study, seeks to solve the immediate problems of observation, gropes its way forward by the help of experience, is always incomplete and always ready to correct or modify its theories. There is no incongruity (any more than in the case of physics or chemistry) if its most general concepts lack clarity and if its postulates are provisional; it leaves their more precise definition to the results of future work.[71]

Freud: I am of opinion that that is just the difference between a speculative theory and a science erected on empirical interpretation. The latter will not envy speculation its privilege of having a smooth, logically unassailable foundation, but will gladly content itself with nebulous, scarcely imaginable basic concepts, which it hopes to apprehend more clearly in the course of its development, or which it is even prepared to replace by others. For these ideas are not the foundation of science, upon which everything rests: that foundation is observation alone. They are not the bottom but the top of the whole structure, and they can be replaced and discarded without damaging it.[72]

The Freudian theme of theoretical fiction, which has often been seen as an oppositional counterpoint to 'positivism and to the substantialisation of metaphysical and metapsychological instances', is in fact a typically positivist trait.[73] Far from leading, as the philosopher Rodolphe Gasché (1997) claims, to 'a dislocation of the exclusive and fundamental value of observation, of the status of objective fact and of the logic proper to theoretical discursivity', speculative fiction was tolerated and encouraged by Freud because it didn't at any moment affect the bare non-theoretical observation of phenomena. The latter continued to furnish the ultimate foundation of science, thanks to its capacity to resist speculations and erroneous hypotheses. Facts are hard, stubborn and intractable and only the theories which can adapt to them survive. Mach, as a good evolutionist, called this the 'adaptation of thoughts to facts'.

> **Mach**: Adaptation of thoughts to facts, as we should put it more accurately, we call observation; and mutual adaptation of thoughts, theory.[74]

However, such an outlook quickly runs aground in psychology and psychopathology, where the 'facts' are the behaviours and actions of pliable human subjects and patients, acutely aware of what is expected of them, and able to adapt themselves to 'thoughts'. By no means can one count upon their resistance to correct the vagaries of metapsychological speculation. This was the constant objection of Freud's peers: by itself, observation in psychology does not prove anything, because it does not provide any 'indication of reality'[75] which allows one to distinguish it from theoretical fictions. Not only is it always theory-laden (which Freud, following Mach, would have been ready to accept, within certain limits),[76] but one cannot separate it from the theory.

John T. MacCurdy: Everyone knows that preconceptions determine observations very largely in all scientific work. We see what we are on the look-out for, and are blind to the unexpected. In psychoanalysis, however, this danger is augmented by the plasticity of the material which is largely produced in accordance with the theory of the analyst.[77]

Jastrow: Psychoanalysis belongs to the equally typical group of therapies in which practice is entirely a derivative of theory ... Here the pertinent psychological principle reads: Create a belief in the theory, and the facts will create themselves.[78]

Here, observation is the *realisation* of the theory. Consequently, one cannot differentiate between objective confirmation and circular self-confirmation, resistance and conformity, fact and speculation, 'truth and fiction that has been cathected with affect'.[79] Hence there is nothing to guarantee that psychoanalysis is not an a priori system, a celibate theoretical machine which produces its own evidence – a positivist's nightmare.

Freud never responded to such objections, always referring to the 'psychic reality' and the 'objective certitude' of the unconscious in a circular manner, rather providing the evidence for this which was requested of him.

Freud, concerning the abandonment of the 'seduction theory': When, however, I was at last obliged to recognize that these scenes of seduction had never taken place, and that they were only phantasies which my patients had made up or which I myself had perhaps forced on them, I was for some time completely at a loss ... When I had pulled myself together, I was able to draw the right conclusions from my discovery: namely, that the neurotic symptoms were not related directly to actual events but to wishful phantasies, and that as far as the neurosis was concerned psychical reality was of more importance than material reality. I do not believe even now that I forced the seduction-phantasies on my patients, that I 'suggested' them.[80]

In his polemic with Popper on the subject of the falsifiablity of psychoanalysis, Adolf Grünbaum reproached Popper with ignoring

that Freud had in fact attempted to reply to the objection of suggestion with his 'tally argument' which 'make[s] him a sophisticated
scientific methodologist, far superior than is allowed by the appraisals
of [his] critics'.[81] It is hard to see what justifies this, for what is striking
is Freud's refusal to address this issue, as the 'tally argument' presup-
poses the non-suggestibility rather than proving it.

> **Woodworth:** Nor can the success of the treatment – regarding which I
> do not pretend to judge – be used as weighty evidence in favor of the
> theory. The 'pragmatic argument' will not work in this case. We have a
> number of other treatments, all more or less successful in treating neu-
> rotic cases, and each one purporting to be based on a different theory.[82]

> **Hart:** This argument has little weight. In the history of medicine many
> structures have been built upon the fallacy of *post hoc propter hoc* . . . It is
> of course true that satisfactory results are achieved by psychoanalysis,
> but it is equally true that satisfactory results are achieved by many,
> indeed by all, other methods of psychotherapy, and by a multitude of
> methods which lie altogether outside the walls of medicine . . . We
> must hence conclude that the argument from therapeutic results can-
> not provide the independent confirmation of psychoanalytic validity
> of which we are in search.[83]

> **Wohlgemuth:** I will now proceed to examine more closely the claim of
> the psycho-analysts that the numerous cures which have been effected
> by means of psycho-analysis constitute an undeniable proof of the
> correctness of their doctrine . . . If a cystitis is due to a calculus, no
> internal antiseptic or lavages will end the cystitis; the calculus itself
> must be removed first, and only the removal of the 'complex,' and
> nothing else, can end neurotic symptoms. But neurotic symptoms have
> been cured before Freud was ever thought of, and are still being cured
> by other means. Hence it follows that Freud's theory as to the cause of
> the hysteric symptoms is wrong . . . Thus it appears rational to assume
> that a common factor is active in the various methods of procedure,
> psychoanalytic or otherwise. And this common factor I hold to be
> SUGGESTION, pure and simple, and nothing else.[84]

> **Aldous Huxley:** Psycho-analysts defend their theory by pointing to its
> practical therapeutic successes. People are cured by psycho-analysis,

they say; therefore psycho-analysis must be correct as a theory. This argument would be more convincing than it is, if it could be shown: first, that people have been cured by psycho-analysis after all methods had failed; and secondly, that they have really been cured by psycho-analysis and not by suggestion somewhat circuitously applied through psycho-analytic ritual.[85]

Hollingworth: Among other things, Freud fails to show why other methods of therapy than his own also succeed. If his own theories are demonstrated by his own therapy, what shall we say of the reported success of the [suggestive] therapy of Babinski, Hurst and Rosanoff?[86]

Confronted by the objection of suggestion, Freud could have responded by trying to elaborate procedures aimed at eliminating artefacts of the psychological equation (control groups, double blind experiments, etc.), as have been widely employed. He could have multiplied his observations, trusted in statistical studies in 'the American manner',[87] or attempted to quantify the results obtained by psychoanalysis and compare them to other psychotherapies, as is done in contemporary outcome studies. He could have encouraged follow-up studies, permitting independent researchers to interview his patients and have access to his analytic notes. Such attempts at statistical and experimental verification were by no means unknown at that time, and figures such as Gattel and Jung attempted to apply them.[88] At the same time, such attempts would not have resolved the fundamental problems posed by the inevitable interaction between the observer and the subject, which continues to haunt the most rigorously controlled studies.[89] But Freud would have at least been true to the positivistic spirit, in trying to test his theories and to separate fact from artefact in the most rigorous manner. By contrast, he refused to take such objections seriously, and continually appealed to the 'observations' and 'facts' produced by his method, when the reliability of the latter was at issue.

Freud to Saul Rosenzweig, 28 February 1934: I have examined your experimental studies for the verification of psychoanalytic propositions with interest. I cannot put much value on such confirmation because the abundance of reliable observations on which these propositions rest makes them independent of experimental verification.[90]

Freud, 1933: Only quite a short while ago the medical faculty in an American University refused to allow psychoanalysis the status of a science, on the ground that it did not admit of any experimental proof. They might have raised the same objection to astronomy; indeed, experimentation with the heavenly bodies is particularly difficult. There one has to fall back on observation.[91]

In this regard Freud's adversaries, who for the most part shared his positivistic convictions, were justified in reproaching him for betraying his own principles.

Wohlgemuth: Experimental psychologists have been trained to walk warily; they know that in their science the pitfalls are far more numerous than in any other of the natural sciences; every experiment has to be carefully scrutinized and the conditions closely watched. The greatest and most insidious enemy is 'suggestion,' and to eliminate this is never easy ... 'Suggestion' is to the psychologist what bacteria are to the surgeon. The psychologist aims, as it were, at an aseptic treatment, whilst the psychoanalyst indulges in deliberate infection. After having waded through the psycho-analysis of little Hans, which is reeking and teeming with suggestion, to read Freud's remarks upon it and upon its critics simply takes one's breath away.[92]

Hart: [The] constant testing by an appeal to objective facts is a *sine qua non* in the development of any scientific theory, and we have seen that it is just this test which is lacking in the growth of psychoanalytical theory, because objective facts will not serve its purpose, but only those facts after they have been prepared by the method of psychoanalysis.[93]

It is exactly here that the legend of the immaculate conception of psychoanalysis came in. Since Freud was not willing to allow the method, which enabled him to obtain the 'facts' which he invoked, to be tested, he had to find another means of dealing with the objection that he had been influenced by his hypotheses or speculations. Hence the claim that he had been completely free of any theoretical pre-conception whatsoever.

> **Freud:** Apart from emotional resistances ... it seemed to me that the main obstacle to agreement lay in the fact that my opponents regarded psycho-analysis as a product of my speculative imagination and were unwilling to believe in the long, patient and unbiased work which had gone into its making.[94]

Metapsychological speculation, in other words, was quite apart from pure observation. It is this absence of presupposition to which the legend gave credence. If Freud had to fight against the prejudices of his teachers and colleagues, if they supposedly refused to grant the least importance to the role of sexuality in the neuroses, if he had to overcome his own resistances, one could hardly accuse him of seeing sexuality everywhere under the influence of a preconceived sexual theory.

> **Freud:** The singling out of the sexual factor in the aetiology of hysteria springs at least from no preconceived opinion of my part. The two investigators as whose pupil I began my studies of hysteria, Charcot and Breuer, were far from having any such presupposition; in fact they had a personal disinclination to it which I originally shared.[95]

> **Freud:** I now learned from my rapidly increasing experience that it was not any kind of emotional excitation that was in action behind the phenomena of neurosis but habitually one of a sexual nature ... I was not prepared for this conclusion and my expectations played no part in it, for I had begun my investigation of neurotics quite unsuspectingly.[96]

Similarly, if Freud worked in total isolation, if he never read what Schopenhauer or Nietzsche had written about active forgetting or the significance of drives, one could not accuse him of having projected preconceptions onto the clinical material. Peter Gay cites a letter from Freud to Lothar Bickel in which he once again insists on his 'lack of talent' for philosophy, affirming that he had 'made a virtue out of necessity' through presenting 'the facts which revealed themselves' to him in an 'undisguised' form, 'without bias and without preparation'.

Freud to Lothar Bickel, 28 June 1938: Hence I have rejected the study of Nietzsche although – no, because – it was plain to me that I would find insights in him very similar to psychoanalytic ones.[97]

Freud: I should not like to create an impression that during this last period of my work I have turned my back upon patient observation and have abandoned myself entirely to speculation. I have on the contrary always remained in the closest touch with the analytic material and have never ceased working at detailed points of clinical or technical importance. Even when I have moved away from observation, I have carefully avoided any contact with philosophy proper.[98]

Freud: If anyone sought to place the theory of repression and resistance among the presuppositions instead of the findings of psychoanalysis, I should oppose him most emphatically. Such premises of a general psychological and biological nature do exist, and it would be useful to consider them on some other occasion; but the theory of repression is a product of psycho-analytic work, a theoretical inference legitimately drawn from innumerable experiences.[99]

The same goes for what Sulloway calls Freud's 'crypto-biology': if Freud so frequently denied having been influenced by the biology of his time, this wasn't, as Sulloway claims, an attempt artificially to disguise psychoanalysis as a 'pure' psychology (which would make little sense of his attempts to point to convergences between his theories and biology'[100]). Rather, this enabled him to deny that his theories on the drives, infantile sexuality or bisexuality preceded and hence shaped the impartial observation of the clinical material. According to Freud, such ideas belonged to the '*clinical* postulates of psycho-analysis',[101] rather than to the biogenetic speculations of his ex-collaborator, Wilhelm Fliess.

Freud to Karl Abraham, 6 April 1914: The subjection of our $\Psi\alpha$ to a Fliessian sexual biology would be no less a disaster than its subjection to any system of ethics, metaphysics, or anything of the sort.[102]

Freud: I must, however, emphasize that the present work [*The Three Essays on the Theory of Sexuality*] is characterized not only by being completely based upon psycho-analytic research, but also by being deliberately independent of the findings of biology. I have carefully avoided introducing my scientific expectations, whether derived from general sexual biology or from that of particular animal species, into this study – a study which is concerned with the sexual functions of human beings and which is made possible through the technique of psycho-analysis. Indeed, my aim has rather been to discover how far psychological investigation can throw light upon the biology of the sexual life of man.[103]

Freud: We have found it necessary to hold aloof from biological considerations during our psycho-analytic work and to refrain from using them for heuristic purposes, so that we may not be misled in our impartial judgement of the psycho-analytic facts before us.[104]

Infantile sexuality, repression, the unconscious and the theory of dreams were thus presented as authentic 'discoveries', products of 'observation' and 'experiences' which arose independently of any heuristic hypotheses, anticipatory interpretations, theoretical contaminations or involuntary suggestions on the part of their discoverer. The myth of the immaculate conception of psychoanalysis corresponds rigorously to what one could call the myth of the immaculate induction of Freudian theory: Freud was not influenced by anyone, hence he couldn't have contaminated the clinical material. The rewriting of history had the effect of transforming Freud's hypotheses and speculations into hard, positive and incontrovertible facts. It legitimated them epistemologically, simply short-circuiting the objection of suggestion.

Whilst difficult to explain in psychological terms, the function of the myth of the immaculate conception becomes clarified when one resituates it within the context of Freud's positivistic rhetoric and the controversies in which he was engaged. To those who criticised the arbitrariness of his hypotheses, Freud opposed the image of the patient collector of empirical facts. To those who suspected him of projecting theories drawn from elsewhere onto clinical material, he replied that he was much too uncultivated to be capable of doing so. To those who accused him of imposing his ideas onto patients, he retorted that he only listened to what they had told him. The Freudian legend was a very effective means of returning critiques to their sender and of inverting the order of research. Hence what was subjective suddenly became objective. What was contingent and historical became atemporal. Interpretation became 'psychic reality'. Constructions became 'historical truth' which emerged from a black box to which only the analyst had the key.

> **Wohlgemuth:** [Freud] makes an assertion, defends it on the grounds of its plausibility, and then on the next page he refers to the assertion as a 'fact,' or, 'as I have shown or demonstrated, etc.'.[105]

> **Huxley:** All the other great 'facts' of psycho-analysis are found on examination to be mere assumptions ... No proofs of any of these assumptions are adduced. But they are all treated as facts.[106]

> **Jastrow:** One ... fallacy permeates pages and volumes of psycho-analysis: the fallacy of attributism. It consists in accepting as a reality an abstract concept devised by the thinker for the convenience of his thinking ... The fallacy of attributism subtly, insidiously, comprehensively invades every phase and phrase of the psychoanalyst's technique. He has forgotten the realities and put in their place a mythology of forces – Ucs., Id, Ego, Super-ego, Oedipus, libido in many guises, and other animated concepts – which he then uses to account for the clinical data which suggested them. As a consequence the sense of hypothesis is lost, and the assurance of reality substituted; that is the essence of delusion.[107]

We propose to call this process of the transmutation of interpretations and constructions into positive facts *interprefaction*. Interprefaction forms the basic element of Freud's scientistic rhetoric and the diverse historical legends which he wove around his so-called 'discoveries'. It makes things and events from words, it fabricates facts from suppositions, conjectures and hypotheses.

Interprefaction represents what Freud was actually doing whilst denying he was doing so.

One can legitimately critique this unwarranted reification in drawing attention to the rhetorical, suggested character of so-called analytic 'facts'. As we have seen, this is precisely what most of Freud's critics did, and still do today: 'Your facts aren't facts, they are artefacts which you have fabricated.' However, in many respects, such critiques remain close to Freud's positivistic outlook, in suggesting that one can clearly separate out fact from artefact in the domain of psychology. Thus many of Freud's initial critics, such as Aschaffenburg, Kraepelin, Hoche, Janet and Morton Prince were by no means free of such reification when they proposed their own rival theories: the divide between what was considered fact and artefact was simply drawn up differently.

But one can also reproach Freud, not so much for having created new facts, but for having denied that this was what he was doing. Rather than view analytic interprefaction as having given rise to false facts, one can see it as having led to true artefacts presented as facts. Rather than viewing the Freudian legend as a pure and simple fiction, one can see it as a fabrication which denies that it is a fabrication. What is at issue here then is the dissimulation of the construction of analytic facts, rather than their construction per se.

The interprefaction of psychoanalysis can thus be read in these two senses. Either one underscores its fictive and illusory character, or one highlights its productive aspects. In the first, one denounces the voluntary or involuntary manipulation of facts by the analyst. In the second, one denounces the veiling of this manipulation. One either considers Freud to have been insufficiently positivist, or to have been too much so. These two critiques diverge profoundly as to their respective implications. At bottom, the issue comes down to how one considers the psychological enterprise, and the status of its constructs. However, before attempting to evaluate this, one needs to follow Freud's procedures more closely.

The manufacture of fantasy

First, let's consider Freud's seduction theory and its abandonment, which was so decisive for the history of psychoanalysis. In his historical recapitulations, Freud repeatedly recounted how he had initially believed the striking accounts of sexual abuse and incestuous perversions which his patients reported to him, before realising that these accounts were really fantasies which expressed infantile 'oedipal' unconscious desires. For a long time, this reversal came to be seen as the inaugural gesture of the Freudian 'break': first, hysterical deceit, then the magisterial reversal which with one stroke revealed the truth of the lie, the reality of fiction and the logic of the fantasy.

Jean Laplanche and Jean-Bertrand Pontalis: It is traditional to look upon Freud's dropping of the seduction theory in 1897 as a decisive step in the foundation of psycho-analytic theory, and in the bringing to the fore of such conceptions as unconscious phantasy, psychical reality, spontaneous infantile sexuality and so on.[108]

Freud: Influenced by Charcot's view of the traumatic origin of hysteria, one was readily inclined to accept as true and aetiologically significant the reports made by patients in which they ascribed their symptoms to passive sexual experiences in the first years of childhood – to put it bluntly, to seduction. When this aetiology broke down under the weight of its own improbability and contradiction in definitely ascertainable circumstances, the result at first was helpless bewilderment ... If hysterical subjects trace back their symptoms to traumas that are fictitious, then the new fact which emerges is precisely that they create such scenes in phantasy, and this psychical reality requires to be taken into account alongside practical reality. This reflection was soon followed by the discovery that these phantasies were intended to cover up the auto-erotic activity of the first years of childhood ... And now, from behind the phantasies, the whole range of a child's sexual life came to light.[109]

Freud: Under the influence of the technical procedure which I used at that time, the majority of my patients reproduced from their childhood scenes in which they were sexually seduced by some grown-up person.

With female patients the part of seducer was almost always assigned to their father. I believed these communications, and consequently supposed that I had discovered the roots of the subsequent neurosis in these experiences of sexual seduction in childhood ... When I had pulled myself together, I was able to draw the right conclusions from my discovery: namely, that the neurotic symptoms were not related directly to actual events but to wishful phantasies ... I had in fact stumbled for the first time upon the Oedipus complex, which was later to assume such an overwhelming importance, but which I did not recognize as yet in its disguise of phantasy.[110]

Freud: In the period in which the main interest was directed to discovering infantile sexual traumas, almost all my women patients told me that they had been seduced by their father. I was driven to recognize in the end that these communications were untrue and so came to understand that hysterical symptoms are derived from phantasies and not from real occurrences.[111]

The impression given by such passages is that it was Freud's patients (or their incestuous unconscious desires) who were responsible for Freud's initial error. However, one need only look at Freud's 1896 articles where he presented his theory to see that his retrospective account does not accord with what he wrote at the time, and is in fact quite tendentious. This was noted in 1966 by the psychiatrist Paul Chodoff,[112] soon followed by the philosopher Frank Cioffi.[113] In these articles, in stark contrast to his subsequent accounts, Freud insisted on the extraordinary difficulty which he had in enabling these 'scenes of seduction' to emerge. According to what he wrote, far from his patients having spontaneously confided that they had been the victims of sexual abuse, they were indignant when Freud proposed this as a hypothesis. He had to fight against their resistances inch by inch and extract the memory of the sexual scene piece by piece.

Freud: the fact is that these patients never repeat these stories spontaneously, nor do they ever in the course of a treatment suddenly present the physician with the complete recollection of a scene of this kind.

One only succeeds in awakening the psychical trace of a precocious sexual event under the most energetic pressure of the analytic procedure, and against an enormous resistance. Moreover, the memory must be extracted from them piece by piece, and while it is being awakened in their consciousness they become the prey to an emotion which it would be hard to counterfeit.[114]

Freud: Before they come for analysis the patients know nothing about these scenes. They are indignant as a rule if we warn them that such scenes are going to emerge. Only the strongest compulsion of the treatment can induce them to embark on a reproduction of them.[115]

Freud's letters to Fliess at this time confirm this point. For example, there is the description of the case of 'Miss G. de B.', a cousin of Fliess whom Freud tried to persuade that the eczema around her mouth and her trouble speaking stemmed from the fact that she had been forced as a child to suck her father's penis. Apparently, she wasn't convinced.

Freud to Fliess, 3 January 1897: When I thrust the explanation at her, she was at first won over; then she committed the folly of questioning the old man himself, who at the very first intimation exclaimed indignantly, 'Are you implying that I was the one?' and swore a holy oath to his innocence. She is now in the throes of the most vehement resistance, claims to believe him, but attests to her identification with him by having become dishonest and swearing false oaths. I have threatened to send her away and in the process convinced myself that she has already gained a good deal of certainty which she is reluctant to acknowledge.[116]

Such procedures seem to be far away from the spontaneous volunteering of traumatic recollections. The available evidence indicates that Freud's patients did not have such 'memories' before they had been reconstructed (or constructed) on the basis of indices, conjectures and interpretations, and they were often not convinced of the reality of such events. As Freud had to recognise later, he had communicated to them the content of the traumatic scene (in other words, his hypothesis and construction).

> **Freud:** It is true that in the earliest days of analytic technique we took an intellectualist view of the situation. We set a high value on the patient's knowledge of what he had forgotten, and in this *we made hardly any distinction between our knowledge of it and his.* We thought it a special piece of good luck if we were able to obtain information about the forgotten childhood trauma from other sources – for instance, from parents or nurses or the seducer himself – as in some cases it was possible to do; and we hastened to convey the information and the proofs of its correctness to the patient, in the certain expectation of thus bringing the neurosis and the treatment to a rapid end. It was a severe disappointment when the expected success was not forthcoming ... Indeed, telling and describing his repressed trauma to him did not even result in any recollection of it coming into his mind.[117]

Even when some patients came to visualise or to 'reproduce' fragments of such scenes under Freud's pressure, they refused to regard them as true memories. Freud's colleague Leopold Löwenfeld saw this sentiment of irreality as the proof that these were false memories, suggested by Freud himself. As was well known, the Nancy school had experimented widely with the implantation of false memories under hypnosis.

> **Freud:** While they are recalling these infantile experiences to consciousness, they suffer under the most violent sensations, of which they are ashamed and which they try to conceal; and, even after they have gone through them once more in such a convincing manner, they still attempt to withhold belief from them, by emphasizing the fact that, unlike what happens in the case of other forgotten material, they have no feeling of remembering the scenes.[118]

> **Leopold Löwenfeld:** These remarks [by Freud] show two things: 1. The patients were subjected to a suggestive influence coming from the person who analyzed them, by which the rise of the mentioned scenes was brought quite close to their imagination. 2. These fantasy pictures

that had arisen under the influence of the analysis were definitively denied recognition as memories of real events. I also have a direct experience to support this second conclusion. By chance, one of the patients on whom Freud used the analytic method came under my observation. The patient told me with certainty that the infantile sexual scene which analysis had apparently uncovered was pure fantasy and had never really happened to him.[119]

Why did Freud feel the need to rewrite history so as to imply that his patients had spontaneously volunteered their memories? Paradoxically, the fact that they didn't recall the events in question would have fitted in better with his subsequent theory of repression. But not to have done so would have laid himself completely open to the charge of suggestion. To concede this here would be to raise the question whether the same was not true of his later theories of neurosis, obtained through the same 'analytic' method? Hence it was critical for Freud to conceal the fact that it was he who had speculated, imagined these scenes of sodomy,[120] sadism, fetishism,[121] analingus[122] and fellatio, and taken them to be real, under the influence of his theoretical presuppositions of the moment.

> **Freud to Fliess, 3 January 1897:** The agreement [of my material] with the perversions described by Krafft[-Ebing][123] is a new, valuable proof of reality.[124]

At the same time, through transforming his own hypotheses and conjectures into the 'communications' of his patients, Freud was able to wash his hands of this whole affair, as the onus of responsibility lay with his patients. His error had simply been one of having trusted their bona fides too much and hence having allowed himself to have been led astray by them. It also enabled him to give body and reality to his speculations, despite their erroneous character. With the seduction theory, Freud had put his scientific reputation on the line, and had failed. However, by converting his mistaken theories into communications received from his patients, he was able to use his new interpretive strategies upon what he now claimed that they had said to him. Rather than being explained as a technical failure due to the unwitting suggestive implantation of false memories, psychoanalytic theory could explain what had really occurred, and what lay behind his patients' alleged communications. Better yet, Freud could now claim having observed something rather than nothing, even if it was only with hindsight that he realised its true significance. In effect, Freud had hypostatised and substantivised his own interpretations.

> **Freud:** By means of analysis, as you know, starting from the symptoms, we arrive at a knowledge of the infantile experiences to which the libido is fixated and out of which the symptoms are made. Well, the surprise lies in the fact that these scenes from infancy are not always true. Indeed, they are not true in the majority of cases, and in a few of them they are the direct opposite of the historical truth. As you will see, this discovery is calculated more than any other to discredit either analysis, which has led to this result, or the patients, on whose statements the analysis and our whole understanding of the neuroses are founded ... We are tempted to feel offended at the patient's having taken up our time with invented stories ... It remains a fact that the patient has created these phantasies for himself, and this fact is of scarcely less importance for his neurosis than if he had really experienced what the phantasies contain. The phantasies possess *psychical* as contrasted with *material reality*, and we gradually learn to understand that *in the world of the neuroses it is psychical reality which is the decisive kind.*[125]

> **Freud:** Whence comes the need for these phantasies and the material for them? There can be no doubt that their sources lie in the instincts; but it has still to be explained why the same phantasies with the same content are created on every occasion ... I believe these *primal phantasies*, as I should like to call them, and no doubt a few others as well, are a phylogenetic endowment ... It seems to me quite possible that all the things that are told to us to-day in analysis as phantasy – the seduction of children, the inflaming of sexual excitement by observing parental intercourse, the threat of castration (or rather castration itself) – were once real occurrences in the primaeval times of the

human family, and that children in their phantasies are simply filling in the gaps in individual truth with prehistoric truth.[126]

One sees here how Freud's rewriting of history subtly objectivised what at the outset was only a set of highly speculative hypotheses, which in his own view were ultimately false. What he called his hunches 'in neuroticis'[127] became 'scenes' reported by his patients, then fantasies expressing their unconscious desires, and finally, through efficient recyling, products of phylogenetic inheritance and prehistoric reality. What this sequence neatly passes over is the status of the unconscious fantasies which Freud claimed to be behind the scenes of seduction which his patients confided in him. If such spontaneous recollections appear not to have taken place, what then of the unconscious fantasies they supposedly expressed? Do they not have a similarly questionable status? What fantasies did his patients actually have? Were the forced recollections which he subsequently claimed had been their unconscious fantasies simply responses to his investigative technique and conjectures? Without further historical records, such questions are difficult to resolve. However, what Freud's narrative strategies achieved is clear: the supposition of spontaneous narration of events presented as memories which then came to be seen as fantasies lent credence to the notion of the existence of unconscious fantasies fuelled by infantile wishes. Far from having been based on the observation of facts which were correctly interpreted after a period of erring, the psychoanalytic theory of fantasy is an interpretation of interpretations, resting on Freud's suppositions. The fact that it has taken so long for this to be seen is testament to the rhetorical effectiveness of Freud's rescripting of history.

Should we then reduce the Freudian interprefaction of fantasies to a deception, to an effect of pure rhetoric? This is the perspective of a number of 'revisionist' scholars, such as Frank Cioffi, Han Israëls, Allen Esterson and Frederick Crews, for whom the account of the discovery of unconscious fantasies is a historical mystification which rests on nothing. From this perspective, the Freudian legend took hold because of our belief[128] in the unconscious, which itself was a ruse of the great sophist. Hence the task of the historian should be one of unmasking the vacuity of Freud's accounts, and with this of psychoanalysis itself. However, such a perspective, whilst unmasking Freud's theories, still partakes of a similar positivism.

Indeed, in many respects, historical demystification has been unable to undo the effects of legendary interprefaction. In recent years, we have seen that despite an increasing number of works of historical criticism, in psychoanalysis it is often 'business as usual'. Individuals continue to confess their fantasies, to rescript their lives in terms of Oedipal conflicts, or to recover repressed memories of infantile sexual abuse, and practitioners continue to conduct their trade in good faith. Is this simply due to human, all too human credulity ('mundus vultus decepit')? Or because psychoanalysts have maintained a still powerful authoritative position in the media, health services and human sciences? Such a perspective would be too simple, and would also fail to account for the success of other psychological theories and other psychotherapeutic systems which have also flourished. In our view, it is important to grasp the productive nature of interprefaction, and the manner in which it has fashioned new forms of self-experience while giving rise to new realities or optional ontologies.

> **G. K. Chesterton:** Psychoanalysis can no longer be dismissed as a fad; it has risen to the dignity of a fashion, and possesses all that moral authority and intellectual finality which we associate with a particular pattern of hats or whiskers ... But in any case, a theory is only a thought, while a fashion is a fact. If certain things have really taken hold of the centres of civilization, they play quite as much a part in history whether their ultimate origin is a misapprehension or not.[129]

This returns us to the two ways of comprehending interprefaction. Revisionist historians have had good grounds for stressing the fabricated character of the so-called psychoanalytic 'evidence', but some have too quickly ended here, as if it were simply a question of denouncing an illusion. What is critical to grasp is that interprefaction *does* something to people. Individuals respond to the interpretations of their analysts and suggestive effects of cultural milieux, and many have rescripted their lives on this basis. As a result, new realities have been fashioned. In other words, there is a becoming-fact of fiction or legend becoming a fact, which escapes the simple opposition of true or false, of the given or constructed, of the real and illusory.

To return to the scenes of seduction, it is evident from Freud's own accounts that his patients did not initially have any recollections. However, this does not exclude the fact that they may have accepted the possibility of entertaining them and followed Freud in his hypotheses. It is otherwise hard to grasp why they would have continued treatment with him (some among them, like Emma Eckstein, Elise Gomperz and Oscar Fellner,[130] had been long-term patients, and had valiantly followed Freud through a number of theoretical turns). From this perspective, one need not evoke transference or suggestibility or the credulity of patients towards Freud for having taken up the constructs he proposed. They played the therapeutic game which he proposed, just as experimental psychology subjects or participants of seances have done in their respective settings. It is likely that the more they joined in the game, the more it became serious, and the more it took on shape and reality. Suddenly, the past was no longer the same; innocent memories of childhood were transformed into 'screen-memories' for more embarrassing or sinister events. Dreams could become confirmations of new realities, and symptoms could take on new significations. Patients themselves could take on the task of reinterpreting their lives through a previously unremembered traumatic event which seemed to offer the hope of explanation and liberation. Hence it is not surprising that scenes of seduction would emerge, just as Freud predicted.

In 1925, in his 'autobiographical study', Freud wrote that 'under the influence of the technical procedure which I used at that time, the majority of my patients reproduced from their childhood scenes in which they were sexually seduced by some grown-up person'.[131] There is no reason to doubt this, though it is important to emphasise that these recollections do not appear to have been spontaneous recollections, but rather small psychodramas which mimed Freud's intentions. As Jean Schimek has noted,[132] the technical procedure which Freud used at that time (the 'pressure method', consisting in pressing the forehead of patients and asking them to evoke an image or idea) was not greatly different from the hypno-cathartic method described in *Studies on Hysteria*, in that the objective continued to be one of provoking the re-emergence or an intense visualisation (a hallucination) of the traumatic event. Since Freud recounts that he had to retrieve the memory 'piece by piece', it is clear that such reproductions were fragmentary, or at least were so initially. But judging from his letters to Fliess, it also seems that some patients ended by offering Freud almost complete scenes, exactly conforming to his expectant attention.

> **Freud to Fliess, 24 January 1897:** Thus I was able to trace back, with certainty, a hysteria that developed in the context of a periodic mild depression to a seduction, which occurred for the first time at 11 months and [I could] hear again the words that were exchanged between two adults at that time! It is as though it comes from a phonograph.[133]

> **Freud to Fliess, 22 December 1897:** The intrinsic authenticity of infantile trauma[134] is borne out by the following little incident which the patient claims to have observed as a three-year-old child. She goes into a dark room where her mother is carrying on and eavesdrops. She has good reasons for identifying herself with this mother. The father belongs to the category of *men who stab women*, for whom bloody injuries are an erotic need . . . The mother *now* stands in the room and shouts: 'Rotten criminal, what do you want from me? I will have no part of that. Just whom do you think you have in front of you?' Then she tears the clothes from her body with one hand, while with the other hand she presses them against it, which creates a very

peculiar impression. Then she stares at a certain point in the room, her face contorted by rage, covers her genitals with one hand and pushes something away with the other. Then she raises both hands, claws at the air and bites it. Shouting and cursing, she bends over far backward, again covers her genitals with her hand, whereupon she falls over forward, so that her head almost touches the floor; finally, she quietly falls over backward onto the floor. Afterwards she wrings her hands, sits down in a corner, and with her features distorted with pain she weeps.[135]

One may ask whether the patients themselves believed in the scenes which they reproduced so impressively? From the moment when patients no longer considered their memories as real, it is possible that they may have viewed them as simulations or role plays: 'as if' enactments to test Freud's hypotheses. This would not have stopped them from having simulated these scenes with conviction, and consequently they would have been convincing enough for Freud to take them as confirming his hypotheses. Freud would have been presented with the scenes which he predicted unfolding before him with a hallucinatory exactitude, presenting what appeared to be total confirmation of his theories. It is not surprising that there would have been a temptation for him to continue to press his point and induce his patients to produce more proof.

In the end, it is undeniable that Freud truly 'observed' something, and that his patients sometimes presented scenes of seduction.[136] In this regard, it is impossible to reduce his later accounts to a lie, as some have argued: he did indeed sometimes hear from his patients what he claimed to have heard. The problem is that we are not informed as to when he heard such statements. It rather appears that they retrospectively confirmed his theoretical hypotheses, only *after* after he had suggested the latter by insistent questions, encouragements, admonishments and the reframing of reality.[137] In presenting the scenes enacted by his patients as spontaneous confessions, the legendary narrative short-circuits the time which was necessary to obtain them. It makes one forget how they became real, the process of their production. These scenes were not waiting to be uncovered by Freud: they were produced, co-produced through a negotiation between the doctor and his patients, between the theory and those who were supposed to ratify it, to make it real. The Freudian legend obliterates this consensual fabrication of reality in favour of indisputable 'facts', 'givens' and 'observations'. By contrast, it appears that what were in play here were realities which were negotiated and subject to revision at each moment.

One sees here how a technical reading of the process of interpre-faction, attentive to the procedures through which psychic reality was produced, is quite distinct from a purely critical reading, attempting to arrange everything under the columns of true or false, fact or artefact. Whilst it appears that the scenes and the phantasms invoked by the Freudian legend were initially fictions, they became real for the patients once they accepted them. The patients reproduced traumatic 'reminiscences' between 1889 and 1895, then scenes of infantile sexual abuse between 1896 and 1897, and then they stopped, once Freud asked them instead to produce Oedipal fantasies or memories of 'primal scenes'. Each time, a new reality was produced, with its own rules and characteristics. Had other hypotheses and theoretical demands been given, other psychological realities and therapeutic worlds may have resulted – which was exactly what took place at the turn of the century in the myriad other schools. Like many other psychotherapies and psychologies, psychoanalysis was an ontology-making practice, which recreated the world in its image.

Delbœuf: The existence of several schools of hypnotism thus is only natural and can be easily explained. They owe their birth to the reciprocal action of the hypnotised on their hypnotisers. Only their rivalry has no reason for being: *they are all in the right.*[138]

Wohlgemuth: If a dream of mine were analysed by Freud he would doubtless unearth some sexual complex, whilst Jung, with the same dream, would discover some 'prospective and teleological function,'

158 • Freud Files: An Inquiry into the History of Psychoanalysis

and Adler would find the 'will to power, the masculine protest.' This I think is sufficient proof that the result is due to the psychoanalyst and that the dream-interpretation is the *via regia* to the *analyst's* unconscious.[139]

Hart: It may be noted in this connexion that, while the pupils of Freud confirm by their clinical observations the findings of their master, the pupils of Jung, working with weapons forged of much the same material and in similar pattern, have no difficulty in finding ample clinical confirmation for the quite disparate tenets of Jung.[140]

Judd Marmor: Depending upon the point of view of the analyst, the patients of each school seem to bring up precisely the kind of phenomenological data which confirm the theories and interpretations of their analysts! Thus each theory tends to be self-validating. Freudians elicit material about the Oedipus Complex and castration anxiety, Jungians about archetypes, Rankian about separation anxiety, Adlerians about masculine strivings and feelings of inferiority, Horneyites about idealized images, Sullivanians about disturbed relationships, etc.[141]

Ellenberger: Patients under Freudian analysis dream Freudian dreams, discover their Oedipus complex, their castration anxieties, and establish strong transferences with their analysts. Patients under Jungian analysis dream Jungian dreams, discover their projections and their animas, and realize their individuations. And so on for every dynamic school and subschool. It is as if Descartes' famous 'evil genius' really existed and self-confirmed all the theories of dynamic psychiatry.[142]

But after all, why speak of an *evil* genius, as if it deceives us? It is not because the scientific legend elaborated by Freud dissimulated the artefactuality and the historicity of analytical phenomena that we are forced to conclude that they are illusory. Does one say that a legal contract is a fiction, simply because the reality which it creates did not pre-exist the contract being signed? Or that a cricket match isn't real because the rules are purely conventional? As the participants agree to play the game and respect the rules and the contract, they make it real. At a structural level, the same holds true for psychoanalysis and other forms of psychotherapy. These consensual practices do not reflect the world, they recreate a segment of it. There is nothing wrong with that as long as protagonists do not seek to impose their world on those who never signed up for it and who don't accept it.[143] After all, as Delbœuf noted, 'they are all in the right'. From a Freudian perspective, everyone who has ever lived and will ever live has an unconscious and an Oedipal complex. There is no possibility of regarding these as optional and opting out of them in favour of other forms of self-narration. Faced with a self-validating system of this type, the significant question is not one of knowing whether it is true or false, real or invented, historical or legendary, but rather of comprehending how it functions, how it produces effects which 'interprefact' inner worlds.

> **Jastrow:** Yet in all the Freudian flood of communications, as copious as unsavoury, recounting the adventures of the Freudian 'Oedipus,' I find no definite statement of how the incest theory arose. One may read and re-read that it was 'discovered' in the analysis. This, stripped to its factual content, means that the theory was found acceptable by some neurotic sufferers submitting to analysis; that incidents and relations in their childhood, including fantasies, could be described in such terms by the usual procedures of the Freudian confession in which fact, fantasy, suggestion and prepossession are intricately interactive. And once started, it was accepted eagerly by the disciples as a shibboleth of their faith.[144]

> **Wohlgemuth:** If I want to cure a man of some hysteric stigma, I must get him *to accept the suggestion*. If it cannot be done by telling him, whether in hypnosis or otherwise, that the stigma will disappear, or, *à la Coué*, by his incessant repetition that he is getting better, I may, perhaps, be more successful in making him believe that he is suffering from some 'complex,' and then 'discover' it by the psychoanalytic method. I must get him to *accept* the suggestion, and this is the *sine qua non*.[145]

Airbrushing Breuer

However, one may raise the question of what happens if people subjected to analysis do not accept the interpretation (the suggestion) which is proposed to them? Would interprefaction be legitimate in this case? The examples which we have considered so far concern cases where both parties have taken on board the constructions and interpretations of the analyst, and have remade the world and rewritten personal history on this basis. But what of cases in which one of the parties rejects the interpretations and even refuses to join in the further game of 'transference resistance'? What of apostate disciples who propose rival interpretations which are incompatible with those of the master? Or the sceptical colleagues who demand proofs before taking psychoanalytic theory on board? In such cases, there is clearly no consensus, and one cannot count on the assent of those to whom theories are proposed to make them true and turn them into facts. On the contrary, one is back in the situation of contestation, where hypotheses and interpretations are hotly debated and the facts in question are not taken as established and hence universally accepted.

Freud's response to such individuals, which he was constantly confronted by, is quite clear. He applied the same treatment in the form of interpretations that he gave to his clients. This appears to have begun with his attribution in private of repressed homosexuality and paranoia to Fliess after his embarrassing dispute with him concerning priority and plagiarism.[146]

> **Freud to Jung, 1 February 1907:** My inclination is to treat those colleagues who offer resistance exactly as we treat patients in the same situation.[147]

If colleagues did not accept his theories, it was because they repressed sexuality (Breuer, and German psychiatry as a whole), because they were perverse (Stekel), neurotic (Rank),[148] paranoiac (Fliess, Adler, Ferenczi),[149] on the edge of psychosis (Jung)[150] or in a psychiatric condition (Rank again).[151] Through attributing the 'resistances' which his adversaries opposed *to his theories* to resistances which they supposedly had *to their own unconscious*, Freud killed two birds with one stone. On the one hand, he very effectively delegitimated those who opposed him, through turning them into marionettes moved by forces outside of their control. On the other hand, he short-circuited all discussion on the subject of his theories and interpretations, since he presupposed what was being debated: the existence of the Freudian unconscious and the exclusive prerogative of the psychoanalyst to decipher its manifestations. We see here the familiar mechanisms of psychoanalytic interprefaction: from being a hypothesis to be confirmed, the Freudian unconscious became an established incontrovertible fact, as if Freud had already won the debate. Hence there wasn't even much need to obtain the assent of his adversaries or take their objections into account. As the psychologist Adolf Wohlgemuth put it, 'Heads I win, tails you lose.'[152]

> **Freud:** Thus the strongest resistances to psycho-analysis were not of an intellectual kind but arose from emotional sources. This explained their passionate character as well as their poverty in logic. The situation obeyed a simple formula: men in the mass behaved to psychoanalysis in precisely the same way as individual neurotics under treatment for their disorders ... The position was at once alarming and consoling: alarming because it was no small thing to have the whole human race as one's patient, and consoling because after all everything was taking place as the hypotheses of psycho-analysis declared that it was bound to.[153]

This confounds two very different types of relations: that of the consensual contract between the therapist and his patients, and that of scientific and scholarly debate where there is the necessity of attempting to convince one's colleagues and rivals. It was one thing to lead patients to accept interpretations in a contractual therapeutic relation which they could terminate at any point. It was another thing to assume that such interpretations were equally applicable to peers, and indeed, to all others, despite their protestations. In deliberately blurring the boundaries between these domains, Freud unjustifiably raised the optional ontology of the psychoanalytic relation, where participants agree between themselves to define a world according to their taste for the sake of therapeutic benefit, into a general ontology, a universal science which would be applicable to all.

It is clear that Freud would never have been satisfied to regard his theories as interprefactions, or his evidence as realities fabricated and negotiated in concert with his patients. This would have reduced psychoanalysis to simply a technique of psychological manipulation, to one form of 'psychic treatment' among others. Freud's aim was to establish psychoanalysis as the only scientific psychotherapy, based on a universally valid psychology. Consequently, 'hard' facts were necessary. It was this will to science which Freud's legendary inter-prefaction presented as already fulfilled, a 'fait accompli', hence short-circuiting the slow work of proof and argumentation.

> **Jung:** A very famous professor, whose assertions I had ventured to criticize, came out with the magisterial dictum: 'It must be right because I have thought it.'[154]

> **Jung, interview with Kurt Eissler, 29 August 1953:** For example, I once had a discussion with him [Freud] about some theoretical topic. And I said to him: 'In my view that is not at all the case!' He said to me: 'But it must be so!' I asked: 'Why then?' 'Because I have thought it!' You know, when he had thought something, he himself was so convinced and therefore it *had* to be correct![155]

> **Jung to Ernst Hanhart, 18 February 1957:** The subjective overvaluation of [Freud's] thinking is illustrated by his dictum: 'This must be correct because I have thought it.'[156]

> **Jung, interview with Hugo Charteris, 21 January 1960:** Imagine! He [Freud] once said to me: 'I thought it – so it must be true.'[157]

From the perspective of contemporaneous scholarly and scientific debate, this form of interprefaction which magically closed controversies before they could properly begin was quite illegitimate, as it no longer required the agreement of those to whom it was proposed. On the contrary, it did violence to them, as it transformed the negotiable performative statements of a therapist into a scientific constative, an

irrefutable dictat. Statements which might be acceptable in a con-
senting psychotherapeutic relation through being taken up by those
to whom they were proposed functioned quite differently outside of
this context, when they were imposed on individuals against their
will. In this way, interprefaction turned into a fallacious rescripting of
history.

> **Ernest Jones:** Two of the members [of the Secret Committee], Rank
> and Ferenczi, were not able to hold out to the end. Rank in a dramatic
> fashion ... and Ferenczi more gradually toward the end of his life,
> developed psychotic manifestations that revealed themselves in,
> among other ways, a turning away from Freud and his doctrines.[158]

> **Peter Gay:** In 1923, Rank went through some distressing episodes that
> hinted at welling-up conflicts; in August, for one, at dinner with the
> Committee in San Cristoforo, Anna Freud witnessed an outburst that
> she later described as 'hysterical hilariousness.' Just as ominously, Rank
> began to espouse techniques and theoretical positions that would
> move him far from the ideas he had been steeped in for two decades
> and had done so much to propagate.[159]

Such statements are examples of the character assassination which was
practised to deligitimate the technical and theoretical innovations of
two of Freud's hitherto most loyal followers. For a less obvious example,
we may consider the manner in which Freud managed the controversy
between himself and his old friend and collaborator Josef Breuer.

In 1909 in his lectures at Clark University, Freud had not hesitated
to attribute the paternity of psychoanalysis to Breuer.

> **Freud:** Ladies and Gentlemen, – It is with novel and bewildering
> feelings that I find myself in the New World, lecturing before an
> audience of expectant enquirers ... If it is a merit to have brought
> psycho-analysis into being that merit is not mine. I had no share in its
> earliest beginnings. I was a student and working for my final examina-
> tions at the time when another Viennese physician, Dr. Josef Breuer,
> first (in 1880–2) made use of this procedure on a girl who was suffering
> from hysteria.[160]

Freud followed this with a long description of the famous 'talking cure' of Anna O., presented as a total therapeutic success and a presentation of the cathartic method developed by Breuer and Freud. However, five years later in his 'History of the psychoanalytic movement', the tone had completely changed.

> **Freud:** Certain opponents of psycho-analysis have a habit of occasionally recollecting that after all the art of psycho-analysis was not invented by me, but by Breuer ... I have never heard that Breuer's great share in psycho-analysis has earned him a proportionate measure of criticism and abuse. As I have long recognized that to stir up contradiction and arouse bitterness is the inevitable fate of psychoanalysis, I have come to the conclusion that I must be the true originator of all that is particularly characteristic in it.[161]

Freud now not only insisted on the disagreements between himself and Breuer on the subject of the 'psychical mechanisms' of hysteria ('defence' versus 'hypnoid state'), but also described his former mentor as a timorous investigator, frightened by sexuality, whom he had to convince to publish the case of Anna O., almost against his will, and who had broken with Freud shortly after the publication of *Studies on Hysteria*. Furthermore, Freud insinuated publicly for the first time that the end of the treatment of Anna had been much more ambiguous than he and Breuer had given it to be understood up till now.

> **Freud:** I am quite sure, however, that this opposition between our views [on the psychical mechanisms of hysteria] had nothing to do with the breach in our relations which followed shortly after. This had deeper causes, but it came about in such a way that at first I did not understand it; it was only later that I learnt from many clear indications how to interpret it. It will be remembered that Breuer said of his famous first patient that the element of sexuality was astonishingly undeveloped in her and had contributed nothing to the very rich clinical picture of the case[162] ... In his treatment of her case, Breuer was able to make use of a very intense suggestive rapport with the patient,[163] which may serve us as a complete prototype of what we call 'transference' to-day. Now I have strong reasons for suspecting that after all

her symptoms had been relieved Breuer must have discovered from further indications her sexual motivation of this transference, but that the universal nature of this unexpected phenomenon escaped him, with the result that, as though confronted by an 'untoward event,' he broke off all further investigation. He never said this to me in so many words, but he gave me enough clues at different times to justify this conjecture of what happened.[164]

What had transpired between 1909 and 1914 to justify such a striking rewriting of the founding episode of psychoanalysis? And why this volte-face on Breuer's role in the matter? Some explanation may be found in the different contexts and moments of Freud's accounts. In 1909, Freud was speaking in front of a very distinguished audience of American neurologists, psychiatrists and psychologists, amongst others,[165] who for the most part only knew him as the co-author of the *Studies on Hysteria* and the promoter of a new psychotherapeutic method, the 'Breuer–Freud method', which was often confounded with other forms of hypno-suggestive therapies derived from Janet's 'psychological analysis'.[166] As Eugene Taylor has emphasised, for many, Freud was thought to be the junior author of the two.[167] Ten years earlier, at his presentation at the tenth anniversary of Clark University, Forel had presented the work of Breuer and Freud as a variation of the hypnotic psychotherapy of which he himself was one of the great proponents in Europe.

> **Forel:** In an obscure but very frequent manner, on the other hand, certain single impulses may leave behind lasting inhibitions, or stimuli, and perhaps disorders of function which may take a pathological character, and seriously tantalize the victim. Such points were used, a few years ago, by Breuer and Freud in Vienna, for the foundation of their doctrine of arrested emotions, which, unfortunately, was developed into a one-sided system, although it started from correct facts. Thus especially violent affects are apt to leave behind all sorts of nervous disorders (convulsions, paralysis, pains, dyspepsia, menstrual disorders). Breuer and Freud tried to lead the patients in a hypnotic condition to the causative, frequently forgotten, and frequently sexual

moment of the trouble, to make them dream over that moment and to give them, once and forever, a counter suggestion, curing the disorder. In many cases this works; but by no means always.[168]

Freud was quite aware of the American context, which Jones had been keeping him abreast of.[169] Thus it was not surprising, speaking from the same podium as Forel ten years earlier, that Freud would have begun his presentation of psychoanalysis with a recapitulation of the treatment of Anna O., passing over his rupture with Breuer on the subject of the exclusive sexual aetiology of hysteria. By contrast, in 1914, as we have seen, he was writing in the context of the heated controversies around psychoanalysis, in which Breuer's name was regularly evoked against him (notably by Forel). Thus it makes sense that Freud emphatically stressed his distance from the Breuerian heritage. It was impossible to continue to present Breuer as the absent father of Freudian psychoanalysis, as he was being frequently cited against Freud. Against the model of continuity and progress, he substituted that of theoretical rupture. In other words, it became necessary to show that the cathartic method had been a dead end, contrary to what Forel, Frank, Bezzola and others were claiming, and that only psychoanalysis (the sexual hermeneutic) could explain why and surmount the shortcomings of the cathartic method.

Proving the first point did not, in itself, present any difficulties, since Freud always knew that the treatment of Bertha Pappenheim (the actual 'Anna O.') had not been an unmitigated success, contrary to what he and Breuer had claimed in *Studies on Hysteria*.[170] At the end of treatment, far from being 'free from the innumerable disturbances which she had previously exhibited',[171] she was committed by Breuer to a private clinic in Kreuzlingen, Switzerland, suffering from facial neuralgia (trigeminal neuralgia), severe convulsions, morphine addiction and a 'slight hysterical insanity'.

Report sent by Breuer to Robert Binswanger, Director of the Bellevue Clinic, mid-June 1882: Today, the patient is suffering from slight hysterical insanity, confessing at the moment to all kinds of deceptions, genuine or not, occasionally still seeing bits of nonsense such as people spying on her, and the like, and exhibiting perfectly odd behavior on visits. She is receiving daily 0.08–0.1 morphine by injection.[172]

Breuer hadn't mentioned his patient's very painful neuralgia in his 1895 case history, nor the morphine addiction that had resulted from his efforts to calm her convulsions. Nevertheless, the neuralgias figured prominently among the symptoms that he and Freud, in their 'Preliminary communication', claimed to have been able to trace back to traumas.[173] It would have been interesting for their colleagues in neurology and psychiatry to learn that the cathartic cure of Breuer's paradigm patient had not eliminated this symptom.

Furthermore, once at Bellevue, Bertha Pappenheim had developed the habit each evening of losing the ability to speak her native language.

> **Albrecht Hirschmüller:** Mention of this last symptom in the Kreuzlingen report is particularly surprising since Breuer states in 1895 that this symptom had been removed at one stroke – and once and for all – with the narration of that first crucial experience.[174]

Bertha Pappenheim subsequently had three other stays at a clinic, each under a diagnosis of hysteria. It was only near the end of the 1880s, six or seven years after the conclusion of her treatment with Breuer, that she began to recover – this recovery having nothing to do with the famous talking cure.[175]

> **Hirschmüller:** What is certain is that the impression [Breuer] gives in *Studies on Hysteria* that the patient was completely cured does not square with the facts.[176]

Freud could therefore have revealed these secrets and thereby undermined the origins of the Forelian's psychanalysis. Indeed, he didn't waste any opportunities to tell the insiders of the psychoanalytic movement, as we know from their various and subsequent 'leaks', or else from recently exhumed archival documents.

> **Poul Bjerre (1916):** I can add that the patient [Anna O.] was to undergo a severe crisis in addition to what was given out in the description of the case.[177]

> **Jung (1925):** There is then a certain untrustworthiness about all these earlier cases [of Freud]. Thus again, the famous first case that he had with Breuer, which has been so much spoken about as an example of a brilliant therapeutic success, was in reality nothing of the kind. Freud told me that he was called in to see the woman the same night that Breuer had seen her for the last time,[178] and that she was in a bad hysterical attack, due to the breaking off of the transference.[179]

> **Jung citing Freud (1953):** At the end [of Breuer's case history] it is said: She was cured – through the chimney sweeping – it is said that she was cured. But she wasn't cured at all! When she came under my hands [Freud's hands] she had a great hysterical attack, as when Breuer let her go.[180]

> **Ferenczi, Clinical Diary, 1 May 1932:** [Freud] must have been first shaken and then disenchanted, however, by certain experiences, rather like Breuer when his patient had a relapse.[181]

> **Freud to Sir Arthur Tansley, 20 November 1932:** In Breuer's case-history, you will find a short sentence: – 'but it was a considerable time before she regained her mental balance entirely' (*Studien über Hysterie*, p. 32). Behind this is concealed the fact that, after Breuer's flight, she once again fell back into psychosis, and for a longish time – I think it was $\frac{3}{4}$ of a year – had to be put in an institution some way from Vienna.[182]

The problem was that Freud couldn't use this argument publicly without calling into question the historical foundation of the talking cure (cathartic *and* analytic) and revealing that he had been complicit in Breuer's dubious declarations of therapeutic success in *Studies on Hysteria*. For that matter, nowhere in Freud's *published* works do we find the miraculous 'healing' of Anna O. drawn into question.[183] On the contrary, what we do find, beginning in 1914 with the 'History of the psychoanalytic movement', is the assertion that this otherwise spectacular healing was *incomplete*: Anna O. was to have developed a 'transferential love' for Breuer, who had failed to recognise and analyse the sexual nature of the 'rapport' that he had used to make the symptoms disappear (this is a summary of the *published* versions).

Freud, however, took great care to present this belated revelation as a reconstruction – made sometime afterwards – of what had really occurred. In the 'History', he spoke of 'conjecture' and 'interpretation' and of 'suspicions' based on 'indications' or 'clues' provided by Breuer, who 'never said this to me in so many words'.[184] In his autobiographical study and Breuer's obituary, he declared that it was a matter of 'reconstruction' and 'suppositions':

> **Freud:** I found reason later to suppose that a purely emotional factor, too, had given him an aversion to further work on the elucidation of the neuroses. He had come up against something that is never absent – his patient's transference onto her physician, and he had not grasped the impersonal nature of the process.[185]

> **Freud:** The patient had recovered and had remained well and, in fact, had become capable of doing serious work. But over the final stage of this hypnotic treatment there rested a veil of obscurity, which Breuer never raised for me; and I could not understand why he had so long kept secret what seemed to me an invaluable discovery instead of making science the richer by it ... It was easy to see that he too shrank from recognizing the sexual aetiology of the neuroses. He might have crushed me or at least disconcerted me by pointing to his own first patient, in whose case sexual factors had ostensibly played no part whatever. But he never did so,[186] and I could not understand why this was, until I came to interpret the case correctly and to reconstruct, from some remarks which he had made, the conclusion of his treatment of it. After the work of catharsis had seemed to be completed, the girl had suddenly developed a condition of 'transference love'; he had not connected this with her illness, and had therefore retired in dismay.[187]

In a letter from Freud to his fiancée dating from this period, though, we find a different story.

Freud to Martha Bernays, 31 October 1883: Breuer too has a very high opinion of her and has given up her care because his happy marriage threatened to come unstuck on account of it. The poor wife could not bear it that he devoted himself so exclusively to a woman, about whom he obviously spoke with much interest, and was certainly jealous of nothing else but the engrossment of her husband by a stranger. Not in the ugly, tormenting way, but in the quietly resigned manner. She fell ill, lost her spirits, until it dawned on him and he learned the reason for it, which of course was a command for him to withdraw completely from his activity as physician of B.P. Can you be silent, Marthchen? It is nothing dishonorable, but rather something very intimate and that one keeps to oneself and one's beloved. *I know it of course from him personally.*[188]

Here, Freud makes a point of mentioning Breuer's 'esteem' for and 'interest' in Bertha Pappenheim (what he termed in his obituary of Breuer 'a large amount ... if the phrase can be allowed, of medical libido').[189] In his published 'reconstructions', however, he speaks of a transferential love *of Bertha Pappenheim* for Breuer. Nothing in the letter to Martha or in any other document, supports this version, which is contradicted by all sorts of information.[190] This appears to be an interprefaction of Freud; while in accordance with psychoanalytic theory, it doesn't tally with what is known about the life of Bertha Pappenheim. All the accounts agree on this subject and they corroborate Breuer's version: Bertha Pappenheim was asexual and remained that way for the rest of her life. But this too, of course, is precisely what the psychoanalytic rewriting of the history was intended to deny, over the objections of Breuer and the Forelians.

As John Forrester and Laura Cameron have rightly emphasised, the case of Anna O. had become for Freud 'a potential *experimentum crucis*' on which the 'correctness of psychoanalytic theory' depended.[191] It was necessary for him to establish that Anna O.'s asexuality, far from 'falsifying' his theory, was only superficial. The legendary interprefaction of the end of Anna O.'s treatment satisfied this exigency: in attributing to Anna O./Bertha Pappenheim a 'transferential love' which Breuer ignored, Freud made her fate as a spinster appear to be a residual symptom of her unanalysed transference. As he was to write to Sir Arthur Tansley, the talking cure had been 'a cure with a defect'. In short, Breuer had botched the treatment, and those who took his side exposed themselves to the same disappointment.

> **Freud to Tansley, 10 November 1932:** Subsequently [to Anna O.'s institutionalisation] the disease had run its course, but it was a cure with a defect. Today she is over 70, has never married, and, as Breuer said, which I remember well, has not had any sexual relations. On the condition of the renunciation of the entire sexual function she was able to remain healthy. Breuer's treatment, so to speak, helped her over her mourning. It is of interest that, as long as she was active, she devoted herself to her principal concern, the struggle against white slavery.[192]

> **Freud:** Breuer's first hysterical patient was ... fixated to the period when she was nursing her father in a serious illness. In spite of her recovery, in a certain respect she remained cut off from life; she remained healthy and efficient but avoided the normal course of a woman's life.[193]

It is noteworthy that this entire construction is based on an interprefaction, and one which was forged without the acknowledgement of the principal parties, who undoubtedly would have vigorously protested had they been consulted (Breuer seems to have done precisely that).[194] Forel, wanting to clarify for himself the episode of Anna O., had at least made the effort to collect Breuer's actual testimony and evidence. As for Freud, he refrained from doing so, just as he refrained from contacting Bertha Pappenheim (which would have been very easy for him to do, since his wife knew her personally). Instead, he had them testify *in absentia* in support of his theory, without asking their opinion any more than he asked Leonardo, Shakespeare or Michelangelo for theirs. In these conditions, how would the jurors (readers, colleagues) have been able to question these accounts, since they were presented not as *ad hoc* interpretations, but as *matters of fact,* 'historical' events that actually took place?

In his published versions, Freud insisted that Breuer hadn't told him everything about what had happened between him and Anna O. In private, though, he claimed that he had received the story from Breuer himself, or else that the latter had at least confirmed his suspicions.

Princess Marie Bonaparte, Diary of 17 October 1925: Breuer and Fräulein Anna O. Confession ten years later.[195]

Bonaparte, Diary of 16 December 1927: Freud told me the Breuer story . . . Breuer's daughter questioned her father about it. He confessed everything that Freud had written in the *Selbstdarstellung.* Br[euer] to Freud: 'What have *you* got me into!'[196]

Freud to Stefan Zweig, 2 June 1932: What really happened with Breuer's patient I was able to guess later on, long after the break in our relations, when I suddenly remembered *something Breuer had once told me* in another context before we had begun to collaborate and which he never repeated . . . I was so convinced of this reconstruction of mine that I published it somewhere. Breuer's youngest daughter (born shortly after the above-mentioned treatment, not without significance for the deeper connections!)[197] read my account and asked her father about it (shortly before his death). He confirmed my version, and she informed me about it later.[198]

Freud to Tansley, 20 November 1932: My guesses about what happened afterwards with Breuer's first patient are certainly correct. He confirmed [them] in full to *his* daughter, who, on reading my Autobiographical Study, had questioned him about them.[199]

The problem, though, is that the account Breuer is supposed to have 'confirmed' or 'confessed' is found nowhere in the *Autobiographical Study,*[200] nor in any other text published by Freud. To Jung, to Marie Bonaparte, to Stefan Zweig and, it seems, to many other colleagues, Freud appears to have related an even more fabulous and explosive story than that of Anna O.'s supposed 'transferential love' for Breuer.

Otto Rank, 1st American Lecture (1924): Psychoanalysis was born in the year 1881. Its father was the late physician, Dr. Josef Breuer, who for nearly ten years kept secret the birth of this illegitimate child.[201] Dr. Breuer then abandoned the child because it might appear a bastard of scientific medicine, of which he himself was a representative, and of psychotherapy, which is still under suspicion at the present time ... The story is this. As Breuer one day revisited his patient [Anna O.], at that time almost recovered, he found her again in bed, in a state of excitement accompanied by violent convulsions whose meaning he had not long to look for. His patient cried out to him that she was now bringing forth the child begotten by him. This was enough to horrify any respectable doctor. Consequently he, so to speak, forgot his cue, took the matter personally, declared the patient insane, and arranged for her to be put into a mental hospital ... There, after some time, this acute condition died away of its own accord.[202]

Abraham Arden Brill, Course of psychiatric psychoanalysis, 1924, the Pathological Institute, Ward's Island: There was another and perhaps even more conclusive reason for Breuer's ultimate retreat. [After her recovery] Anna O. kept coming to see him for advice and assistance with her problems; and Breuer, following his custom, used to hypnotize her. One day the young woman came to him in a hysterical state, and while he was going through the hypnotizing formulas she suddenly grabbed him, kissed him, and announced that she had become pregnant by him. Of course the old man was shocked. He decided that the girl must be crazy, or, at all events, that the treatment had its dangers. The experience was too much for Breuer. He had not been able to brave the world of prudery to begin with, and this final incident was the climax. There and then he decided to separate from Freud.[203]

Bonaparte, Diary of 16 December 1927: Freud told me the Breuer story. His wife tried to kill herself towards the end of Anna–Bertha's treatment. The rest is well known: Anna's relapse, her fantasy of pregnancy, Breuer's flight.[204]

Freud to Stefan Zweig, 2 June 1932: On the evening of the day when all her symptoms had been disposed of, he was summoned to the patient again, found her confused and writhing in abdominal cramps.

Asked what was wrong with her, she replied: 'Now Dr. B.'s child is coming!' At this moment he held in his hand the key that would have opened the 'doors to the Mothers,' but he let it drop.[205] With all his intellectual gifts there was nothing Faustian in his nature. Seized by conventional horror he took flight and abandoned the patient to a colleague. For months afterwards she struggled to regain her health in a sanatorium.[206]

Jung, citing Freud (1953): When [Anna O.] came into my care she had, she had the same as when Breuer left her as cured, she had a great hysterical attack, and cried, Now Breuer's child is coming! We need the child, no? But that doesn't feature in the case history! . . . he said, that makes a bad impression, and so on.[207]

We know that on 20 June 1925, on the occasion of Breuer's death, Freud sent a letter of condolence to his son Robert Breuer, who in response mentioned the esteem in which his father had held Freud's recent works. This, Freud wrote back, 'was like balm on a painful wound which had never healed'.[208] In the polite exchange of letters which followed between Freud and the Breuer family,[209] there is no trace of a 'confirmation' by Breuer of Freud's allegations in the *Autobiographical Study*; and we reflect that it is improbable that Dora Breuer would have confided such sensitive information to some-one her father had been estranged from for almost thirty years and who had a very poor reputation in the family circle.[210] Whatever the case, and even if we were to suppose that Breuer had indeed con-firmed what Freud had written in his autobiography, such a confir-mation at most could only have applied to the emotional imbroglio in which Bertha Pappenheim's treatment was carried out, and not to the story of the hysterical childbirth Freud was spreading in private. Presenting this history as a corroborated fact seems to be the drama-tisation of a tendentious and improbable interpretation, intended to discredit Breuer and his followers.

The first to reformulate Bertha Pappenheim's treatment in terms of the libido theory in public was not Freud, however, but Max Eitingon.

Eitingon had begun corresponding with Freud in 1906, while he was at the Burghölzli hospital, and in 1907 he went to visit him in Vienna.[211] In December 1910, at the moment when the Freudians were beginning to get nervous about Forel's initiatives, Eitingon gave a talk on Anna O. (Breuer) considered from the psychoanalytic point of view,[212] at a conference organised by Freud in Vienna on the theme 'Theory of the Neuroses and Psychotherapy'. In this text, discovered by Albrecht Hirschmüller in the Archives of Erich Gumbel (director of the Max Eitingon Institute of Jerusalem[213]), Eitingon provided a critical revision of Breuer's case history in which he emphasised its pre-psychoanalytic character, that is to say its incompleteness. Breuer had insisted on the 'asexual' character of Anna O.'s symptomology; Eitingon, though, retranslating Breuer's report in the 'language of psychoanalysis', had no difficulty recognising the sexuality within it: Anna O., at the bedside of her ailing father, had nourished incestuous fantasies, as well as a *fantasy of pregnancy* which she subsequently repressed and transferred onto Breuer, who was transformed into a substitute for her dead father.

> **Max Eitingon, 1909:** Anna got into a state of faintness, anemia and disgust at eating, and this became so bad that in her great pain she wanted to distance herself from the care of the sick person. So she fled, and at the same time due to her condition became bedridden herself. Thus she also got into bed, although into another one, and the above symptom complex looks not only similar to the expression of a pregnancy fantasy.[214]

Eitingon, after criticising Breuer's blindness to the transference of which he was the object, wondered *in fine* about the true reasons for Anna O.'s healing, concluding that the cathartic method used by the Forelians was unsophisticated and outdated (this, of course, was the point of his whole talk).

> **Eitingon:** For a long time the cathartic method . . . despite the fact that it still has proponents, can no longer be seen as a rational psychotherapeutic method.[215]

It is unclear to what extent Eitingon was simply echoing conversations he had had with Freud, or if he was proposing an original interpretation of his own. Whatever the case, it is clear enough that this rereading of Breuer's case history was essentially intended retroactively to make it fall in line with the subsequent developments of psychoanalytic theory. The fantastic tale of Anna O.'s hysterical childbirth lent colour to this theoretical interpretation. Even Kurt Eissler, at the end of a life dedicated to defending Freud's probity and moral rectitude against his detractors, was forced to recognise this fact, speaking in this regard of a 'hardly believable derailment' by his hero.[216]

> **Kurt Eissler:** Freud's version is false throughout, as is reliably documented ... Freud was a fairly reliable reporter of events, sometimes amazingly accurate ... But here is an incident in which he became the victim of an extensive paramnesia ... Freud's documented ambivalence to Breuer, the extreme improbability of the actions he attributed to Breuer, and the several fatal contradictions of his own account by documentary evidence leave no doubt that Freud was a victim of his own personal imagery in his letter to Zweig. Breuer's alleged remark, whatever it may have been, must have been submitted in Freud's unconscious to elaboration until the reconstruction suddenly appeared, decades later, with its convincing impression of reality ... [Freud] must have expected that his correction of Zweig's portrait of Breuer would find its way into print. Why this urge to denigrate Breuer after so many decades? It was not only an act of ingratitude but also an act of indiscretion. He divulged intimate matters which, so he claimed, he had obtained at a time of Breuer's trusting friendship. Freud acted here in a way that is in contrast to his usual fidelity of character: he was ungrateful, indiscreet, and slanderous.[217]

Eissler, of course, tries to psychologise the whole affair, viewing it as the symptom of Freud's unconscious ambivalence towards his old friend – which once again gives psychoanalysis the last word. However, the episode cannot be reduced to the 'personal', for it clearly had a strategic role. The rewriting of Anna O.'s history, as well as the origins of psychoanalysis, came at exactly the right time to settle a scientific controversy and to get rid of a bothersome fact, which carried with it the risk of 'falsifying' Freudian theory and giving ammunition to its adversaries. Asexualised, Anna O. refuted Freudian psychoanalysis. On the other hand, rolling about on the ground, holding her lower abdomen, she refuted Forelian psych-analysis and made Breuer look like a fool. Freud's narrative victory over Breuer was total, as the conflict of interpretations that divided them no longer even appeared as such. Readers were presented with a historical event that put an end to the discussion – a matter of fact that no one could henceforth draw into question.

But it was an interprefaction. For those upon whom it is foisted, an interprefaction (without *uptake*) is at best a forgery, at worst a cal-umny. In 1953, Ernest Jones brought out the first volume of his biography of Freud, in which he revealed the true identity of Anna O. and, for the first time, enlightened the public at large on the history of her 'hysterical childbirth (pseudocyesis), the logical termi-nation of a phantom pregnancy'.[218] Jones claimed to have received this account directly from Freud; but in a note, he added that his source, insofar as the biography of Bertha Pappenheim was con-cerned, had been one of her cousins, Mrs Ena Lewisohn. On 20 June 1954, *Aufbau*, the newspaper of German-speaking immigrants in New York City, printed a letter from Paul Homburger, the executor of Bertha Pappenheim's will.

> **Paul Homburger:** I am one of the rare members of Bertha Pappenheim's close family circle who is still living and I have the duty as her executor to speak in the name of the family and to establish that the family is not capable of an inexcusable lack of piety to authorise the lifting of a medical secret which Bertha had guarded during her life. But much worse than the revelation of her name as such is the fact that Dr. Jones on p. 225 adds on his own account a completely superficial and misleading version of Bertha's life after the

conclusion of Dr. Breuer's treatment. Instead of informing us how Bertha was finally cured and how, completely mentally reestablished, she led a new life of active social work, he gives the impression that she was never cured and that her social activity and even her piety were another phase of the development of her illness ... Anyone who has known Bertha Pappenheim during the decades which followed will regard this attempt at interpretation on the part of a man who never knew her personally as defamation.[219]

It may be objected that what is at issue here is nothing other than 'human, all too human' failings of Freud, which were hardly particular to him. However, our aim here is not to stand in judgement concerning Freud's conduct, nor to evaluate it morally. Rather it is to show the significant strategic functions of Freud's interprefactions in establishing how psychoanalysis became, for so many, a reality.

3

Case histories

Freud to Fliess on the 'Dora' case, 25 January 1901: 'It is the subtlest thing I have written so far.'

Freud (1985), 433

Freud's account [of the Rat Man case] remains exemplary as an exposition of a classic obsessional neurosis. It brilliantly serves to buttress Freud's theories, notably those postulating the childhood roots of neurosis, the inner logic of the most flamboyant and most inexplicable symptoms, and the powerful, often hidden, pressures of ambivalent feelings.

Peter Gay (1988), 267

The case history known as that of the 'Wolfman' is assuredly the best [of Freud's case histories]. Freud was then at the very height of his powers.

Jones (1955), 274

The legend of Anna O.'s hysterical childbirth is a typical example of the psychoanalytic rewriting of history. Here, as elsewhere, Freud applied to the history of psychoanalysis (and later to history itself, if we consider *Totem and Taboo*, *Moses and Monotheism* and *Woodrow Wilson*) the same method of interpretation that he used in the privacy of his office to 'reconstruct' his patients' forgotten and repressed memories. From this point of view, there is little difference between the 'case' of Anna O. and the Breuer 'case', the Schreber 'case', the Fliess 'case', the 'case' of the Wolf Man and the 'cases' of Jung, Rank or Ferenczi. Everyone – colleague or patient, sane or raving mad, dead or alive – was subjected to the same deciphering from the same hermeneutics of unconscious desire. In this sense, we can well say that Freud's 'case histories' (*Krankengeschichten*) are no less mythical than the fabulous 'history of the psychoanalytic movement' narrated in his autobiographical writings or the history of humanity described in his phylogenetic and anthropological fictions. No matter where we look, we find the same rewriting of history, the same narrativising of arbitrary interpretations, the same transformation of hypotheses into facts.

One may object that there is, nevertheless, a difference between Freud's polemical fictions and his case histories, a difference that we emphasised several times in the previous chapter: the vicious analyses of opponents, which completely disregard the protests of those concerned, are merely interprefactions; while the case histories and clinical observations record the results of an analytic deciphering to which the patients have, if not actively participated in, at least given their consent. As today's psychoanalysts freely admit, in the end what matters in analysis is not so much the 'historical truth' of the construction proposed by the analyst, but its 'narrative truth';[1] that is, the fact that patients make use of it to rewrite their histories in a way that 'makes sense' for them. In other words, it matters little that this construction is a fiction; it only matters that the patients accept and understand this fiction as *their* history and their truth.

> **Jacques Lacan:** Let's be categorical: in psychoanalytic anamnesis, what is at stake is not reality, but truth, because the effect of full speech is to reorder past contingences by conferring on them the sense of necessities to come.[2]
>
> **Lacan:** History is not the past ... the fact that the subject relives, comes to remember, in the intuitive sense of the word, the formative

events of his existence, is not in itself so very important. What matters is what he reconstructs of it . . . What is essential is reconstruction, the term he [Freud] employs right up until the end . . . I would say – when all is said and done, it is less a matter of remembering than of rewriting history.[3]

Jürgen Habermas: [The analyst] makes interpretive suggestions for a story that the patient cannot tell. Yet they can be verified in fact only if the patient adopts them and tells *his own story* with their aid.[4]

Roy Schafer: The analyst establishes new, though often contested or resisted, questions that amount to regulated narrative possibilities. The end product of this interweaving of texts is a radically new, *jointly authored* work or way of working.[5]

We could say a lot about these reformulated versions ('structuralist', 'hermeneutical', 'narrativist') of psychoanalysis – and especially about the fact that they continue to present themselves as being *psycho-analysis*, even as they seem to disregard Freud's pretensions of revealing the objective truth of the psyche. If the final criterion for the fiction proposed by the therapist is that the patient accept (*veri*-fy) it, why insist on perpetrating Freudian fictions in accordance with psychoanalytic theory as opposed to any others? Why the inevitable interpretation of the patient's biography in terms of desire, repression, resistance or transference – and not, let's say, in terms of class struggle, astrological constellations, the evil eye, diet or psychopharmacology? And in what way is the psychoanalytic account superior to others, especially if its truth value comes not from *what* it recounts, but only from its assimilation by the one *to whom* it is recounted?

Schafer: People going through psychoanalysis – analysands – tell the analyst about themselves and others in the past and present. In making interpretations, the analyst retells these stories . . . *This retelling is done along psychoanalytic lines.*[6]

The truth is that, despite appeals for collaboration with the patients (designated as 'analysands', to better emphasise their active participation), psychoanalytic theory always provides the framework for the stories to be recounted on the couch, and later in the case history. There is nothing inherently wrong with this (after all, the therapist has to start from somewhere), but we at least need to recognise that little has fundamentally changed since Freud's more authoritarian and 'suggestive' psychoanalysis, in which the patient was indoctrinated.

> **Raymond de Saussure:** Freud was not an excellent psychoanalytic technician . . . First of all, he had practised suggestion for too long not to have retained certain reflexes. When he was persuaded of a truth, he wasted little time in awakening it in his patient's mind; he wanted to quickly convince him, and because of this, he talked too much. Secondly, one rapidly sensed the theoretical question with which he was preoccupied, because he often developed at length new points of view that he was in the process of clarifying in his own mind. It was beneficial for the mind, but not always to the treatment.[7]

> **Paul Roazen, citing Helene Deutsch:** Freud may have been a holy figure to Helene, but she had her reservations about him as a therapist; he thought to teach more than to cure.[8]

> **Joan Riviere, on her analysis with Freud:** He was much more interested in the work in general, than in me, as a person. He was interested in the translations [for the *Collected Papers*]. He was interested in the *Verlag* [blotted out] and he would as soon as one came in be quite prepared to show me a German letter and discuss it with me, you see, and argue, and that sort of thing. Well, from my point of view now it is completely impossible to see it as an analysis! . . . I was also frustrated and deprived because he practically devoted the whole session to business.[9]

> **Freud, analysis notes for the Rat Man, 8 October 1907:** He [the patient] is sure of having *never* thought that he could wish the death of his father. – After hearing these words pronounced with growing vigour, I believe it necessary to provide him with a piece of the theory. The theory asserts that because all anxiety and anguish corresponds to an earlier, repressed wish, we must assume exactly the contrary. It is likewise certain that the unconscious is the contrary of the conscious. – He is extremely disturbed, extremely incredulous . . . [Four pages later:] But it is now time to abandon the theory and return to the self-observation and memories. *Seventh Session [Wednesday 9 October]* He takes up the same subject. He can't believe that he has ever had this wish against his father.[10]

Whether the patient chooses to collaborate with the analyst or, on the contrary, resist his interpretations, the fact remains that everything originates from the theory informing these interpretations – no matter if it be the 'ready-made' theory inherited by Freud's successors or else, as in the case of the founder himself, hypotheses and speculations tried out on patients. We thus have the right to wonder, as Albert Moll was already doing in 1909,[11] if the case histories are actually at the core of the theory or if it isn't rather the inverse. In the end, what do these case histories tell us? What the patient says or does? Or rather what the analyst reconstructs of what transpired, filling gaps and discontinuities with interpretive connections – that is, what the analyst *interprefacts*?

'The famous padded door . . .'[12]

Freud, for his part, surely would have protested vigorously. According to him, case histories and clinical vignettes are limited to 'observations' and 'experiments', into which no speculation, presupposition or theoretical anticipation is allowed to enter. The Freudian legend, as we have seen, exists to bolster and give credibility to this constantly reaffirmed, positivistic thesis: the theory (the meta-psychology) comes after the observation or, at the least, it never interferes with it. The psychoanalyst observes what patients say (or don't say) to him, how they behave in relation to him and how their symptoms evolve – all of this being done in an absolutely neutral and objective manner, without ever interfering with the clinical 'data'.

> **Freud**: It is not a good thing to work on a case scientifically while treatment is still proceeding – to piece together its structure, to try to foretell its further progress, and to get a picture from time to time of the current state of affairs, as scientific interest would demand. Cases which are devoted from the first to scientific purposes and are treated accordingly suffer in their outcome; while the most successful cases are those in which one proceeds, as it were, without any purpose in view,

allows oneself to be taken by surprise by any new turn in them, and always meets them with an open mind, free from any presuppositions. The correct behaviour for an analyst lies in swinging over according to need from the one mental attitude to the other, in avoiding speculation or brooding over cases while they are in analysis, and in submitting the material obtained to a synthetic process of thought only after the analysis is concluded.[13]

It is this impartial observation, the fundamental cornerstone of psychoanalysis, that case histories are supposed to represent for those not present at the analysis, just like, say, the Royal Society's seventeenth-century *Philosophical Transactions* or the modern reports we make of experiments today. These documents *take the place* of what happened in the analyst's office; they *report* to the public the psychical 'events' brought to light during analysis – and the theory subsequently attempts, somehow or other, to make sense of these events. We immediately see the enormous role these case histories play in the official epistemology of Freudianism, inasmuch as they are equated with the analytical experience itself. They are, as Kurt Eissler proudly declared, 'the pillars on which psychoanalysis as an empirical science rests'.[14] To take this declaration seriously, though, is to admit that the entire metapsychological edifice rests on a handful of cases that were observed and described by Freud himself: Dora, the Rat Man, the Wolf Man, the Homosexual (we hesitate to add Little Hans to this extremely short list, because, with the exception of one session with Freud, his analysis was conducted entirely by his father).[15] This is rather extraordinary,[16] a fact acknowledged by Freud himself in his foreword to the Dora case.

> **Freud:** It is, on the contrary, obvious that a single case history, even if it were complete and open to no doubt, cannot provide an answer to all the questions arising out of the problem of hysteria . . . It is not fair to expect from a single case more than it can offer. And anyone who has hitherto been unwilling to believe that a psychosexual aetiology holds good generally and without exception for hysteria is scarcely

likely to be convinced of the fact by taking stock of a single case history.[17]

Michael Sherwood: This situation is almost unique: in perhaps no other field has so great a body of theory been built upon such a small public record of raw data.[18]

The problem, though, is not that Freud published so few of these 'observations', since one observation, if it is well executed, can revolutionise an entire discipline. (Ian Hacking,[19] quite rightly, points out that Michelson and Morley's famous experiments on the Earth's motion relative to ether – in which we see an anticipation of the theory of relativity – were comprised of Michelson's observations made in the space of a few hours on the days of 8, 9, 11 and 12 July 1887.) What is problematic about Freud's observations is the fact that he was the only one who had access to them, contrary to the demands of publicity which have characterised science since the seventeenth century. As Steven Shapin has shown,[20] this demand is an entirely integral aspect of the 'Scientific Revolution', not to mention the modern sciences among which psychoanalysis is supposedly situated. For Boyle and his colleagues at the Royal Society, only an experiment visually certified by multiple competent and credible witnesses was sufficient to establish a fact: a *matter of fact*, around which a consensus could be made. The experiments of Boyle, Hooke and Oldenburg, for this reason, were carried out in a public location (a laboratory in the halls of the Royal Society), and they were open to their peers, who were called upon to sign the official report. As for colleagues who lived far away, they were furnished with detailed experimental protocols so that they could reproduce the experiment themselves, and thus, in their turn, be witnesses to the *matter of fact*.

This ideal of direct observability and possible replication – whether ultimately realised or not – is one of the traits that most efficiently distinguishes modern science from the initiatory and secretive practices that preceded it, and it continues to define the scientific ethos, whatever the field. Thus, even during Freud's time, any doctor or researcher could attend Charcot's patient demonstrations or Bernheim's hypnosis sessions, both to verify the authenticity of the phenomena they described, and to train in their techniques. It was after a visit to the Salpêtrière, for example, that Delbœuf became convinced of the artefactual nature of Charcot's *grande hystérie* and *grand hypnotisme*.[21] Likewise, it was after their return from a visit to Bernheim's clinic in Nancy that Forel, Freud and several others began practising 'suggestive psychotherapy' in their clinics or private offices.

> **Bernheim:** The many French and foreign colleagues who have done me the honor of visiting my clinic have been able to appreciate that my greatest concern has been not to go beyond the limits of the most scrupulous observation, and not to cross beyond the frontiers of demonstrable truths. Those of my colleagues who retain some doubts, either because they have not seen my cases or because they know about them incompletely, display a wise and scientific skepticism. But if they are willing to visit my clinic they will find here the continuing demonstration of the facts I report.[22]

At the beginning of the twentieth century, this ease of access to clinical materials and training techniques (which is to say, of reproducibility) naturally continued to characterise the majority of European clinics in which psychotherapy was practised. This is especially true at the Burghölzli clinic, where psychoanalysis, as we have seen, was taught just like any other medical technique. Researchers who came there for an internship could have on-the-job training in the new techniques by witnessing analytic interviews with patients, by undergoing analysis with Jung, Riklin or Maeder, or again by collectively analysing their dreams and slips of the tongue during the meals they took together.

> **Bleuler, 1910:** The doctors of the Burghölzli have not only interpreted one another's dreams, they have paid attention for years to those complex indicators which have been offered: mistakes, slips of the pen, a word written over the line, symbolic actions, the humming of unconscious melodies, acts of forgetting, and so on. In this manner we

have got to know one another, and have mutually obtained an integrated portrait of our character and our conscious and unconscious strivings.[23]

Again: in 1909 the title of Jung's lectures for the summer semester was 'Course in Psychotherapy with Demonstrations',[24] making clear the open nature of the teaching being done in Zurich.

In Vienna, however, things were done much differently. Owing to the confidentiality that Freud's private clientele demanded, no one was allowed to come into his office to verify *de visu* the exactitude of his observations or to learn the finer points of his technique. To be honest, though, this obstacle wasn't insurmountable. Freud quite easily could have asked his patients for their permission to have a colleague witness the sessions and, undoubtedly, it would have been obtained on the condition that this colleague also respect medical confidentiality (which went without saying: the observations doctors published at this time never revealed the names of the patients, even when aliases were used). It was in this way, for example, that Breuer had asked Krafft-Ebing to observe his patient Bertha Pappenheim;[25] and there was nothing extraordinary about this. Even the first analysts found it completely natural to allow their colleagues to attend analysis sessions.

Ernest Jones, on Otto Gross: He was my first instructor in the practice of psychoanalysis and I used to be present during his treatment of a case.[26]

Ferenczi, 5 February 1910: I believe I have found a recruit of some importance for our cause in the person of a young student. His name is . . . Vajda . . . Currently, I am undertaking an experiment with him. I have chosen . . . an exemplary case of anxiety hysteria, and I am analyzing the patient in Vajda's presence, three times a week. He acts as my 'secretary.' And the arrangement works! This is not without interest for the *teaching* of psychoanalysis.[27]

Angelo Hesnard: We remember our astonishment when, during our first research studies in collaboration with some of Freud's disciples, we attended several . . . interviews between the analyst and analyzed, during which the former was practically silent for hours at a time, while the second, orienting his reverie little by little in a personal direction, naturally, and sometimes without any intervention by the doctor, yielded confidences of perfect transparency.[28]

Freud, however, strongly insisted that the delicate nature of his patients' confidences meant that such 'scientific uses' of 'their admissions' were entirely out of the question.

> **Freud:** The presentation of my case histories remains a problem which is hard for me to solve ... If it is true that the causes of hysterical disorders are to be found in the intimacies of the patients' psycho-sexual life, and that hysterical symptoms are the expression of their most secret and repressed wishes, then the complete elucidation of a case of hysteria is bound to involve the revelation of those intimacies and the betrayal of those secrets. It is certain that the patients would never have spoken if it had occurred to them that their admissions might possibly be put to scientific uses; and it is equally certain that to ask them themselves for leave to publish their case would be quite unavailing ...[29] I am aware that – in this city, at least – there are many physicians who (revolting though it may seem) choose to read a case history of this kind not as a contribution to the psychopathology of the neuroses, but as a *roman à clef* designed for their private delectation. I can assure readers of this species that every case history which I may have occasion to publish in the future will be secured against their perspicacity by similar guarantees of secrecy, even though this resolution is bound to put quite extraordinary restrictions upon my choice of material.[30]

It will be remarked that here Freud speaks of the necessity of hiding his patients' identities from the public, which is an entirely legitimate concern. But why expand this embargo to include those colleagues bound by professional secrecy? It's one thing to protect a patient's privacy from the public; it's something else to shield their analyses from any peer evaluation or 'case presentation'. No one, in fact, would push the principle of medical confidentiality to such an extreme, and apply it in such a rigid manner, as Freud and his successors did.[31] Psychoanalysis is a strange, confidential science, in the sense that the direct and public presentation of the *matter of fact* is quite literally *forbidden*, tabooed and scandalised. From this point of view, Freud's private office was indeed closer to the laboratory of the ancient alchemists, where a "secret art" was practised, than to the open and transparent space of the modern laboratory. No one penetrated his lair; no one saw the 'transmutations of psychological values' achieved by the scientist; and thus no one would know how to reproduce them independently. Freud is the sole witness to what transpired behind the padded doors of 19 Berggasse, and of his cases we know only what he wanted to tell us in his case histories. For the rest of us, all we know about his method of working comes from the sparse technical writings that he left us.

> **Freud:** I have as a rule not reproduced the process of interpretation to which the patient's associations and communications had to be subjected, but only the results of that process. Apart from the dreams, therefore, *the technique of the analytic work has been revealed in only a very few places* ... Before the technical rules, most of which have been arrived at empirically, could be properly laid down, it would be necessary to collect material from the histories of a large number of treatments.[32]

> **Strachey:** An examination of the list of Freud's technical writings ... will show that after [the publication of the *Studies on Hysteria* in 1895], apart from two very sketchy accounts dating from 1903 and 1904, he published no general description of his technique for more than fifteen years ... The relative paucity of Freud's writings on technique, as well as his hesitations and delays over their production, suggests that there was some feeling of reluctance on his part to publish this kind of material. And this, indeed, seems to have been the case, for a variety of reasons ... Behind all his discussions of technique, however, Freud never ceased to insist that a proper mastery of the subject could only be acquired from clinical experience and not from books. Clinical experience with patients, no doubt, but, above all, clinical experience from the analyst's own analysis.[33]

One of the most immediate consequences of this 'secretist' practice was the elevation of Freud's case histories to the status of paradigms for analytic practice (the term *Paradigma* is often used by Freud himself).[34] Insofar as third-person observation of an analysis was out of the question, those who wanted to be trained in analysis were forced to fall back on Freud's case histories and/or put themselves on the master's couch (as the observed, not as observers). Even today, analysts in training learn psychoanalysis not by observing a senior practitioner's analyses, but by studying Freud's case studies, and by making a didactic analysis with an analyst who learned the same way. As a result, climbing back up the chain we always find ourselves with Freud and his canonical case histories – endlessly copied and 'confirmed' by successive generations of analysands/analysts. In this respect, it is not exactly accurate to say, as Sulloway has,[35] that the non-scientific character of the new technique Freud developed is marked by the fact that his peers couldn't replicate it. On the contrary, there are undoubtedly few domains where the replication has been so well cultivated and with so much success. In other sciences, practitioners rarely take the time to repeat experiments that have already been conducted, and when they do attempt to do so the replication is almost never perfect, owing to the inadequate transmission of the 'implicit knowledge' necessary to make the equipment work.[36] What is replicated in psychoanalysis, however, is not the experiment itself, but *Freud's report* of it – which is obviously quite different. Those who accept this report as the thing itself certainly have little difficulty finding the phenomena it describes wherever they look: it's simply a matter of reciting it, and having it recited to them. But for the more sceptical, if they want to verify the accuracy of the report, they will have about as much luck catching their own shadow. In several cases, when Freud's colleagues tried to apply the psychoanalytic method to see for themselves, they ended up with much different observations and reports.

Adolf Friedländer: In my 'Brief Remarks on Freud's Doctrine relative to the Sexual Etiology of the Neuroses,' and in an address before a medical society in Frankfurt, I have reported that in order to be impartial I have decided to apply Freud's psychoanalytic method in several cases. The results were not of a nature to change my [critical] views.[37]

Janet: If the psychoanalytical method means, at any cost, and with aid of the most improbable and most ridiculous interpretations, the discovery of sexual fixed ideas, it is clear that the authors I have quoted, and I myself, have not practised psychoanalysis. Are we to blame for that? The very thing we are discussing is the justification for pushing this method of sexual interpretation to an extreme . . . Who is entitled to insist upon us using a method which is discredited by our own observations?[38]

Forel: I now intend to briefly provide three examples of psychoanalyses, two of them practiced by myself, and one by Frank. The question of knowing if, in the first case, sexual anaesthesia is a purely individual and innate trait or if it is caused by a Freudian 'repression' wasn't resolved by the analysis; the woman remained as frigid as before. For the Freudian School, *every* case of this type concerns repression. But such a supposition is completely arbitrary and I contest its validity.[39]

Here we touch upon another consequence of Freudian secrecy: the necessity of taking Freud at his word. As the philosopher Frank Cioffi aptly remarks, psychoanalysis is a *testimonial science*,[40] based on the veracity of its founder. With Freud as the sole witness to the phenomena invoked by the theory, it is extraordinarily important that his case reports and clinical observations be absolutely reliable. If they aren't – if, for example, it turns out that Freud let himself be influenced by preconceived ideas, personal considerations or the desire to contradict an adversary – then the entire edifice would be threatened. We would no longer have clinical 'data', only biases. This is why, from very early on, the Freudian legend doubled as a personality cult. Freud, Jones thus tells us, was a man of 'absolute honesty' and 'flawless integrity';[41] a man who was ready to sacrifice friendships and theories upon the altar of Science. (Jones, with some difficulty, concedes that the murky Swoboda–Weininger scandal, in which Fliess caught Freud red-handed in a lie, was the exception which proved the rule: 'It was perhaps the only occasion in Freud's life when he was for a moment not completely straightforward.'[42]) This personality cult may seem a harmless accessory, but it corresponds to a profound epistemological necessity. If it wasn't possible for Freud to lie, it's simply because, in the absence of the thing itself, we have only the witness's good faith to rely upon.[43] As Lacan might have said: the Freudian field is structured by a symbolic pact with the founding Father, whose Word, which his sons constantly return to, is the sole guarantor of their practice. This is what explains, for example, why the question of knowing whether Freud cheated on his wife with his sister-in-law is so significant for psychoanalysts. In any other scientific discipline, such a preoccupation with the vulgar details of the founder's biography would seem trivial and inappropriate; but not in psychoanalysis, where such questions stir up a tide of polemics and erudite commentaries.[44] They go directly to the reliability of the Witness of the Unconscious: how could we believe someone whose soul and desire weren't pure? Here again, it's Lacan who sums it up.

> **Lacan:** What is it that makes us say at once that . . . alchemy, when all is said and done, is not a science? Something, in my view, is decisive, namely, that the purity of soul of the operator was, as such, and in a specific way, an essential element in the matter. This remark is not beside the point, as you may realize, since we may be about to raise something similar concerning the presence of the analyst in the analytic Great Work, and to maintain that it is perhaps what our training analysis seeks. I may even seem to have been saying the same thing myself in my teaching recently, when I point straight out, all veils torn aside, and in a quite overt way, towards that central point that I put in question, namely – *what is the analyst's desire?*[45]

Narrating the unconscious

Was the founding analyst's desire pure? Let's suppose for a minute that it was. Let's suppose, in other words, that we could respond negatively to Frank Cioffi's famous question: 'Was Freud a liar?'[46] Would his case histories, because of this, be any more reliable? By no means. It is essential to understand that a written report is not a simple 'observation' of reality. All narration, as sincere as it may be, implies a selection, a montage, a 'configuration'[47] and a 'retrodiction'[48] of events from the narrator's point of view (this is what we could call, in honour of Kurosawa's beautiful film, the Rashomon effect). This is the reason why Boyle and his colleagues at the Royal Society were so insistent that experiments and observations be made in public. In their eyes, only a convergence of multiple testimonies was capable of correcting the errors of individual witnesses.

> **Robert Boyle:** For, though the testimony of a single witness shall not suffice to prove the accused party guilty of murder; yet the testimony of two witnesses, though but of equal credit ... shall ordinarily suffice to prove a man guilty; because it is thought reasonable to suppose, that, though each testimony single be but probable, yet a concurrence of such probabilities (which ought in reason to be attributed to the truth of what they jointly tend to prove) may well amount to a moral certainty, i.e. such a certainty as may warrant the judge to proceed to the sentence of death against the indicted party.[49]

As judges and historians know quite well, the narrated event is a (re)construction, fabrication and interpretation of an event, whose meaning is determined by the plot or storyline in which it is embedded – it is not a naked event that could satisfy us by simply being recorded. From the outset, then, psychoanalysis's official epistemology runs into all the well-known problems that prevent us from dreaming of any objectivity in history or criminal law. This is all the more true in that Freud's case studies are long, complex and, above all, well written. While the 'observations' of a Bernheim or even a Janet limit themselves to transmitting events in a quasi-telegraphic style, Freud tells us actual stories, using all the narrative resources available to the fiction writer (some of which we will take a look at later on).

> **Freud:** It still strikes me myself as strange that the case histories I write should read like short stories and that, as one might say, they lack the serious stamp of science ... A detailed description of mental processes

such as we are accustomed to find in the works of imaginative writers enables me, with the use of a few psychological formulas, to obtain at least some kind of insight into the course of that affection. Case histories of this kind are intended to be judged like psychiatric ones; they have, however, one advantage over the latter, namely an intimate connection between the story of the patient's sufferings and the symptoms of his illness – a connection for which we still search in vain in the biographies of other psychoses.[50]

But is this truly an advantage? After all, how can we be sure that the Freudian novelist hasn't discarded a certain element and unduly insisted upon another? Or established arbitrary links to better form his rough material into a coherent storyline, with 'a beginning, a middle and an end'?[51] In short, what proof do we have that he didn't sacrifice 'observation' – always untidy and disorganised – to the impeccable narrative *demonstration* of his theories? Nothing, once again, but the assurances of Freud himself.

> **Freud:** The case history itself was only committed to writing from memory after the treatment was at an end, but while my recollection of the case was still fresh and was heightened by my interest in its publication. Thus the record is not absolutely – phonographically – exact, *but it can claim to possess a high degree of trustworthiness*. Nothing of any importance has been altered in it except in some places the order in which the explanations are given; and this has been done for the sake of presenting the case in a more connected form.[52]

> **Freud:** Taking notes during the session with the patient might be justified by an intention of publishing a scientific study of the case. On general grounds this can scarcely be denied. Nevertheless it must be borne in mind that exact reports of analytic case histories are of less value than might be expected. Strictly speaking, they only possess the ostensible exactness of which 'modern' psychiatry affords us some striking examples. They are, as a rule, fatiguing to the reader and yet do not succeed in being a substitute for his actual presence at an analysis. Experience invariably shows that *if readers are willing to believe an analyst* they will have confidence in any slight revision to which he has submitted his material.[53]

In a moment we shall consider what to think of this 'slight revision', and if readers are indeed justified in placing their faith in the narrative accuracy of analysis's Arch-Witness. For the moment, let's read, as a forewarning, the more sober assessments of James Strachey – esteemed expert on Freud's writings, if ever there was one.

> **Strachey to Jones, date unknown:** Freud was quite extraordinarily inaccurate about details. He seems to have had a delusion that he possessed a 'photographic memory'.[54] Actually . . . he constantly contradicts himself over details of fact. When we did the case histories [for the *Collected Papers*] we sent him a long list of these – most of which he then put right in the Ges.[ammelte] Schriften and later editions.[55]
>
> **Strachey to Jones, 9 November 1955:** I enclose two extracts from the original report of the 'dritte Fall'[56] . . . It also shows how utterly incapable of accuracy over details the Professor was. He'd actually got the correct facts in front of him, and simply couldn't copy them out.[57]

But there is something more serious than this carelessness of Freud, the sole eyewitness. Beyond the inevitable distortions introduced by the narrative presentation of observed clinical data, we need to understand that Freud's reports don't merely describe, with more or less precision, what has taken place in his office. They also relate 'events' (real or fantastical: it matters little here) that he himself *reconstructed*: Elisabeth von R.'s love for her brother-in-law, Dora's love for Mr K., the Wolf Man's 'primal scene'. These psychical events share the distinction of having never been observed in the analyst's office. They are, Freud tells us, unconscious, repressed beyond his patients' consciousness. Patients have no memory of these events – they never even mentioned them – although they may find these memories as a result of accepting the analyst's construction (which, we should remark in passing, was not the case with Elizabeth von R., Dora or the Wolf Man). In reality, it's the *analyst* who puts these psychical events in their mouth (or in their unconscious); he's the one who, in their place, says *to them* what they can't say themselves. In this sense, Freud's case histories are anything but an objective report of clinical data that the analyst merely records through the method of passive listening and attentiveness known as 'free-floating attention'.

> **Freud:** [The analyst] must turn his own unconscious like a receptive organ towards the transmitting unconscious of the patient. He must adjust himself to the patient as a telephone receiver is adjusted to the transmitting microphone.[58]

Contrary to what Freud's positivistic rhetoric would have us think, there is not, nor can there be, any 'observation' of the unconscious, since, by its very definition, the unconscious never appears or presents itself as such to consciousness (this, clearly, is why Freud, in the passage cited above, appeals to the analyst's *unconscious*, without telling us how this unconscious gets to his consciousness). As his 1915 article on 'The unconscious' succinctly explains, the unconscious only becomes phenomenal in becoming conscious, thus disappearing in the same moment as it appears.

> **Freud:** How are we to arrive at a knowledge of the unconscious? It is of course only as something conscious that we know it, after it has undergone transformation or translation into something conscious.[59]

How, then, does this 'transformation or translation into something conscious' operate; this process by which the 'thing-in-itself' of the unconscious is transformed into observable phenomenon? How do we know, for example, that the sensation of pressure Dora felt on her chest represents the pressure of Mr K.'s erect member against her clitoris, or that the Wolf Man's anxiety, experienced during his famous dream, expresses in an inverted form his desire to be sexually satisfied by his father? Better yet, how do we know that Dora and the Wolf Man even have an unconscious? How do we know that there actually is a Freudian unconscious? The key reason is that the analyst's interpretations tell us so: making use of the grammatical rules of transformation called displacement, condensation, projection, identification, reversal into the opposite, symbolism, etc., he translates his patients' symptoms and dreams into 'unconscious thoughts' unknown to them. The following passage, again from 'The unconscious', explains all of this very clearly.

> **Freud:** Psycho-analytic work shows us every day that translation of this kind is possible. In order that this should come about, the person under analysis must overcome certain resistances – the same resistances as those which, earlier, made the material concerned into something repressed by rejecting it from the conscious.[60]

The unconscious thus appears in the interpretations of the analyst who *says* that there is something to be translated – the concerned parties know nothing about it, and consequently some are quite sceptical. Here we arrive at a difficulty or ambiguity which is absolutely essential for psychoanalysis, and which Freud's positivistic epistemology (his legendary epistemology) functioned to dissimulate: ultimately, this theory has no facts, no observations to get one's teeth into. It is a theory supported by itself: a celibate speculative machine producing, with its hypotheses and 'constructions', its own reality. Whatever he might claim, Freud never 'observed' the unconscious or repression anymore than he 'discovered' the Oedipus complex, infantile sexuality or the meaning of dreams. He only wagered that they existed, acting 'as if' these conjectures were real and then asking his patients to confirm them.

> **Binswanger, report of his visit to Vienna, 15–26 January 1910:** On one occasion I referred to the statement he [Freud] had made during a Wednesday meeting that 'the . . . unconscious is metaphysic, we simply posit it as real,' meaning, of course, that we acted *as if* the unconscious were something real, like the conscious. Being a true scientist, Freud said nothing about the *nature* of the unconscious, precisely because we know nothing certain about it; rather, we merely deduce it from the conscious. He thought that just as Kant postulated the thing in itself behind the phenomenal world, so he himself postulated the unconscious behind the conscious that is accessible to our experience, but that can never be directly experienced.[61]

The ambiguity of this 'as if' confided to Binswanger is rather remarkable. On the one hand, Freud seemed anxious to maintain the hypothetical character of his theoretical 'simulations', insisting on the impossibility of revealing the Thing Itself of the unconscious. But on the other hand, and in the same motion, he asks us to act '*as if* the unconscious were something real', while transgressing the limit he had just demarcated between speculation and possible experience, hypothesis and observation, theory and empiricism. Instead of presenting his interpretations as interpretations (and nothing else), he immediately transforms them into psychical events attributed to his patients. Instead of presenting us with his 'constructions' as constructions (and nothing else), he makes of them *reconstructions*, *reconstitutions* of the past. Suddenly, we no longer have an 'as-if unconscious', but the unconscious pure and simple – without the precautionary quotation marks – whose topography and vicissitudes are described to us with the utmost seriousness and gravity.

> **Freud:** [The] work of construction, or, if it is preferred, of reconstruction, resembles to a great extent an archaeologist's excavation of some dwelling-place that has been destroyed and buried or of some ancient edifice. The two processes are in fact identical, except that the analyst works under better conditions and has more material at his command to assist him, since what he is dealing with is not something destroyed but something that is still alive ... All of the essentials are preserved; even things that seem completely forgotten are present somehow and somewhere, and have merely been buried and made inaccessible to the subject. Indeed, it may, as we know, be doubted whether any psychical structure can really be the victim of total destruction. It depends only upon analytic technique whether we shall succeed in bringing what is concealed completely to light.[62]

It is this second action, that of reifying interprefaction, which defines psychoanalysis, while ultimately providing the material (the legendary material) of clinical observations and Freudian case histories. Despite appearances, these case histories don't recount what happened or was said in the analyst's office. Instead, they provide a narrative presentation of that which the patient is not in any way aware of having experienced, thus systematically obfuscating the borders between the material supplied by the patient and the highly speculative conjectures the analyst injects into this material. Without this narrative interference – which places the data observed on the same plane as the interpretation of this data – psychoanalysis would never have been able to present itself as an empirical discipline, or establish its theories as indisputable facts. It is, therefore, worthwhile to study in greater detail this work of narrative interprefaction, to which we owe so many astonishing 'discoveries'.

The mind reader

Let's first take some examples in which the narrative transformation of hypotheses into positive facts is particularly evident.

Example 1: Ida Bauer ('Dora', in Freud's case history) bitterly complains of her father encouraging Mr K.'s advances towards her to better pursue his own liaison with Mrs K. Over the years, however, she had done everything to encourage this very same liaison.

> **Freud:** The same inference was to be drawn ... namely, that she had all these years been in love with Herr K. When I informed her of this conclusion she did not assent to it.[63]

Some nineteen pages later, we are informed that Ida Bauer had been very close to Mrs K. and that Mrs K. had taken her as an ally and confidant in her conjugal difficulties with her husband. How, then, do we reconcile this with the love of the young woman for Mr K.?

> **Freud:** How Dora *managed to fall in love with the man* about whom her beloved friend had so many bad things to say is an interesting psychological problem. We shall not be far from solving it when we realize that thoughts in the unconscious live very comfortably side by side,

and even contraries get on together without disputes – a state of things which persists often enough even in the conscious.[64]

All of a sudden, the 'inference' from nineteen pages before has become a reality, eliciting all sorts of contradictions and problems. However, who ever said that Ida loved Mr K.? Only Freud. It is obvious that Freud's interesting 'psychological problem' would instantly vanish if he consented to abandon his hypothesis instead of projecting it onto Ida's unconscious – in spite of her protests. (This reveals, incidentally, that the indifference to the contradictions he attributes to the unconscious could be said to be Freud's own.)

Example 2:[65] Ida had developed asthma (dyspnoea) at the age of eight, after a hike in the mountains. Freud, who at this period (1899–1900) has a complete theory of hysteria – which he attributes to the repression of infantile masturbation accompanied by incestuous fantasies[66] – seeks to learn more about her condition.

> **Freud:** Now the only light she was able to throw upon this first attack was that at the time of its occurrence Daddy (*Papa*) was away from home for the first time since his health had improved. In this small recollection there must be a trace of an allusion to the aetiology of the dyspnoea. *Dora's symptomatic acts and certain other signs gave me good reasons for supposing* that the child, whose bedroom had been next door to her parents', had overheard her father in his wife's room at night and had heard him (for he was always short of breath) breathing hard while they had intercourse.[67]

To this point, the interpretation is only a 'supposition' based on 'signs' about which Freud tells us very little. But just a few lines later, this supposition has already become a certainty providing the foundation for a long case history.

> **Freud:** A little while later, when her father was away and the child, devotedly in love with him, was wishing him back, she must have reproduced in the form of an attack of asthma the impression she had received. She had preserved in her memory the event which had occasioned the first onset of the symptom, and we can conjecture from it the nature of the train of thought, charged with anxiety, which had accompanied the attack. The

first attack had come on after she had over-exerted herself on an expedition in the mountains, so that she had probably been really a little out of breath. To this was added the thought that her father was forbidden to climb mountains and was not allowed to over-exert himself, because he suffered from shortness of breath; then came *the recollection of how much he had exerted himself with Mummy (Mama)* that night, and the question whether it might not have done him harm; next came concern whether she might not have over-exerted herself in masturbating – an act which, like the other, led to a sexual orgasm accompanied by slight dyspnoea – and finally came a return of the dyspnoea in an intensified form as a symptom. Part of this material I was able to obtain directly from the analysis, but the rest required supplementing.[68]

It is important to note the great pains taken by Freud not to specify the extent to which he has 'supplemented' the material provided by Ida – and for good reason: not only is the 'primal scene' his own supposition, but furthermore Ida 'denied flatly'[69] having the slightest memory of masturbating before the age of eight, or having been in love with her father.[70] Even if we keep her memories of the mountain excursion in mind, we are nonetheless led to the conclusion that Ida's contribution to Freud's case history was quite minimal. The rest is pure speculation on Freud's part; however, he narrates all of this as if the events had actually occurred in Ida's mind. So how, under these conditions, is the reader to know the difference?

Example 3: Sergius Pankejeff (a.k.a. the 'Wolf Man') had a nightmare at the age of four, in which he saw white wolves seated on the branches of a tree. After a long and acrobatic deciphering, involving all sorts of tentative hypotheses, Freud is about to reveal its secret.

> **Freud:** I have now reached the point at which I must abandon the support I have hitherto had from the course of the analysis. I am afraid it will also be the point at which the reader's belief will abandon me.[71]

What follows is an exposition of the famous 'primal scene': the infant, at the age of one and a half, observes with interest his parents engaged in coitus *a tergo*; it is repeated three times and he greets the event with a jubilatory defecation. Having arrived at this point, Freud recognises that he is asking a lot of the reader; but he doesn't let this hinder him. On the contrary, he asks the reader to suspend his critical faculties, just as one would do with a book of fiction.[72]

> **Freud:** I can assure the reader that I am no less critically inclined than he towards an acceptance of this observation of the child's, and I will only ask him to join me in adopting a provisional belief in the reality of the scene.[73]

Fortified by the indulgence he has extorted from his reader, Freud then proceeds as if the reality of this 'constructed primal scene'[74] (constructed by him) had been definitively established, *blackboxed*: 'the postures which he saw his parents adopt';[75] 'the picture of sexual satisfaction afforded through his father's agency, just as he had seen it in the primal scene';[76] 'the patient was longing for some one who should give him the last pieces of information that were still missing upon the riddle of sexual intercourse, just as his father had given him the first in the primal scene long before',[77] etc. In two places, the reader is even asked to believe that the primal scene is an authentic memory of Pankejeff himself.

> **Freud:** When the patient entered more deeply into the situation of the primal scene, he brought to light the following pieces of self-perception. He assumed to begin with, he said, that the event of which he was a witness was an act of violence, but the expression of enjoyment which he saw on his mother's face did not fit in with this; he was obliged to recognize that the experience was one of gratification.[78]

> **Freud:** Then suddenly, in connection with a dream, the analysis plunged back into the prehistoric period, and led him to assert that during the copulation in the primal scene he had observed the penis disappear, that he had felt compassion for his father on that account, and had rejoiced at the reappearance of what he thought had been lost.[79]

One chapter later, the reality of the primal scene is so well established that it is used to explain another scene the analyst has constructed – this time with the maid Grusha.[80]

Freud: When he saw the girl on the floor engaged in scrubbing it, and kneeling down, with her buttocks projecting and her back horizontal, he was faced once again with the posture which his mother had assumed in the copulation scene.[81]

Accepting that Freud's construction was hypothetical at first, one could argue that what is critical is that the patient eventually corroborated it: even if we assume that the patient's assent was the product of transference and/or suggestion and that his 'self-perceptions' and 'assertions' were retrospective illusions, Freud did not invent everything. On the contrary, he seems to have taken great care not to put anything forward that hadn't first been confirmed by the patient himself.

Freud: Many details, however, seemed to me myself to be so extraordinary and incredible that I felt some hesitation in asking other people to believe them. I requested the patient to make the strictest criticism of his recollections, but he found nothing improbable in his statements and adhered closely to them. Readers may at all events rest assured that I myself am only reporting what I came upon as an independent experience, uninfluenced by my expectation.[82]

It's certainly plausible that many of Freud's patients didn't raise any objections to his interpretations – even his most daring and racy ones – and indeed, we have many examples attesting to this. Pankejeff's case, however, is quite a different matter. As it happens, we have his own testimony which plainly contradicts Freud's version of events. Sixty years later, he confided to the Austrian journalist Karin Obholzer that he had never been able to recall the scene imagined by Freud, in spite of the latter's assurances that the memory would reappear after a certain period of time. How, then, do we reconcile this with the 'self-perceptions' of the scene, the 'memories' and the 'statements' and the 'assertions' that Freud so freely attributed to him?

Sergius Pankejeff: That scene in the dream where the windows open and so on and the wolves are sitting there, and his interpretation, I don't know, those things are miles apart. It's terribly farfetched ... But that primal scene is no more than a construct ... The whole thing is improbable because in Russia, children sleep in the nanny's bedroom, not in the parents'. It's possible, of course, that there was an exception, how do I know? But I have never been able to remember anything of that sort . . . He [Freud] maintains that I saw it, but who will guarantee that it is so? That it is not a fantasy of his? . . . Well, I also have to look at psychoanalysis critically, I cannot believe everything Freud said, after all. I have always thought that the memory would come. But it never did.

Karin Obholzer: One might say that your resistance up to the present day is so strong that you didn't want to remember.

Pankejeff: Well, that would also be a supposition, wouldn't it? But it is no proof.[83]

Free indirect style

The examples we have cited to this point all have one thing in common: they systematically confuse the limits between the analyst's heuristic hypotheses and the 'psychical reality' of the person on the couch. What was initially an idea of Freud's is, in the end, presented as the patient's unconscious or latent thought, in such a manner that we no longer know who thinks what. Everything, in fact, proceeds as if Freud were reading into the thoughts of others; or, more precisely, as if he were reading them for us. This last trait is what brings his case histories closer to fictional narration, and further distances them from the 'psychiatric observations' they claim to be. Indeed, as Käte Hamburger points out,[84] only in fictional narrative can the intimate thoughts and feelings of someone other than the one who speaks be described as if they were said out loud. Neither non-fictional narrative nor non-narrative fiction allows for such a transgression of the 'barriers that rise between each single ego and the others',[85] and undoubtedly this is what makes this literary genre so charming – and, let us add, psychoanalysis so seductive.

In his case histories, Freud acts exactly like the omniscient narrator of novels and short stories who enters into the minds of his characters at will and reveals their most intimate thoughts to us. Just like Balzac or Stendhal, he knows the hidden motives behind their actions, and he even has access to thoughts and feelings that they themselves are hardly aware of, or else refuse to acknowledge. But while the omniscient narrator of classic novels takes centre stage, often intervening with conspicuous commentary or irony, Freud constantly tries to efface himself as narrator in order better to create the illusion of having immediate access to the thoughts of his 'characters' (which, literarily speaking, actually places him in the company of such realist novelists as Flaubert, Zola and Henry James). Thus, instead of writing: 'Our hero, entangled in his contradictions, didn't yet dare to admit that he had been a witness to the coupling of his parents', he writes more plainly: 'the expression of enjoyment which he saw on his mother's face ...'. Instead of writing: 'Shaken, Dora said nothing, but inside she was ready to give her belief to the interpretation of her cough that the doctor had proposed', he writes: 'this tacitly accepted explanation',[86] etc. Certainly there is a narrator, no less omniscient than before, but he makes himself increasingly discreet and transparent as he penetrates deeper into his characters' intimate thoughts, thus creating a marked 'reality effect'. The reader, who is asked to suspend his disbelief, now has the impression of directly witnessing the patient's inner life.

The problem, of course, is that Freud's case histories are not fictional stories. His patients are people in flesh and bone, not imaginary creatures whose minds he could enter into at will. Reading sentences of this type: '[in Grusha] he was faced once again with the posture which his mother had assumed in the copulation scene', we are therefore made to think that Freud is narrating thoughts *reported to him by the patient*, while, in reality, he is doing nothing of the sort (as we have seen, Freud narrates his own thoughts). There is, therefore, a particularly subtle abuse of narrative confidence here, for by granting himself licence to enter into other people's minds while claiming not to be doing so, Freud hedges his bets, simultaneously working in two genres at once: fictional narrative and non-fictional narrative.

Most of the time, Freud carefully avoids stating explicitly that he cites statements made by the patient. More prudently, he prefers to remain in the ambiguous zone of 'free indirect style' so dear to realist novelists, which has the precise effect of *confounding* quotation and narration, direct discourse and indirect discourse.[87] Instead of writing in the mode of *oratio recta*: [Dora said:] 'I remember how much Papa had exerted himself that night with mother', or else in the mode of *oratio obliqua*: 'Dora remembered that her father had exerted himself a great deal that night with her mother', he writes, like a novelist narrating the inner thoughts of a character: 'Then came the recollection of how much he had exerted himself *with Mummy* that night.'

Obviously the advantage of this last formulation is that we don't know who is speaking. Is it the analyst-narrator, reporting in the third person how the memory came to Ida Bauer? Or is it Ida, who uses the deictic 'Mummy', which is characteristic of first-person direct discourse? As noted by all people who have studied it, free indirect style (also called *erlebte Rede*[88] or *narrated monologue*[89]) is fundamentally equivocal in that it merges the voice of the narrator and that of the character.

> **Gérard Genette:** We see here the key difference between first-person monologue and free indirect style, which are sometimes mistaken for each other, or inappropriately equated: in free indirect discourse, the narrator assumes the character's speech, or, if we prefer, the character speaks through the narrator's voice, and thus the two voices are *confounded*; in immediate discourse, the narrator effaces himself and the character *takes his place*.[90]

> **Dorrit Cohn:** The narrated monologue holds a mid-position between quoted monologue (restitution of the person's thought in the mode of direct discourse) and psycho-narration (restitution in the mode of indirect discourse) ... Imitating the language a character uses when he talks to himself, it casts that language in the grammar a narrator uses in talking about him, thus superimposing two voices that are kept distinct in the other two forms.[91]

It is of course this ambiguity which makes free indirect style so attractive to the novelist, as it allows the narrator surreptitiously to slide into the characters' skins and to reconstruct their intimate or subliminal thoughts as though they had expressed them themselves. This is the same for Freud, since this form allows him to ventriloquise his patients, and to suggest that the thoughts he attributes to them are in fact their own, without quoting in direct discourse (which would have been impossible). The last point is very important: all this continues to be narrated in the third person and the narrator, as Genette aptly remarks, doesn't entirely disappear into the character, even if he does all he can to create the illusion of doing so. It is thus difficult to catch Freud making things up, since he rarely declares explicitly that he reproduces words spoken by his patients. To those, like Max Scharnberg[92] or Allen Esterson,[93] who would accuse him of deceitfully presenting his interpretations as if they were the actual accounts given by his patients, he could always reply that he did nothing of the sort: these critics were adopting an extremely literal and legalistic reading of what is, in fact, only literary licence. Flaubert's trial, it has been said,[94] would never have taken place if the authorities had had enough literary sense to understand that *Madame Bovary*'s immorality was that of his character Emma's thoughts, narrated in free indirect style, and not those of the author-narrator Flaubert. Likewise and conversely, Freud would be right to argue, from a strictly grammatical point of view, that he never *explicitly* attributed his own thoughts to his patients.

All the same, this is inevitably the reader's impression; and, grammatical defence aside, it is obviously the reason Freud makes use of this very special form. By virtue of its indeterminacy, free indirect style allows him simultaneously to concretise his theoretical hypotheses, by creating the illusion that he is reproducing his patients' thoughts, *and* to protect himself in case he was to be accused of fabricating 'observations' when there was nothing to be observed: is it his fault if his readers take at face value what he, the conscientious scientist, was merely suggesting? The argument is clearly specious, but it is enough to counter accusations of fabrication. It does not, however, immunise such a scientist from the inevitable conclusion to be drawn from it: if everything we read in Freud's case histories can be reduced to a simple suggestion, then the famous 'experience' on which psychoanalysis rests turns out to be a pure stylistic *effect*.

Who speaks?

In the examples we have considered up to this point, narrative interprefaction left traces in the Freudian text, even if the effect it produced on readers was to make them forget these traces. With a little investigation we were still able to see the narrator's projection into his character, and to follow the path leading from the analyst's interpretations to the thoughts he attributed to his patients. But is this always how it works? Let's suppose for a moment that Freud had succeeded in completely erasing these traces. In this hypothesis, there would be nothing besides the indeterminacy of the free indirect style. Severed from its source, the statement would, so to speak, float in the air, without anyone knowing exactly *who* is speaking in the text – the patient, or the analyst? Confronted with such an ambiguous passage, we would be justified in asking ourselves if it isn't Freud who gives us his own interpretations, while passing them off as associations or declarations made by the patient herself. But since we weren't present in his office and are reluctant to grant ourselves the same omniscience he grants to himself, we would only be making unverifiable hypotheses. If Freud did efface the traces of the work of interprefaction from his text, we can't, by definition, know anything about it.

At least most of the time. It just so happens that we have, by a fortuitous coincidence, notes taken by Freud during the first four months of the Rat Man's analysis.[95] Admittedly, these notes, composed from memory in the evening after each session, don't constitute a verbatim account of his analysis,[96] and we do have every reason to believe that Freud included only those points specifically concerned with the story he was in the process of constructing. Indeed, the notes from the first seven sessions seem to have been written with an eye towards a presentation to be made three weeks later at the Psychoanalytic Society of Vienna on the 'Beginning of a patient history'.[97] In no way, then, can we consider these notes to be a pure and unmediated record of how the analysis unfolded akin to a legal transcript, and we may be justified in having doubts about their reliability. Nevertheless, as they are, they represent a less developed and less refined version than the one that was published, and consequently, they provide us with a more precise understanding of the narrative reworking employed by Freud in this case history – and presumably in others.

> **Ernest Jones:** It was Freud's custom to destroy both his manuscript and the notes on which it was based, of any paper he published. By some odd chance, however, the day-to-day notes of this case, written every evening, were preserved, at least those for the best part of the first four months of the treatment . . . This material is invaluable as affording a unique opportunity for watching Freud at his daily work so to speak: his timing of interpretations, his characteristic use of analogies to illustrate a point he was making, the preliminary guesses he would make privately which might subsequently be either confirmed or disproved, and altogether the tentative manner in which such piecemeal work proceeded.[98]

Let's take a look at this process, then.

Example 4: The patient Ernst Lanzer (a.k.a. the 'Rat Man') is deeply in love with his cousin Gisela (the 'woman' or 'friend' of Freud's published case history), but, as the notes from the session of 8 October 1907 inform us, 'it wasn't possible to consider a union between them due to material difficulties'[99] – apparently his cousin wasn't wealthy enough. On 8 December, Lanzer mentions in passing how his mother, six years earlier, had planned to have him married to a rich distant relative. Here, first of all, are the notes taken by Freud.[100]

> **Freud, analysis notes of 8 December 1907:** By all sorts of detours, under the cure's transference, story of a temptation whose <u>significance</u>

seems to escape him ... It was related to his mother's old plan, according to which he was supposed to marry one of the Saborskys' daughters, a charming girl now 17 years old. He doesn't suspect that to avoid this conflict [between his mother's plan and his love for Gisela], he took refuge in the illness, the path towards which had been paved by the childhood choice between an elder sister and a younger one, as well as by the return to the story of the father's marriage. The father was in the habit of humorously describing himself as a young suitor; the mother sometimes mocked him by saying that he had once courted a butcher's daughter. He found the idea [implied: suggested by Freud] intolerable that his father was willing to abandon his love to protect his material interests by the alliance with the Saborskys. He becomes very irritated with me; this manifests itself through insults that are only expressed with great difficulty ... He visibly resists the temptation to fantasize about marrying my daughter instead of his cousin, and about insulting my wife and my daughter. A transference crudely expressed [implied: can be translated] as follows: Mrs. F[reud] can lick his ass (revolt against the more respected family). Another time he sees [implied: fantasises] my daughter who, in place of her eyes, has two patches of dung, **which means that he has fallen in love not with her eyes, but her money.**[101]

On this evening, Freud is already sketching out a narrative form for the material provided by his patient, but in his notes his patient's reactions are allowed to spill over into his own interpretations. In particular, it is clear that Lanzer had rejected the idea advanced by Freud that his father had married his mother for her money. Likewise, he didn't 'suspect' that he had fallen ill in order to avoid having to choose between the poor girl and the rich girl, and it had completely 'escaped' him that his irritation with the analyst's unpleasant interpretation actually expressed a transferential 'temptation' to marry the rich girl, following his father's example. Let us note, too, that all of this sums up *one session* of analysis. Let's now look at the published version.

Freud, case history of the Rat Man: One day the patient mentioned quite casually an event which I could not fail to recognize as the precipitating cause of his illness, or at least as the immediate occasion of the attack which had begun some six years previously and had persisted to that day. He himself had no notion that he had brought forward anything of importance ... His mother was brought up in a wealthy family with which she was distantly connected. This family carried on a large industrial concern. His father, at the time of his marriage, had been taken into the business, and had thus by his marriage made himself a fairly comfortable position. The patient had learnt from some chaff exchanged between his parents (whose marriage was an extremely happy one) that his father, some time before making his mother's acquaintance, had made advances to a pretty but penniless girl of humble birth ... After his father's death the patient's mother told him one day that she had been discussing his future with her rich relations, and that one of her cousins had declared himself ready to let him marry one of his daughters when his education was completed ... This family plan stirred up in him a conflict as to whether he should remain faithful to the lady he loved in spite of her poverty, or whether he should follow in his father's footsteps and marry the lovely, rich, and well-connected girl who had been assigned to him. And he resolved this conflict, which was in fact one between his love and the persisting influence of his father's wishes, by falling ill; or, to put it more correctly, by falling ill he avoided the task of resolving it in real life.

... As was to be expected, the patient did not, to begin with, accept my elucidation of the matter. He could not imagine, he said, that the plan of marriage could have had any such effects: it had not made the slightest impression on him at the time. But in the further course of treatment he was forcibly brought to believe in the truth of my suspicion, and in a most singular manner. With the help of a transference phantasy, he experienced, as though it were new and belonged to the present, the very episode from the past which he had forgotten, or which had only passed though his mind unconsciously. There came an obscure and difficult period in the treatment; eventually it turned out that he had once met a young girl on the stairs in my house and had on the spot promoted her into being my daughter. She had pleased him, and he pictured to himself that the only reason I was so kind and incredibly patient with him was that I wanted to have him for a son-in-law ... After we had gone through a series of the severest resistances and bitterest vituperations on his part, he could no longer remain blind

to the overwhelming effect of the perfect analogy between the transference phantasy and the actual state of affairs in the past. I will repeat
one of the dreams which he had at this period, so as to give an example
of his manner of treating the subject. He dreamt that *he saw my
daughter in front of him; she had two patches of dung instead of eyes.* No
one who understands the language of dreams will find much difficulty
in translating this one: it declared that *he was marrying my daughter not
for her 'beaux yeux' but for her money.*[102]

Let's not dwell on the young girl encountered in the stairway, something which is not to be found in the analysis notes. Let's disregard the
fantasy, equally absent from the analysis notes, of becoming the
analyst's son-in-law. What is most striking is the casualness with
which Freud juggles the treatment's chronology. In the notes,
Lanzer *rejected* the idea that his father had married his mother out
of self-interest; furthermore, he was visibly irritated – a fact that Freud
(during or after the session, it's not clear) had interpreted as the
transferential enactment of the conflict he attributed to his patient.
In the case history, however, the Rat Man *accepts* Freud's interpretation *after a long and 'obscure' period of resistance.*[103] Furthermore, one
of the aggressive fantasies revealed during the session (or rather,
constructed by the analyst after the fact) becomes, in the case history,
a *dream* of confirmation that Lanzer had *later on*, which, incidentally,
enables Freud to justify and explain the arbitrary elements of his
interpretation by appealing to an alleged 'language of dreams'.[104]
The result is that Lanzer's resistance is, so to speak, temporally
diluted, until the moment where it evaporates, transforming itself
into a *confirmation* of the analyst's hypotheses. We would be hard-
pressed to find a better illustration of Lacan's thesis, according to
which 'psychoanalysis is a dialectical experience' in which 'truth is
transmuted for the subject'[105] – except that here the 'dialectical
reversal'[106] which transforms the 'no' of the subject into the liberating
'yes' appears to be entirely imaginary. But the reader, of course, is not
informed of this. On the contrary, he is made to believe that this

interpretive projection by the analyst is a dialectical self-reflection of the patient himself.[107]

The pretty postal worker and the unscrupulous gambler

With this last example, we come close to what could taken to be the falsification of observations. Previously, we had seen Freud in acts of interpretive projection, such as when he attributed his own thoughts to his patients, or else when he transformed his own constructions into memories reported by patients on his couch. In the preceding example, though, he appears surreptitiously to modify his own analysis notes better to construct his story, just like an unscrupulous historian who alters a document to make it correspond to his version of events. Now we leave the ambiguous domain of poetic licence and narrative projection and enter into a domain where reports, and even the patients' words, are simply rewritten.

Example 5: On 3 October 1907, during his second session with Freud, Lanzer recounts with a great deal of repugnance how the 'rat idea', to which he owes his alias, came to him. He had become obsessed with the idea in August while in Galicia, where he was participating in military manoeuvres as a reserve officer. During a march, a captain Nemeczek told him of reading about an oriental torture method, in which a bowl filled with rats was attached to the posterior of the condemned man, so that the rats would gnaw a path through his anus. This evocation had elicited an obsessional fear in Lanzer that the same torture might be inflicted upon Gisela; a fear which he fended off, in no less an obsessional manner, with the help of an apotropaic formula or 'sanction' intended to ensure that such a thing never happened.

In this same session, Lanzer also related how Captain Nemeczek, on the following evening, had told him to reimburse Lieutenant David a certain sum that the latter had paid for a postal package containing a pince-nez sent to Lanzer. A second 'sanction' had then

formed in his mind: not to repay the money, because, if he did, his
beloved would be submitted to the rat torture. This was immediately
supplanted by an equally solemn counter-'sanction': to return the
money to Lieutenant David, as Captain Nemeczek had suggested. But
when he tried to settle his debt with Lieutenant David, he learned
that Nemeczek was mistaken – it wasn't, in fact, David who had lent
him the money.

> **Freud, analysis notes of 3 October 1907:** 'I went to find my account-
> ant, a noncommissioned officer, and gave him the order to bring the 3
> crowns 80 to Lieutenant David . . . He came back and told me that the
> aforementioned David was at an advanced post . . . An officer who was
> going to go into the small town offered to go to the post office and pay
> for me; but I was opposed to this, because I was sticking to the letter of
> the oath [you will give the money to David].' (David's relationship to
> the post office is not clear.) 'I ended up meeting David and I offered
> him the 3 crowns 80 he had paid for me. He declined the offer: "I didn't
> pay for anything for you." At this moment, I was struck by this thought:
> there are going to be consequences, *everyone* will be doomed to suffer
> this penalty' (because he couldn't keep his oath). 'Everyone' especially
> means his deceased father and this woman.[108]

On 4 October 1907, during the third analysis session, Freud had
Lanzer again explain to him the episode of the non-reimbursement
of the postal package, as he had had difficulty comprehending it
during the previous session. Was the money to be given to
Lieutenant David, as Captain Nemeczek had said, or else to the
post office, as had been suggested to him by the officer who had
gone to the 'small town' (Spas), which was near to where the military
manoeuvres were taking place?

> **Freud, analysis notes of 4 October 1907:** I asked him if in fact he
> really hadn't believed that the money should be handed over, not to
> the post office, but to David; he responded that he had had some
> doubts, but that in the interest of his oath, he had believed in the last
> hypothesis. Here there is an obscurity and uncertainty to the memory,
> as if he had sorted something out after the fact. Basically, at the

beginning of the story – which he adds later – there was another captain, to whom he had previously been introduced, who told him that he had been asked at the post office if he knew a certain second lieutenant Lanzer, for whom there was a package to be paid for on delivery. This captain had said 'no,' and thus he hadn't taken the package. Then comes the episode with Captain Nemeczek. In addition, he explains in more detail the meeting with David, who tells him that he wasn't the one responsible for the mail, but lieutenant Engel. Here, an oversight on my part: during the afternoon nap, he had reasoned out, so to speak, in his dream, how to sort everything out and he stated the following: he would go to the post office with the two officers, David and Engel; there, David would give the 3.80 to the young woman (*Postfraülein*) working there, the young woman would hand it to Engel, and he himself [Lanzer], in accordance with the oath, would pay 3.80 to David.[109]

To make things clear, let's emphasise some salient points. The anonymous Captain didn't pick the package up at the post office, and he wasn't the one who paid for Lanzer. Furthermore, it wasn't Lieutenant David, contrary to what Captain Nemeczek had mistakenly told him, nor the person behind the counter (which would be absurd). As the context clearly indicates, it's Lieutenant Engel, 'who was responsible for the mail' bound for soldiers on manoeuvres, who paid for the package – which explains why, in the quasi-delirious circuit of restitution worked out in Lanzer's half-dream, Engel, and not 'the young woman at the post office', is the final recipient of the 3.80 crowns. As for this young woman at the post office, it's not the anonymous Captain who mentions her (he only speaks of the 'post office'), but Lanzer (even though he hadn't been to the post office and thus had no way of knowing if the person behind the counter was a man or woman). In reality, this 'young woman' only appears in the *fantasy* of restitution which Lanzer, during his restless nap, had 'reasoned out, so to speak, in his dream'.

Lanzer's story continues. After hesitating a long time to ask Lieutenant David to take part in his incredible fantasy of restitution, he takes the train and returns to Vienna in a state of great agitation. There, calmed by his friend Galatzer, he finally succeeds in overcoming his inhibition to pay the debt, and he sends the money 'to the post office in Galicia'.[110] This last point, we should note, in no way contradicts the fact that the sum was owed to Lieutenant Engel. In fact, he should address the money order to the post office in Spas, because this is where Engel came to pick up mail for the soldiers on manoeuvres.

If we now turn to the published case history, we notice that Freud ignores this fact to argue, in a completely unexpected manner, that the sum was, in reality, owed 'to no one but the official at the post office'.

Freud, case history of the Rat Man: It was this last statement which provided me with a starting-point from which I could begin straightening out the various distortions involved in his story. After his friend had brought him to his senses he had dispatched the small sum of money in question neither to Lieutenant A. [David] nor to Lieutenant B. [Engel], but direct to the post office. He must therefore have known that he owed the amount of the charges due upon the packet *to no one but the official* [in the masculine: *dem Postbeamten*] *at the post office*, and he must have known this before he started on his journey. It turned out that in fact he had known it before the captain [Nemeczek] made his request and before he himself made his vow; for he now remembered that a few hours before meeting the cruel captain he had had occasion to introduce himself to another captain, who had told him how matters actually stood. This officer, on hearing his name, had told him that he had been at the post office a short time before, and that *the young lady there* (*Postfräulein*) had asked him whether he knew a Lieutenant L. (the patient, that is), for whom a packet had arrived, to be paid for on delivery. The officer had replied that he did not, but the young lady (*das Fräulein*) had been of the opinion that she could trust the unknown lieutenant and had said that in the meantime she would pay the charges herself. It had been in this way that the patient had come into possession of the pince-nez he had ordered. The cruel captain had made a mistake when, as he handed him over the packet, he had asked him to pay back the 3.80 kronen to A. [David], and the patient must have known it was a mistake. In spite of this he had made a vow founded upon this mistake, a vow that was bound to be a torment to him.[111]

We cannot help but be struck by the liberties Freud takes with his patient's story, as well as by the improbability of the narrative he substitutes for it. The young woman at the post office whom Lanzer fantasised in his half-sleep becomes a definitive actor, whose words are reported to us. Better yet, this bureaucrat of the Austro-Hungarian Empire decides to pay the postage fee for this unknown soldier in transit. And Freud now claims – contradicting his own notes – that it was the anonymous Captain who had explained all this to Lanzer, and that the latter had known all along that the money was neither owed to David nor to Engel. (But to whom had the generous post office worker given the package, and how did it finally end up in Captain Nemeczek's hands? It remains a mystery.)

Why did Freud engage in this retelling? And why did he so forcefully maintain that Lanzer owed the money to the imaginary young woman at the post office, rather than to Lieutenant Engel? We needn't look very far to find the answer. In the section titled 'The paternal complex and the solution to the rat idea', Freud explains that the story of the anonymous Captain had revived in Lanzer's unconscious his identification with his father.

> **Freud, case history of the Rat Man:** But the information that the young lady at the post office at Z [Spas] had herself paid the charges due upon the packet, with a complimentary remark about himself, had intensified his identification with his father in quite another direction. At this stage in the analysis he brought out some new information, to the effect that the landlord of the inn at the little place where the post office was had had a pretty daughter. She had been decidedly encouraging to the smart young officer, so that he had thought of returning there after the manoeuvres were over and of trying his luck with her. Now, however, she had a rival in the shape of the young lady at the post office. Like his father in the tale of his marriage, he could afford now to hesitate upon which of the two he should bestow his favours when he had finished his military service.[112]

We now understand why Freud seems to have been impelled to insert the generous postal worker in the narrative: to establish a counterpart for the pretty innkeeper's daughter, and thus create an otherwise nonexistent symmetry with the (no less constructed – see example 4) story of Lanzer's father, who had supposedly hesitated between a poor girl and a rich girl.[113] Freud appears to have made up this episode to make his patient's narrative coincide with his Oedipal hypothesis. One might ask whether this doesn't apply also to what is said about the innkeeper's daughter, who is mentioned nowhere in the handwritten notes. Regardless, whether there was no girl or only one girl, the fact remains that there is no evidence for a competition between two girls, nor, consequently, any symmetry between the father's and son's stories. This symmetry, which is integral to the ingenious 'solution to the rat idea' proposed by Freud, appears not to exist.

Example 6: On 30 November 1907, Lanzer recounts various anecdotes from the period when his father was a soldier.

> **Freud, analysis notes of 30 November 1907:** On one occasion, his father had ten florins of regimental money in his hands to meet certain expenses. He lost some of it in a game of cards with some other men, let himself be tempted to go on playing and lost the whole of it. He lamented to one of his companions that he would have to shoot himself. 'By all means shoot yourself,' said the other, 'a man who does a thing like this ought to shoot himself,' but then lent him the money. After ending his military service, his father tried to find the man, but failed. (Did he ever pay him back?)[114]

We should note that the patient says only that his father had tried in vain to find this man after leaving the army, not that the goal of his search had been to reimburse him (there is nothing in the text to dissuade us from thinking that he had already settled his debt before that). It appears to be *Freud* who, composing his notes that same night, wonders in parentheses if the father had ever repaid his debt, and who, on subsequently reviewing these notes, underlines in pencil this passage that catches his attention.[115] It's easy to understand why he asks this question: the symptom that had led Lanzer to consult him was a compulsive inhibition preventing him from reimbursing a sum that had been advanced during military manoeuvres. Freud, reflecting on that day's session, is therefore struck by the analogy between the two situations;[116] he wonders if the father repaid his debt before leaving the army or if, on the other hand, he sought in vain to do it later – in which case the symmetry between father and son would be perfectly clear. But there are no signs that he asked Lanzer: the following session, which takes place after the space of a week, takes off in a completely different direction, and the question never reappears elsewhere in his notes.

Four months later, Freud plunges back into his notes in preparation for a four-hour lecture on the Lanzer case, which he is to give on 27 April 1908 at the 'Meeting of Freudian psychologists' of Salzburg.[117] Meanwhile, Jung had been asking him repeatedly to present one of his cases, rather than a 'declaration of principle',[118] as he originally intended.

> **Jung to Freud, 11 March 1908:** I ask you for a *casuistic* presentation. We can all follow this. To my taste I would still prefer this to your suggestion to speak about psychanalysis.[119]

Jung, clearly, was hoping that Freud would finally provide the detailed description of a completed analysis that everyone had been waiting for. Freud, who, surprisingly, seems to have been short on completed analyses (in 1908!), decided at the last moment to give a lecture on Lanzer, despite the fact that this latest analysis wasn't 'finished'.

> **Freud to Jung, 13 March 1908:** Now about my lecture – I give in ... A report on a case I am now engaged in might at a pinch be compressed into an hour, but the case is not finished, the decisive phase and outcome are still lacking, one mustn't count one's chickens, etc. If it should turn out badly, I want to be free to substitute something else; who knows what may happen in six weeks?[120]

This case also provided Freud with a felicitous opportunity to present a 'defence and illustration' of his theory of obsessional neurosis, which Janet had criticised in his monumental work *Obsessions and*

Psychasthenia.[121] Thus, given the stakes, it was urgent that Freud 'finish' Lanzer's analysis. On 8 April, during a meeting of the Psychoanalytic Society of Vienna, Freud announced that he had discovered the solution to the 'rat idea' (a 'solution', let us note, which is only a preliminary draft of what he will put forward in the published case history).

> **Minutes of the Psychoanalytic Society of Vienna, meeting of 8 April 1908:** Prof. Freud reports on the solution of the rat idea in the obsessional neurotic; it means . . . the identification with his father, who also was in the army and contracted a gambling debt there; a friend loaned his father money to settle his debt; his father probably never paid this debt since he was a '*Spielratte*' ('gambling rat').[122]

Evidently, Freud still hadn't made the effort to question his patient on this rather crucial point. In his notes, Lanzer asserted that his father had never located his friend, which left only two possibilities open: either his father had repaid the debt *before* the end of his military service, or else he had *never* repaid him. Nevertheless, Freud says here that he had *probably* never paid him back, which makes it rather clear that he didn't know anything more about this point than before.[123] The only reason Freud provides to make us believe that the father had 'probably' never settled his debt is that he was a *Spielratte* – certainly a very striking association, but one which is absent from his handwritten notes. Are we to suppose, therefore, that this association came to Lanzer during a session after 20 January? Let's continue following the evolution of the case history.

> **Freud, case history of the Rat Man:** As always happened with the patient in connection with military matters, he had been in a state of unconscious identification with his father, who had seen many years' service and had been full of stories of his soldiering days . . . His father, in his capacity as non-commissioned officer, had control over a small sum of money and had on one occasion lost it at cards. (Thus he had been a '*Spielratte*'.) He would have found himself in a serious position if one of his comrades had not advanced him the amount. After he had

left the army and become well-off, he had tried to find this friend in need so as to pay him back the money, but had not managed to trace him. The patient was uncertain whether he had ever succeeded in returning the money. The recollection of this sin of his father's youth was painful to him ... The captain's words, 'You must pay back the 3.80 kronen to Lieutenant A.,' had sounded to his ears like an allusion to this unpaid debt of his father's.[124]

Freud, case history of the Rat Man: In this way rats came to have the meaning of '*money*' ... All his ideas connected with that subject were, by way of the verbal bridge '*Raten – Ratten*' ['instalments' – 'rats'], carried over into his obsessional life and brought under the dominion of the unconscious. Moreover, the captain's request to him to pay back the charges due upon the packet served to strengthen the money significance of rats, by way of another verbal bridge '*Spielratte*,' which led back to his father's gambling fault (*Spielverfehlung*).[125]

This last passage tends to reinforce our suspicion about the *Spielratte* association, as the context in which it appears clearly indicates that it functions as a 'verbal bridge', of which the patient was not aware – and thus was 'constructed' by the analyst for the demands of his line of reasoning. It appears to be Freud rather than Lanzer who characterises the father as a *Spielratte* in order to increase the 'probability' that he had never settled his debt. All the same, Freud now treats this probability as a certainty: the case history speaks of the father's '*unpaid debt*', of his 'sin' and of his '*gambling fault*'. We are even told that he had tried, in vain, to locate his friend '*so as to pay him back the money*' – something that there are no indications that the son had said to Freud (if he had, why would Freud, in his notes, wonder if the father had ever repaid his debt?).

Freud regretfully adds: 'The patient was uncertain whether he had ever succeeded in returning the money', thus attributing an uncertainty to Lanzer that was in fact his own at the moment he was composing his notes. Had Freud in the meantime questioned Lanzer on the matter, and had the latter informed Freud that he didn't know if his father had settled his debt? But this question only increases our confusion, because if Lanzer wasn't sure whether his father ever 'succeeded' in locating his friend to return the sum he owed him, how does Freud know that he had *not* found him – if it's not from his notes, the version of which he maintains on this point without realising that he unwittingly contradicts himself? And above all, what authorises Freud to proceed by attributing his patient's uncertainty to the fact that 'the recollection of this sin of his father's youth was painful to him', if the patient himself didn't know whether or not his father had repaid his debt – in short, if he had sinned or not? In reality, the patient's testimony is only invoked in order for Freud immediately to disqualify it in favour of the hypothesis he prefers. In the process, Freud will have nevertheless created the illusion *that there was such an account provided by Lanzer, and that his insistence that the father's debt was never repaid comes from Lanzer himself.* But there is no evidence in the analysis notes to support this perception, while the contradictions in the published version suggest that Freud hadn't any confirmation of his hypothesis from the patient. The father's unpaid debt, this key element of the 'solution to the rat idea' – and of so many other post-Freudian reinterpretations of this case – appears to have only ever existed in Freud's mind. And yet, we are all prevailed upon to believe that it was, in fact, a memory reported by the famous 'Rat Man'.

> **Lacan:** It is by recognising the forced subjectivisation of the obsessive debt – in the scenario of futile attempts at restitution, a scenario that too perfectly expresses its imaginary terms for the subject to even try to enact it, the pressure to repay the debt being exploited by the subject to the point of delusion – that Freud achieves his goal. This is the goal of bringing the subject to rediscover – in the story of his father's lack of delicacy, his marriage to the subject's mother, the 'pretty but penniless girl,' his wounded love-life, and his ungrateful forgetting of his beneficent friend – to rediscover in this story, along with the fateful constellation that presided over the subject's very birth, the unfillable gap constituted by the symbolic debt of which his neurosis is the act of protest.[126]

> **Lacan:** [The Rat Man's 'deeper truth'] is situated solely in what Freud refers to here as the 'word chain' – which, making itself heard both in the neurosis and in the subject's destiny, extends well beyond him as an

individual – and consists in the fact that a ... lack of good faith presided over his father's marriage and that this ambiguity itself covered over a breach of trust in money matters which, in causing his father to be discharged from the army, determined the latter's decision whom to marry.[127] Now this chain, which is not made up of pure events (all of which had, in any case, occurred prior to the subject's birth), but rather of a failure (which was perhaps the most serious because it was the most subtle) to live up to the truth of speech and of an infamy more sullying to his honor – the debt engendered by the failure seeming to have cast its shadow over the whole of his parents' marriage, and the debt engendered by the infamy never having been paid – this chain provides the meaning by which we can understand the simulacrum of redemption that the subject foments to the point of delusion in the course of the great obsessive trance that leads him to ask Freud for help.[128]

The return of the Wolf Man

Let's now consider a final example. Up until now, we have used Freud's analysis notes to reveal, by simple comparison, the rewriting of observational data in his case histories. This is not, however, the only means available to the historian to unearth the interprefactive work hidden behind the narrative façade of Freud's 'patient histories'. If one is ready to assume the role of detective, one can also defy the medical secret invoked by Freud and attempt to find the patients themselves – or their friends and relatives – to ask them *their* version of the story. It's a long-drawn-out task, full of uncertainty (some have spent their research careers doing so), but in the absence of the analysis notes it's often the only means available to find an external point of reference for Freud's case histories. Over the years, the identifications of 'Anna O.',[129] 'Emmy von N.',[130] 'Elisabeth von R.',[131] 'Cäcilie M.',[132] 'Katharina',[133] 'Mr E',[134] 'Dora',[135] etc. have allowed historians to reopen the black boxes of these famous 'cases', revealing the often considerable discrepancies between Freud's histories and the testimony of the patients themselves, or else that of their close friends and family.

Example 7: The most brilliant 'coup' in this regard is undoubtedly the discovery of the Wolf Man's actual identity in 1973 by the Austrian journalist Karin Obholzer. The previous year, the philanthropist/psychoanalyst Muriel Gardiner had published the anonymous 'Memoirs' of the Wolf Man, a moving document honouring psychoanalysis. This piece was sandwiched between a preface by Anna Freud and two articles by Ruth Mack Brunswick and Gardiner herself devoted to Freud's exemplary patient – the single one, among all his peers, to be 'willing to cooperate actively in the reconstruction and follow-up of his own case'.[136] The Wolf Man, we learned in this book, led a peaceful life retired in Vienna, where he had spent his career in an insurance company after the loss of his fortune in Russia. His identity, as it happens, didn't seem to be a secret for the series of psychoanalysts who had come to visit and question him about his analysis with Freud. Intrigued, Karin Obholzer decided to find him in order to write an article about him.

> **Karin Obholzer:** It was relatively easy. Freud, in his case history, gives the Wolfman's name as Sergei P. and I knew from Muriel Gardiner's book that he was still living in Vienna. So I started by looking up under 'P' in the telephone book. He wasn't listed, but then he might just not have the telephone (which he didn't, as I found out later). I therefore looked him up in the so-called 'address-book.' I don't think this address-book exists anymore, but at that time, anybody who rented an apartment in Vienna in any given year would be listed in it. I was looking for a Russian name and since the second letter of the Wolfman's true name is 'A,' I didn't have to look for too long: Pankejeff, Sergius. It had to be him![137]

Sergius Constantinovitch Pankejeff, who received money from the Sigmund Freud Archives,[138] and around whom Kurt Eissler and Muriel Gardiner had established a tight sanitary cordon,[139] seems to have been rather excited to be discovered by someone outside the

International Psychoanalytic Association. Having gained his confidence, Obholzer succeeded in convincing him to agree to a series of interviews, despite pressure exerted on him by Eissler and Gardiner to deny her request.[140] Pankejeff, however, made the condition that these interviews were not be published until after his death. Reading them, we quickly understand why: near the end of a life spent obediently conforming to the role of the 'Wolf Man', Pankejeff turned against his benefactors and invalidated, with a touch of vindictiveness, much that Freud, Mack Brunswick and Gardiner had written about him. Essentially, these three claimed that his different periods of analysis with Freud (1910–14, 1919–20) and Mack Brunswick (1926–7, 1929–?, 1938) had allowed him to lead a normal and productive life.

> **Freud, 1923:** I parted from him [in 1914], regarding him as cured . . . Since then [the Wolf Man's reanalysis in 1919–20] the patient has felt normal and has behaved unexceptionally.[141]

> **Freud, 1937:** His good state of health has been interrupted by attacks of illness which can only be construed as offshoots of his perennial neurosis. Thanks to the skill of one of my pupils, Dr. Ruth Mack Brunswick, a short course of treatment has on each occasion brought these conditions to an end.[142]

> **Ruth Mack Brunswick:** The therapeutic results [of Pankejeff's analysis with Mack Brunswick] were excellent and remained so, according to my last information in 1940, despite major personal crises.[143]

> **Muriel Gardiner:** There can be no doubt that Freud's analysis saved the Wolfman from a crippled existence, and Dr. Brunswick's reanalysis overcame a serious acute crisis, both enabling the Wolfman to lead a long and tolerably healthy life.[144]

Not so, Pankejeff retorted. Sixty years after his first analysis with Freud, he was still suffering from obsessional ruminations and bouts of deep depression,[145] despite the subsequent and almost constant analytic treatment he had received since then (after the war, he had been in successive analyses with Alfred von Winterstein,[146] an unidentified female analyst (Eva Laible?) and Wilhelm Solms; to this ought to be added a stay at a psychoanalytic counselling clinic in 1955,[147] as well as daily 'analytically directed conversations'[148] with Kurt Eissler when the latter returned to Vienna during the summer).

> **Pankejeff:** In reality the whole thing looks like a catastrophe. I am in the same state as when I first came to Freud, and Freud is no more.[149]

> **Pankejeff:** Instead of doing me some good, psychoanalysts did me harm ... That was the theory, that Freud had cured me 100 percent ... And that's why [Gardiner] recommended that I write memoirs. To show the world how Freud had cured a seriously ill person ... It's all false.[150]

What then about Freud's interpretation of his childhood nightmare, the 'primal scene', his parents' coitus *a tergo* thrice repeated? Pankejeff had never believed it, and he had never remembered it, contrary to what Freud led his readers to believe in the case history (see our example 3 above).

Pankejeff	That scene in the dream where the windows open and so on and the wolves are sitting there, and his interpretation, I don't know, those things are miles apart. It's terribly farfetched.[151]
Obholzer	He [Pankejeff] would come back to this subject very often, and he always insisted that he had never remembered the scene postulated by Freud. Freud told him that the memory would come back eventually, but it never did.[152]

What about the scene with the maid Grusha, crouched on all fours, which had supposedly reminded him of his mother's position during the primal scene, and to which Freud attributed his compulsive attractions to women of a lower social status? Once again, Pankejeff had no memory of it.

> **Pankejeff:** I cannot remember. I cannot even remember this Grusha. She was a maid, I believe. But I cannot remember details.[153]

And his exclusive taste for coitus *a tergo*, in which Freud also saw an echo of the primal scene? Pankejeff categorically denied having had a particular preference for this sexual position.

Obholzer	To get back to sexuality: Freud says somewhere that you preferred a certain position during intercourse, the one from behind ...
Pankejeff	Well, that was no absolute, you know ...
Obholzer	... that you enjoyed it less in other positions.
Pankejeff	But that also depends on the woman, how she is built. There are women where it is only possible from the front. That's happened to me ... It depends on whether the vagina is more toward the front or toward the rear.
Obholzer	I see. In any event, Freud writes, 'He was walking through the village which formed part of their estate, when he saw a peasant girl kneeling by the pond and employed in washing clothes in it ...'[154] He thought that you involuntarily fall in love when you come across something like that. And 'even his final choice of object, which played such an important part in his life, *is shown by its details (though they cannot be adduced here)* to have been dependent upon the same condition ...'[155]
Pankejeff	That's incorrect.
Obholzer	How so?
Pankejeff	No, it's incorrect.
Obholzer	Then why does Freud write it?
Pankejeff	With Therese, if you insist on details, the first coitus was that she sat on top of me.
Obholzer	That would be the exact opposite ...[156]

Likewise, Freud reduced Pankejeff's intestinal problems and persistent constipation to his desire to be penetrated by his father, as his mother had been during the primal scene, and to the castration anxiety that this feminine fantasy had elicited in him. As for Pankejeff, he had a much more prosaic explanation, which he couldn't have neglected to share with Freud at the time.

Pankejeff	I once [before the analysis] had diarrhea, and Dr. Drosnes came to the estate ... He takes a little bottle wrapped in paper from his pocket and says, 'This is calomel.' He pours some into a cup and says, 'Take it.' The result was that it got worse ... The next time, I tell him that it didn't help, it just got worse. And he says, 'I didn't give you enough' ... Later, a general practitioner told me that it [calomel] is only given to horses, not humans. I am telling you that what happened was that I couldn't eat anything all winter long .... It was terrible. All the mucous membranes were torn. And what happened as a consequence?...
Obholzer	Constipation, I imagine?
Pankejeff	Yes, a constipation that nothing could be done with ... And that has stayed with me to the present day: My intestines don't work by themselves. I have to take something twice a week. At times, I take it only twice a week, but then I have pains. It's terrible what this man did.
Obholzer	You had no intestinal difficulties before that?
Pankejeff	Before that, everything functioned perfectly.[157]

Freud, however, claimed to have definitively succeeded in eliminating this symptom during Pankejeff's second analysis. Indeed, in a note appended to his case history in 1923, he wrote that Pankejeff had come back to see him in Vienna to work through a remainder of the transference that hadn't been resolved.

> **Freud:** He then came to Vienna and reported that immediately after the end of the treatment he had been seized with a longing to tear himself free from my influence. After a few months' work, a piece of the transference which had not hitherto been overcome was successfully dealt with.[158]

Freud doesn't say anything else about this 'piece of transference', but Ruth Mack Brunswick tells us in her 'Supplement to Freud's "History of infantile neurosis"' that this referred to his constipation, which Freud seems to have considered a transferential identification with his own chronic constipation.[159]

Mack Brunswick: He [Pankejeff] returned to Freud for a few months of analysis, with the purpose, successfully accomplished, of clearing up his hysterical constipation.[160]

Here again, protests from Pankejeff. Not only had his constipation never been cured, but it wasn't even the reason he went to see Freud. It was actually Freud who had insisted that he undergo a second period of analysis, despite his desire to return to Odessa to save his fortune which was threatened by the Bolshevik Revolution.[161]

Pankejeff: When I visited Professor Freud in the spring of 1919, on my way to Freiburg, I was so thoroughly satisfied with my mental and emotional condition that I never thought of the possibility of needing more psychoanalytic treatment.[162]

Pankejeff to Gardiner, 14 September 1970: My reanalysis in 1919 took place not at my request, but at the wish of Professor Freud himself.[163]

Obholzer	[Pankejeff] often told me that his first four years of analysis with Freud had helped him . . . The mistake he did was to go and see Freud again in 1919.
M. B-J	Why do you say the second analysis was a mistake?
Obholzer	Because he agreed to resume the analysis in spite of the fact that he didn't want to. He had paid a visit to Freud on his way to Freiburg, where his wife Theresa was staying with her dying daughter, and Freud persuaded him to come back [from Freiburg] to Vienna for a reanalysis. *This* was the 'catastrophe.' The Wolfman always reproached Freud for this.[164]
Pankejeff	That intestinal thing was really the reason I stayed with Freud at that time. He said, 'That's something we still have to deal with' . . .
Obholzer	And what became of your intestinal disorders?
Pankejeff	I somehow got it to come by itself, a few times. And he wrote, 'We've been successful!' No such thing! . . . And I said to him [Freud], 'I would like to go because of my financial affairs.' And he answered, 'No, stay here. There is this and that still to be resolved.' And so I stayed. And that's why it became too late.[165]

In the end, what remains of Freud's psychoanalytic construction? Not much. Without corroboration from the patient, the primal scene remains a foundationless hypothesis, as does the castration anxiety to which it supposedly gave rise – and just about everything else that followed in Freud's analysis. Without the scene with Grusha, there is no way to explain the specifics of Pankejeff's love life. Without the exclusive preference for coitus from behind, there is no reason to believe that these sexual practices re-enacted the primal scene. Without a cure for the constipation, there is no reason to give credence to Freud's psychogenetic explanation of it. And without the 'piece of transference' to overcome, what, in the end, are we talking about?

Freud's case history holds together solely because he invented, at every narrative intersection, what was necessary for him to make Pankejeff's life coincide with the theoretical fable he was in the process of spinning. The history of the Wolf Man is not that of Sergius Pankejeff, no more than the histories of the Rat Man and Dora are those of Ernst Lanzer and Ida Bauer. It's a 'psycho-analytic novel'[166] that gives form to hypotheses, animates theoretical characters and cloaks the analyst's conjectures in the bright colours of reality. That Pankejeff spent much of his life playing the role of the Wolf Man doesn't change anything: quite simply, he confounded himself with the character written for him in Freud's novel – until the moment he decided to get out of the story and speak in his own name.

Freud the novelist?

In an academy filled with scepticism concerning the scientificity of psychology, and populated with semiotic, hermeneutic, post-structural and deconstructive literary theories, one can imagine the following retort: 'So, you've picked apart some of the narrative strategies Freud uses in his case histories to support his positivistic rhetoric and create the illusion of an empirical science. But we've known for ages that Freud wasn't a scientist, but a phenomenal man of letters, one of these writers who change the world by giving us a new language to describe it … Of course his case histories were novels! If not, how could he have worked out the incredible complexity of our deepest thoughts, their overdetermination, their signifying absurdity? We don't go to the laboratory to provide an account of the ambiguity and ambivalence of desire – the desire that turns against itself or loses itself in the other – we do so with the pen of the great writer. Do we reproach Stendhal, Dostoevsky or Proust for not being scientists? Freud shouldn't be measured against Copernicus or Darwin; rather, he should be measured against Dante, Shakespeare, and all these great narrators of the human soul. Come to speak of it, didn't Freud receive the Goethe Prize?'

This hermeneutical-narrativistic defence of Freud and psychoanalysis has become commonplace today, but it does come up against a stubborn fact: nothing irritated Freud so much as to be compared to a novelist.

> **Freud:** A recent book by Havelock Ellis … includes an essay on 'Psycho-Analysis in relation to sex.' The aim of this essay is to show that the writings of the creator of analysis should be judged not as a piece of scientific work but as an artistic production. We cannot but regard this view as a fresh turn taken by resistance and as a repudiation of analysis, even though it is disguised in a friendly, indeed in too flattering a manner. We are inclined to meet it with a most decided contradiction.[167]

This rejection of literariness is in no way anecdotal, since it is directly related to the 'will to science' (Isabelle Stengers' formulation) which has historically defined psychoanalysis. A refusal to take this seriously is a refusal to take seriously the project of psychoanalysis as such, banishing it to complete insignificance. As with so many other attempts at the end of the nineteenth century to found a scientific psychology, psychoanalysis claimed to supplant all previous forms of knowledge. Literature, in this respect, presented a unique problem for psychoanalysis. Indeed, what subject could be found that hadn't already been treated by novelists, poets and dramatists? What recess of the human soul could psychoanalysis illuminate that they hadn't already explored in great depth? How could one hope to rival – and submit to universal laws – the inexhaustible knowledge of humanity deposited in world literature? In literature, psychoanalysis ran into a mirror: a strange and unnerving double.

> **Freud to Arthur Schnitzler, 14 May 1922:** I have tormented myself with the question why in all these years I have never attempted to make your acquaintance and to have a talk with you . . . I think I have avoided you from a kind of reluctance to meet my double . . . Whenever I get deeply absorbed in your beautiful creations I invariably seem to find beneath their poetic surface the very presuppositions, interests, and conclusions which I know to be my own. Your determinism as well as your skepticism – what people call pessimism – your preoccupations with the truths of the unconscious and of the instinctual drives in man, your dissection of the cultural conventions of our society, the dwelling of your thoughts on the polarity of love and death; all this moves me with an uncanny feeling of familiarity.[168]

In what way, then, were psychoanalysis' stories and characters so different from those of literature? In what way were they more 'true'? What could justify the psychoanalyst's claim to know more about human nature than the writers? Only by dogmatically asserting an 'epistemic rupture' between psychoanalysis and literature, thereby re-establishing an asymmetry between Freud and his doubles, could psychoanalysis settle this question to its satisfaction.

> **Freud, on the occasion of his seventieth birthday:** The poets and philosophers before me discovered the unconscious. What I discovered was the scientific method by which the unconscious can be studied.[169]

> **Freud:** Now in this dispute as to the estimation in which dreams should be held, imaginative writers seem to be on the same side as . . . the author of *The Interpretation of Dreams*. . . creative writers are valuable allies and their evidence is to be prized highly, for they are apt to know a whole host of things between heaven and earth of which our philosophy has not yet let us dream . . . If only this support given by writers in favour of dreams having a meaning were less ambiguous! A strictly critical eye might object that writers take their stand neither for

nor against particular dreams having a psychical meaning; they are content to show how the sleeping mind twitches under the excitations which have remained active in it as off-shoots of waking life.[170]

In 1909, there was a discussion within the Psychoanalytical Society of Vienna on the subject of Richard Strauss' *Elektra*, which had just been performed at the Vienna Opera. The libretto was written by Hugo von Hofmannstahl, who was fairly knowledgeable about psychoanalysis. Freud, however, hadn't liked it a bit.

Freud, Minutes of the Psychoanalytic Society of Vienna of 31 March 1909: We have the right to analyze a poet's work, but it is not right for the poet to make poetry out of our analyses. Yet, this seems to be a sign of our times. The poets dabble in all possible sorts of sciences, and then proceed to a poetic working up of the knowledge they have acquired. The public is fully justified in rejecting such products.[171]

The will to assert an asymmetry between psychoanalysis and literature is especially self-evident here: Freud proceeds by diktat, denying the poet the right to use psychoanalysis as a source of inspiration, while granting himself the right to put the poet on his couch. Psychoanalysis affirmed its hegemony over literature by unilaterally subjecting it to its interprefactions. A century of 'psychoanalytic literary criticism' followed. It was essential for Freud to make his readers believe in the scientific nature of his interpretations and constructions – this was the only way to establish psychoanalysis' supremacy over its hermeneutical rivals, and thus to represent psychoanalysis as the only possible way for people to comprehend their own life, and those of others.[172] Without these scientific pretensions, psychoanalysis is nothing more than one interpretation among many others in the large market of psychological, philosophical, religious and literary hermeneutics. The question, therefore, is not to know if Freud's writings allow us to shed some light on the human condition, as indeed any talented writer can. It is, instead, to know why we should attribute a special and incomparable status to his writings, and why so many people did just this during the twentieth century. We might add: if we are to evaluate psychoanalysis on purely hermeneutical or aesthetic criteria, there are grounds for finding it wanting. Simulating science may not be the best way to write great literature.

> **Jean Cocteau:** We must not confuse the darkness I am speaking of and that into which Freud asks his patients to descend. Freud burglarized some shabby apartments. He removed some mediocre pieces of furniture and erotic photographs. He never sanctified the abnormal as transcendence. He never paid tribute to the great disorders. He provided a confessional for the unfortunate ... Freud's key to dreams is incredibly naïve. Here, the simple christens itself as the complex. His sexual obsession was destined to seduce an idle society for which sex is its axis ... Sexuality is not, we infer, without some role in it. Da Vinci and Michaelangelo proved it, but their secrets have nothing to do with Freud's removals ... Freud's mistake was to have made our darkness into a storage unit that brings it into disrepute, and for having opened it when it is fathomless and can't even be opened part way.[173]

4

Policing the past

I have a wide experience in what people report as having discussed with my father, or heard him say, and it is always untrue.
Anna Freud to Kurt Eissler, 27 January 1951[1]

At the outset of this book, we posed the question as to why psycho-analysis – a discipline apparently dealing with the past – is so allergic to history. The reason has now become clear: historical inquiry, by its very nature, poses a threat to the foundations of psychoanalysis, to its very identity. This is not only because historians have separated Freud's theory from the plethora of legends which surrounded it, as if it was a question of freeing the rational and empirical kernel of psycho-analysis from its mythical, political and speculative coverings. Through making evident the discrepancies between Freud's accounts and the material of which he spoke, through demonstrating the process of construction which his legendary narratives were deployed to conceal, through showing the fabrication of psychoanalytic facts prior to their crystallisation into objects of cultural consensus, the work of Freud historians has made it apparent that there never was a kernel.

This is not to suggest that historians have finally unveiled the truth of Freud's accounts or of his patients. That Sergius Pankejeff or Ernst Lanzer, for example, may have rejected this or that interpretation of

Freud tells us nothing about the validity or utility of the latter. Freud's patients are not necessarily any more trustworthy than Freud[2] and their disagreements with him were part and parcel of the game of analysis, of the conflict of interpretations. However, through bringing to light the arbitrariness behind Freud's narrative interprefactions, historical study relativises and delegitimates the theory of psychoanalysis much more effectively than any epistemological critique. Instead of attempting to demonstrate that Freud could not prove (verify, test, validate) what he proposed – which has never stopped people from being convinced of the persuasive force of his accounts – historical critique calls into question the hermeneutic pact between Freud and his readers through revealing the unreliability of his texts and rendering them suspect. How is one supposed to continue to believe everything he says, when faced with the accumulation of half-lies, misleading assertions, stylistic equivocations and significant omissions? Why should one continue to attribute him a privileged access to the 'unconscious', once it has become clear how he continually evokes this to silence those who were not in agreement with him? And why should we continue to have faith in his self-portrayals, rather than the contrary statements of some of his patients and former colleagues and adversaries, once it has transpired that at times he manipulated the clinical givens to make them say what he wanted them to? In sum, Freud can no longer be regarded as an always reliable witness. Or rather, he is one witness amongst others, and one with particular stakes and interests.

Given this, it is not surprising that Freud's successors did all they could to impede the work of historians, through censuring documents, blocking access to the archives of the psychoanalytic movement and launching campaigns of denunciation against scholars. It was essential to protect Freud's narrative monopoly against the alternative accounts proposed by some of his patients, his rivals and historians. Without this, psychoanalysis would have soon returned to being one therapeutic narrative amongst others in the competing and burgeoning private-sector marketplace for psychological well-being. Psychoanalysis would have dissolved into a plethora of divergent contested accounts rather than laying claim to being the sole science of the mind and the pre-eminent form of psychotherapy. Thus the proliferation of narratives had be stopped to maintain the sole unquestionable and non-negotiable account. This was not because Freud's successors necessarily believed all his accounts – but they had to be maintained to continue to sustain and protect psychoanalysis and to make it true. How else to make it true than to declare it to be such – and to play the game of truth, the game of science? The official history of psychoanalysis has been a constant defence of the Freudian legend. As such, it has played an important theoretical and institutional role, protecting the 'facts' and 'observations' upon which psychoanalysis is supposed to reside. In such a situation, it is evident that historians would be seen as trouble makers who had to be silenced.

Kürzungsarbeit

After Freud's death on 23 September 1939, his heirs had to confront the question of how to deal with his literary remains. In keeping with his style, Freud had requested that all his papers be burnt after his death, but his widow could not bring herself to do this.[3] What should one do with all these documents – leave them in an attic, place them in an archive or publish them? This question had already arisen when Freud's letters to Fliess re-emerged and were purchased by Marie Bonaparte. As we have seen,[4] she had acquired them on the express condition that they would not enter Freud's possession and she had kept this promise, resisting Freud's pressure to have them burnt.

> **Marie Bonaparte's Diary, entry of 24 November 1937:** Freud, when I wrote to him from Paris that Ida Fliess had sold his letters and that I acquired them from Reinhold Stahl, was very moved. He judged this act to be highly inimical on the part of Fliess's widow. He was happy

to know that at least the letters were in my hands, and not sent off to someplace in America where they would no doubt have been published immediately ... Ida Fliess was determined that the letters not reach the hands of Freud.[5]

Whilst the letters did not fall into Freud's hands, his family got hold of them and could decide what to do with them. As Freud had destroyed Fliess' letters,[6] there was no need for negotiations between two literary estates, as later happened with the Freud–Jung letters. Marie Bonaparte thought that 'this material, so important for the history of psychoanalysis',[7] should be published in its entirety. At the beginning of May 1946, she sent the letters to Anna Freud. The latter hesitated to disregard the expressed desire of her father, but she agreed that the 'the material is indescribably interesting', as she described them to Ernst Kris.[8] It was finally decided to have Kris prepare an edition under the joint supervision of Anna Freud and Marie Bonaparte. Kris seemed well placed for this task, as a historian of art and a psychoanalyst trained by Anna Freud. Furthermore, he was married to the child analyst Marianne Rie, who had also been analysed by Anna Freud, and was the daughter of Freud's old friend Oscar Rie and Melanie Bondy, the sister of Ida Fliess. Kris was clearly 'one of the family'.

Kris commenced work in the summer of 1946.[9] A critical problem which confronted him was the addressee of the letters. Wilhelm Fliess was not a nobody. He was an ambitious theoretician and the author of works which had once been quite well known. An oto-rhino-laryngologist by training, Fliess had discovered that through applying cocaine to the nasal mucous membrane he could suppress symptoms such as migraines, diverse neuralgias, and digestive, cardiac and respiratory difficulties. He concluded by affirming the existence of a 'nasal reflex neurosis', a clinical syndrome which he attributed to the sequellae of infectious diseases having affected the nasal pathways and to vaso-motor difficulties of the genital zone. Having observed a regular increase of nasal mucous during menstruation, and, inversely, the disappearance of dysmenorrhoea following the application of cocaine to the nasal mucous membrane, Fliess postulated a particular reflex relation between the nose and the female genital organ. In the measure in which he had managed to suppress neurasthenic symptoms in certain of his male patients through applying cocaine to the 'genital points' of the nasal mucous membrane, he deduced that the same reflex relation between the nose and the genital zone existed in men and that neurasthenia had a sexual aetiology (masturbation). In a work published in 1897,[10] he expanded these observations into a vast theory on the role of biorythms in human life. Alongside the female menstrual cycle of twenty-eight days, he posited another group of masculine periodic phenomena which reproduced themselves every twenty-three days. Both these cycles existed in everyone, corresponding to what Fliess called our 'bisexual disposition',[11] and their combination, which gave rise to all sorts of complicated calculations, was supposed to determine the events of our biological existence, from the day of our birth (hence infantile sexuality existed) up to the day of our death.

By the time Kris came to edit the letters, Fliess' theories (aside from an interest in biorhythms in alternative circles) had long been rejected, and no one believed in the nasal reflex neurosis or a twenty-three-day masculine cycle. However, when Freud and Fliess were writing to each other, these hypothesis were far from absurd.

> **Sulloway:** Let's just take ... for instance the notion that life is regulated by rhythms, biorhythms and so on. Well, you can go right back to Charles Darwin's *The Descent of Man* and find an elaborate discussion about why the gestation cycles of all higher vertebrates follow periods of either weeks or a month and always multiples of seven, fourteen and twenty eight days. Darwin argued that this is simply an evolutionary consequence of our having evolved from some kind of invertebrate progenitor which lived in tidal zones, for in tidal zones the food cycles and therefore the reproductive cycles are dependent on the phases of the tides and therefore of the moon. Now, if Charles Darwin is taking this stuff seriously, why shouldn't all of Fliess's contemporaries?[12]

For his part, Freud took Fliess' ideas completely seriously. As the letters demonstrate, the most minor and major events in Freud's family life, from Martha's menstruations to the decrease in Freud's libido[13] and the death of Jakob Freud[14] were interpreted in the light of Fliessian cycles and offered to Fliess as confirmations of his theories. Freud did not hesitate to diagnose nasal reflex neuroses in his patients and to apply the treatment advocated by Fliess (*cocainum, dosim repetatur*), and sometimes sent patients to Berlin to be treated directly by Fliess. Moreover, he had Fliess operate on his nose several times and directly applied cocaine there for a period of at least three and a half years[15] to treat migraines, cardiac problems and functional difficulties (anxiety, depression, breathlessness) which his friend attributed to a nasal origin.

> **Freud to Fliess, 24 January 1895:** Last time I wrote you, after a good period which immediately succeeded the reaction, that a few viciously bad days had followed during which a cocainization of the left nostril had helped me to an amazing extent. I now continue my report. The next day I kept the nose under cocaine, which one should not really do; that is, I repeatedly painted it to prevent the renewed occurrence of swelling; during this time I discharged what in my experience is a copious amount of thick pus; and since then I have felt wonderful, as though there never had been anything wrong at all . . . I am postponing the full expression of my gratitude and the discussion of what share the operation had in this unprecedented improvement until we see what happens next.[16]

More generally, it is evident that Freud and Fliess were engaged in an intense intellectual collaboration, considering their ideas as complementary and joint (in a 1893 letter, Freud spoke of 'our aetiological formula' for neurasthenia). Freud was visibly impressed by Fliess' theories, to the point of designating him as the 'Kepler of biology'.[17] In 1901, he proposed a co-signed work entitled *Human Bisexuality*[18] (which ultimately became the *Three Essays on the Theory of Sexuality*). In 1904, he invited Fliess to join him in setting up 'a scientific journal that will be devoted to the "biological and psychological exploration of sexuality"'.[19] However, there is little mention of Fliess in Freud's publications after 1905. Apart from a few references to the theory of periodicity and some notes where he acknowledged the Fliessian origins of the concept of bisexuality,[20] Fliess was an absentee in Freud's references, and most notably in Freud's account of his 'splendid isolation' during the formation of the theory of psychoanalysis.

For his part, Fliess had publicly implicated Freud in his priority dispute with Otto Weininger and Hermann Swoboda, through publishing the embarrassing letters in which Freud protested that he hadn't used the concept of bisexuality in his *Three Essays* and defended himself for having indiscretely communicated Fliess' ideas to his patient Swoboda, and through him to Weininger, who utilised them in his book *Sex and Character*.[21] In private, Freud fended off Fliess' detailed accusations through attributing them to a paranoia brought about by repressed homosexuality (the origin, Freud added, of his ideas on paranoid psychosis).[22]

Ernst Kris was confronted with the problem of how to square the content of Freud's letters to Fliess with the legend of the immaculate conception proposed by Freud in his public works. The simplest manner was to employ Freud's private strategy of pathologising Fliess, and hence portraying his theories as the expression of his paranoia. How could Freud have possibly been influenced by such manifestly delirious speculations? In his 'introduction', Kris cited several authors critical of Fliess, claiming that the latter's scientific pretensions belonged to the 'realm of the psychopathological',[23] that he suffered from 'paranoid "overvaluation of an idea"',[24] that his clinical works had a 'mystical tendency',[25] that his doctrines moved further away from observation and 'had grown more and more remote from fact and observation'.[26] Kris even did some family research to try to get an authorised corroboration of his diagnoses from Fliess' son Robert, who was his wife's cousin. This did not prove to be difficult. Robert Fliess had turned against his father, notably after a 'long conversation'[27] with Freud in 1929. He had been trained by Karl Abraham, and was now installed as a psychoanalyst in New York.

> **Ernst Kris to Anna Freud, 18 October 1946 (with a copy to Robert Fliess):** I thank the conversation with Dr. Fliess for information only on a small number of concrete questions. The most important of this information is the fact that Wilhelm Fliess's mother was living at the time of the correspondence, that she suffered a great deal and already then, or later, became ill with paranoia ... Dr. Fliess's report on his own experience with nasal therapy was extremely interesting ... Dr. Fliess added your father recalled the illness of his grandmother and spoke to him about it in a conversation in Tegel.[28]

> **Kris to Anna Freud, 18 October 1946 (without a copy to Robert Fliess):** Robert Fliess described precisely the nature of the paranoia of his father, and portrayed in details his views on where reality testing functioned and where it didn't, as well as describing the later attitude of his father towards Freud entirely in the same sense as Marianne ... In his view Wilhelm Fliess lied pathologically. He asserted that your father had informed him about this in Tegel.[29]

> **Anna Freud to Kris, 29 October 1946:** I find the position of Robert Fliess to be thoroughly understandable and also see no reason why he should not read the letters, before he decides to collaborate on the commentary. The more he knows about the illness of his father, the more cautious he must naturally be in his conduct, since it would not do well in any respect if he is just placed as the son of the father.[30]

Once transformed into someone mentally ill, Fliess could be neutralised and nullified, and his collaboration with Freud presented in an asymmetrical manner. As Kris maintained to John Rodker of Imago Publishing, who had wanted to publish the letters under the title *Letters to Fliess*, Fliess played no role in the elaboration of psychoanalysis.

> **Kris to John Rodker, 26 May 1953:** First, I remain absolutely and unconditionally opposed to 'Letters to Fliess' as title of the publication. There are serious and not only sentimental reasons against this. Fliess was an accident. The friendship was a required outlet ... Alternately to 'Dawn of Psychoanalysis', it seems to me that 'The Origins of

Psychoanalysis' would be an apt title, but at any rate, the name of Fliess in the main title has to be avoided.[31]

However, these manoeuvres were hardly sufficient. It was necessary to eliminate the most evident traces of Freud's interest in the 'delirious' theories of his friend. In other words, to censor the letters. It is not clear when this decision was taken, but in October 1946 the first abridged manuscript was ready[32] and this 'shortening work' (*Kürzungsarbeit*), as Kris called it,[33] continued until the end of 1947, with some further revisions. It was only in 1985 when the complete letters were published that the scale of the censorship became fully apparent: of the 284 letters which Kris had at his disposal, only 168 escaped being totally eliminated, and of these only twenty-nine were published intact. The others (including some of the accompanying manuscripts, such as 'Manuscript C') were shortened in differing proportions, often without indication. Nearly two thirds of the letters were discarded. As James Strachey later confided to Max Schur with British understatement, 'the censorship of Freud's letters in the *Anfänge* was rather extreme'.[34]

> **Editor's note to the abridged edition of the letters to Fliess**: The selection was made on the principle of making public everything relating to the writer's scientific work and scientific interests and everything bearing on the social and political conditions in which psycho-analysis originated; and of omitting or abbreviating everything publication of which would be inconsistent with professional or personal confidence.[35]

> **Ernest Jones:** The letters and the passages omitted in publication, which the present writer has also read, refer to uninteresting details about arranging meetings, news about the health of various relatives and patients, some details of the efforts Freud made to follow Fliess's 'law of periods,' and a number of remarks about Breuer which show that Freud harbored more vigorously critical opinions about him than has generally been supposed.[36]

However, when one looks at the censored passages, it is clear that a large share of them, far from being solely concerned with Freud's private life, relate directly to the theoretical interests which he shared with Fliess. Thus one finds no mention in the first edition of his use of cocaine for therapeutic ends, to eliminate either his patients symptoms or his own. There is no mention of Emma Eckstein, one of Freud's favourite patients who became a psychoanalyst, and who nearly died after a disastrous operation on her nose by Fliess carried out at Freud's request.[37]

> **Anna Freud to Kris, 11 February 1947**: One more: From the beginning I had the greatest pleasure in omitting the Eckstein case history. I do not believe that it will be missed by the reader and it seems to me that there is a long series of considerations against it.[38]

The same goes for Freud's and Fliess' exchange in 1904 on the Swoboda–Weininger episode. In the censored version, the correspondence ended with an innocent postcard sent by Freud to Fliess in 1902 from Paestum, giving the reader no inkling of the priority dispute which led Fliess to break relations with Freud.

> **Anna Freud to Suzanne Bernfeld, 15 December 1951**: With the edition of the Fliess letters, Ernst Kris and I have naturally considered where the theme of the Weininger conflict should be drawn out, but then we have decided, and I think correctly, against it. This continuation of the Fliess history is very instructive for the character transformation of Fliess, but it brings very little for the other side.[39]

More seriously, the cuts in the letters between 1892 and 1896 and Kris' notes obliterated the connections between Fliess' theory on the nasal-sexual aetiology of neurasthenia and Freud's growing interest during these crucial years in the role of sexual 'noxae' in the actual neuroses (neurasthenia and anxiety neurosis), and then in hysteria, obsessional neurosis and paranoia.

> **Freud to Fliess, 6 December 1896**: Finally, I cannot suppress the conjecture that the distinction between neurasthenia and anxiety neurosis, which I detected clinically, is connected with the existence of the two 23-day and 28-day substances.

> **Kris' note:** An assumption from which Freud soon freed himself. It represented the climax of his efforts to connect Fliess' views with his own.[40]

It was the initially speculative and biologising character of Freud's theories on the role of sexuality in the neuroses that was erased, in favour of a selection more in keeping with the official myth of the unexpected discovery in the clinical material.

> **Freud (1910):** Even workers who are ready to follow my psychological studies are inclined to think that I over-estimate the part played by sexual factors ... Far from this position having been postulated by me theoretically, at the time of the joint publication of the Studies with Dr. Breuer in 1895 I had not yet adopted it; and I was only converted to it when my experiences became more numerous and penetrated into the subject more deeply.[41]

At the same time, apart from an important letter of 14 November 1897, one finds hardly any trace in Kris' edition of the 'scatology' (*Dreckologie*) which preoccupied Freud in the months following the abandonment of the seduction theory, and which concerned the derivation of normal repression from the passage of the human species to the upright posture and to the correlative disgust for the anal and oral 'erogenous zones' which were abandoned then.

> **Anna Freud to Kris, 11 February (list of passages to cut):** Letter 154. Omit: dreckology. Letter 155: ditto.[42]

Here again, the result of this omission obscured the connections between these scatological hypotheses on the ontogenic recapitulation by the individual of the erotogenic zones abandoned in the course of phylogenesis and the theory of infantile sexuality put forward in the *Three Essays* in 1905. Confronted with concepts such as those of the 'erotogenic zones', of 'polymorphous perversity', of 'reaction formation', of 'the latency period', of 'regression' to the anal and oral stages, a reader would be unlikely to grasp that these notions were not derived from infant observation, but directly stemmed from the biogenic speculations which Freud shared with Fliess.[43]

> **Freud to Fliess, 11 February 1897**: I had been meaning to ask you, in connection with the eating of excrement [by] [illegible words] animals, when disgust first appears in small children and whether there exists a period in earliest infancy when these feelings are absent. Why do I not go into the nursery and experiment [omitted text: with Annerl (Anna Freud)]? Because with twelve-and-a-half hours' work I have no time, and because the womanfolk do not back me in my investigations.[44]

> **Freud to Fliess, 22 December 1897**: Have you ever seen a foreign newspaper which passed Russian censorship at the frontier? Words, whole clauses and sentences are blacked out and the rest becomes unintelligible.[45]

However it wasn't only the most overtly speculative passages of the correspondence which succumbed to the censor, but also clinical vignettes. To Fliess, Freud described what transpired in his office in a raw manner. This makes the correspondence indispensable for reconstructing Freud's practice at this time, notably during the period of the 'seduction theory'. One can see how he threw ideas in the air and then 'tested' them on his patients,[46] through insisting upon them until he had obtained the desired confirmation, and how he treated the slightest refusal as a 'resistance' to be conquered by all means possible.[47] One also sees how his 'pressure technique' provoked spectacular states of trance in some of his patients, during which they 'relived' with intensity the scenes of seduction which he made them remember.[48]

> **Freud to Fliess, 6 December 1896:** In association, she recovered from her unconscious the memory of a scene in which (at the age of 4) she watched her papa, in the throes of sexual excitement, licking the feet of a wet nurse.[49]

> **Freud to Fliess, 17 December 1896:** Will you believe that the reluctance to drink beer and to shave was elucidated by a scene in which a

nurse sits down *podice nudo* [with bare buttocks] in a shallow shaving bowl filled with beer in order to let herself be licked, and so on?[50]

Freud to Fliess, 3 January 1897: She is suffering from eczema around her mouth and from lesions that do not heal in the corners of her mouth . . . (Once before I traced back entirely analogous observations to sucking on the penis.) In childhood (12 years) her speech inhibition appeared for the first time when, with a *full* mouth, she was fleeing from a woman teacher. Her father has a similarly explosive speech, as though his mouth were full. *Habemus papam!*[51]

Freud to Fliess, 12 January 1897: Would you please try to search for a case of childhood convulsions that you can trace back (in the future or in your memory) to sexual abuse, specifically to *lictus* [licking] (or finger) in the anus . . . For my newest finding is that I am able to trace back with certainty a patient's attack that merely resembled epilepsy to such treatment by the tongue on the part of his nurse. Age 2 years.[52]

Freud to Fliess, 11 February 1897: Hysterical headache with sensation of pressure on the top of the head, temples, and so forth, is characteristic of the scenes where the head is held still for the purpose of actions in the mouth . . . Unfortunately my own father was one of these perverts and is responsible for the hysteria of my brother (all of whose symptoms are identifications) and those of several young sisters.[53]

It was evidently not seen fit to publish such details, which, aside from the insight into Freud's actual practice, serve to demonstrate how Freud extensively rewrote his seduction theory and the events leading to its abandonment in his subsequent historical recapitulations.

Anna Freud to Kris, 11 February 1947: I am sending you notes which Martin [Freud] had given me, after he had read the unabridged correspondence. Naturally, the cuts were noted and it was only with a few points that he was not sure how far the cuts went . . . He is in favour of striking out the case histories which are not used in later works and have a purely perverse character, and as far as I can see it, the other sister endorses him . . . We were already in agreement not to leave everything from the period in which perverse fantasies appear as the precursor to infantile sexuality. But we have still left much.

List of passages to eliminate:

Letter 112 [6 December 1896] Paragraph "Hyst ..." Omit! In the
same letter: pages 10 and 11. Strike out the history of
perversions!

Letter following letter 113, dated in pencil 17.12.96. Page 2, second
paragraph, the perversions with the governess 'will you believe'
etc., strike out!

Letter 119, page 249. 'Unfortunately my father is' absolutely strike out!

Letter 141. The father as perverse, the words 'not excluding my own
father', strike out.

(one of the most beautiful letters!)[54]

Kris to Anna Freud, 29 April 1947: It was my intention to leave out
everything which could give an impression of excessive intimacy,
everything which the details and the extent of the nose and heart
complaints draws out before the death of his father ... Further, I have
left out what gives the impression of wildness in the case histories ...
and what here and there is too intimate in connection with these
abridgements ... I also think that the abridgement must go further ...
I have no bad conscience with the abridgements which I now recommend to you. On the contrary, perhaps we will decide to be still more
radical.[55]

Thus passages where Freud appeared to credit the possibility of a
satanic sexual cult were omitted. Freud had been intrigued by the
resemblance of the 'scenes' of perversion which he provoked in his
patients and the accounts of diabolic debauchery extorted under
torture by the judges in the Inquisition. Rather than being more
circumspect concerning the 'scenes' of his patients, he ended by
believing the veracity of the accounts of the poor 'witches', effectively
taking sides with their torturers. Furthermore, he floated the hypothesis that the perverse acts which his patients had allegedly submitted
to were part of a ritual practised by a secret satanic sect still active.
Fliess was sceptical.[56] As for Kris and Anna Freud, it was clear that the
striking similarity between Freud's therapy and the Inquisition would
not go down well before the public. The passages reproduced here in
italics corresponds to those which were eliminated.

Freud to Fliess, 17 January 1897: But why did the devil who took possession of the poor things invariably abuse them sexually and in a loathsome manner? Why are their confessions under torture so like the communications made by my patients in psychic treatment? . . . *Eckstein has a scene where the diabolus sticks needles into her fingers and then places a candy on each drop of blood. As far as blood is concerned, you are completely without blame!*[57]

Freud to Fliess, 24 January 1897: I am beginning to grasp an idea: it is as though in the perversions, of which hysteria is the negative, we have before us a remnant of a primeval sexual cult, which once was – *perhaps still is* – a religion in the Semitic East (Moloch, Astarte). *Imagine, I obtained a scene about the circumcision of a girl. The cutting off of a piece of the labium minor (which is even shorter today), sucking up the blood, after which the child was given a piece of the skin to eat. This child, at age 13, once claimed that she could swallow a part of an earthworm and proceeded to do it. An operation you once performed was affected by a hemophilia that originated in this way* . . . I dream, therefore, of a primeval devil religion with rites that continue to be carried on secretly, and understand the harsh therapy of the witches' judges. Connecting links abound.[58]

However, despite all the efforts of the censors, Freud's letters to Fliess remained explosive. One could not conceal the fact that Freud had had an extremely intense friendship with Fliess. Furthermore, this relation appears more strange if one simultaneously depicts Fliess as a dangerous paranoiac: the further one tried to separate Freud from Fliess, the more pathological their intimacy appeared. Members of the Freudian family were concerned about this.

Anna Freud to Kris, 29 October 1946: The Hoffers have both read the abridged version and seem to be impressed very positively, if also hesitating about the effect on the outer work in many points, almost identically as we did at that time. Ernst [Freud] is just now reading the unabridged version ... But he seems to be more dismayed than impressed and thought that the manner of the friendly admiration for a man who in the end did not turn out to be a great man somehow gives a compromising impression.[59]

Heinz Hartmann to Anna Freud, 17 March 1947: The story of the creation of psychoanalysis is at the same time the story of the creator's crisis. This certainly does not surprise us; it would surprise us if this were not the case. But to the public these things are little known and somewhat incredible.[60]

Siegfried Bernfeld to Anna Freud, 18 January 1950: I hope the book comes out soon. In my opinion it is great and important. On the other hand one may safely predict that the book will be followed by any number of publications explaining that Freud was a very sick man and that psychoanalysis fits only his own case.[61]

Strachey to Jones, 24 October 1951: It's really a complete instance of *folie à deux*, with Freud in the unexpected role of hysterical partner to a paranoia.[62]

Jones to Strachey, 11 January 1954 (concerning the essay on Leonardo da Vinci): I don't quite agree with what you say about Freud gradually reconciling himself to bisexuality. I think myself he was over-reconciled to it, if you see what I mean. He never really emancipated himself from Fliess and was *avowedly* struggling with that question in 1910 in Sicily. A lot of it then got passed on to Adler, Stekel, Jung and most of all to Ferenczi.[63]

One had to have a therapy for this pathology. The solution had already been indicated by Freud, who had explained to some of his disciples that he had 'succeeded' where Fliess had sunk into delirium.

Freud to Ferenczi, 6 October 1910: I no *longer* have need for that full opening of my personality . . . This need has been extinguished in me since Fliess's case . . . A piece of homosexual investment has been withdrawn and utilized for the enlargement of my own ego. I have succeeded where the paranoiac fails.[64]

In other words, Freud cured himself of his affection for Fliess. The 'therapy' that Kris was in search of had already been found, as it was nothing other than Freud's self-analysis. This had enabled Freud to free himself from Fliess' influence and to find his own original thoughts and psychic health at the same time. Consequently, the texts had to be presented in a manner to support this thesis. As one has seen, Freud's self-analysis did not have a critical place in his letters to Fliess (six weeks of self-interpretation followed by an avowal of failure).[65] Through Kris' interpretation and censorship, it was elevated into the centre of the correspondence and featured as the *fons et origo* of psychoanalysis. This conformed with its progressive mythification in the psychoanalytic movement. In 1947, Kris had already claimed for psychoanalysis that 'no other large body of hypotheses in recent science reveals to a similar extent the influence of one investigator'.[66] In his introduction to the Fliess letters, he explained that it was due to the self-analysis begun in the summer of 1897 that Freud was able to gain 'insight into the structure of the Oedipus complex, and thus into the central problem of psycho-analysis';[67] it enabled 'the step from the seduction theory to full insight into the significance of infantile sexuality'[68] (summer and autumn 1897), and then led to 'insight into the role of erotogenic roles in the development of the libido',[69] to the interpretation of dreams (spring 1898), to the solution of the problem of forgotten acts (summer 1898) and finally to the comprehension of the relation between the theoretical investigation of dreams and the therapy of the neuroses (beginning of 1899). In this elegant chronology, it was necessary artificially to start the self-analysis in August rather than October 1897 (that is to say, after the first doubts concerning the seduction theory), to ignore that the erotogenic zones had already emerged in December 1896, to prolong the self-analysis until 1899, and to censor all the passages which showed that Freud continued to flirt with the hypothesis of 'paternal aetiology' until April 1898,[70] well after the official abandonment of the seduction theory and the actual end of the self-analysis (November 1897). Above all, it was critical to attribute all these developments to Freud himself,[71] to detach his theories from anything which connected them to those of Fliess, and more generally, from their historical and intellectual contexts. By making the self-analysis the mono-source of Freud's theories, Kris promoted the myth of the self-engenderment of psychoanalysis as an 'independent science'[72] in a very effective manner. The so-called Freudian 'epistemological break',[73] was, quite literally, the product of the censors' scissors.

There was a further advantage of Kris' operation: it furnished an impeccably psychoanalytic explication of the origins of psychoanalysis, through making Freudian theory the product of a successful self-analysis. Thus therapy and science converged: Freud cured himself through unveiling the truth, and he saw the truth because he was cured. Thus the madness and folly of the letters were redeemed, as they were simply detours on the way to the cure that was truth, obstacles which Freud had to surmount in a heroic manner. In private, Kris thought that Freud had voluntarily made himself ill so as to be able to resolve the problem of the neuroses.

> **Kris to Anna Freud, 7 December 1947**: I think that Freud's transformation after his self-analysis was so splendid because his neurosis became for him an instrument of research. I often think to myself that he allowed it so as to be able to solve the riddle. But I know very well that one can't say such a thing and consider it as my private version of the hero cult I otherwise avoided.[74]

In his introduction, Kris underlined the painful and uneven course of the self-analysis, the alternation of progress and resistance,[75] and Freud's mood swings during this period. But this simply underscored the fact that it was analytic work which enabled him to separate progressively from Fliess, through overcoming the unconscious conflicts which were the origin of his pathological attraction for his friend's theories. (Ironically, it was actually Fliess who detached himself from Freud.) Kris' explication was highly efficacious, and was immediately taken up by most of the Freudian family, who saw it as a riposte to the potential critiques that the publication of the letters could occasion. Bernfeld, to whom Kris showed his introduction in July 1949, proposed to accompany the publication of the letters with an article on Freud's self-analysis, to drive this point home.

Bernfeld to Anna Freud, 18 January 1950: That's why I think of a paper on 'Freud's self-analysis' showing how very small and irrelevant the neurotic symptoms are and clarifying the relationship between the self-analysis – which in my opinion is a great deed in itself – and the whole body of psychoanalytic method and content.[76]

This consensus had been the effect of a compromise. In actual fact, in the first version of his introduction, Kris had gone much further in his description of the symptoms which Freud's self-analysis was supposed to have cured. This had considerably alarmed Anna Freud and Marie Bonaparte, who feared that Freud would appear as 'a serious and uncured neurotic'.[77] To judge by a long letter addressed by Kris to Marie Bonaparte in November 1947, one of the contentious points[78] between him and his two co-editors was his reference to the homosexual nature of the friendship between Freud and Fliess.

Kris to Marie Bonaparte, 6 November 1947 (with a copy to Anna Freud): Your second concrete comment refers to a passage that reads (pp. 77/78): 'Freud mentions repeatedly that his relationship with Fliess played a part in his self-analysis (see Letter 66, for instance). Several passages permit one to assume that Freud realized that his relationship with Fliess was connected with the chief problem of the first phase of his self-analysis, his relations with his father (Letter 134), and the progress of the self-analysis seems to have facilitated his estrangement from Fliess.' Your comments to this passage read: 'People would conclude that Freud was homosexual. We know what you mean, others not.' To this I should like to reply: Everybody who reads the letters – and I am referring only to the selection we publish – has got the impression of an unusually intimate friendship and of an attachment which, seen from the outside, suggests the proximity of sublimated homosexual tendencies. I am purposely here not referring to the unabridged text in which the reference to the nasal therapy tends to reinforce this impression. Freud himself repeatedly mentioned that the relation to Fliess played a role in Freud's self-analysis (see for example Letter 66). From a few passages one is permitted to suspect that Freud came to the insight that his relation to Fliess was connected to the main problem of the first phase of his self-analysis, that is, the relation to the father and the feminine inclination (Letter 134). And it seems that the progress of the self-analysis made the separation from Fliess easier.[79]

The second contentious point was the nature of the numerous ailments which plagued Freud in the 1890s: migraines, nasal symptoms, gastro-intestinal symptoms, rapid mood swings and above all cardiac arrhythmia accompanied by dyspepsia and anginal pains. Concerning the cardiac symptoms which worried Freud, Breuer had been of the opinion that they were due to a 'chronic myocardia'. As for Fliess, he considered them due to nicotine intoxication, and then diagnosed them with a nasal aetiology for which he prescribed his habitual cure: cocainisation of the nasal mucous membrane and turbinate operations. Others, such as Elisabeth Thornton,[80] have suggested that they were due to effects of cocaine, which Freud, following Fliess' advice, had taken initially to calm his migraines.[81] From this perspective, Fliess' cocaine therapy was an illness which it pretended to cure, as Karl Krauss once famously characterised psychoanalysis.[82] Even to suggest such connections would have been unacceptable, given the level of concern over any mention of nasal therapy in the letters. Having previously accepted Max Schur's (who was subsequently Freud's personal physician) diagnosis of coronary thrombosis, Kris came to the conclusion that the cardiac and other symptoms were of a neurotic nature, which he explained in the first version of his introduction.

Kris, extract from the unpublished version of his introduction to the letters to Fliess: Freud did not indicate the immediate cause which induced him to his self-analysis. At the end of the half year which followed the death of his father, in spring 1897, he mentioned neurotic disturbances, in which Fliess 'was drawn in' (Letters 65ff). This is not the first occasion in which Freud touches on the theme of his own neurotic difficulties. Already in the year 1894 – thus at the time of the tense and conflictual collaboration with Breuer and often since that time – Freud reported fluctuations of health and moods. The heart complaints which Freud suffered from in these years and which Fliess tended to think led back to nicotine abuse were never certainly diagnosed.[83] Freud's own conception fluctuated; but the letters strengthen the impression that Freud was correct in his supposition of a psychic cause or a psychic contribution. This impression is strengthened by the success of the self-analysis. Already in the year 1898 Freud felt 'much more normal' and 'healthier'.[84]

Anna Freud and Marie Bonaparte were strongly against any mention of a 'neurosis' of the founder, which risked giving weapons to the adversaries of psychoanalysis. So the official diagnosis remained one of organic cardiac symptoms. Anna Freud reprimanded her former analysand.

> **Anna Freud to Kris, 4 June 1947**: But in all the sentences which refer to the self-analysis, one notices that you are still in an inner conflict, and with this there is too much explanation and apology and this arouses in the reader the impression, which you do not want to arouse: namely that with his thirst for knowledge, he found himself in forbidden territory. I think that we must solve the question of conscience before you give this paragraph its definitive form. We decided that it is not correct to convey certain points, since one must omit them. We decided in favour of the opposite, since there is no ground for the apology and the reader will find it more natural that he came to know these things.[85]

Anna Freud proposed to ask Max Schur to write a note on the diagnosis of thrombosis, explicitly citing the letter mentioning the myocardia postulated by Breuer (she added that this letter should not be cut).[86] This would have undercut Kris' construction, as it removed one of the reasons for the self-analysis. Shaken by this rebuff, Kris wrote several letter to plead his case and invoked other members of the Freudian family. He noted that Heinz Hartmann agreed with him that Freud suffered from a 'cardiac neurosis' and Felix Deutsch, who had been Freud's doctor in the early 1920s, was also inclined to exclude a prior coronary incident. Even Schur had changed his opinion, as, after reading the letters, he 'suddenly felt that he never really believed in the thrombosis of the 1890s'.[87] Anna Freud was not disposed to give way.

> **Anna Freud to Kris, 12 November 1947**: After the many fluctuations from one to another view, I feel that Schur's opinion loses its value for the decision. Hartmann, who has no physical evidence, can know no more of it than any other reader of the letters. And Felix Deutsch is, as you know, not impartial on this point.[88]

There was nothing to do but to give in. The censor was now censored, and Kris removed references to Freud's 'feminine tendency' and his various 'neurotic' symptoms, and only left a vague reference to his mood swings and the alternation of progress and resistance. Consequently, the reader remains in the dark as to precisely what Freud was cured of. The self-analysis, which Kris had brought to centre stage to provide a therapy for the errancy of the letters, now became a cure without an illness nor much in the way of discernable symptoms. The mystification of the origins of psychoanalysis was complete. It was only in 1966 that Max Schur discretely revealed some fragments from the unpublished parts of the correspondence[89] and only in 1985 that the letters appeared intact, apart from anonymising the names of patients.[90] However, the myth of the immaculate self-analysis had already taken root and become embedded and enshrined in the literature of psychoanalysis and spread to other disciplines, including in figures as sophisticated as Derrida and Ricoeur. The censors had won. To this day, how many people bother to read the complete edition of the letters to Fliess?

A biography in search of an author

The Origins of Psychoanalysis appeared in German in 1950 and in English in 1954. However, this was only the first step in establishing the official history of psychoanalysis. In the same letter in which he sent Anna Freud his final correction, Kris announced the next task.

> **Kris to Anna Freud, 7 December 1947**: The two 'biographies,' of which I have not read Ludwig's, will hopefully have satiated the greedy interest so fully and have satisfied the hostility so fully, that the

appearance of our volume will pass without sensation. Then Bernfeld will have the time to write a correct biography and we will have time to publish a selection of further letters or write the biography of psychoanalysis instead of Freud.[91]

Bernfeld to Kris, 11 July 1949: I received today the first installment [of *Aus den Anfänge der Psychoanalyse*], and have read through it in a hurry. My impression is that you have done a great job with the introduction. The biography of Freud starts to take shape.[92]

As we have seen,[93] Freud had been profoundly allergic to any intrusion in his private life and his heirs shared this attitude, systematically refusing all cooperation with projects such as the fictional biography of Irving Stone,[94] a Hollywood film planned by Anatole Litvak or the historical researches of Dr von Hattingberg of Baden-Baden.

Anna Freud to Eissler, 26 February 1952: I know about the plan of Hattingberg's and have been asked to help him a year ago already. But I refused outright. I do not see how a complete stranger like Hattingberg has the right to write a biography, how he can have the knowledge to do so. It seems to me that he had much better be left to his own devices, and perhaps he will [illegible] so little that he will drop his plan.[95]

However, this rigorously obstructionist attitude became untenable when unauthorised biographies and memoirs began to appear. These threatened to diminish Freud's public image. In 1946 and 1947, two critical biographies of Freud appeared, from Emil Ludwig[96] and Helen Puner,[97] soon followed by other incursions into Freud's private life. Anna Freud was outraged by these. She described Ludwig's work as 'labour of hate',[98] while that of Puner was 'horrible';[99] Erik Erikson's article on the Irma dream in *The Interpretation of Dreams* 'literally turn [ed] [her] stomach';[100] Leslie Adams, a New York psychiatrist who had done researches on Freud's youth,[101] was a 'full-time crank';[102] Joseph Wortis deserved being taken to court for having published his memoirs of his analysis with Freud,[103] and so on. Thus it was imperative to produce a 'true biography', as Kris described it, to form a bulwark against the proliferation of unauthorised accounts.

> **Heinz Hartmann to Anna Freud, 17 March 1947:** There will be biographies of Freud. The question is only whether among these biographies there will be a work which one can accept.[104]

> **Jones, preface to vol. 1 of his Freud biography:** Freud's family understandingly respected his wish for privacy, and indeed shared it. They often sheltered him from a merely inquisitive public. What changed their attitude later was the news of the many false stories invented by people who had never known him, stories which were gradually accumulating into a mendacious legend.[105]

But who should write the true life of Freud? On October 1946, Jones was contacted by Leon Shimkin, the director of Simon & Schuster, who wanted to know if he was interested in writing a biography of Freud.[106] Jones immediately contacted Anna Freud, who was ambivalent about this prospect. Jones had recently taken sides against her in the conflict with Melanie Klein.[107] He had never truly been part of the 'family' and she was not sure how much she could trust him. So she suggested that Jones collaborated with Siegfried Bernfeld, an old friend of her youth in Vienna,[108] thinking that Bernfeld could direct the project or at least control his collaborator. Moreover, Bernfeld was particularly qualified for this task, as, following his emigration to the United States, he had begun to undertake very detailed investigations with his wife Suzanne of Freud's youth and the intellectual context of his early work.[109]

> **Anna Freud to Kris, 13 March 1947:** Jones is not averse to seeking collaborators, as he is not at all suited to do this work alone on account of his state of health. He himself had thought of Bernfeld, which is no bad idea, if the task can be divided . . . Somehow I do not believe in the reality of this project. I don't consider Jones to be healthy enough. But if in this way his material could be preserved for us, it is probably worth the trouble to be interested in this matter. In any case I do not want to

appear negative towards it ... since I do not want to lose all influence on this affair.[110]

Anna Freud to Bernfeld, 4 March 1947: [Shimkin] is very interested in publishing a biography of my father and has been in connection here with Ernest Jones who is not unwilling to use the material (letters, personal memories, etc.) in his possession to write at least part of one if he can find somebody to co-operate with him. The idea was that you might be interested in the proposition of being that person and that you might like to write about the development of analytic thought in the manner in which you did it in your articles which have already been published.[111]

Bernfeld was more suspicious than Anna Freud of Jones. Furthermore, it is clear that he conceived of his historical articles as drafts of chapters of his own Freud biography,[112] so a collaboration with Jones would come into conflict with his project. Nevertheless, he was willing to work with Jones.

Bernfeld to Anna Freud, 19 March 1947: Confidentially: I am concerned about Jones' contribution. In England – back in 1937 – Jones made some remarks on Freud's personality and life which shocked me, not only because they were made in a hostile and careless way at the dinner table but mainly because they reveal that Jones, at that time, lacked the kind of sympathy and reverence for Freud which is essential for an objective historian. I know that he doesn't like me a bit and I doubt therefore whether he would be able to cooperate with me. I don't like him either but I have sufficient appreciation of his contributions to psychoanalysis to be willing to try.[113]

Anna Freud to Bernfeld, 26 March 1947: Jones' negative attitude, as it revealed itself to you, is no secret and only too well known to me. But I believe it was mainly the result of jealousy and a feeling that he was not appreciated enough and it has probably greatly diminished since my father's death ... I do not know whether he will really have the strength and length of life to finish anything of the kind, but I feel sure that his material is very valuable and that he should at least collect it and thereby prepare the way for further work on it. But that is, of course, not the way in which one could present the task to him.[114]

Several months later, however, Jones wrote a preface for Freud's study *The Question of Lay Analysis* which did not please Anna Freud. The issue was one where Jones had disagreed with Freud, and he referred to Freud's anti-medical prejudices. On 16 May, she asked Kris to inform Shimkin that she was considering withdrawing her agreement to Jones as Freud's biographer.[115] In reply, Shimkin proposed entrusting Bernfeld with the role, aided by Anna Freud herself.[116] As she did not want to participate directly in it, she proposed instead a collaboration between Bernfeld and Kris, with Jones reduced to being an informer.[117] Finally, in September, the publisher decided to offer Jones a contract for a volume of 300,000 words.[118] The project appears to have lain fallow for two and a half years, until Jones wrote to Bernfeld on 23 March 1950 to ask for his collaboration, in line with the original project.[119] Jones wondered how he could integrate the work in Bernfeld's already published articles into his biography. Bernfeld, faithful to the promise which he had made to Anna Freud, reassured him on this point and offered to place his published and unpublished researches at Jones' disposal.

> **Bernfeld to Jones, 24 April 1950:** I do not see how my studies could possibly interfere with your work and I do not see why you could not or should not use my publications exactly in the way they fit into your plan. If you wish to quote paragraphs or pages of my publication this can be arranged with the bearer of the copyright ... I shall be glad to cooperate when you wish to receive unpublished information from me.[120]

As their correspondence between 1950 and 1953 reveals, their collaboration was very close, and much greater than one would have been led to imagine by Jones' acknowledgement in the first volume.[121]

> **Peter J. Swales:** volume one of the Jones Biography was very largely a rewrite of Bernfeld, who was the very first to do genuine historical research on Freud ... Bernfeld was the true illuminator ... Chunks of Jones's book are just an out and out plagiarism of Bernfeld.[122]

Jones questioned Bernfeld on all sorts of questions, such as Freud's date of birth, his disguised autobiographical essay on 'Screen memories',[123] and his relations with Brentano and Meynert. Bernfeld gave detailed answers or undertook researches to help Jones. He corrected the drafts of chapters which Jones sent him, as did James Strachey, who was another concealed collaborator on the biography. In return, Bernfeld asked Jones about matters which he could perhaps answer with the documents to which he had access: what was the distance between Freud's birthplace, 117 Schlossergasse, and the market? Were there police records about Freud's nanny who was reported for theft by his half-brother? What was known of the criminal activities of his uncle, Josef Freud? When did Freud go to Wandsbeck to visit his fiancée during his researches on cocaine? (Jones' reply: Freud's train arrived at Hamburg station on 2 September 1884 at 5.45 in the morning.)

However it is clear that the main direction of the information flow was from Bernfeld to Jones, who knew little about Freud's infancy and youth. The situation started to change when Jones gained the confidence of the family, after showing his first chapters to Anna Freud.

> **Jones to Strachey, 27 October 1951:** It is amazing how converted to enthusiasm the whole Freud family have become for the Biography. They keep pouring in information.[124]

In April 1952, the family agreed to show Jones the *Betrothal Letters* – nearly 2,000 letter between Freud and Martha Bernays during their four-year engagement, and then their 'secret journal', which was a supreme mark of confidence. Bernfeld was impatient to know what they contained, and asked Jones to send him a microfiche of the *Betrothal Letters* and offered to transcribe them. However, Jones could not oblige, as he said that they had been sent to him 'only after heartbreaking discussions and after exacting all kinds of pledges . . . not another living soul . . . etc.'.[125] The truth was that, as Jones' stock with Anna Freud rose, Bernfeld's fell. For reasons that are not entirely clear but appear to have been connected to her relations with Suzanne Bernfeld, Anna Freud thought that his wife exercised a bad influence on him and led his researches towards what was sensational. Already in 1947, Anna Freud was disturbed that Kris had promised to show the Fliess letters to Bernfeld, arguing that one couldn't count on the discretion of his wife.[126] Two years later, when Bernfeld had announced his intention to publish an article with his wife on Freud's self-analysis, Anna Freud wrote to Kris to ask him to ask Bernfeld not to cite the letters to Fliess without authorisation and to send them a draft 'for criticism'.[127] But the final straw was that Bernfeld had mentioned that he was researching on Freud's uncle Josef, of whom Freud had written in *The Interpretation of Dreams* that he had run-ins with the law, to Kurt Eissler, which the latter indiscretely passed to Anna Freud (at that time, neither Bernfeld nor Jones knew that he had been found guilty in a counterfeit money scandal, in which Freud's elder brothers were also suspected).

> **Bernfeld to Eissler, 4 January 1951:** What criminal acts did Uncle Josef, the brother of Jakob Freud, commit? When? What was his sentence?[128]

This was too much. Anna Freud was 'appalled'[129] by this intrusion into the secret of the Freud family, and she decided no longer to reply to Bernfeld's requests for information.[130] As Bernfeld was writing an article on Freud's experiences with cocaine, the embargo of the *Betrothal Letters* which covered this period was highly irritating. Just as he had told Jones, who was surprised to learn this, the young Freud published an article in July 1884 in which he championed the use of cocaine, which had recently been introduced on the market, for diverse ailments, such as gastric disorders, seasickness, neurasthenia, facial neuralgias, asthma and exhaustion. Freud also wrote that he had succeeded in completely detoxing a patient with morphinomania through orally administering cocaine, and he repeated this in a talk given in March 1885 and published the following month. Here, he also recommended administering cocaine with subcutaneous injections, adding that 'no addiction to cocaine developed; on the contrary, a growing antipathy was evident'.[131] Albrecht Erlenmeyer, a specialist in morphinomania, tested this on some of his patients. In May 1886, he published an article which was extremely critical of Freud. He argued that administering cocaine did not lead to a withdrawal from morphine, and, furthermore, that it resulted in an addiction to cocaine. He concluded that Freud had unleashed a 'third blight'[132] on humanity, after alcohol and morphine. In a rejoinder to Erlenmeyer, Freud attributed Erlenmeyer's results to the fact that the latter had administered cocaine subcutaneously rather than orally, as Freud had recommended. This was clearly misleading, as Freud had indeed recommended the first method in his article of April 1885. Apart from some veiled allusions in *The Interpretation of Dreams*, where he evoked the figure of a 'very dear friend' who had become intoxicated by cocaine through administering injections contrary to his advice,[133] Freud never mentioned this embarrassing episode in his writings, preferring to recount how he just failed to be the first to discover the anaesthetic properties of cocaine, which his friend Carl Koller did through following up some of Freud's indications, whilst Freud went to visit his fiancée.[134]

Bernfeld, obviously basing his work on the passage in *The Interpretation of Dreams*, succeeded in identifying the anonymous morphinomanic whom Freud claimed to have cured. It was Ernst von Fleischl-Marxow, a colleague and a friend of Freud who had used morphine to combat the extreme pain following the amputation of a finger. Exactly as Erlenmeyer had found in his own patients, Fleischl-Marxow developed a cocaine addiction thanks to Freud's treatment. He died six years later, addicted to both morphine and cocaine.[135] Bernfeld asked Jones if the *Betrothal Letters* shed further light on this episode. Jones confirmed that the letters contained 'valuable and unexpected' information[136] on this subject, and added that he would plead Bernfeld's case with Anna Freud, to enable him to consult at least this part of the correspondence.

Jones to Bernfeld, 28 April 1952: What a company they were. Meynert drank. Fleischl was a bad morphinomanic and I am afraid that Freud took more cocaine than he should though I am not mentioning that.[137]

Jones to Strachey, 27 May 1952: The way Freud thrust the cocaine on everybody must have made him quite a menace; even Martha had to take it to bring some bloom into her cheeks! ... He was only interested in the magical internal effects of the drug, of which he took too much himself. Even years later he and Fliess were always cocainising each other's nose.[138]

Jones to Anna Freud, 3 May 1952: I daresay you know that Bernfeld is writing up the cocaine episode. Should you agree to my sending him the extracts from the Br.Br. [*Braut Briefe*] on the subject? There would be nothing personal in them, but there is a full account of his experiences with it.[139]

Anna Freud gave her permission, presumably because she hadn't considered the implications. The letters revealed several 'unexpected' matters:[140]

1   Fleischl's treatment had been a failure: ten days after the demorphinisation cure prescribed by Freud, cocaine had not suppressed the suffering nor the symptoms of lack. The physician Theodore Billroth tried a new operation on the amputated stump, prescribing morphine to Fleischl.[141] Freud's claims in his article which appeared the following month that he had cured his patient of his morphine addiction were baseless.

2   Fleischl continued to take cocaine 'regularly'[142] in the summer, progressively increasing the dose during the winter and autumn of 1884–5. Thus, contrary to Freud's affirmation in his talk in March 1885, it was simply not the case that Fleischl had not developed any addiction to cocaine.

3   Contrary to what he later claimed in his rejoinder to Erlenmeyer and in the passage of *The Interpretation of Dreams* concerning

his 'unhappy friend', Freud did indeed administer injections of cocaine to Fleischl in January 1885 to try to calm his persistent pain, after which Fleischl started to inject himself with excessive doses of cocaine.

Bernfeld dealt with these issues with an exemplary tact in his article, which appeared posthumously in 1953.[143] The first point was purely and simply passed over in silence and the second was hardly touched on. He simply noted, without drawing the obvious conclusion, that the passages of Ernest Jones' forthcoming biography led him to 'think that it was probable'[144] that Fleischl's addition to cocaine began to be noted in the winter of 1884–5. As for the third point, Bernfeld underlined the contradiction between Freud's response to Erlenmeyer and his defence of subcutaneous injections in his article of 1885, as well as the fact that Freud never subsequently referred to this article. But these points were used to concentrate on this omission and to see it as 'an *unconscious* dishonesty – a forgotten act'[145] due to his feeling of guilt of having realised his unconscious desire to kill Fleischl (Bernfeld invoked the dream of 'Brücke's laboratory' in *The Interpretation of Dreams*). This effectively diverted attention from what Freud had said about the use of the syringe. Bernfeld concluded his article by affirming that Freud had abandoned all his research on cocaine from 1887, whilst still citing a passage from Freud's *The Interpretation of Dreams* on the topic of his practice of nasal cocain-isation in 1895, conceding that Freud had for some time maintained a 'limited and skeptical' interest in the question for some time.[146]

Despite these evasions, the article provoked a veritable 'fizz'[147] with Anna Freud.

Anna Freud to Jones, 19 September 1952: I did not like it at all, except the facts which are very interesting. But the interpretations, with which the facts are intermingled (hers, I am sure), are loose, wrong and sometimes ludicrous. Please do not let him publish it in this form. After all, you know now how all these things really happened and it should be your role to silence the other biographers, who have to invent half of their facts.[148]

Jones to Strachey, 22 September 1952: How did you know Anna's reaction to Bernfeld's cocaine? By the same post I get a letter from her begging me to stop him.[149]

To prevent a similar explosion regarding the chapter he was preparing on the same episode, Jones quickly dissociated himself from Bernfeld.

Jones to Anna Freud, 22 September 1952: The more I know of the history the less do I think of Bernfeld's work. The evil genius is certainly that pest Suzanne ... I have written a chapter on cocaine (not finished) which I hope you will like better than theirs.[150]

Jones to Anna Freud, 31 October 1952: I hope you will like my cocaine chapter better than Suzanne's melodramatic and badly informed effort ... There has been a good deal of speculation about the mystery people have sensed in the cocaine story, so I am sure the best way to dispel it is to give a straightforward account that will make it quite intelligible.[151]

In reality, Jones' chapter reproduced Bernfeld's article, sometimes nearly word for word, adding further information gleaned from the *Brautbriefe*. Jones gave a more detailed and vivid description of Fleischl and his disastrous demorphinisation cure. In a rash manner, he made explicit some points which Bernfeld had been careful to avoid. 'For a short time', he claimed, Fleischl's demorphinisation had been 'very successful'[152] and 'the cocaine had for some time helped' to control[153] some of his symptoms. These were vague and misleading statements, aimed at explaining how Freud could have made false claims for success in his 1884 and 1885 articles. Jones underlined that Freud had affirmed in his April 1885 article that his patient had not developed any addiction to cocaine, but added in a fallacious manner that '(this was before Fleischl had suffered from cocaine intoxication)'.[154] As for Freud's denials of the use of the syringe, Jones simply reiterated Bernfeld's psychoanalytic exculpation, through appealing to an 'unconscious repression'[155] and to 'unconsciously determined' behaviour (but he omitted references to Freud's death wishes towards Fleischl).[156]

Fortunately for Jones, this was enough to soften Anna Freud, who gave his chapter her imprimatur.

> **Jones to Bernfeld, 22 December 1952:** Yes, A. F. has, rather to my surprise, passed all my chapters. For what it is worth I may tell you that she hopes you will not publish your cocaine one, so I don't know what to advise you about it. She asked me to influence you not to.[157]

Bernfeld didn't understand why Anna Freud had objected to his article and not to Jones' chapter, which, he noted, went much further than his.

> **Bernfeld to Jones, 31 December 1952:** Don't try further to influence me not to publish it. I have written to Miss Freud and asked for her comments.[158]

This was Bernfeld's last letter to Jones. In December 1951, he had survived a coronary thrombosis. He died in April 1953. Ironically, it was Jones, whom Anna Freud had considered too frail for the task, who survived Bernfeld, and who profited from Bernfeld's research in writing *the* Freud biography.[159]

The Jones biography: the definitive form of the legend

The episode of the collaboration between Bernfeld and Jones illustrates the manner in which the Freud biography was a communal enterprise of Freudian insiders, and how the historical information on which it was based was centralised, filtered and controlled by Anna Freud. From her house in Hampstead (now the location of the Freud Museum), she decided in a sovereign manner who could have access to what, which documents could be published or cited, and which events of her father's life could be mentioned or rather should be omitted. Thus Jones was able to read complete correspondences and documents which were restricted for other researchers, in part or completely, for decades, and in some cases remain so: the complete letters to Fliess (published in 1985), the *Betrothal Letters*, the *Secret Chronicle* (accessible to researchers since 2000), the correspondences with Minna Bernays, Karl Abraham, Oskar Pfister, Sándor Ferenczi, C. G. Jung, Max Eitingon and Abraham Brill, as well as the journals of Marie Bonaparte. Just like Kris with the Fliess letters, Jones submitted the chapters of his biography to Anna Freud for her approval and critique. Her censure sometimes concerned trivial as well as significant points. For example, Jones was instructed not to mention Freud's chronic constipation.[160] This was one of the rare points on which he disobeyed. He was interdicted from mentioning that Martha's brother, Eli Bernays, had illegitimate children (his legitimate son, the famous publicist Eli Bernays, threatened a law suit).[161] In other letters, Anna Freud demanded that Jones should remove or modify passages on Abraham,[162] and Pfister,[163] and complained that Ferenczi 'comes off badly'.[164] However, in the main, she didn't have to censor much, as Jones had already done the bulk of this. Much smarter in this regard than Bernfeld, he knew how to anticipate her desires and to avoid contentious issues or at least present them from the most favourable angle.

> **Jones to Anna Freud, 28 November 1951:** Your father used to call me the diplomat of the [International Psychoanalytic] Association, but sinking myself in his thoughts in this work makes me absorb something of his ruthless integrity and aversion to compromise. In the matter of his neurosis, for example, I naturally lay the chief stress on the mighty achievement of overcoming it single-handed, for I really think his self analysis was his greatest feat. But I don't want critics to say, 'Naturally Jones, being a blind admirer, gives a one-sided picture and omits this, that and the other.'[165]

Jones' biography was a brilliant dramatisation of the Freudian legend. As we have seen with his treatment of Bernfeld's article on cocaine, Jones was past master in the art of utilising documents and accounts to which he alone had access to flesh out and confirm Freud's accounts whilst eliding the contradictions. When Kris abridged the letters to Fliess, he deliberately cut their anecdotal aspects, rendering them 'more arid' and 'austere' than they actually were.[166] By contrast, Jones did not hesitate to be a raconteur, embroidering the anecdotes narrated by Freud and adding more striking details. These embellishments never contradicted the master-narrative proposed by Freud and the troika of Ernst Kris, Anna Freud and Marie Bonaparte. Indeed, they fleshed it out and made it more vivid. Consequently Anna Freud, who had been irritated by the 'sensationalism' of the unauthorised biographies, was not troubled by them.

This method of dramatisation is particularly evident in the treatment Jones reserved for what he called the 'Fliess period'. Relying on the unpublished portions of the correspondence, he did not hesitate to divulge all sorts of details about the famous 'neurosis' that Anna Freud had suggested Kris keep quiet or at least downplay. Freud, he revealed, had for almost ten years suffered from a 'very considerable psychoneurosis'[167] – characterised by a 'passionate relationship of dependence'[168] with Fliess – from bouts of severe depression,[169] from fears of death and travelling,[170] from an inhibition about going to Rome,[171] as well as from cardiac problems that were psychosomatic in origin[172] (Jones thus repeated the diagnosis Kris had made in private). Freud, quite literally, had suffered as a martyr.

> **Jones:** His sufferings were at times very intense, and for those ten years there could have been only occasional intervals when life seemed much worth living. He paid very heavily for the gifts he bestowed on the world, and the world was not very generous in its rewards.[173]

Jones even went so far as to mention that Freud had taken cocaine prescribed to him by Fliess to treat a nasal infection. The two men, he said in jest, evinced 'an inordinate amount of interest . . . in the state of each other's nose'.[174] But everywhere else, Jones systematically minimised Freud's enthusiasm for nasal therapy and Fliess' theories. These ideas belonged to the 'realm of psychopathology'[175] and Fliess, in fact, had developed 'persecutory ideas'[176] about Freud at the time of their falling out. The emphasis Fliess placed on the somatic processes at work in sexuality 'must have been a drag on Freud's painful progress from physiology to psychology',[177] while their discussions were 'duologues rather than dialogues'.[178] Freud's strange infatuation with Fliess' wild imaginings is explained by his 'unconscious identification'[179] of his friend with his father – and this had faded away when Freud undertook an analysis of his 'deeply buried hostility'[180] towards his father after the latter's death, discovering in quick succession the Oedipus complex, the meaning of dreams and the role of infantile sexuality that, until then, had been concealed by the (neurotic) theory of paternal seduction. In thus making self-analysis the key to Freud's strictly *psychological* discoveries, Jones faithfully conformed to the version of events sketched out by Freud and consolidated by Kris,[181] while giving them an even more pronounced psychoanalytic turn. History was put at the service of the scientific myth, embellished with the trappings of archives and documents.

> **Jones:** In 1897 [Freud] embarked, all alone, on what was undoubtedly the greatest feat of his life. His determination, courage and honesty made him the first human being not merely to get glimpses of his own unconscious mind – earlier pioneers had often got as far as that – but actually to penetrate into and explore its deepest depths. This imperishable feat was to give him a unique position in history.[182]

We find the same method in the chapter dedicated to the 'Breuer period'. In his edition of the letters to Fliess, Kris had systematically eliminated all the passages in which Freud rather viciously maligned Breuer, despite all the professional and financial assistance that his ex-friend had given him over the years. Jones, on the other hand, didn't hesitate to point out the ingratitude and 'bitterness'[183] of Freud's comments – something he found difficult to explain. Better yet, he scrupulously quoted all the passages in which Breuer insisted on the role of sexuality in the neuroses, thereby contradicting what

Freud had written about the resistance of his collaborator. But Jones also cited the less than flattering descriptions of Breuer in Freud's letters: that of a 'weak' and indecisive man whose 'pettifogging kind of censoriousness'[184] prevented him from him from fully assenting to the revolutionary theories of his young colleague. And above all, the major 'leak': Jones made public the fable of Anna O.'s hysterical childbirth which Freud, as we have seen, had been spreading in private to discredit Breuer and counter his objections to the exclusively sexual aetiology of the neuroses. Jones even gave the real name of Breuer's patient, which he had discovered in the *Betrothal Letters*, and he claimed that one of these letters 'contain[ed] substantially the same story'[185] that Freud had told him – which was false.[186] For good measure, he added his own embellishments, claiming that Breuer, after fleeing the hysterical childbirth 'in a cold sweat', had departed the next day with his wife for Venice where they conceived a daughter who, 'born in these curious circumstances',[187] was fated to commit suicide sixty years later in New York City (absolutely nothing in this sensational story is true).

Just as with Bernfeld, Jones regularly sent drafts of his chapters to James Strachey, who was working on the volumes of the *Standard Edition* (this project, begun immediately after Freud's death, can be considered the third pillar of psychoanalysis' official history, after *The Origins of Psychoanalysis* and Jones' biography). In response to receiving the three chapters to be included in the first volume, Strachey sent Jones ten pages of very detailed commentary on many points, one of which was the story of Anna O.'s hysterical childbirth.

Strachey to Jones, 24 October 1951: Breuer's adventure. Freud told me the same story with a good deal of dramatic business. I remember very well his saying: 'So he took up his hat and rushed from the house.' – But I've always been in some doubt of whether this was a story that Breuer told Freud or whether it was what he inferred – a 'construction' in fact. My doubts were confirmed by a sentence in the *Selbstdarstellung* (G. W. 14, 45): 'Aber über dem Ausgang der hypnotischen Behandlung lastete ein Dunkel, das Breuer mir niemals aufhellte . . .' [But over the final stage of this hypnotic treatment there rested a veil of obscurity, which Breuer never raised for me] And again (*ibid*, 51): 'Er hätte mich durch den Hinweis auf seine eigene erste Patientin schlagen oder irre machen können, bei der sexuelle Momente angeblich keine Rolle gespielt hatten. Er tat es aber nie; ich verstand es lange nicht, bis ich gelernt, mir diesen Fall richtig zu deuten und . . . zu rekonstruiren.' [He might have crushed me or at least disconcerted me by pointing to his own first patient, in whose case sexual factors had ostensibly played no part whatever. But he never did so, and I could not understand why this was, until I came to interpret the case correctly and to reconstruct . . . it.] But you seem on p. 20 to have further evidence on the subject. Were Freud's published remarks put in that form for reasons of discretion?'[188]

Strachey, quite perceptively, puts his finger on the oddities that we have already encountered:[189] if Freud heard the story directly from Breuer, why would he have needed to 'reconstruct' it? Obviously, Strachey suspected Freud of having improperly presented, under the guise of historical fact, what was merely an interpretation. Jones, who knew perfectly well that this was the case – since he was able to use the letter to Martha as a means of comparison – nevertheless decided to stay the course.

> **Jones to Strachey, 27 October 1951:** Freud gave me two versions of the Breuer story. The theatrical one about his grabbing his hat, and then the true one that Breuer hypnotized Anna and calmed her before leaving. I have left out the hat; 'rushed from the house' seems to me legitimate, since it conveys the spirit of the situation.[190]

The nasty rumour started by Freud now became the official public version. Strachey, in a note appended to his translation of the Anna O. case, aligned himself with Jones, an example of the synchronisation between the biography and the 'standard' edition.

> **Strachey:** On this point (said Freud one day to the present translator, with his finger on an open copy of the book), there is a hiatus in the text. What he was thinking of and proceeded to describe was the

episode that had marked the end of Anna O.'s treatment. The story is told by Ernest Jones in his biography of Freud and it will suffice here to say that once the treatment had seemingly been crowned a success, the patient suddenly exhibited to Breuer the presence of a strong, positive, and unanalyzed transference that was indubitably sexual in nature.[191]

In the same way, Jones also took up the theme of Freud's 'splendid isolation' and the 'boycotting'[192] of his work by his colleagues, systematically blowing out of proportion the negative reviews of his works, while treating the several positive reviews that he cited as courageous 'exceptions': *Studies on Hysteria* hadn't been well received by the medical community,[193] *The Interpretation of Dreams* had been greeted with 'a most stupid and contemptuous review'[194] by Burckhardt, who had halted outright its sales in Vienna, and the *Three Essays on the Theory of Sexuality* along with the case history of 'Dora' had caused their author to be ostracised from his profession.

> **Jones:** *The Interpretation of Dreams* had been hailed as fantastic and ridiculous, but the *Three Essays* were shockingly wicked. Freud was a man with an evil and obscene mind ... At about the same time Freud filled his cup of turpitude in the eyes of the medical profession by ... deciding to publish a case history which is generally referred to as the 'Dora analysis' ... But his colleagues could not forgive the publication of such intimate details of a patient without her permission, and still more the imputing to a young girl tendencies towards revolting sexual perversions.[195]

Quite strangely, this rehashing of the puritanism which supposedly confronted the nascent psychoanalysis went hand in hand with Jones' launching of a new myth, that of *Freud's* puritanism. Freud, if we are to believe his biography, was an 'unusually chaste person – the word "puritanical" would not be out of place':[196] he was a father and family man with Victorian morals and he was an 'uxorious'[197] and 'quite peculiarly monogamous' husband,[198] who had very early on renounced all sexual activity,[199] while personally condemning the familiarities that his writings seemed to justify. Consideration of

Freud's correspondences is sufficient to repudiate this legend[200]– what is worth noting is that it corresponded with a dramatisation of the positivistic legend Freud had forged.

> **Jones:** To his own great surprise, and against his personal puritanical predilections, Freud was finding himself more and more compelled by the results of his investigations to attach importance to the sexual factors in aetiology ... It was no sudden discovery, and – in spite of what his opponents have suggested – it was quite unconnected with any preconceptions.[201]

The creation of psychoanalysis had thus been *literally* immaculate and asexualised. As Bruno Bettelheim noted in regard to the first two volumes of the biography, Jones paradoxically ended up shielding Freud from all psychoanalysis.

> **Bruno Bettelheim:** How unpsychoanalytic Jones, as biographer, can be is further illustrated by the way he disposes of what may have been one of Freud's most intimate relations. Speaking of Freud's sister-in-law, who, for forty-two years, was part of his household circle, Jones simply says, 'There was no sexual attraction on either side.' One must wonder about the man Freud who traveled for long periods alone with this mature woman, roomed in hotels with her, but did not find her sexually attractive; one wonders even more how it was possible for this woman not to become sexually attractive to Freud.[202]

Faithful lieutenant of the first Freud wars, Jones also revived the strategy of pathologisation mobilised by Freud against his adversaries with renewed vigour. Any person who had ever had the misfortune of being opposed to Freud at one point or another was systematically presented as a 'case', or else as having a personality deficiency: Fliess was a 'paranoiac', Meynert was 'highly neurotic',[203] Breuer had a 'weakness in his personality',[204] Stekel suffered from 'moral insanity'[205] and a 'troublesome neurotic complaint, the nature of which I need not mention',[206] Jung had a 'confused mind',[207] Morton Prince was 'rather stupid',[208] Ferenczi was 'haunted by a quite inordinate and insatiable longing for his father's love',[209] Adler was a 'cantankerous person ... constantly quarreling ... over points of priority in his ideas',[210] Rank had 'unmistakable neurotic tendencies',[211] Aschaffenburg and Vogt were subject to revealing Freudian slips,[212] Moll's 'vehemence' almost justified a 'libel action',[213] Joseph Collins was 'notorious for his proclivity to indecent jokes',[214] Oppenheim was affected by a 'severe anxiety condition' and his wife was a 'bad case of hysteria',[215] Friedländer was 'a doubtful personality with a shady past'[216] and Hoche was 'both a secret admirer and bitter enemy' of Freud's.[217] Even Dora was a 'disagreeable creature who consistently put revenge before love'.[218] All sorts of anecdotes were mobilised to ridicule opponents and trivialise their arguments, preventing them from being heard with their own voices. Thus Wilhelm Weygandt, at a psychiatry conference held in 1910 supposedly shouted, while hitting his fist against the table, that psychoanalysis ought to be tried in a courtroom; in 1908 and in 1909, two lectures given by Abraham had successively provoked a 'furious outburst' by Oppenheim and another 'angry outburst by Ziehen against these monstrous ideas';[219] Friedländer had threatened Freud with a lawsuit;[220] Raimann had criticised *The Interpretation of Dreams* without having even read the book;[221] Collins had protested to the American Neurological Association for allowing James Putnam to give a presentation full of 'pornographic stories about pure virgins'.[222]

> **Jones:** Freud lived in a period of time when the *odium* theologicum had been replaced by the *odium* sexicum ... In those days Freud and his followers were regarded not only as sexual perverts but as either obsessional or paranoiac psychopaths, and the combination was felt to be a real danger to the community ... No less than civilization was at stake. As happens in such circumstances, the panic aroused led in itself to the loss of that very restraint the opponents believed they were defending. All ideas of good manners, of tolerance and even a sense of decency – let alone any thought of objective discussion or investigation – simply went by the board.[223]

Jones received the assistance of Lilla Veszy-Wagner – an analyst in training being analysed by Balint[224] – who compiled and catalogued the contemporary literature of the period on psychoanalysis. It is clear, to judge from the abstracts which she had prepared for him,[225] that he systematically discarded all the nuanced assessments of Freudian theory (Warda, Gaupp, Möbius, Binswanger, Näcke, Stern), while holding onto only the most negative formulations – which were made even more so by detaching them from any context: Spielmeyer described psychoanalysis as 'mental masturbation',[226] Hoche claimed that it was 'an evil method born of mystical tendencies',[227] Rieger saw a 'simply gruesome old-wives' psychiatry',[228] etc. Thus reduced to an exchange of epithets, the intense scientific controversy that had taken place around psychoanalysis was trivialised to the point of sinking into total insignificance.

With most of the protagonists in the Freudian wars no longer around to defend themselves, Jones clearly had an easy go of it. Still, it was necessary to verify that all these people were definitely in cemeteries. In January 1955, just as the second volume of the biography was going to print, one of the lawyers for Hogarth Press, J. E. C. Macfarlane, sent Jones a list of around sixty 'defamatory passages'[229] that he insisted be removed or modified in order to protect the publishing house against future lawsuits. Since British libel law did not protect the dead, Jones could keep these passages as they were if he succeeded in establishing that the persons concerned were deceased. Adler, Rank, Ferenczi were no longer alive, but what about Oppenheim, Ziehen, Collins, Vogt, etc.? Jones had already asked Lilla Veszy-Wagner to research Freud's former adversaries.

> **Lilla Veszy-Wagner:** When writing Freud's biography, Jones carefully checked whether (and how many) of these bugbears were still alive. I had expressed doubts about the death of one individual, and in a letter to me dated December 13, 1954, Jones could scarcely conceal his pique when he wrote: 'I don't care when he died so long as I can be sure he is thoroughly dead now, since I am libeling him severely.'[230]

To Jones' delight, most of the slandered parties turned out to be dead and buried. Those who remained were spoilsports. With regret, Jones was forced to remove a note on Gezá Roheim, which was 'capable', said the lawyer, 'of an extremely uncomplimentary interpretation'.[231] It was also necessary to tone down certain passages on Helen Puner and Adler's biographer, Phyllis Bottome. Then there was Jung, about whom Jones had a long series of discussions with Peter Calvocoressi, one of the Hogarth Press directors.

> **Peter Calvocoressi to Jones, 17 February 1955**: We now come to the much more tricky subject of Jung. Broadly speaking, there are two serious allegations against Jung which cannot stand: that he was anti-Semitic and that when he and Freud parted company there was not merely a parting of the ways but also an element of disloyalty or turpitude in Jung's action . . . I have been through a great number of questionable references to Jung and must raise a dozen of these with you. If we can settle these principal items, then I think we can let the others go.[232]

Several of the passages that Calvocoressi advised removing concerned Jung's 'racial prejudice', his 'antagonistic attitude' towards Freud and finally his putative mental derangement.

> **Calvocoressi to Jones, 17 February 1955**: The expression: 'Jung is crazy' must come out. As I have already explained, the fact that this is Freud's remark does not make it less defamatory or make us less liable to an action.[233]

Jones, though, wasn't ready to sacrifice these passages which he held particularly dear, and he thus negotiated tooth and nail. And if 'Jung is cracked' was used in place of 'Jung is crazy', would this be more acceptable? 'National prejudice', instead of 'racial prejudice'? 'Disagreeable look', instead of 'sour look'? Finally, Jones offered to accept all financial responsibility for the costs of a future lawsuit.

> **Jones to Calvocoressi, 17 February 1955**: I am so completely convinced from all I know of Jung's personality and career that he would

be the last person to expose himself to the ridicule of a libel action that I feel like guaranteeing to pay the expense myself in such an extra-ordinarily unlikely eventuality.[234]

In the end, Hogarth Press accepted this proposal, which allowed Jones to keep certain contentious passages. As Jones had predicted, Jung did not pursue any legal action, and thus the claims about him entered the public domain without the slightest protest.

> **Jung to Jones, 19 December 1953**: Of course you have permission to read Freud's letters copies of which are in the Freud Archives ... it would have been advisable to consult me for certain facts. For example, you got the story of Freud's fainting attack quite wrong. It also was by no means the first one; he had such an attack before in 1909 previous to our departure for America in Bremen, and very much under the same psychological circumstances.[235]

> **E. A. Bennet, 15 September 1959**: C. G. [Jung] spoke of Ernest Jones and some of the inaccuracies in his biography of Freud ... When Jones was writing his book on Freud, he never asked him (C. G.) anything about the early years when he and Freud were working together. As Freud and Ferenczi were dead C. G. was the only person who could have given him accurate information, and he could easily have done so. Jones was not there, and there were a number of errors in his book.[236]

Jung was still alive, but this was not the case for Rank and Ferenczi, who could be easily assassinated post-mortem. Rank and Ferenczi, Jones recalled in the last volume of his biography, were both members of the famous Secret Committee created to defend psychoanalysis against doctrinal deviations (it was Ferenczi who had had the idea, even if Jones happily credited himself with its founding).

> **Jones:** Adherence to what psychoanalysis had revealed signifies the same as retaining one's insight into the workings of the unconscious, and the ability to do so presupposes a high degree of mental stability. My hope when founding the Committee naturally was that the six of us were suitably endowed for that purpose. It turned out, alas, that only

four of us were. Two of the members, Rank and Ferenczi, were not able to hold out to the end. Rank in a dramatic fashion presently to be described, and Ferenczi more gradually toward the end of his life, developed psychotic manifestations that revealed themselves in, among other ways, a turning away from Freud and his doctrines. The seed of a destructive psychosis, invisible for so long, at last germinated.[237]

On what basis did Jones make this impressive diagnosis? Had Rank and Ferenczi sunken into delirium? Had they been committed? Had they been hearing voices? Not at all: Ferenczi had died in 1933 of pernicious anaemia, while he was testing a new psychoanalytic technique ('neo-catharsis'), and Rank, after his break with Freud, had become a prolific author, while also developing a form of short therapy ('will therapy'). In reality, Jones once again made himself the mouthpiece for Freud's polemical diagnoses, which he nonchalantly presented as if they were proven facts.

It seems that Rank, who was extremely energetic, was also subject to bouts of despondency, this being the reason that Freud, in 1920, described him to Ferenczi as a 'periodical'[238] (that is, a person afflicted by manic-depression). It was this diagnosis, completely innocent to begin with, that Freud several years later seized upon during his dispute with Rank over the latter's arguments in *The Trauma of Birth*. Shortly after Rank temporarily renounced his heresies and confessed his Oedipal sins,[239] Freud wrote to Ferenczi that their colleague had emerged from a serious 'psychiatric state'[240] – and he stood by this diagnosis of manic-depressive psychosis once Rank definitively broke with him.

> **Freud to Eitingon, 13 April 1926:** The demon in him has now carried him along a slow tranquil path to the goal he tried to reach at first in a pathological attack . . . I confess I was very deceived in my prognosis of the case – a repetition of fate.[241]

> **Freud quoted by Joseph Wortis:** I can say one thing, because it is generally known: since leaving me, Rank has been having periodic

bits of depression, and in between, sort of manic phases – periods in which he does a great deal of work, and others in which he cannot do any at all.[242]

This is the ad hoc diagnosis that Jones revisited, which he thus transformed into the key for Rank's entire biography: if his personality had changed after the war, 'it must have been a hypomanic reaction to the three severe attacks of melancholia he had suffered while in Krakow';[243] if he had become authoritative and domineering in his relations with Jones, it was because a 'manic phase of his cyclothymia was gradually intensifying';[244] the 'hyperbolic' style of *The Trauma of Birth* 'accorded with the hypomanic phase through which Rank was then passing';[245] as for Freud, he had been mistaken in thinking that Rank's repudiation of his errors was definitive, because his 'present melancholic phase was again replaced by another manic one only six months later, with the usual oscillation in later years'.[246] Jones concluded his long chapter on Rank by insisting, 'we are not concerned here with Rank's further career'[247] – which was extremely opportunistic, since an attentive examination of this career would have made it abundantly clear that the 'mental trouble that wrecked Rank' and prevented him from leading a 'fruitful and productive life'[248] was a complete fabrication.

We can say much the same thing about the 'psychosis' Ferenczi supposedly suffered from at the end of his life. Here again, Freud was at the origin of this mean-spirited fiction. Irritated by Ferenczi's 'neo-cathartic' innovations, he had begun to suggest, during the autumn of 1932, that the latter's physical deterioration was also accompanied by a 'psychical and intellectual' deterioration.[249] In April of the following year, while Ferenczi struggled against death, Freud wrote to Max Eitingon that their friend had had a 'grave delusional outbreak'.[250] Five days after Ferenczi's death, he put the final nail in the coffin: the pernicious anaemia that had taken away his disciple was the 'organic expression' of delusions of persecution.

Freud to Jones, 29 May 1933: It is now easier to comprehend the slow process of destruction to which he fell victim. During the last two years it *expressed itself organically* in pernicious anemia, which soon led to severe motor disturbances ... Simultaneously a mental degeneration in the form of paranoia developed with uncanny logical consistency. Central to this was the conviction that I did not love him enough, did not want to acknowledge his work, and also that I had analyzed him badly. His technical innovations were connected with this ... These were indeed regressions to his childhood complexes.[251]

It was well known that, near the end of his life, Ferenczi had bitterly complained about Freud, and some of his students, like Izette de Forest and Clara Thompson, had noted Freud's hostile behaviour towards his ex-friend. In the biography, Jones assured his readers that there was absolutely nothing to this idle gossiping, though, he added, it was 'highly probable that Ferenczi himself in his final delusional state believed in and propagated elements of it'.[252]

Jones: [Ferenczi's] mental disturbance had been making rapid progress in the last few months ... Then there were the delusions about Freud's supposed hostility. Toward the end came violent paranoiac and even homicidal outbursts, which were followed by a sudden death on May 24 ... The lurking demons within, against whom Ferenczi had for years struggled with great distress and much success, conquered him at the end, and we learned from this painful experience once more how terrible their power can be.[253]

Outraged by this description of Ferenczi's last moments, the executor of his estate, Michael Balint, vigorously protested to Jones.

Michael Balint to Jones, 28 November 1957: I think what you say about him [Ferenczi] is in many ways out of true and misleading. This is especially so about what you say of his mental condition during his last period. I saw Ferenczi during the last months of his life on many occasions, once or twice every week, and I never found him deluded, paranoid or homicidal. On the contrary, though he was physically incapacitated by his ataxia, mentally most of the time he was quite fresh and often discussed with me the various details of his controversy with Freud and his plan to revise some of his ideas published in his last papers . . . I saw him on the Sunday before his death and though he was very weak, his mind even then was completely clear.[254]

Balint to Jones, 12 December 1957: As mentioned, I have received several letters from all over the world urging me to do something; the last being from Elma and Magda, Ferenczi's step-daughters, who are, as you know, the legal owners of the Freud–Ferenczi correspondence, asking me to get either a rectification by you or to withdraw the permission to use his correspondence.[255]

In his defence, Jones responded that he had received his information from an 'eyewitness' whom he did not wish to name. Balint, though, refused to accept this explanation.

Balint to Jones, 30 December 1957: Several people, among them Clara Thompson, Alice Lowell, Izette de Forest, and so on, have already written to me strongly criticising your description. If you now state that your description is based on the evidence of an eye witness, I am afraid all of them will come forward with their testimony, perhaps even challenging the trustworthiness of your witness . . . By the way, just to satisfy my curiosity, I would like very much to know who your eye witness was. I thought I knew practically all the people who had any contact with Ferenczi during his last weeks and I can't imagine which amongst them could get in touch with you and describe Ferenczi's state.[256]

Forced into a corner, Jones sent an evasive response; but his letter leaves little doubt as to the identity of this mysterious 'eyewitness'.

Jones to Balint, 16 December 1957: Freud himself was in no doubt at all that the changes of views [in Ferenczi] as well as his inexplicable estrangement were due to personal mental changes. It is true that I have come to accept this opinion also, but it did not come from me.[257]

Freud had thought so, therefore it was true. The Biography, as we see, was history as seen through the eyes of Freud, the 'eyewitness' of the unconscious: on the one hand, there were the colleagues, disciples and patients, literally blinded by their 'demons' and their resistances;

on the other, the serene self-analyst, capable of seeing what they themselves could not. Perfectly asymmetrical and partisan, Jones' biography described, quasi-cinematically, the unconscious of adversaries and turncoats *as if one were there*. History, in turn, became interprefaction. Under the guise of a historical account, the Biography provided Jones the occasion to take up his early battles on behalf of the Freudian cause, and settle scores with his (preferably dead) opponents.

> **Eric Fromm to Izette de Forest, 31 October 1957:** [This is a] typically Stalinist type of re-writing history, whereby Stalinists assassinate the character of opponents by calling them spies and traitors. The Freudians do it by calling them 'insane'.[258]

> **Frank Knopfelmacher:** It is all there: the miraculous purity of the Founding Personage, the preordained diabolism of Judas (Jung), dazzling vistas of humanity redeemed with apocalyptic visions of perdition and death ... The steadfast centre (Jones) fighting against the left deviationists (Glover), the right deviationists (Horney, Fromm), and against the unspeakable renegades whose deviations have led them on and on along the slippery path of treachery, until they ended up in the camp of the enemy (Adler, Jung). Yet somehow, nobody gets killed in all this – only character-assassinated. The psychoanalytic game seems to be a sort of unpolitical bolshevism without teeth.[259]

And then there is everything we do *not* find in the Biography's three thick volumes. We vainly search for the episode of Emma Eckstein's catastrophic 'nasal therapy' (there is only a mention, in passing, that she was one of the women with whom Freud maintained an intellectual relationship[260]). No mention of the unbelievable erotic-analytic triangle of Ferenczi, Gizella Pálos and her daughter Elma, to which Freud had played the role of family therapist.[261] Nothing about the analysis of Anna Freud by her own father.[262] Nothing about the suicides of Viktor Tausk and Herbert Silberer, which the analytic rumour attributed to their relationships with Freud.[263] Nothing about the murder of Hermine von Hug-Hellmuth, the pioneer of child psychoanalysis, by her nephew-patient; and nothing either about the fact that the so-called *A Young Girl's Diary*, which she had edited and Freud had glowingly prefaced, was in reality a complete fabrication.

> **Strachey to Jones, 3 March 1956:** By the way, can you give me any low down on the Halbwüchsige Mädchen [allusion to the German title of the *Diary*: *Tagebuch eines halbwüchsigen Mädchens*]? It always from the first seemed to me it must be a swindle. Was it, as I suppose, another example of Freud's simpleminded gullibility? (His letter to H.-H. [Hug-Hellmuth], which was used as the preface to the book, will come into Vol. XIV [of the *Standard Edition*], the metapsychol. [ogical] volume.)[264]

> **Jones to Strachey, 5 March 1956:** There was a lot of talk about the Halbwüchsige Mädchen after the war when Rank and Storfer made desperate efforts to check its authenticity.[265] Unfortunately H.H. was murdered just then and carried to the grave the secret of who the author was, which was never found out. My own impression is that the diary started by being genuine, but got touched up by either the author or H.H. Cyril Burt and others, I think William Stern in Germany, pointed out some chronological contradictions.[266]

Let's compare with the single mention of Hug-Hellmuth's *Journal* in the Biography.

> **Jones:** The anti-German prejudice was of course only part of the general opposition to psychoanalysis, and the years 1921–22 ... were particularly difficult ones for us in London ... Sir Stanley Unwin narrowly escaped a police prosecution for publishing the translation of a book issued by the [*Internationaler Psychoanalytischer*] *Verlag*, *A Young Girl's Diary*, which I had luckily refused to incorporate in our Library Series.[267]

The first volume of the Biography appeared in early autumn of 1953. Jones had worked feverishly to make sure it came out before the English translation of the letters to Fliess.

> **Jones to Bernfeld, 4 February 1952:** The Anfänge [Origins] translation will appear in both London and New York this autumn[268] and I am anxious to counteract in time any bad impression it may produce,

especially among the critics. I am therefore racing against time to get my Vol. I out first.[269]

The effect was immediate, exceeding all expectations. In New York City alone, 15,000 copies were sold in the first two weeks.[270] Everywhere, Jones' work was acclaimed, and the glory of Sigmund Freud immediately spread throughout the world: from London to Sydney, passing through Paris and Frankfurt. The Freudian legend had finally penetrated the masses.

> *Sunday Times*, 20 September 1953: Changes in the fundamental categories in terms of which we interpret the world and each other, in the very framework of our thought and language, are rare in history; and more rarely still can we attribute such a change to one man. Not to Newton certainly – for mechanism is mature in Galileo and Descartes; to Darwin and perhaps to Marx. But about Sigmund Freud, the inventor of psychoanalysis, there can be no doubt; the word 'inventor' can be used without any of the qualifications so common in the history of ideas.

> *Scotsman*, 8 October 1953: It is difficult to think of any scientific discoverer who so completely revolutionized the field in which he worked as Freud.

> *Manchester Guardian*, 9 October 1953: Dr. Ernest Jones has drawn the portrait of a man who deserves to be acclaimed, by general consent, among the greatest of any age, a man whose luminous mind shed light on the dark corners of human experience and whose extraordinary personal integrity . . . led him to a path of exploration from which the boldest had previously shrunk. He discovered a new continent of the mind and became its first cartographer.

> *World of Books*, November 1953: Sigmund Freud has certainly had more influence on our culture than any other mind of our own time – so much influence that it is quite incalculable.

> *Griffin*, December 1953: This is undoubtedly what gives Freud his place among the greatest thinkers of mankind, that he re-iterated,

after Lucretius and Rabelais and Swift and Nietzsche, that thought is conditioned; and that he was able to point to conditions we knew nothing of – for the good reason that we knew them too well and had them under masks.

It was much the same story after the publication of the second volume.

> **New York Post, 18 September 1955:** Sigmund Freud had no Newton before him. If the theory of relativity is said to be the greatest feat the human intellect achieved, it is difficult to find words for the attainment of Freud: because Freud also had no Max Planck, no Nernst, no Niels Bohr around him – nobody close to his own level of comprehension except the students whom he later taught.

> **Bournemouth Daily Echo, 21 October 1955:** Sigmund Freud must be bracketed with Karl Marx and Charles Darwin as one of the three most influential thinkers of modern time.

> **Standard, January–February 1955:** Today it is a commonplace that Freud's was one of the seminal minds of all times. As with Darwin and the theory of evolution, it is less significant that he was right or wrong about this or that detail or emphasis, than that he pointed the way. For the way he pointed is one which no conscientious student of human behavior will ever be able to ignore.

'Top secret'[271]

One of the very few individuals to adopt a more critical stance was Bruno Bettelheim. Bettelheim, a Viennese immigrant who was not part of the Freudian inner circle, pointed out multiple 'errors and omissions' in the biography of Jones – 'a man', he said, 'who is now old and whose personal participation and obvious partisanship have dimmed objectivity'.

> **Bettelheim:** Despite the deficiencies which must have been obvious to all sophisticated readers, the reviewers have outdone themselves in praise of this biography . . . This is not the definitive biography of Freud,

but it is definitely an official biography, presenting that picture of him which members of the Freud family and official psychoanalysis have accepted as definitive. What a splendid history of this great man could now be written if official psychoanalysis had not sealed the Freud archives with twenty-five hundred of his letters for fifty years![272]

Bettelheim appears to have been the first to put his finger on what should have immediately been apparent to the specialised critics: Jones, in his biography, relied on correspondences and documents that were not only unedited, but also *prohibited* to the public and other researchers. Indeed, no one could verify the accuracy of the facts he reported because the documents he had used were locked away in the 'Sigmund Freud Archives' at the Library of Congress in Washington, DC, for a period going well beyond the fifty years indicated by Bettelheim. Jones' advantage over the other historians was a result of this overwhelming fact: how could his version of events be drawn into question when he alone had had access to the archives of Freudianism? Thanks to the policy of retention practised by Anna Freud and the administrators of the Freud Archives, the Holy Scripture was, very literally, incontestable and irrefutable.

> **Anna Freud to Jones, 23 September 1952:** Only [the] appearance [of your book] will silence the self-appointed biographers since the difference in available material will become apparent. I shall certainly do what I can to discourage others, actually I do it all the time.[273]

> **Anna Freud to Jones, 25 November 1952:** I look forward to your book stopping all the impossible attempts at biography of my father which are in the air (and on paper) now.[274]

The idea of an archive that brought together all the documents of the Freudian family seems to have taken shape in July 1950, in close connection with the abridged edition of the letters to Fliess and the preparations for the 'true biography'. Bernfeld, who had just obtained archival documents on Freud's studies in Vienna, wrote to Anna

Freud, suggesting that they join their respective archives in a 'center of biographical documentation'.

> **Bernfeld to Anna Freud, 24 July 1950:** I would be curious to know if you intend to create a sort of center of biographical documentation. In other words, if you wish to add to the voluminous collections of letters, etc., that you already possess, the information that is currently in other hands.[275]

The idea rapidly took hold, because, in November of the same year, Kurt Eissler, in the name of Anna Freud, contacted Luther Evans, the Librarian of Congress, to inquire about the possibility of depositing the Freudian Archives at the American Library of Congress. One month later, Eissler informed Anna Freud that the articles of incorporation for the 'Sigmund Freud Archives', signed by Heinz Hartmann, Bertram Lewin, Ernst Kris, Herman Nunberg and himself, had been registered in the state of New York.

> **Eissler to Anna Freud, 23 December 1950:** I want to inform you of the progress of our efforts to create the Sigmund Freud Archives. We have submitted the statutes in preparation for setting up the Archives as a registered company in the state of New York, and a contract is going to be signed with the Library of Congress that will allow the Archives to deposit all the assembled documents in the Library's vaults. The board of directors will have the right to determine who can access the documents and at what date. Consequently, any possibility of indiscretion has been ruled out ... The person that you designate could then be Vice-President and become an important liaison between you and the Archives, while making the rest of us carry out all of your wishes concerning the Archives.[276]

At the same time, Eissler had written to Bernfeld to ask him for advice on the founding of such an archival centre. Bernfeld, in his response, drew up a list of various collections that he believed should be part of the archives: I. Freud's published works in every language (books, articles, interviews, witticisms and opinions expressed in public); II. Correspondences, manuscripts, personal journals, handwritten notes, annotated texts, personal papers; III. Photographs, portraits, films, family trees of the Freud, Nathanson and Bernays families, interviews with people who had known Freud; IV. Works of those (teachers, friends or associates) who had influenced Freud; V. Reviews of his works, as well as books, articles and pictures that had been approached psychoanalytically. Bernfeld also sketched out two types of possible operations, which he called 'type A' and 'type B'. According to 'type A', the Archives would limit themselves to colligating the documents and the testimonials in order to send them directly to the Library of Congress, where they would be 'accessible to certain people under certain conditions'.[277] According to 'type B', the Archives would be a genuine research centre managed by a curator, 'where the documents – under certain conditions – would be made accessible to certain people', with the exception of those that had been donated sealed, which would be deposited at the Library of Congress. As Bernfeld noted, 'type A' would cost practically nothing, since the administrative and archival expenses would be entirely covered by the American taxpayers, while 'type B' would require a substantial budget. Nevertheless, Bernfeld made it clear that he preferred 'type B', adding that he would be willing to serve as curator, despite the financial sacrifice it would mean for him. Then, in a postscript to which we have already alluded, he suggested the type of research that such a curator would engage in.

> **Bernfeld to Eissler, 4 January 1951:** There are dozens of things, such as: 'Did Freud personally meet Richard Avenarius?',[278] or 'What crimes were committed by his uncle Joseph, the brother of Jakob Freud? When was this? What was he sentenced to? What did he do afterwards?' Etc., etc.[279]

In his response, Eissler indicated that the decision had already been made to opt for a centre of 'type A' and that the documents assembled by the Archives would be sent directly to the Library of Congress, without any examination. Bernfeld, disappointed that his proposition had not been accepted, warned against the dangers of not processing the documents before depositing them at the Library of Congress.

> **Bernfeld to Eissler, 19 January 1951:** The plan you describe in your letter of 13 January naturally has my approval, since it conforms to one of the alternatives I suggested ... I don't like the idea of assembling letters and sending them unprocessed to the Library of Congress. I understand the advantages of this procedure. But I think that it should only be used as a last resort and it would be better not to make things easy for donors wishing to lock them up and bury them in Washington. I know enough about Freud as a letter writer to understand that many of his correspondents would prefer to keep secret some of his blunt remarks regarding them and their colleagues. It's mostly excessive sensitivity, but at times there is, in fact, food for devastating gossip ... If the Archives come to fruition, they are probably going to suck up all these documents and keep them sealed for an undetermined duration. And this is a point, in my opinion, that deserves serious reflection by the Directors of the Archives; they shouldn't begin to assemble the documents before deciding on a policy that reduces this danger.[280]

Involved as he was in his historical research, Bernfeld doesn't seem to have understood that what he perceived as a 'danger' was precisely the objective Anna Freud had conceived for the Archives. In this affair, Eissler, a young analyst trained by August Aichhorn, was simply an executor of Miss Freud's wishes – he had sent her a copy of Bernfeld's first letter and was awaiting her instructions.

> **Eissler to Anna Freud, 13 January 1951:** I hope that I am not committing an indiscretion in including a copy of the letter that Dr. Bernfeld wrote to me, insofar as I am sending it without having asked his permission ... It's clear in reading this letter that he would like to be the curator of the letters. I think that this is absolutely impossible since the Archives operate according to the principle of not favoring any publication and of handling everything personal with the greatest discretion. Of course, I could imagine that there may be among the letters certain ones that aren't of a personal nature and that essentially deal with Freud's scientific work, and undoubtedly the

question will eventually be to know the extent to which you and the future proprietors of the letters would be favorably disposed to a study of such letters by a reliable biographer. For that reason, it would be very important for me to know if you would prefer to have a contemporary analyst writing a biography of Freud or if the Archives should, from the start, adopt a policy of not making any documents available to anyone, not even those that contain no personal references.[281]

Anna Freud to Eissler, 27 January 1951: Frankly, I was appalled by his suggestions [those of Bernfeld]. They are extremely far from what I was envisaging for 'the Archives' and I think that it goes without saying for you as well. I find it difficult to imagine something more contrary to the life of my father, to his habits, to his conceptions and attitudes than this sort of detailed study of his biography . . . I believe it necessary to very clearly distinguish between 'the Archives' as a safe place and archives conceived as a way of assembling materials for a biography. The letters that I and, I suppose, the Princess [Marie Bonaparte] intended to deposit there would have gone there in order to *not* be used at this time by a biographer.[282]

Things couldn't be any clearer. Eissler, while also sending a copy of Bernfeld's second letter, thus assured Miss Freud that the Archives would be a tomb.

Eissler to Anna Freud, 4 February 1951: Following up on my indiscretion, I am sending you a copy of another letter from Bernfeld . . . I am sure that the majority of the letters will be given [to the Freud Archives] on the sole condition that no contemporary will be able to read them and you can be sure that I will not grant Bernfeld's demand 'not to make things easy for donors wishing to lock them up and bury them in Washington' . . . Of course, the personal letters will only have been read by the donor and will be sent sealed to the representative of the Archives, which will not have the right to open the letter and which will send it sealed to the Library of Congress, where it will remain sealed for as long as the donor or the board of directors stipulate. *Broadly speaking, the board of directors will stipulate a longer duration than the donor has intended,* in order to prevent any possibility of an embarrassing situation in the future.[283]

Henceforth, Bernfeld's fate within the movement's inner circle was sealed. On 28 March, Eissler, somewhat ashamed, told Anna Freud that he had met Bernfeld in New York and that the latter had expressed his surprise that Anna, as she had formerly done, no longer responded to his letters and requests for information.[284] Bernfeld had clearly fallen into disfavour; now, his rival Jones was going to have access to the treasures of House of Freud.

On 16 February, Eissler announced to Anna Freud the formation of the Sigmund Freud Archives, Inc.'s board of directors, which included, among others, Bertram Lewin (President), Ernest Jones, Heinz Hartmann, Willi Hoffer, Princess Marie Bonaparte (Vice-Presidents), Ernst Kris, Herman Nunberg and Siegfried Bernfeld (members). Albert Einstein, Thomas Mann and Anna Freud were honorary members. Eissler himself settled for the more modest position of 'Secretary'. Anna Freud was delighted.

> **Anna Freud to Eissler, 27 February 1951:** This wonderful list contains so many of our old friends that this alone should guarantee that all goes well as far as our future plans are concerned.[285]

The goal of the Freud Archives had never been to make the documents of Freudianism available to the public, as Luther Evans, the Librarian of Congress, undoubtedly believed when Eissler approached him. In reality, the Library of Congress and the American people had been duped. What Anna Freud and the Freudian Family sought, quite simply, was a safety deposit box where they could lock up the archives, *their* archives, and protect them from the curiosity of outsiders. If their choice was the Library of Congress, it was because the American government and its legendary bureaucracy presented, in this respect, extremely solid guarantees of reliability and security. Not to mention the fact that the costs of archiving and safekeeping the materials were entirely thrust upon the American taxpayers: as Bernfeld had said, a 'type A' Archives wouldn't cost a dime. Better yet, donations to the Library of Congress were tax-deductible, making for an excellent business, insofar as the 'expert' designated to appraise their value for the American Internal Revenue Service was none other than ... Kurt Eissler.[286]

Paul Roazen: Eissler went around and suggested to all the people concerned that they could get tax deductions on what they donated to the Freud archives. A good deal for everybody, right? It was a wholly crooked set-up. The gifts were made to the Freud Archives, then Eissler, as head of Freud Archives, gave them to the Library of Congress. The archives was a conduit. The documents are housed at the Library of Congress at taxpayers' expense, but the Library of Congress has to turn to the Freud Archives before they can release anything.[287]

M. B-J: So it is a situation in which the Freud Archives use taxpayers' money to pursue its own goals, without being accountable to anybody?

Roazen: Yes. Thanks to this setup, everything went through Eissler's hands and is now under the Freud Archives' control. For instance, Eissler went around and conducted interviews with anyone who would see him, only to lock up these tapes at the Library of Congress. At the same time, there have always been exceptions to this policy of secrecy. For instance, Eissler would send some of the material to Jones – which is how I was able to read it in the Jones files, before those were restricted in their turn.[288]

But it wasn't simply the American taxpayers who were taken advantage of, but also, in many cases, the donors themselves. Even though certain donors were obviously in on the secret, many others undoubtedly believed that they were making a gift of their archives to a public entity, the Library of Congress, considering that the Library's current 'Freud Collection' was initially called 'The Sigmund Freud Archives'. As article 2 of the contract signed on 5 July 1951 between the Sigmund Freud Archives, Inc. and the Library of Congress, the latter promised to 'protect [the] identity [of the donations] by marking the name "The Sigmund Freud Archives" on all the publications and on the cartons containing other documents, and [to] administer these donations under the title "The Sigmund Freud Archives"'.[289] It must have been difficult, therefore, for the donors to distinguish between the 'Sigmund Freud Archives' of the Library of Congress and the 'Sigmund Freud Archives, Inc.' – all the more so since the paper in front of them proudly stated: 'Conservator of the Archives: the Library of Congress' (later changed to 'Guardian and Proprietor of the Sigmund Freud Collection: the Library of Congress').

In reality, the donations were being made *to the Sigmund Freud Archives, Inc.*, a private organisation which then became their legal owner and could thus impose any restrictions on access that it wished from the moment they were deposited at the Library of Congress (in the catalogues, we still read: 'Donor: Sigmund Freud Archives' or 'Donor: Kurt Eissler'). In regard to this, Peter Swales speaks of 'donor impostership',[290] insofar as Eissler was to have deliberately maintained the ambiguity surrounding the donations' actual destination. It is hard to prove such an intention to mislead; nevertheless, the ambiguity Swales is concerned with is quite real, and we can find many examples of it. To the British psychiatrist E. A. Bennet, who in 1972 asked if the Freud Archives would be interested in two letters that Freud had addressed to him, Eissler nonchalantly responded that it depended on the Library of Congress.

> **Eissler:** Of course, we take in all the documents ... The original or a photostat is deposited in the Library of Congress. *The Archives are not independent*, everything goes to the Library of Congress in Washington.[291]

To the donors, then, the Archives passed themselves off as representatives of the Library of Congress and of the American people, in order, as Bernfeld said, to 'suck up' the documents and testimonials. To the Library of Congress, on the other hand, they passed themselves off as the representatives of donors and medical confidentiality, imposing restrictions on access, as well as arbitrary declassification dates, which the donors themselves had not often demanded.

Marvin W. Kranz, Supervisor of the Freud Collection at the Library of Congress: In certain cases, we know that the [original] donor imposed restrictions on access ... As a general rule, the documents were given to Eissler [and] he imposed restrictions. Presumably, he would say to the person: 'We are going to classify that for a period of twenty-five, fifty years, okay?' and the person would say yes. We don't know how exactly it worked, but in my opinion, it was Eissler who suggested the restrictions.[292]

Eissler, Notes on His First Interview with Sergius Pankejeff in Vienna, 1952: He always has the idea that his Memoirs could be published and is rather disappointed, that this material will first be read by others in 200 years.[293]

Eissler to the Pastor Oskar Pfister, 20 December 1951: When your report is opened in 150 years, I believe that it will no longer be able to cause even the slightest indiscretion.[294]

Eissler, Interview with Carl Gustav Jung, 29 August 1953: I believe that the historical development of depth psychology will at one time have a great interest, and your relation to Freud, your observations of Freud whom you knew in such an important phase, in such an important epoch, will very much interest historians, if there are still historians in 200 years /laughs/.[295]

Eissler to Bonaparte, 1 April 1960: At The Library of Congress you would only see a row of boxes which concern The Sigmund Freud Archives. The boxes are filled with sealed envelopes and, since we have an agreement with The Library of Congress that the envelopes may be opened only after many years they would not be permitted to show you anything of their contents ... if you plan to visit The Library of Congress solely out of your desire to see The Sigmund Freud Archives, I would strongly advise against it because, as I have said before, there is nothing to see other than a row of boxes.[296]

Yes, the Freud Archives were very much a tomb, a crypt, where, as Bernfeld said, the radioactive waste of psychoanalysis' history could be 'buried'. Therefore, as we see with the X (formerly Z) series of the Sigmund Freud Collection, the slow process of declassification (we are almost tempted to say: of decontamination) only began in 1995, with the correspondence between Freud and Max Eitingon, and will continue for the most part until 2057, when Eissler's inteviews with Elsa Foges, Harry Freud, Oliver Freud, Judith Bernays Heller,[297] Clarence Oberndorf, Edoardo Weiss and the mysterious 'Interviewee B' are due to be released. In the 1990s one letter to Freud from an unidentified correspondent was restricted till 2113 (and not 2102, as the 1985 catalogue anticipated[298]). Now, many such items do not even have a stipulated derestriction date, and are listed simply as 'closed'.

> **Sulloway:** Just think of the secrecy associated with the documents of the Freud Archives at the Library of Congress and the oddity of their dates of release. Some documents are sealed away until 2013, others until 2032, others until 2102, 2103, etc., and you wonder how they came up with these strange dates. If you look up the birth and death dates of the persons concerned, you are almost tempted to apply Fliessian periodicities of 23 and 28 to see what these numbers mean, because it is not 100 or 150 years from anybody's death, it's not 150 or 200 years from anybody's birth – it's just some weird number that someone thought up! It is totally arbitrary, but that is how censorship has always worked.[299]

In certain cases, the restrictions on access have been imposed *despite* the wishes expressed by the donors. As Peter Swales has noted, Eissler's interview with Freud's granddaughter, Sophie Freud, will not be available until the year 2017, even though she has declared herself, on several occasions, in favour of a complete and immediate opening of the Archives. Paul Roazen, likewise, relates how Eissler refused to let the psychoanalyst Helene Deutsch take a look at *her own donation* when she had wished to show it to Roazen.

> **Roazen:** I wrote a letter to the Freud Archives, which Helene co-signed, in which I requested to have access to this material. The letter that I got back was not signed by Eissler himself, but by Edward Kronold, who was technically head of the Freud Archives at the time. He didn't actually deny our request, he just said that they would postpone their decision till the next meeting of their board of

directors . . . This was totally absurd, of course, for what we were asking for was perfectly obvious and straightforward.[300]

Roazen: During my own research on Freud and his circle, I met numerous donors who were not only completely unaware that their donation was now locked away, but who also clearly disapproved of the secrecy Eissler was determined to maintain around Freud in order to protect him from the curiosity of independent historians.[301]

Eissler to Borch-Jacobsen, 13 November 1996: Doctor P[ankejeff] wanted the recordings of our conversations to be published while he was alive. I refused.[302]

The Freud Archives, obviously, do not represent the wishes of their donors, contrary to what they made the Library of Congress and the public believe. In reality, they only represent themselves, which is to say, the interests of the Freudian Family and Cause. And these interests have never coincided with those of the public interest, of the *res publica*. The function of the Archives has never been one of openness and publication, but rather one of selection and censorship: controlling access to the documents, filtering information, monitoring interpretation and debate, and, above all, stopping material passing unrestricted into the public domain. Nothing could be further from the democratic ideal of 'free and open access to knowledge and information'[303] that guides the Library of Congress. Kurt Eissler spent his life amassing archives and testimonials, not in order to share them and reveal their contents, not even to preserve them for future generations, but with the single goal of being able to determine who would have access to what – all this in the interests of a private society: the true Freudians.

There was, in the end, a method in this madness. If Eissler censored anything and everything, it wasn't because there was something to hide – some skeletons in the closet or compromising photos. It was because the Archives, despite the portions open to the public, had never been intended for the public. Anna Freud perhaps said it best: these documents are going to be deposited at the Library of Congress 'in order to not be used by a biographer'. Meaning: by a non-accredited, non-authorised biographer, since, for the historians in the Freudian family, it was never a question of hiding anything from them. At the same time that Anna Freud was locking up the Archives and refusing Bernfeld access to it because he was judged to be too independent, Jones was allowed wide access, aiding him with his work on the Biography. He certainly wasn't going to be the one to contradict the version of events Freud had put down in his writings, whether in his case histories or his historical-autobiographical presentations of psychoanalysis.

Above all, what mattered was preserving psychoanalysis' narrative monopoly, preventing any other accounts from entering into competition with Freud's, and dissuading all rival interpretations. In this sense, the censorship of the Archives must be understood in relation to the concurrent promotion of the Freudian legend. If it was necessary to establish a sanitary cordon around the 'Wolf Man', seal the testimony of the children of 'Cäcilie M.' or 'Elisabeth von R.', and censor the patients' names, it wasn't necessarily because all these people had explosive secrets to reveal, but because their accounts ran the risk, first, of differing from Freud's and, second, of making them less certain, and more open to disputation. Subjected to comparison and debate, Freud's interprefactions would no longer be able to present themselves as the transparent and indisputable narration of 'facts', 'discoveries' and 'observations'.

From this point of view, the censorship of the Freud Archives is by no means an arbitrary absurdity with no wider import. Explaining it away by means of Anna Freud's excessive filial piety or Eissler's lovable eccentricity[304] is decidedly too simple. Eissler executed the orders of Anna Freud, and Anna Freud continued a policy of dehistoricisation and narrative decontextualisation which had been her father's – as, for example, when he burned his correspondences or destroyed his analysis notes. The important thing was to keep everyone else's hands off the Freudian narrative and to rid it of all the parasitic 'noises' liable to cloud its message, in order to immunise Freud's testimony – which is to say psychoanalytic theory – against all doubts and questions. Without this excessive dehistoricisation, psychoanalysis would never have succeeded in establishing itself as the Holy Scripture of psycho-therapy, nor Freud as the Solitary Hero of the unconscious. The Archives' censorship, so absurd at first glance, is absolutely essential to the system it and psychoanalysis' legendary epistemology together constitute. It's not surprising that the Freudians have considered the work of historians of their discipline among their most serious adver-saries: psychoanalysis is vulnerable to its history.

Coda: what was psychoanalysis?

The fashion this winter is psychoanalysis.

André Breton (1990 [1924]), 94

Freudian psychology had flooded the field like a full rising tide and the rest of us were left submerged like clams buried in the sands at low water.

Morton Prince (1929), ix

I know of no other example of a system of unjustified beliefs which has propagated itself so successfully as Freudian theory. How was it done?

Alasdair MacIntyre (1976), 35

The censorship of Freud's correspondences, the sequestering of documents and reminiscences in sealed boxes in the Freud Archives, the compilation of the official Freud biography and the preparation of the *Standard Edition of the Complete Psychological Works of Sigmund Freud* was a systematic and concerted enterprise, intended to consolidate and disseminate the Freudian legend. The legend was now everywhere, massive and virtually unassailable. Texts available to researchers and the general public had been carefully filtered and reformatted to present the image of Freud and psychoanalysis that the Freudian establishment wanted to promote. Thus it is no surprise that the apotheosis of psychoanalysis took place in the 1950s, and that it was from America and Britain, the new centres of the psychoanalytic family, that the Freudian wave spread through the world.

For half a century, this artificial construction has formed the basis of our knowledge of Freud and the origins of psychoanalysis. It is striking to see how widely it was accepted, even by those who otherwise had a critical and sceptical view of psychoanalysis. Even when Freud's works were reread and reinterpreted in heterodox ways, it was always on the basis of the sanitised and dehistoricised version propagated by Anna Freud, Ernst Kris, Ernest Jones, James Strachey and Kurt Eissler. Lacan's famous 'return to Freud' was simply a return to the version of Freud that they had canonised. The same goes for all the more recent hermeneutic, structuralist, narrativist, deconstructivist, feminist and post-modern reformulations of psychoanalysis. Despite their sophistication and their refusal of Freud's positivism, the Freud which they interpreted/deconstructed/narritivised/fictionalised was always the same legendary Freud, dressed up in the new garments of the latest intellectual fashion.

The success of this propaganda mission rested on its invisibility, on the dissimulation of the 'Kürzungsarbeit': cuts in letters weren't indicated, inconvenient facts were omitted, skeletons were hidden in closets, critics were silenced, the names of patients were disguised, recollections were sequestered, tendentious interpretations were presented as real events, calumnies and rumours were taken as facts. The mythification of the history of psychoanalysis gave it a simplicity which rendered it suitable for mass dissemination. At the same time, the formidable obstacles which confronted historians rendered a wholesale challenge of the legend impossible.

The consequences of this state of affairs went far beyond the confines of the history of psychoanalysis and had profound effects on the way the enterprise of modern psychology as a whole was perceived. The legend effectively delegitimated the psychotherapies which psychoanalysis competed with in the mental health market place. At the same time it led to the rescripting of the history of ideas in the twentieth century, giving psychoanalysis a prominence that it never properly had. To the extent to which psychoanalysis was placed at the centre and the origin of the critical developments in depth psychology, dynamic psychiatry and psychotherapy, psychoanalysis became everything – and at the same time nothing. All clothing suited it, because it all bore the label 'Freud'. Already in 1920, Ernest Jones noted that the public only had the vaguest ideas of what psychoanalysis really was, and what distinguished it from other approaches.

> **Jones to the Secret Committee, 26 October 1920:** From various recent reports I have had from America and from reading their recent literature I am sorry to say that I get a very bad impression of [the] situation there. Everything possible passes under the name of $\Psi\alpha$, not only Adlerism and Jungism, but any kind of popular or intuitive psychology. I doubt if there are six men in America who could tell the essential difference between Vienna and Zurich, at least at all clearly.[1]

Ninety years later, the situation has hardly changed: 'any kind of popular or intuitive psychology' is precisely what passes for psychoanalysis, whether it be in university seminars, specialist journals and magazines, or on television or the radio. However, it is precisely this confusion and the manner in which Freudians successfully exploited it to promote 'psychoanalysis' that significantly contributed to the success of the brand. If it appears to be everywhere, it is because so much has been arbitrarily Freudianised, franchised by psychoanalysis: slips, dreams, sex, mental illness, neurosis, psychotherapy, memory, biography, history, language, pedagogy and teaching, marital relations, politics.

> **John Burnham:** In the United States Freud became the agent not so much of psychoanalysis as of other ideas current at the time. Psychoanalysis was understood as environmentalism, as sexology, as a theory of psychogenic etiology of the neuroses. Likewise when Freud's teachings gained attention and even adherents, his followers often

believed not so much in his work as in evolution, in psychotherapy, and in the modern world.[2]

But if psychoanalysis is everything and nothing at the same time, what are we ultimately speaking about? *Nothing* – or nearly nothing: it is precisely because it has always been vague and floating, perfectly inconsistent, that psychoanalysis could propagate as it did and embed itself in a variety of 'ecological niches', to use Ian Hacking's expression, in the most diverse array of environments.[3] Being nothing in particular, psychoanalysis has functioned like Lévi-Strauss' famous 'floating signifier':[4] it is a 'machine', a 'whatsit', a 'thingumajig' which can serve to designate anything, an empty theory in which one can cram whatever one likes. To take an example, Freud's unilateral insistence on the pre-eminence of sexuality was objected to from all sides. No matter, he then developed his theory of narcissism and the analysis of the ego, silently borrowing from some of his critics, Adler and Jung. The traumatic neuroses of the First World War appeared to have conclusively demonstrated that one could suffer from hysterical symptoms for non-sexual reasons. Freud then came up with the theories of the repetition compulsion and the death drive from the ever ready unconscious. Such radical theoretical shifts have often been cited in praise of Freud's conscientious empiricism, but this is to confound falsificationist rigour with damage limitation. No 'fact' was likely to refute Freud's theories, as he could adapt them to objections made to him, according to the exigencies of the moment, in continual shadow-boxing with his critics.

D. H. Lawrence, 1923: Psychoanalysis has sprung many surprises on us, performed more than one volte-face before our indignant eyes. No sooner had we got used to the psychiatric quack who vehemently demonstrated the serpent of sex coiled round the root of all our actions, no sooner had we begun to feel honestly uneasy about our lurking complexes, than lo and behold the psychoanalytic gentlemen reappeared on the stage with a theory of pure psychology. The medical faculty, which was on hot bricks over the therapeutic innovations, heaved a sigh of relief as it watched the ground warming under the feet of the professional psychologists.[5]

Frank Cioffi: Sometime about 1912 Freud felt that Adler was attempting to disarm criticism of his 'masculine protest' by representing it as a corollary of Freud's own apparently well-established castration complex. How did Freud deal with this embarrassment? This is how: 'I find it impossible to base the genesis of neuroses on so narrow a foundation as the castration complex... I know of cases of neurosis in which the castration complex plays no pathogenic part or does not appear at all' (1914, SE 14, pp. 974–93). And yet once Adler had been seen off the castration complex was reinstated to its position of centrality and Freud became amnesic for the fact that he had treated patients in which the 'castration complex play[ed] no pathogenic part.' In an essay of 1928 he assures readers with respect to the influence of the castration complex: 'Psychoanalytic experience has put these matters in particular beyond the reach of doubt and has taught us to recognize in them the key to every neuroses' (1928, SE 21, p. 184).[6]

Jones' statement cited earlier suggests that he believed that there was something radically distinctive about psychoanalysis that enabled it to be rigorously distinguished from Jung's or Adler's work and all other forms of 'popular psychology'. But what held psychoanalysis together – both theoretically and institutionally – was a legend, and it was this that constituted its very identity. In reality, as we have seen, psychoanalysis was riven from its inception by contradictory interpretations as to what psychological analysis/psychoanalysis/psychanalysis/psychosynthesis/free psychoanalysis/individual psychology/ analytical psychology were, and to wherein they differed. This situation has not ceased. Fundamentally, it has not been possible to demonstrate the properly 'Freudian unconscious' in a manner convincing to all. After the ruptures with Fliess, Forel, Bleuler, Adler, Stekel and Jung, there were those with Rank, Ferenczi and many others. Within the movement itself, divergent tendencies and schools multiplied, while views initially championed by dissidents and critiques of psychoanalysis were silently recuperated and presented as 'developments' of psychoanalysis, as progress.[7] Under such conditions, how can one continue to speak of 'psychoanalysis', as if it were a matter of a coherent doctrine, organised around a series of clearly articulated theses, principles or methods? Psychoanalysis in the singular never existed. What is there in common between Freud's theories and those of Rank, Ferenczi, Reich, Klein, Horney, Winnicott, Bion, Bowlby, Kohut, Kernberg, Lacan, Laplanche, Zizek or Kristeva? Even psychoanalysts have recognised that psychoanalysis has become an umbrella term covering the most diverse and mutually contradictory perspectives. In 1988, Robert Wallerstein, then president of the International Psychoanalytic Association, asked with disquiet whether there was still *one* psychoanalysis, after the multitude of post-Freudian developments and the failure of several initiatives to create a consensus within American psychoanalysis in the 1950s.

> **Robert Wallerstein:** We live in a world of increasing psychoanalytic diversity, of many (and differing) psychoanalyses, which then – with their boundaries then drawable in conceptually differing ways – of course makes more difficult any clear overall distinction of psychoanalysis from psychotherapy.[8]

Whilst conceding that the theories of psychoanalytic metapsychology were finally nothing other than 'articles of psychoanalytic faith', Wallerstein nevertheless claimed that the Freudian field continued to present a unity at the level of clinical theory and the givens of the consulting room.[9] However, his definition of the psychoanalytic clinic was so expansive and vague that it could be applied to many other forms of dynamic psychotherapy.

To highlight this diversity is not to evaluate or criticise the plethora of diverse practices and conceptions which have been associated with the label 'psychoanalysis', nor is it to cast doubt on the fact that many have found something in these which have facilitated their lives (the same goes for other forms of psychotherapy). A recognition of the heterogeneity of the field signals that each form of psychoanalysis or psychodynamic therapy needs to be adequately characterised and separately evaluated. Similarly, critiquing the positivistic scientific pretensions of psychoanalysis does not invalidate it (to take this view would simply be to partake of the same positivism from the opposite side) but indicates that different forms of evaluation – philosophical, ethical, political and aesthetic – come into play. But such an undertaking is not our present brief, and would require a wider comparative historical study of the wider field of the psychotherapies and dynamic psychologies.

The truth is that the unity of psychoanalysis was provided by the institutional allegiance to the Freudian legend, that is to say to the notion that Freud's creation of psychoanalysis was an unprecedented event that revolutionised human understanding. Psychoanalysis maintained itself to the extent to which this legend held. Without the legend, its disciplinary identity and radical difference from other forms of psychotherapy collapse. This is precisely what we witness today: the legend is losing its hold, fraying from all sides. Despite delaying tactics, primary materials have been entering the public sphere: correspondences have been re-edited without censorship, archival collections have been declassified (even if on a drip feed), historians have identified patients, documents and recollections have resurfaced. Little by little, the puzzle is being reconstituted, forming portraits quite different from that fashioned by the censors and hagiographers. This is not to say that there is a consensus among historians – it is simply to note that the cumulative effect of their work has been to dismantle the monomyth. Today defenders of the legend have vigorously protested this, at times resorting to the old tactics which once served so well in the first Freudian wars (the pathologisation of adversaries, *ad hominem* attacks, etc.), but without the same success. Readers approaching Freud simply have a wealth of documentation and critical historical studies which simply wasn't available in the 1970s and 1980s, together with an increasing number of studies which have demonstrated that Freud's professional rivals, adversaries and former colleagues weren't all the fools they were painted to be.

Thus there is little point in searching to 'kill' Freud, as some have done, or starting another 'Freud war', which in all likelihood would add little to its antecedents.[10] Ironically, this would only serve to continue to give life and identity to psychoanalysis, whereas one could say that psychoanalysis, in a certain sense, no longer exists – or rather, never did.[11] The Freudian legend is being effaced before our eyes, and with it, psychoanalysis, to make way for other cultural fashions, other modes of therapeutic interaction, continuing and renewing the ancient ritual of patient–doctor encounter. We should hurry to study Psychoanalysis whilst we can,[12] for we will soon no longer be able to discern its features – and for good reason: because it never was.

Notes

ACKNOWLEDGEMENTS

1. Some extracts were published in Meyer (2005), and two interviews were reproduced in Dusfresne (2007).

INTRODUCTION

1. Freud (1916–17), 284–5. The same idea is more fully developed in Freud (1917a), 140.
2. Kant (1787), 21: 'Thus far it has been presumed that all our cognition must conform to objects . . . Let us, therefore try to find out by experiment whether we shall not make better progress in the problems of metaphysics if we assume that objects must conform to our cognition . . . The situation here is precisely the same as was that of *Copernicus* when he first thought of explaining the motions of celestial bodies. Having found it difficult to make progress there when he assumed that the entire host of stars revolved around the spectator, he tried to find out by experiment whether he might not be more successful if he had the spectator revolve and the stars remain at rest.'
3. Cited by Porter (1986), 291.
4. Cohen (1976); Porter (1986).
5. Brentano (1874), 2.
6. Flournoy (1896), 1.
7. Stengers (1992).
8. Freud (1933), 159.
9. McIntyre (1958), 2.
10. James (1999), 53.
11. James (1892), 468.
12. Stern (1900), 415.

13. Flournoy (1903b). Flournoy republished this in his 1911 book, *Esprits et médiums*, a copy of which is to be found, not insignificantly, in Freud's library. This passage is found on page 266.
14. Hall (1909), cited in Shakow and Rappaport (1968), 67.
15. Gesell (1912), 20.
16. Hall (1923), 360. In 1923, Hall wrote to Freud, 'in fact history will show that you have done for us a service which you are not at all extravagant in comparing with that of Darwin for biology'. In John Burnham (1960), 313.
17. Jung (1907), 3–4.
18. Sigmund Freud Collection, Manuscript Division, Library of Congress, Washington, DC; cited in Alexander and Selesnick (1965), 5.
19. Eder (1913), 1.
20. Jones (1913), xii; (1957), 345.
21. Jones (1918), 256.
22. Sulloway (1992a), 484. See Jones to Freud, 15 January 1931, in which he revealed that Huxley was 'the chief hero of my youth. As you doubtless know, he was nicknamed "Darwin's bulldog," and you would perhaps agree that my identification with him has not been entirely fruitless' (Freud and Jones 1993, 682).
23. McDougall (1936), 149.
24. Hoche (1910), 1009.
25. Weygandt (1907), 302.
26. Freud (1914a), 43. Columbus was added by Freud in 1924 in the second edition of this text. For Ferenczi's likening of Freud to Columbus, see below, p. 80.
27. Wohlgemuth (1923), 227–8.
28. Freud (1916–17), 20.
29. Freud (1926a), 190–1.
30. Assoun (1981), 191ff.
31. Haeckel (1876), vol. 1, 38–9. As pointed out by Assoun (1981), 198 and 205, Haeckel did not differentiate between Lamarck and Darwin.
32. Haeckel (1876), vol. 2, 264.
33. Haeckel (1920), 19.
34. Huxley (1926), cited in Ellenberger (1970a), 252, n. 139.
35. Du Bois-Raymond (1883), 500.
36. Haeckel (1920), 66.
37. Haeckel (1902), 288–9.
38. Freud and Abraham (2002), 344–5.
39. Freud and Abraham (2002), 346.
40. *The Lancet*, 231 (1938), 1341.
41. Gould (1989), 44.
42. Ellenberger (1973), 54.
43. Freud (1914a), 22.
44. Sulloway (1992a), 489–95.

45. Strachey (1976), 23–4.
46. Strachey, in Freud (1953–74), vol. 1, 257.
47. Jones (1956), 122–3.
48. Schwartz (1999), 40. It seems that, for Schwartz, the history of humanity before Freud was one long aphasia.
49. Grubrich-Simitis (1997), 25.
50. Lacan (2005), 334.
51. *Ibid.*, 429–30.
52. Ricoeur (1974), 172.
53. Kuhn (1970), 4.
54. On the notion of the 'black box', see the introductory chapter of Latour (1987).
55. Blum and Pacella (1995), 105.
56. Bloor (1976).
57. For a useful overview, see Golinski (1998).
58. See for example the corrections of Jung (1925), 16, and Janet (1919), vol. 2, 215ff.
59. Janet (1919).
60. In the following, we propose to reopen the controversies which surrounded psychoanalysis from the beginning. We do not necessarily subscribe to the positions advanced by Freud on the one hand nor his critics on the other, which are at times as problematic as his. To find cogency in the criticisms of psychoanalysis by figures such as Gustav Aschaffenburg, Eugen Bleuler, Alfred Hoche, August Forel, Pierre Janet, C.G. Jung, Emil Kraepelin or William McDougall does not imply that one accepts their diverse positions on psychiatry, psychology and psychotherapy. Similarly, in the contemporary context, criticising psychoanalysis does not mean that one is in favour of psychotropic medication or against psychotherapy.
61. Ellenberger (1973), 54. The notebooks of this research are at the Centre Henri Ellenberger, Hôpital Sainte-Anne, Paris; see also Ellenberger (1970a), xiv.
62. Ellenberger (1970b), 27–8.
63. Ellenberger (1961).
64. 'Individual legends – elements', typed notes, Centre Henri Ellenberger, Hôpital Sainte-Anne, Paris.
65. Zilboorg (1941); Wyss (1961); Veith (1965).
66. Ellenberger (1970a), 548.
67. 'The uncertainties of psychoanalysis', typed notes, Centre Henri Ellenberger, Hôpital Sainte-Anne, Paris. See also 'Chapitre VII Freud Conclusion', manuscript notes, *ibid.*: 'That which Freud introduced ... return to the system of the antique "sect" ... the most intimate initiation, considerable sacrifices of money, communal doctrine, cult of the Founder.'
68. Sulloway (1992a).
69. Interview with Frank J. Sulloway, Cambridge, MA, 19 November 1994.

70. *Ibid.*
71. Campbell (1968).
72. Freud (1939), 139.
73. Ellenberger (1973), 56.
74. Interview with Frank J. Sulloway, Cambridge, MA, 19 November 1994.
75. This term seems to have been used for the first time in Freud studies by Sulloway (1992a), xvii. It is important not to confound it with 'revisionism' in the Marxist sense, or even less with the 'revisionism' of Holocaust deniers.
76. Cioffi (1974); (1984). John Forrester (1980) also showed the gap of more than a decade between Freud's comments on the significance of the Oedipus tragedy and its elevation into the core complex of the neuroses, the Oedipus Complex (in the meantime borrowing the term 'complex' from Jung).
77. Lothane (1989), 215; Spector (1972), 58.
78. Mahony (1986), 69, 81, 215; (1996), 8–9, 55–6, 139–40; Anthony Stadlen cited by Macmillan (1997), 640.
79. Israëls and Schatzman (1992) and Mahoney (1992b).
80. Bernfeld (1946); Swales (1982b); Skues (2001).
81. Ellenberger (1972); Hirschmüller (1989); Borch-Jacobsen (1996).
82. Ellenberger (1977).
83. Swales (1986).
84. Swales (1995); see also the 'Memorandum for the Sigmund Freud Archives' drawn by this patient's daughter, Sigmund Freud Collection, Manuscript Division, Library of Congress, Washington, DC.
85. Obholzer (1982).
86. Masson (1992), 241–58.
87. Vogel (1986).
88. Falzeder (1994a).
89. Mahony (1992a).
90. Lynn (1993).
91. Edmunds (1988).
92. On 'Katharina', see Swales (1988); on 'Dora', Stadlen (1989).
93. *Time*, 29 November 1993.
94. Webster (1995).
95. Israëls (1999).
96. Forrester (1997a).
97. Meyer (2005).
98. The most striking example is the exchange which followed the publication of a series of articles by Frederick Crews on Freud in the *New York Review of Books*, collected in Crews (1995).
99. Smith (1995).
100. Malcolm (1984), 7.

101. Eissler (1971), 91–2; allusion to Freud's diagnosis of Daniel Paul Schreber as paranoid, on the basis of his *Memoirs of my Nervous Illness* (Schreber 1955 [1903]).
102. Major (1999), 76.
103. Yerushalmi (1996), 144.
104. Available online at http://users.rcn.com/brill/swales.html.
105. Available online at www.zetetique.fr/index.php/dossiers/94-critique-psychanalyse.
106. France has since witnessed no less than two other 'guerres des psys' on the occasion of the publication of *The Black Book of Psychoanalysis* (Meyer 2005), and of Michel Onfray's *The Twilight of an Idol. The Freudian Fabrication* (Onfray 2010).
107. For more on this comic episode, see Mikkel Borch-Jacobsen and Sonu Shamdasani, 'Une visite aux Archives Freud,' in Borch-Jacobsen (2002), 271–6.

I PRIVATISING SCIENCE

1. Marie Bonaparte Collection, Manuscript Division, Library of Congress, Washington, DC.
2. On the differences between the old sociology of science of Robert K. Merton and the new science studies, see Callon and Latour (1990), 13–14; Latour (1987), 387–92; Golinski (1998), 48–55.
3. See the preface of Jonas Salk (the developer of the polio vaccine) to Latour's inquiry in his laboratory (Salk 1979, 11–14). For an example of a scientist integrating science studies in his work, see Rose (1993).
4. Interview with Isabelle Stengers and Didier Gille, Linkebeek, 25 August 1993.
5. Mijolla (1993).
6. Gay (1988), xv: 'In later years, Freud repeated this destructive gesture more than once, and in the spring of 1938, preparing to leave Austria for England, he threw away materials that an alert Anna Freud, abetted by Princess Marie Bonaparte, rescued from the wastebasket.'
7. Wilkinson (1985), 27: 'Freud had wished his papers to be destroyed, but his widow, Martha, could not comply with his request. Before her own death she left the task to Anna [Freud], and the daughter was similarly unable to effect the loss of such valuable materials.'
8. Cited by Jeffrey Masson in Freud (1985), 9.
9. *Ibid.*
10. Freud (1960), 140–1.
11. Freud (1900), 214, n. 1.
12. Freud (1960), 346.
13. Freud (1923), 235.
14. Freud (1925a), 7.

15. Wundt (1921); Hall (1923); Forel (1935); Moll (1936); Ellis (1939); Jung and Jaffé (1962); on the unreliability of Jung's 'memories' recorded and edited by Aniela Jaffé, see Elms (1994), ch. 3; Shamdasani (1995) and (2005a).
16. Murchison (1930–).
17. See the dismantling of Piaget's autobiographical essay by Vidal (1994a).
18. Murchison (1930–), vol. 3, 277–8.
19. On this question see Shamdasani (2003a), section 1.
20. Freud (1914a), 7.
21. Ibid., 60.
22. Luhmann (1979); Giddens (1990), particularly 26–36.
23. Shapin (1994), 412. Shapin himself complicates this in showing how the verification procedures of the English experimentalists of the seventeenth century were rooted in the gentlemanly culture of time and also how, in the present day, personal status continues to play a role within the specialised networks and core-sets of scientists working within a given domain.
24. Manuscript note of Marie Bonaparte, c. 1927–8 (on this document, see Borch-Jacobsen 1996, 100).
25. Freud (1914a), 21.
26. Ibid., 19.
27. Freud and Ferenczi (1993), 261–2; Ferenczi's emphasis.
28. Wells (1960), 189.
29. Freud (1954), 33–4.
30. Jones (1953), 351–2.
31. Eissler (1971), 306–7.
32. Hobbes (1968 [1651]), 82.
33. Kant (1985 [1786]), 8.
34. Comte (1830–42), vol. 1, 34–5.
35. James (1890), vol. 2, 64.
36. Brentano (1874), 29.
37. Maury (1861); Delbœuf (1993b [1885]).
38. On this question, see Danziger (1991). Self-experimentation was still widely used in medicine. For example, in 1872, George Beard and Alphonso Rockwell wrote concerning electrotherapeutics: 'To all who for the first time enter upon the study of this branch of science, we cannot too strongly recommend the practice of self-experimentation. Better than any experiments on animals, better even, in many features, than extended investigations in the treatment of disease, is the precise and peculiar knowledge of the modus operandi of the applications, and the sensations which they produce, which is obtained through personal experience' (1880 [1872], x–xi). Another example would be Freud's experiments with cocaine, cf. Freud (1885a).
39. Freud (1985), 261.

40. See the letter to Fliess of 14 November 1897: 'Before the vacation trip I told you that the most important patient for me was myself; and then, after I came back from vacation [Freud returned to Vienna on 27 September], my self-analysis, of which there was at the time no sign, suddenly started' (Freud 1985, 279). See also Sulloway's judicious comments (1992a, 208–9), noting that Freud's self-analysis could not have been the reason for his abandonment of the seduction theory, as the legend has it.
41. Freud (1985), 281.
42. Ibid., 299.
43. Jones mentions that Freud had noted his dreams since his youth – none of the notebooks containing these survived Freud's periodic destruction of his papers (Jones 1953, 351–3).
44. Freud (1901), 49.
45. Delbœuf (1993b), 109–18.
46. See the judicious remarks of Duykaerts (1993), 241.
47. Mayer (2001).
48. The self-observations of Bleuler and Forel were reproduced in Forel (1889), under the title 'Two hypnotisers hypnotised'. In subsequent editions, Forel omitted the section concerning himself (in which he had recounted auditory hallucinations and sensory confusion under hypnosis). Freud wrote a laudatory review of Forel's work when it appeared (Freud, 1889).
49. Another slightly later example can be found in Marcinowski (1900).
50. Forel (1910b), 308.
51. Freud (1900), 101–2.
52. Gay (1988), 97.
53. Freud (1900), 105.
54. Ibid., 477.
55. Ibid., xxvi. Jakob Freud died on 23 October 1896, one year before the beginning of the self-analysis proper.
56. Freud (1910a), 32.
57. Clearly taken aback by this passage, the psychoanalysts Jean Laplanche and Jean-Bertrand Pontalis affirm in their The Language of Psycho-Analysis that 'It is not possible, however, to be sure from the term Freud used on this occasion – "Selbstanalyse" – whether he meant a true self-analysis or an analysis conducted by another person' (Laplanche and Pontalis, 1973, 454).
58. Freud (1910b), 145.
59. Freud and Jones (1993), 112.
60. Adler (1972), 56.
61. An allusion to Wilhelm Fliess.
62. Stekel (1925), 563.
63. Baron von Münchhausen pulled himself by his hair to get out of a swamp into which he and his horse had fallen.

64. Jung (1912b), CW 4 § 449. Jones immediately interpreted this as an attack on Freud (see Freud and Jones 1993, 212). Andrew Paskauskas notes: 'The comment may also have been taken personally by Jones. It certainly hit a nerve, for Jones had spent a great deal of energy in undertaking his own self-analysis between 1909 and 1913 and would have resented the implication that he was practicing pseudopsychology' (*ibid.*, 213–14).

65. Freud (1912), 116–17. Freud's article appeared at the beginning of June 1912, before Jung recommended training analysis in his September lectures at Fordham University in New York (Jung 1912b). It is nevertheless clear that it was adopted under the influence of Jung and the Zurich school.

66. Putnam (1911).

67. See amongst others Roustang (1986); Falzeder (1994b; 1998); Shamdasani (2002).

68. Freud (1915a), 166: 'How are we to arrive at a knowledge of the unconscious? It is of course only as something conscious that we know it, after it has undergone transformation or translation into something conscious. Psycho-analytic work shows us every day that translation of this kind is possible.'

69. Sigmund Freud Copyrights, Wivenhoe.

70. Freud and Jung (1974), 526.

71. Freud and Jones (1993), 180.

72. Freud and Jung (1974), 533.

73. *Ibid.*, 534; Freud's emphasis.

74. *Ibid.*, 535.

75. Freud and Ferenczi (1993), 446. On Maria Moltzer and her relations with Jung, see Shamdasani (1998).

76. Freud and Jones (1993), 186.

77. Towards the end of his life, Ferenczi changed his view on this. See Ferenczi (1988).

78. Freud and Ferenczi (1993), 470–1; Ferenczi's emphasis.

79. Lacan (1981), 232; Lacan's emphasis.

80. Freud (1914a), 20.

81. Abraham (1954 [1919]), 308.

82. Freud to Paul Schilder, 26 November 1935, Sigmund Freud Collection, Manuscript Division, Library of Congress, Washington, DC; cited in Gay (1988), 97. Ernst Falzeder notes that Freud, irritated by Rank's *The Trauma of Birth*, insinuated that he wouldn't have written it if he had been analysed. Rank replied: 'I have felt curiously touched by the fact that you, of all persons, suggest that I would not have adopted this concept had I been analyzed. This might well be so. But the question is whether this is a cause for regret. I, for one, can only consider myself lucky, after all the results I have seen with analyzed analysts' (Rank to the former secret committee members, 20 December 1924, cited by Falzeder 1998, 147).

83. Anzieu (1986), 564–5. Anzieu also presented a contemporary psychoanalytic interpretation of Freud's self-analysis: 'Throughout the systematic self-analysis . . . Freud used theory as a defense against depression. Freudian psychoanalytic theory was the product of a working over of the depressive position, whereas Kleinian psychoanalytic theory was the product of a working over of the schizo-paranoid position' (577).

84. Schur (1972).

85. Noted by Falzeder (2000), 44.

86. Freud (1914a), 23–4.

87. Wittels (1924), 118.

88. The mythologisation of the relation between Freud and Jung has quite eclipsed that between Bleuler and Freud on the one hand and Bleuler and Jung on the other, with deleterious effects. In many crucial respects, the relationship and subsequent separation between Bleuler and Freud was more consequential for the subsequent history of psychoanalysis, and its separations from psychiatry, than that between Freud and Jung; second, the relationship and subsequent separation between Bleuler and Jung was more important for Jung than his relation with Freud; third, no account of the relation between Freud and Jung is complete without grasping the complex triangulations between them and Bleuler.

89. Löwenfeld (1904).

90. Bleuler (1904), 718.

91. Freud (1985), 461.

92. Bernheim (1892); Bleuler (1892), 431.

93. Bleuler (1896).

94. Forel was French Swiss, and wrote in French and German. His research was many-faceted, and he was well known for playing a key role in the formulation of the concept of the neurone, for his research on ants and on the sexual question, and for his militant anti-alcoholism. On Forel, see Shamdasani (2006). On his relations with Freud, see Tanner (2003), 83–95.

95. Freud (1889).

96. As Tanner notes, the editorial committee was a veritable Who's Who of figures associated with the Nancy school: aside from Freud, one finds Hippolyte Bernheim, Ambroise Liébeault, Joseph Delbœuf, Max Dessoir, Albert Moll, Paul Möbius, Albert Freiherr von Schrenck-Notzing and Otto Wetterstrand (2003, 80). It was in the Zeitschrift für Hypnotismus that Freud published his first case history, 'A case of successful treatment by hypnotism' (Freud 1892–3).

97. Forel (1891), 26–7.

98. Forel (1899), 412–13.

99. There is nothing surprising in this – as Tanner noted, it was not till the following year that Freud (1904) made public his abandonment of the hypnotic method (2003, n. 124).

100. Forel (1907), 221–2.

101. '[Manfred] Bleuler when I interviewed him told me that he hesitates to give copies to the Archives since he fears for Freud's reputation in view of what Freud wrote to his father about Jung' (Kurt Eissler, manuscript notes in the margin of the translation of a letter from Freud to Bleuler of 17 November 1912, Sigmund Freud Collection, Manuscript Division, Library of Congress, Washington, DC).

102. Sigmund Freud Collection, Manuscript Division, Library of Congress, Washington, DC.

103. Cited in Bleuler (1979), 21.

104. Ernst Falzeder, English manuscript of Falzeder (2004).

105. Jung (1906–9).

106. In 1905 Freud had written: 'I cannot admit that in my paper on "The aetiology of hysteria" (1896) I exaggerated the frequency or importance of that influence' (Freud 1905a, 190). It was only in the following year that he admitted that he had made an error ten years earlier: 'I thus over-estimated the frequency of such events (*though in other respects they were not open to doubt*)' (Freud 1906, 274; our emphasis). To Jung, he seems to have continued privately to affirm that these seductions had been real: '[Jung:] For example, I read his article on the thirteen cases of so-called traumatic hysteria and I asked him, tell me, Professor, are you sure that these people really told you the truth? How do you know that these traumas took place? He said to me [laughs]: But these were good people! And I: Excuse me, but they are hysterics! . . . I was a psychiatrist . . . and I know what hysterics were capable of in this regard! But he denied this . . . He admitted nothing, nothing! Corrected nothing.' Interview typescript of 29 August 1953 with Kurt Eissler, Sigmund Freud Collection, Manuscript Division, Library of Congress, Washington, DC, 17.

107. Jung (1905), CW 2, § 717.

108. Interview with Kurt Eissler (see note 214 above), 33.

109. Aschaffenburg (1906), 1797; Aschaffenburg's emphasis.

110. *Ibid.*, 1798.

111. On 5 October 1906 Jung wrote to Freud about Aschaffenburg and noted: 'it seems to me that though the genesis of hysteria is predominately sexual, it is not exclusively' (Freud and Jung 1974, 4–5). In his reply, Freud by no means assented to this, replying that he was aware that Jung did not share all his views, but hoped that in the course of years he would come closer to them.

112. Jung (1906), § 16.

113. Vogt (1898; 1899). On Vogt's use of hypnosis and causal psychotherapy or causal analysis, see Satzinger (1998), 100–32. Against Breuer and Freud, Vogt argued that it was the task of the patients themselves to discover the causal connections, rather than having them interpreted for them by the physician (*ibid.*, 118–19).

114. In 1900 Warda published an account of a case of hypnoid hysteria treated by Breuer and Freud's cathartic method (Warda 1900).
115. Contrary to general opinion, the word psycho-analytical had been employed prior to Freud. In 1979, Kathleen Coburn noted that the term had been used by Coleridge in his notebooks (cited in Eng 1984, 463). Coleridge had written about the need for a psycho-analytical understanding. As Erling Eng noted, Coleridge understood this as what was 'needed to recover the presence of Greek myth hidden with Renaissance epic verse, this for the sake of realizing a purified Christian Faith' (*ibid.*, 465). Whilst Coleridge's diaries were not published till the twentieth century, the *OED* also notes a published use of the word in 1857 in *Russell's Magazine*: '[Poe] chose ... the psycho-analytical. His heroes are monstrous reflections of his own heart in its despair, not in its peace.' Whether the word may have been in wider circulation has not yet been established.
116. Freud (1896a), 151. The German *Psychoanalyse* is used for the first time in Freud (1896c), 162.
117. Janet (1919), 601–2.
118. This was signalled by Horst Gundlach (2002), who noted the embarrassed reception of the malformed term psychoanalysis by Freud's colleagues and followers. See also Shamdasani (2005b).
119. Bezzola archives.
120. Forel (1919), 218.
121. Frank (1910), 19.
122. Bezzola archives.
123. Frank (1908), 127–8; this article appeared in a volume in honour of Forel.
124. Hoche (1908), 184–5.
125. Bezzola (1908), 219.
126. Freud and Jung (1974), 29.
127. The italicised phrase was deleted from the published version of the correspondence. The originals are on access at the Library of Congress.
128. Freud and Jung (1974), 26 May 1907, 53.
129. Forel and Bezzola (1989), 74.
130. *Ibid.*, 64. Frank's response is reproduced in Forel (1968), 393–5.
131. Forel and Bezzola (1989), 66.
132. *Ibid.*, 69.
133. *Ibid.*, 71.
134. *Ibid.*, 73. Bezzola never wrote this book, to Forel's great chagrin.
135. *Ibid.*, 67.
136. Cited in Cranefield (1958), 320.
137. Cited in *ibid.*, 320. It seems that Breuer continued to correspond with Forel up to 1908, but this correspondence has been lost (see Tanner 2003, n. 125). It is worth quoting here Ludwig Binswanger's recollection of his visit to Breuer, to whom he conveyed the salutations of his father (Robert Binswanger, to whom

Breuer had sent Bertha Pappenheim after her treatment): 'I do not recall Breuer's exact words, but I do remember the vivid gestures and facial expressions with which he responded to my naive question of what his position was regarding Freud since the *Studies*. His look of downright pity and superiority, as well as the wave of his hand, a dismissal in the full sense of the word, left not the slightest doubt that in his opinion Freud had gone scientifically astray to such an extent that he could no longer be taken seriously, and hence it was better not to talk about him' (Binswanger 1957, 4).

138. Forel and Bezzola (1989), 67.
139. *Ibid.*, 70.
140. Forel (1908), 268.
141. Freud and Jung (1974), 33.
142. Vol. 21, 1907, 563.
143. *Ibid.*, 566.
144. Jung (1908a), § 28.
145. Jung deleted this when he republished the paper.
146. Jung (1908b), 277. In the version published in the same year, under the title 'The Freudian theory of hysteria', Jung deleted the passage on Bezzola.
147. Jones (1955), 126.
148. Janet (1908), 301–2. Janet expressed the same position in 1913 in London at the 17th International Medical Congress: 'I have to admit to my great shame that I did not fully comprehend the importance of the [Freudian] upheaval and I naively considered the first studies of Breuer and Freud as a very interesting confirmation of my studies: "We are happy," I wrote at that time, "that Breuer and Freud have recently verified our already old interpretation of fixed ideas in hysterics".... At most these authors changed a few words in their psychological description: they called psycho-analysis what I had called psychological analysis ... Again today if one leaves the adventurous discussions to one side and only examines the observations published by Freud students on traumatic memories, one finds again descriptions very close to those I had previously published. In considering these first theories and these observations, one has difficulty in understanding how psycho-analysis differs from psychological analysis and where one is supposed to find the new viewpoint which it brings to psychiatry' (Janet 1913, 8).
149. Since the publication of the French edition of this book (2006), George Makari's *Revolution in Mind. The Creation of Psychoanalysis* (2008) has appeared. This work is the most significant history of psychoanalysis to date and his analysis converges at a number of points with that developed here, particularly in this section and chapters 6 and 7 of his book. Our main point of difference is with Makari's argument that, after the first schisms, Freud did a volte-face from his prior authoritarian position, and thereafter maintained a relatively loose hold on the psychoanalytic movement. We would rather

emphasis the fact that greater latitude developed regarding the range of per-
missable divergence on aspects of theory (in part necessitated by the damage
limitation exercise vis-à-vis the work of figures such as Adler and Jung) only as
long as the Freud legend and Freud's fundamental authority remained
unchallenged.

150. Freud and Jung (1974), 157.
151. Jung (1973), 7.
152. Introduction to Freud and Abraham (2002), xxvii; Falzeder's emphasis.
153. Forel (1908).
154. *Ibid.*, 266.
155. Forel (1910a), 42 and 44.
156. Forel (1910b), 315–16.
157. Forel and Bezzola (1989), 70.
158. Among those present were: Bernheim, Janet, Forel, Vogt, Jones, Leonhard Seif
(then a Freudian), Loÿ, de Montet, Muthmann, van Renterghem and Warda.
Bezzola and Frank weren't able to attend.
159. Forel (1910b), 313.
160. Forel (1910a), 44.
161. The society was officially founded at Salzburg on 19–25 September 1909. The
president was Fulgence Raymond, Charcot's successor at the Salpêtrière, with
Frank, Forel and Vogt as secretaries. The society comprised not fewer than fifty-
six members.
162. One can follow this discussion in Freud and Jung (1974), 247, 249, 253,
257, 259.
163. Freud and Jung (1974), 268.
164. Forel (1910c); noted by Tanner (2003), n. 128.
165. Freud and Jung (1974), 288 and 295.
166. *Ibid.*, 294–5.
167. Freud and Ferenczi (1993), 119. See also Freud and Jung (1974), 282.
168. Freud and Ferenczi (1993), 120.
169. *Neurologisches Centralblatt*, 1910, 660.
170. Ferenczi (1911), 299. In Jung's terms, 'the great Freud battle' (Freud and Jung
1974, 50).
171. Ferenczi (1911), 301.
172. Freud (1910c), 226–7.
173. Freud (1914a), 43–4.
174. Sigmund Freud Collection, Manuscript Division, Library of Congress,
Washington. DC; cited in Alexander and Selesnick (1965), 4.
175. Frank (1910).
176. Freud and Jung (1974), 310.
177. *Ibid.*, 300.
178. Freud and Jones (1993), 65.

179. Freud and Jung (1974), 300.
180. Isserlin (1907).
181. Freud and Jung (1974), 299–300; Jung's emphasis.
182. *Ibid.*, 300.
183. *Ibid.*, 308.
184. Hoche (1910), 1009.
185. Sigmund Freud Collection, Manuscript Division, Library of Congress, Washington, DC.
186. Freud and Jung (1974), 371.
187. *Ibid.*, 373.
188. *Ibid.*, 376. Freud attributed his public priority dispute with Fliess (see Fliess 1906a) to the latter's paranoia brought about by repressed homosexuality: 'The paranoid form is probably conditioned by restrictions to the homosexual components . . . My one-time friend Fliess developed a dreadful case of paranoia after throwing off his affection for me, which was undoubtedly considerable. I owe this idea to him, i.e., to his behaviour' (Freud and Jung 1974 121). See also Freud's letter to Ferenczi of 10 January 1910, in which Freud attributed his final rupture with Fliess to an interpretation which Freud had made to him: 'This piece of analysis, very unwelcome to him, was the real reason for the break between us which he engineered in such a pathological (paranoic) fashion' (Freud and Ferenczi 1993, 122).
189. Freud and Jung (1974), 376.
190. Freud and Ferenczi (1993), 243.
191. Freud and Jones (1993), 93; see also 101: 'He is a paranoiac I am sorry to say.'
192. Freud and Ferenczi (1993), 262.
193. Freud and Jung (1974), 376.
194. Stekel (1950), 141.
195. Nunberg and Federn (1974), 145, 146 and 148.
196. Stekel (1950), 142.
197. Freud and Jung (1974), 399.
198. 'An der Leser' [To the reader], in Furtmüller (1912), iii; cited in Stepansky (1993), 203.
199. Somewhat overstatedly, though with some justice, Alexander and Selesnick (1965) argued that, without the dissension which led Bleuler to resign, the subsequent isolation of psychoanalysis from the universities and medical schools would not have taken place (1–2).
200. Alphonse Maeder papers.
201. Sigmund Freud Collection, Manuscript Division, Library of Congress, Washington, DC.
202. Freud and Jung (1974), 468.
203. Sigmund Freud Collection, Manuscript Division, Library of Congress, Washington, DC; cited in part in Alexander and Selesnick (1965), 5.

204. Sigmund Freud Collection, Manuscript Division, Library of Congress, Washington, DC; Bleuler's emphasis; cited in part in Alexander and Selesnick (1965), 7.
205. Forel (1919), 221. Ambroise-Auguste Liébeault was the doctor near Nancy who initiated Bernheim into hypnosis.
206. Forel's *The Sexual Question* (1905) appeared the same year as Freud's *Three Essays on the Theory of Sexuality*, and received far more attention and was widely translated. Forel also published a book on *Ethical and Legal Conflicts of the Sexual Life Inside and Outside of Marriage* (1909). Jung reviewed it favourably, noting: 'The author introduces his book with the following words: "The following pages are for the most part an attack, based on documentary material, on the hypocrisy, the dishonesty and cruelty of our present-day morality and our almost non-existent rights in matters of sexual life." From which it is apparent that this work is another contribution to the great social task to which Forel has already rendered such signal service' (Jung 1909, CW 18, § 921).
207. Freud and Ferenczi (1993), 281.
208. Ellenberger (1970a), 810–14.
209. Jung, letter to the *Neue Zürcher Zeitung*, 10 January 1912, CW 18, §§ 1034–8.
210. 'On psychoanalysis', letter of Jung to the *Neue Zürcher Zeitung* of 17 January 1912 (Jung, CW 18, § 1039–40).
211. In English in the original.
212. This official protestation appeared in the *Neue Zürcher Zeitung* of 27 January 1912, signed by Jung and Franz Riklin for the IPA and Alphonse Maeder and J. H. W. van Ophuijsen for the Zurich Psychoanalytical Society. On 28 January, Jung published a heated letter on the debate in the journal *Wissen und Leben* (Jung 1912a).
213. 'A word about psychanalysis', letter of Forel to the *Neue Zürcher Zeitung* of 25 January 1912.
214. 'Psychanalysis and psychoanalysis, or Science and Lay understanding', letter of Forel to the *Neue Zürcher Zeitung* of 1 February 1912.
215. Freud and Binswanger (2003), 79.
216. Cf. above, pp. 47–52.
217. Hale (1971b), 146.
218. *Ibid.*, 153.
219. Since the appearance of the French edition of this book (2006), Ernst Falzeder and John Burnham (2007) have published an article on the Breslau conference, which overlaps at certain points with our study here.
220. Freud and Jung (1974), 545.
221. *Internationale Zeitschrift für ärztliche Psychoanalyse*, 1913, vol. 1, 199.
222. Hoche (1913), 1068.
223. Burnham (1983), 74.
224. Bleuler (1913), 665.

225. Bleuler (1910).
226. Hoche (1913), 1057.
227. *Ibid.*, 1059.
228. *Ibid.*, 1060.
229. Stekel (1911), 36; Stekel's emphasis.
230. Freud and Jones (1993), 146.
231. *Ibid.*, 147–8.
232. *Ibid.*, 149.
233. Jones (1955), 172.
234. Hoche (1913), 1068.
235. Kraepelin (1913b), 787.
236. Weygandt (1913), 787.
237. Kohnstamm (1913), 790–1.
238. Stern (1913), 785.
239. Stransky (1913), 786.
240. Freud and Abraham (2002), 184.
241. Ferenczi (1914), 62–3. Freud took up this reductive explanation in his autobiographical study of 1925: '[Bleuler] strove too eagerly after an appearance of impartiality; nor is it a matter of chance that it is to him that our science owes the valuable concept of ambivalence ... He resigned from it as a result of misunderstandings with Jung and the Burghölzli was lost to analysis' (Freud 1925a, 51). Three years later, Bleuler rejoindered: 'A small correction is permitted. The reviewer did not leave the International Psychoanalytic Association "due to differences with Jung," but he considered the impossible demands of the association that his assistants either joined it or should stay away from the meetings taking place in the Burghölzli as a sign, that he no longer wanted to belong; and he understood the latter easily, because he had warned at that time before its founding that this would lead to secessions, and he considered the striving towards orthodoxy to be incorrect in science. It was a matter of principles, not of persons. I do not know of any differences with Jung' (Bleuler 1928, 1728).
242. Freud and Jones (1993), 199.
243. *Ibid.*, 482–3.
244. *Ibid.*, 234.
245. Freud and Ferenczi (1993), 519.
246. Freud and Jones (1993), 242.
247. Freud and Ferenczi (1993), 550.
248. Freud and Abraham (2002), 251.
249. Archives of the Psychological Club, Zurich.
250. Freud (1914a), 50.
251. Szasz (1989), 149–50; Szasz's emphasis. One may compare what Freud wrote in his final letter to Fliess: 'nor can ideas be patented ... Once they have been let loose, they go their own way' (Freud 1985, 466).

252. Ellenberger (1970a), 638.
253. Stekel (1925), 570.
254. Stekel (1950), 138.
255. Protocols of Aniela Jaffé's interviews with Jung in preparation of *Memories, Dreams, Reflections*, 154; Jung Collection, Manuscript Division, Library of Congress, Washington, DC. On Jung's influence on Freud's analysis of the ego and second theory of drives, see Borch-Jacobsen (1988).
256. Freud and Ferenczi (1993), 133.
257. Freud (1914a), 7. Freud was taking over control of the *Jahrbuch für psycho-analytische und psychopathologische Forschungen*, after Bleuler and Jung had resigned from the editorship.
258. Freud (1914a), 11–12.
259. *Ibid.*, 13.
260. *Ibid.*, 21–3.
261. Freud (1925a), 48.
262. Freud (1914a), 15. One wonders how Freud could have known that he would have had great pleasure from Nietzsche without having read him.
263. Freud (1925a), 59–60.
264. Scherner (1861).
265. Popper [Lynkeus] (1899).
266. Freud (1914a), 19–20.
267. Janet (1894), vol. 2, 68.
268. James (1929), 234.
269. Ellis (1898a), 279.
270. Ellis (1898b), 608–9 and 614.
271. Bleuler (1896), 525.
272. Freud (1985), 448.
273. On the correspondence between Freud and Ellis, see Sulloway (1992a), 464; and Makari (1998a), 654; on the correspondence with Löwenfeld, see Freud (1985), 413, n. 3.
274. On Gattel, see Sulloway (1992a), 513–15; Schröter and Hermanns (1992); on Bárány, see Jones (1955), 189; Gicklhorn and Gicklhorn (1960), 187; on Swoboda, see Freud (1985), 461–4, 466–7.
275. The myth of the universally hostile reception of Freud's work was demolished by Bry and Rifkin (1962); Ellenberger (1970a), 448, 450, 455, 508, 772–3; Decker (1971); Cioffi (1973); Decker (1975; 1977); Sulloway (1992a), 449–67; Tichy and Zwetter-Otte (1999). See also Norman Kiell's anthology of reviews of Freud (Kiell 1988).
276. See Macmillan (1997), ch. 5, notably 129–30.
277. Makari (1998a), 646–7.
278. Micale (1990) and (2008).
279. Hirschmüller (1989), 100.

280. Donkin (1892), 620; cited in Cioffi (1973).
281. King (1891), 518.
282. Clarke (1896), 414.
283. Binet and Simon (1910), 95.
284. Alt (1908).
285. Breuer and Freud (1895), 246; Breuer's emphasis.
286. Hirschmüller (1989), 316–17.
287. Breuer (1895), 1718.
288. Sulloway (1992a), 509.
289. Ritvo (1990); Sulloway (1992a); Makari (1997).
290. Bell (1902), cited by Freud himself (Freud 1910a, 42). Five years earlier, Freud had cited another passage from the same article to illustrate the *absence* of knowledge of infantile sexuality in scientific literature (Freud 1905a, 173, n. 2).
291. Sand (1992); on the embeddedness of Freud's work on dream in the history of the study of dreams, see the remarkable neglected study of Raymond de Saussure (1926), and Ellenberger (1970), 303–11; Kern (1975); and Shamdasani (2003a), section 2.
292. Freud (1925a), 43. See also Freud (1916–17, 84): 'But to concern oneself with dreams is not merely unpractical and uncalled-for, it is positively disgraceful. It brings with it the odium of being unscientific and rouses the suspicion of a personal inclination to mysticism.'
293. See also the note Freud added in 1911 to *The Interpretation of Dreams*: 'However much Scherner's view of dream-symbolism may differ from the one developed in these pages, I must insist that he is to be regarded as the true discoverer of symbolism in dreams' (1900, 359).
294. Scherner (1861), 192; cited in Massey (1990), 571.
295. One may compare this with the famous passage in Freud's *Introductory Lectures*: 'The ego is not master in its own house' (1917a, 143).
296. Hildebrandt (1881), 55; noted by Kern (1975), 85.
297. See McGrath (1967). Freud cited Schopenhauer's 'Essay on visions' three times in *The Interpretation of Dreams* (Freud 1900, 36, 66, 90). On the significance of the German philosophy of the unconscious in the nineteenth century, see Ellenberger (1970a), 208–10, 275–8, 542–3; Shamdasani (2003a), section 3; Liebscher and Nicholls (2010); on Freud's philosophical Schopenhauerianism, see Henry (1993), chs. 5 and 6.
298. Already in 1930 H. L. Hollingworth noted: 'The modern psychoanalytic movement, and what is often referred to as the Freudian psychology, consists chiefly in an elaboration and application of Herbart's doctrines, and their amplification with a wealth of clinical detail' (Hollingworth, 1930, 48). See also Jones (1953), 281, 371–6; Andersson (1962); Hemecker (1987).
299. McGrath (1967).
300. Nietzsche (1895–1904).

301. Freud (1985), 398.
302. Jones (1957), 100.
303. Merton (1976).
304. Freund (1895).
305. Freud (1893).
306. Freud (1985), 152. On the question of intellectual priority, Ernst Kris noted in his edition of Freud (1954) that the article of C. S. Freund reproduced in part an article by Heinrich Sachs published in 1893 (Sachs 1893), at a time when Freud had not made public his ideas on the principle of psychic constancy. Freud, characteristically, never cites Sachs in the texts in which he refers to this principle.
307. Freud (1985), 252.
308. Nunberg and Federn (1967), 48; cited and commented on in Sulloway (1992a), 469–72.
309. Actually, *Névroses et idées fixes* [Neuroses and Fixed Ideas] (Janet 1898).
310. Freud (1985), 302.
311. *Ibid.*, 325.
312. *Ibid.*, 463.
313. In the section of the first edition of the *Three Essays* devoted to bisexuality, Freud cited Gley (1884), Kiernan (1888), Lydston (1889), Chevalier (1893), Krafft-Ebing (1895), Hirschfeld (1899), Arduin (1900) and Herman (1903). Only in the second edition of 1910 did Freud add Fliess' name: 'Fliess (1906) subsequently claimed the idea of bisexuality (in the sense of *duality of sex*) as his own.' However, it goes without saying that Freud was aware that the idea of bisexuality figured prominently in Fliess (1897). In 1924 he went further: 'In lay circles the hypothesis of human bisexuality is regarded as being due to O. Weininger, the philosopher, who died at an early age, and who made the idea the basis of a somewhat unbalanced book [1903]. The particulars which I have enumerated above will be sufficient to show how little justification there is for the claim' (Freud 1905a, 143, n. 1). The Weininger–Swoboda episode is discussed by Sulloway (1992a), 223–32.
314. Freud (1985), 466–7.
315. Swales (1995).
316. Freud (1920b).

2 THE INTERPREFACTION OF DREAMS

1. Hoche (1910), 1009.
2. Aschaffenburg (1911), 754.
3. Hitschmann (1911).
4. Forel (1919), 224, 232 and 235. See Dessoir (1889).

5. Cited by Ellenberger (1970), 806.
6. Prince (1911), 348–9.
7. Haberman (1914–15), 278–9.
8. Wohlgemuth (1923), 246.
9. Breuer (1895), 1717.
10. Freud (1985), 447.
11. Moll (1913), 190.
12. James (1920), vol. 2, 327–8.
13. Binet and Simon (1910), 94–5.
14. Kronfeld (1912), 194.
15. Janet (1919), vol. 2, 262.
16. Haberman (1914–15), 276.
17. Forel (1919), 229 and 234.
18. Kraepelin (1913a), 938.
19. Undated, Adolf Meyer papers, Johns Hopkins University, Baltimore.
20. Wohlgemuth (1923), 246.
21. Hollingworth (1930), 149.
22. Jastrow (1932), 37–8; Jastrow's emphasis. Compare this with Wittgenstein's commentary in 1942: 'Freud is constantly claiming to be scientific. But what he gives is *speculation* – something prior even to the formation of an hypothesis' (Wittgenstein 1966, 44; Wittgenstein's emphasis).
23. Clarke (1896), 414.
24. Gaupp (1900), 234.
25. Forel (1906a), 214.
26. Putnam (1906), 40.
27. Muthmann (1907), 51. Muthmann didn't intend this as a critique of Freud, which is reflected in Freud's relatively benevolent response: 'He [Muthmann] still lacks perspective, he treats discoveries made in 1893 in the same way as the most recent developments' (Freud and Jung 1974, 64).
28. Hoche (1910), 1008.
29. Moll (1913 [1909]), 278–9.
30. Hart (1929), 73–4.
31. Popper (1963), 37–8.
32. See Collins (1985).
33. Pickering (1995).
34. Delbœuf (1993a), 259.
35. Bernheim (1892 [1891]), 168–9.
36. On this question of the artefact in experimental psychology and psychoanalysis, see Borch-Jacobsen (2009); Stengers (2002).
37. On the 'personal equation' in psychology, see Boring (1929), ch. 8, and Shamdasani (2003a), section 1.
38. Devereux (1967).

39. See Kohler's study (1994) on the laboratory fly *Drosophila melanogaster*, which continues in a literal manner the programme of an 'ecology' of experimental practices proposed by Clark and Fujimura (1992).
40. Wohlgemuth (1923), 221.
41. Freud (1925a), 41; our emphasis.
42. Freud and Jung (1974), 6.
43. Forel (1906b), 314.
44. Prince (1911), 347.
45. Cited in Adam (1923), 47.
46. Hart (1929), 73.
47. Woodworth (1917), 179–80.
48. Jastrow (1932), 249–50.
49. Freud (1925a), 42.
50. On this subject, see the excellent remarks of Stengers (2002), ch. 4; as well as Borch-Jacobsen (2009), ch. 2.
51. On this question of hypnosis *in* psychoanalysis, see Borch-Jacobsen (1987), reprinted in Borch-Jacobsen (1992).
52. Frank (1961), 168.
53. Freud (1925a), 42–3.
54. Freud (1905b), 261; Freud's emphasis.
55. Freud (1914b), 148–9 and 155–6.
56. Freud (1916–17), 452.
57. Grünbaum (1985), ch. 2, B.
58. This point is well demonstrated by Assoun (1981), ch. 3. See also Siegfried Bernfeld to Hans Ansbacher, 26 May 1952: 'Freud belonged to the group of physicists and physiologists around Brücke, who prepared the way for the positivism of Mach and Avenarius. He certainly knew the *Zeitschrift für wissenschaftliche Philosophie*. In the 1890s, Mach struck him . . . In one form or another positivism was unquestionably his "natural" mode of thinking' (Siegfried Bernfeld Collection, Manuscript Division, Library of Congress, Washington, DC; cited by Ilse Grubrich-Simitis in Bernfeld and Cassirer Bernfeld, 1981, 260). Freud mentions his reading of Mach's *The Analysis of Sensations* in his letter to Fliess of 12 June 1900 (Freud 1985, 417).
59. Freud (1915b), 117.
60. Freud (1900), 598; (1926a), 194.
61. Freud (1933), 95.
62. Freud (1925a), 32.
63. Freud (1917a), 142.
64. Freud (1915b), 124.
65. Mach (1976), 178; Mach's emphasis.
66. Freud (1937a), 225.
67. Freud (1920a), 60.

68. Mach (1976), 8–9.
69. Freud (1915b), 116.
70. Mach (1976), 9.
71. Freud (1923), 253–4.
72. Freud (1914c), 77.
73. Jacques Derrida, in Derrida and Roudinesco (2004), 282–3: 'Among the gestures that convinced me, seduced me in fact, is its indispensable audacity of thought, what I do not hesitate to call its courage: which here consists in writing, inscribing, signing "theoretical fictions" in the name of a knowledge without alibi (therefore the most "positive" knowledge). One thus recognizes two things at once: *on the one hand*, the irreducibile necessity of the strategem, of the transaction, the negotiation in knowledge, in the theorem, in the *positing* of truth, in its demonstration, in its "making known" or its "giving to understand," and *on the other hand*, the debt of all theoretical (but also juridical, ethical and political) *positing*, to a performative power structured by *fiction*, a figural invention ... The "friend of psychoanalysis" in me is mistrustful not of positive knowledge but of positivism and of the substantialization of metaphysical or metapsychological agencies' (Derrida's emphases). On the supposed 'athetic' and non-positional structure of Freudian speculation, see Derrida's 'To specu-late – on "Freud"' in Derrida (1987). It seems that Derrida confounded the positivistic critique of metaphysics (evinced in Freud) with its Heideggerian deconstruction.
74. Mach (1976), 120.
75. Freud (1985), 264; (1895), 325–8.
76. Mach (1976), 120: 'Observation and theory too are not sharply separable, since almost any observation is already influenced by theory and, if important enough, in turn reacts on theory.'
77. MacCurdy (1923), 132.
78. Jastrow (1932), 261.
79. Freud (1985), 264.
80. Freud (1925a), 34.
81. Grünbaum (1985), 128.
82. Woodworth (1917), 194.
83. Hart (1929), 79 and 81.
84. Wohlgemuth (1923), 162–3; Wohlgemuth's capitalisation.
85. Huxley (1925), 319.
86. Hollingworth (1930), 322.
87. Freud (1910a), 42. Freud refers here to Bell's study of infantile sexuality (1902), which was based on 'no fewer than 2,500 positive observations in the course of fifteen years'.
88. Gattel (1898) had tried to verify Freud's hypotheses on the subject of 'actual neuroses' on a cohort of 100 patients in Krafft-Ebing's psychiatric clinic. As we

330 • Notes to pages 139–50

have also seen, Jung's association experiments were presented as an experimental verification of Freud's theory of repression.

89. See Borch-Jacobsen (2009), ch. 6.
90. Cited in Rosenzweig (1986), 38. Rosenzweig had sent Freud offprints of two of his articles, one of which was devoted to an experimental study of repression. According to Roy Grinker, who was present when Freud read Rosenzweig's articles, 'Freud threw the reprints across the table in a gesture of impatient rejection' (*ibid.*).
91. Freud (1933), 322.
92. Wohlgemuth (1923), 245.
93. Hart (1929), 77.
94. Freud (1925a), 49–50.
95. Freud (1896b), 199.
96. Freud (1925a), 23–4.
97. Sigmund Freud Copyrights, Wivenhoe; cited in Gay (1988), 46.
98. Freud (1925a), 59.
99. Freud (1914a), 16–17.
100. Freud (1913a), 182.
101. Freud (1913a), 182; our emphasis.
102. Freud and Abraham (2002), 229.
103. Freud (1905a), 131.
104. Freud (1913a), 181–2.
105. Wohlgemuth (1923), 237.
106. Huxley (1925), 319.
107. Jastrow (1932), 227 and 229–30.
108. Laplanche and Pontalis (1974), 405.
109. Freud (1914a), 17–18.
110. Freud (1925a), 33–4.
111. Freud (1933), 120.
112. Chodoff (1966), 508.
113. Cioffi (1974).
114. Freud (1896a), 153.
115. Freud (1896b), 204.
116. Freud (1985), 220–1.
117. Freud (1913b), 141; our emphasis.
118. Freud (1896b), 204.
119. Löwenfeld (1899), 195–6.
120. See for example Freud (1985), 227–8, 288–9.
121. Freud (1985), 213.
122. Freud (1985), 218, 223–4.
123. An allusion to the ninth edition of Krafft-Ebing's *Psychopathia sexualis* (1894), which Freud was reading at the time (see Swales 1982a and 1983).
124. Freud (1985), 219.

125. Freud (1916–17), 367–8; Freud's emphasis.
126. *Ibid.*, 370–1; Freud's emphasis.
127. Freud (1985), 226.
128. For a critique of the debunking of belief, see Latour (1996), which intersects with the argument here.
129. Chesterton (1923), 34–5.
130. Alias Mr E in the letters to Fliess; the identity of this important patient was established by Swales (1996).
131. Freud (1925), 32.
132. Schimek (1987), 940–4.
133. Freud (1985), 226.
134. One should note that this 'confirmation' of the theory of seduction occurs two months after Freud's letter to Fliess in which he announced that he no longer believed in his 'neurotica'.
135. Freud (1985), 288–9; Freud's emphasis.
136. This only makes his abandonment of the seduction theory more enigmatic. Since he obtained 'confirmations' from his patients and could attribute the instances where he didn't do so to resistance, what led him to repudiate his theory? Certainly not 'adverse evidence', as Grünbaum contends (1985, 117), because he couldn't have had any (see Cioffi's refutation of Grünbaum's argument, 1988, 240–8). Neither the seduction theory nor its abandonment corresponded to the positivist model of 'adaptation to facts' (Mach).
137. See Borch-Jacobsen (2009), ch. 2.
138. Delbœuf (1886), 169; our emphasis.
139. Wohlgemuth (1924), 499; cited by Cioffi (1998a), 18–19.
140. Hart (1929), 74; cited by Cioffi (1998a), 18.
141. Marmor (1926), 289.
142. Ellenberger (1973), 56.
143. One could say of psychotherapeutic practices what William James said of religious experience in general, which he described as self-validating states of transformation: 'No authority emanates from them which should make it a duty for those who stand outside of them to accept their revelations uncritically' (James 1929 [1902], 327). On this question and on the issue of 'optional ontologies', see Shamdasani (2004).
144. Jastrow (1932), 202.
145. Wohlgemuth (1923), 165; Wohlgemuth's emphasis.
146. See above, chapter 1, p. 85.
147. Freud and Jung (1974), 18.
148. Freud and Ferenczi (2000), 192.
149. Freud and Jones (1993), 3721.
150. Freud to Ferenczi, 9 December 1912: 'Jung is crazy (*meschugge*)' (Freud and Ferenczi 1993, 460); Freud to Abraham, 1 June 1913: 'Jung is crazy' (Freud and

Abraham 2002, 186). Jones to Freud, 25 April 1913: 'Jung's recent conduct in America makes me think more than [ever] that he does not react like a normal man, and that he is mentally deranged to a serious extent; he produced quite a paranoiac impression on some of the Psa psychiatrists in Ward's Island' (Freud and Jones 1993, 199). Brome (1984), 140–1: 'Jung said that the Freudians circulated rumours about his possible schizophrenia, and so adept and sustained were these rumours that it caused him some damage to his practice and "lost me some of my students".' On the continuation of the myth of Jung's madness by his biographers, see Shamdasani (2005a), 72ff.

151. Freud to Ferenczi, 21 December 1924 (Freud and Ferenczi 2000, 195).

152. Wohlgemuth (1923), 69 and 238. It seems that Wohlgemuth was the anonymous 'certain well-known man of science' whom Freud alluded to in 1937: 'He said that in giving interpretations to a patient we treat him upon the famous principle of "Heads I win, tails you lose." That is to say, if the patient agrees with us, then the interpretation is right; but if he contradicts us, that is only a sign of his resistance, which again shows that we are right. In this way we are always in the right' (Freud 1937b, 257).

153. Freud (1925b), 221.

154. Jung (1956), CW 14, § 695.

155. Transcription of Eissler's interview with Jung of 29 August 1953, 19–20; Sigmund Freud Collection, Manuscript Division, Library of Congress, Washington, DC.

156. Jung (1975), 176.

157. Charteris (1960).

158. Jones (1957), 45.

159. Gay (1988), 470–1.

160. Freud (1910a), 9.

161. Freud (1914a), 8.

162. Breuer and Freud (1895), 21–2: 'The element of sexuality was astonishingly undeveloped in her. The patient, whose life became known to me to an extent to which one person's life is seldom known to another, had never been in love; and in all the enormous number of hallucinations which occurred during her illness that element of mental life never emerged.' In the report which he sent to Robert Binswanger at the admission of Bertha Pappenheim (Anna O.) to Bellevue Sanatorium, Breuer wrote: 'The sexual element is astonishingly undeveloped; I have never once found it represented even amongst her numerous hallucinations' (Hirschmüller 1989, 277).

163. One may compare this with what Breuer and Freud wrote in Studies on Hysteria: 'It is plausible to suppose that it is a question here of unconscious suggestion: the patient expects to be relieved of his sufferings by this procedure, and it is this expectation, and not the verbal utterance, which is the operative factor. This, however, is not so. The first case of this kind that came under observation

dates back to the year 1881, that is to say to the "pre-suggestion" era' (Breuer and Freud, 1895, 7).

164. Freud (1914a), 11–12.

165. Among the participants in the celebration of the twentieth anniversary of Clark University were Franz Boas, William James, Adolf Meyer, James Jackson Putnam, William Stern and E. B. Titchener.

166. On the initial reception of Freud in the United States, see Hale (1971), ch. 8, and Burnham (1967).

167. Personal communication.

168. Forel (1899), 412–13.

169. As his letter to Jones of 1 June 1909 demonstrates, Freud was familiar with the text which Forel delivered at Clark University: 'I got the University's publication at the former celebration ten years ago and could see that none of the five foreigners (Forel, Picard, Boltzmann, Mosso, Ramon y Cajal) had lectured in English' (Freud and Jones 1993, 25).

170. For more details on this affair, see Borch-Jacobsen (1996), chs. 3 and 4. Since the publication of the French edition of this book (2006), Richard Skues has published a critical reconsideration of the historical literature on the subject. The points raised are too detailed to go into here and have not led us to revise our argument (Skues 2006).

171. Breuer and Freud (1895), 40.

172. Hirschmüller (1989), 293.

173. Breuer and Freud (1895), 4.

174. Hirschmüller (1989), 114.

175. To those who would object to Borch-Jacobsen (1996) that this was a 'delayed' cure (Green 1995; Talbot 1998, 60), one may ask why one should attribute Bertha Pappenheim's recovery to her treatment by Breuer, rather than to her subsequent hospitalisations, which seems more likely. As for exonerating Breuer on the grounds that he and Freud never proposed a 'causal' therapy but simply a method to suppress symptoms (Hale 1999, 246), one may note that they wrote in their 'Preliminary Communication' that 'each individual hysterical symptom immediately and permanently disappeared when we had succeeded in bringing clearly to light the memory of the event by which it was provoked' (Breuer and Freud 1895, 6). Moreover, it is clear that Breuer went beyond the assertion of a purely symptomatic treatment when he wrote in his case history: 'In this way, too, the whole hysteria was brought to a close' (*ibid.*, 40), or when he talks about 'the end of the illness' and 'the final cure of the hysteria' (46–7).

176. Hirschmüller (1989), 106–7.

177. Bjerre (1920), 86.

178. Nothing has come to light which would corroborate this element of Freud's account, which is somewhat improbable, as he was a medical student at the time.

179. Jung (1925), 16.
180. Transcription of Eissler's interview with Jung of 29 August 1953, 18, Sigmund Freud Collection, Manuscript Division, Library of Congress, Washington, DC.
181. Ferenczi (1988), 93.
182. Cited in Forrester and Cameron (1999), 930. Bertha Pappenheim was interned for just over three months at the Bellevue clinic.
183. On the contrary: in 1917, Freud recalled how 'Breuer did in fact restore his hysterical patient – that is, freed her from her symptoms . . . This discovery of Breuer's is still the foundation of psycho-analytic therapy' (Freud 1916–17, 279–80). In 1923, Freud again stated that Breuer 'succeeded in freeing her [Anna O.] from all her inhibitions and paralyses, so that in the end he found his trouble rewarded by a great therapeutic success' (Freud 1923, 235; the same assertion occurs in Freud 1925a, 20, and again in Freud 1926b, 263).
184. Freud (1914a), 12.
185. Freud (1925c), 280.
186. At least publicly. In private, as we have seen (p. 70), Breuer didn't hesitate to state that the case of Anna O. refuted Freud's theory.
187. Freud (1925a), 20–1 and 26.
188. Our emphasis. On the provenance of this document, see Borch-Jacobsen (1996), 39–42. The German original has been accessible in the Library of Congress since 2000, and is reproduced in Borch-Jacobsen (1997), 51.
189. Freud (1925c), 279.
190. See Borch-Jacobsen (1996), 33–4; Eissler (2001), 174–5.
191. Forrester and Cameron (1999), 931.
192. Cited in Forrester and Cameron (1999), 930.
193. Freud (1916–17), 274.
194. See above, note 70.
195. Cited by Élisabeth Roudinesco in Ellenberger (1995), 15. In the absence of context, it is not clear when this 'confession' took place.
196. Document supplied by Élisabeth Roudinesco, see Borch-Jacobsen (1996), 100.
197. False: Dora Breuer was born on 11 March 1882, which was three months before the end of the treatment (7 June 1882).
198. Freud (1960), 413; our emphasis. Peter Gay introduced the fragments of this letter to Zweig as follows: 'This, [Freud] reported, is what Breuer told him long ago' (Gay 1988, 67).
199. Cited in Forrester and Cameron (1999), 930; Freud's emphasis.
200. See Hirschmüller (1989), 127, who refers to Fichtner (1988).
201. Breuer was still alive at this time.
202. Rank (1996), 50 and 52.
203. Brill (1948), 38. We thank Richard Skues for signalling this passage.
204. Document communicated by Élisabeth Roudinesco.

205. Goethe, *Faust*, part 2, act 1. As Eissler notes (2001, 176), Breuer himself had cited the same passage in *Studies on Hysteria*: 'I must ask to be forgiven for taking the reader back to the basic problems of the nervous system. A feeling of oppression is bound to accompany any such descent to the "Mothers"' (Breuer and Freud 1895, 192).
206. Freud (1960), 413.
207. Transcription of Eissler's interview with Jung of 29 August 1953, 18.
208. Freud's letter of 26 June 1925 to Robert Breuer, reproduced in Hirschmüller (1989), 322.
209. On 13 May, Freud wrote to Mathilde Breuer, who had sent greetings on his 70th birthday (Freud 1960, 222–3). Hirschmüller reproduces a letter of Freud of 14 December 1928 to Robert Breuer to thank him and his sister for sending a biographical note on their father (Hirschmüller 1989, 322–3).
210. See for example Hannah Breuer's letter to Jones, reproduced in Borch-Jacobsen (1996), Appendix 2.
211. Freud and Eitingon (2004).
212. Eitingon (1998).
213. Hirschmüller (1998).
214. Eitingon (1998), 20.
215. *Ibid.*, 27.
216. Eissler (2001), 174.
217. *Ibid.*, 174–7.
218. Jones (1953), 224. Jones wasn't the first, as Brill had published a less elaborate version of the hysterical pregnancy in his *Lectures on Psychiatric Psychoanalysis* in 1948.
219. Homburger (1954).

3 CASE HISTORIES

1. For a good exposition of this point of view, see Spence (1982).
2. Lacan (2005), 213.
3. Lacan (1988), 13–14.
4. Habermas (1971), 260; our emphasis. Also see Loch (1977), 238.
5. Schafer (1980), 36; our emphasis.
6. *Ibid.*, 35; our emphasis.
7. Saussure (1957), 138–9. Raymond de Saussure had been analysed by Freud.
8. Roazen (1985), 193.
9. Joan Riviere's typed interview with Kurt Eissler, 1953, 9–10, Sigmund Freud Collection, Manuscript Division, Library of Congress, Washington, DC; the document was initially classified until 2020, but has recently been made accessible to researchers.

10. Freud (1907–8b), 76 and 84; Freud's emphasis. We refer to Hawelka's complete French–German edition of Freud's notes whenever the passage is not to be found in Strachey's truncated edition of the 'Original Record'.

11. See above, p. 120.

12. 'Interview with Professor Freud', André Breton (1990 [1924]), 94–5.

13. Freud (1912), 114.

14. Eissler (1965), 395.

15. Freud (1909a), 5: 'The case history [of 'Little Hans'] is not, strictly speaking, derived from my own observation.'

16. To take only a few examples from the era, Bernheim's work (1980 [1891]) included 103 observations; the second volume of Janet's book on psychasthenia (1903) had 236.

17. Freud (1905c), 13. It is true that to this Freud added: 'He would do better to suspend his judgement until his own work has earned him the right to a conviction.'

18. Sherwood (1969), 70.

19. Hacking (1983), 174.

20. See Shapin's classic article (1984), and Shapin and Schaffer (1986).

21. Delbœuf's first chapter (1993a) describes a visit to the Salpêtrière, the second a visit to 'Liébeault's clinic', the third a visit to 'Bernheim's clinic'.

22. Bernheim (1980), ix.

23. Bleuler (1910), 660. For more on this, see also the recollections of Brill (1944), 42, and Hilda Abraham (1976), 62; as well as Falzeder (1994b) and Shamdasani (2002).

24. 'Verzeichnis der Vorlesungen an der Hochschule Zürich', Staatsarchiv, Zurich.

25. See Breuer's report quoted in Hirschmüller (1989), 285. Krafft-Ebing's visit isn't mentioned in the case of 'Anna O.' in *Studies on Hysteria*.

26. Jones (1955), 29.

27. Freud and Ferenczi (1993), 143.

28. Hesnard (1925), quoted in Ohayon (1999), 101.

29. This is indeed true for Ida Bauer ('Dora'), who had fled from the treatment, but not for Ernst Lanzer (the 'Rat Man') or for Sergius Pankejeff (the 'Wolf Man'), who, if we are to believe a note added by Freud in 1923, had both given their formal consent to the publication of their case histories (Freud 1905c, 14).

30. Freud (1905c), 7–9. One will note that Freud's 'assurances of secrecy' were not sufficient to prevent historians from identifying most of his patients. We now know the names of Cäcilie M. (Anna von Lieben), Emmy von N. (Fanny Moser), Elisabeth von R. (Ilona Weiss), Katharina (Aurelia Kronich), Emma (Emma Eckstein), Mr E (Oscar Fellner), Dora (Ida Bauer), the Rat Man (Ernst Lanzer), Little Hans (Herbert Graf) and the Wolf Man (Sergius Pankejeff).

31. As well as regularly transgress – Lynn and Vaillant (1998) have shown that on the basis of data available to them on the subject of Freud's analyses, he had kept

third parties informed on the progress of the treatment in more than half the cases. Indeed, one need only look at almost any correspondence between Freud and his disciples to be struck by the continual stream of indiscretions about his patients, as well as by his polemical use of confidences learned during analysis. Freud even publicised disparaging comments by one of his patients (Pastor Oskar Pfister) concerning Jung, his previous analyst: '[The patient] gave me this information quite spontaneously and I make use of his communication without asking his consent, since I cannot allow that a psycho-analytic technique has any right to claim the protection of medical discretion' (Freud 1914a, 64, n. 2). To Poul Bjerre, Jung wrote: 'In a breach of medical discretion, Freud has even made hostile use of a patient's letter – a letter which the person concerned, whom I know very well, wrote in a moment of resistance against me' (17 July 1914, Jung 1975, xxix–xxx). For the identification of Pfister, see the letter from Abraham to Freud of 16 July 1914 in the new, unexpurgated edition of their correspondence, which shows at which point the medical secret was shared among insiders: 'I think Pf is completely unreliable. His letter quoted in "History" was written in opposition to Jung; with a change of attitude he goes back to Jung, and now back to you again!' (Freud and Abraham 2002, 258). Even a loyal supporter like Jones complained in private of several analytic 'indiscretions' by Freud: 'Here are a few more examples. Not to mention the Swoboda case which is different, there was an occasion when he related to Jekels (when in his analysis) the work on Napoleon on which I had been engaged for two years. Jekels immediately published it in such a good essay that I never wrote anything on the subject. Then Freud told me the nature of Stekel's sexual perversion, which he should not have and which I have never repeated to anyone' (Ernest Jones to Max Schur, 6 October 1955; Jones Papers, Archives of the British Psycho-Analytical Society). We wonder what Jones' reaction would have been had he known of the 1953 interview granted by Joan Riviere to Kurt Eissler about her analysis with Freud – carefully kept under lock and key at the Library of Congress until its recent declassification: 'He [Freud] wanted to get out the emotional reaction to Jones ... He then read me a letter from Jones which made some uncomplimentary remarks about me. And he *expected* me to get very angry. And I was merely hurt that Freud should take the attitude of [*censored word*]' (Sigmund Freud Collection, Manuscript Division, Library of Congress, Washington, DC; Riviere's emphasis).

32. Freud (1905c), 12–13; our emphasis.
33. Strachey (1958), 87.
34. Stadlen (2003), 144–5.
35. Sulloway (1992b), 172–4.
36. On this subject, see Collins' edifying elaboration (1985).
37. Friedländer (1911), 309. See also Friedländer (1907).
38. Janet (1913), 38; included in Janet (1925), vol. 1, 627.

39. Forel (1919), 227.
40. Cioffi (1998b), 182.
41. Jones (1955), 433; Jones (1953), 327.
42. Jones (1953), 315.
43. Once again, psychoanalysis comes back to a pre-modern system of knowledge: 'English "moderns" – repeatedly insisted upon the epistemic inadequacy of testimony and authority. Truth could be guaranteed by going on individual direct experience and individual reason; reliance upon others' testimony was a sure way to error' (Shapin 1994, xxix).
44. See, for example: Swales (1982b); Kuhn (1999); Skues (2001). See Maciejewski (2006) for the reportage of Freud's signing into a room at Hotel Schweizerhaus in Maloja, Switzerland, in August 1898 with his sister-in-law as 'Mr and Mrs Freud'.
45. Lacan (1981), 9; Lacan's emphasis.
46. Cioffi (1974).
47. Mink (1965).
48. Danto (1965), ch. 8; Veyne (1971), ch. 8.
49. Robert Boyle, 'Some considerations about the reconcileableness of reason and religion', quoted in Shapin (1984), 488.
50. Breuer and Freud (1895), 160–1.
51. Aristotle, *Poetics* 1450b.
52. Freud (1905c), 10; our emphasis.
53. Freud (1912), 113–14; our emphasis.
54. See the Preface to Freud (1933), 5: 'At that time I still possessed the gift of a phonographic memory.'
55. Jones Papers, Archives of the British Psycho-Analytical Society.
56. Allusion to the handwritten notes related to a 'third case' that Freud initially intended to append to his text on 'Psychoanalysis and telepathy' (Freud 1921), but which ended up forming the basis for his lecture on the case of Dr Forsyth in 'Dreams and occultism' (Freud 1933). We should note what Strachey wrote about this in his 'Editorial note' to his translation of 'Psychoanalysis and tele-pathy' in the 18th volume of the *Standard Edition*: 'The two versions of the [Forsyth] case agree very closely, with scarcely more than verbal differences; and it has therefore not seemed necessary to include it [the manuscript version] here.' In reality, a comparison between the published version and the original manu-script deposited at the Library of Congress shows that Freud, for no apparent reason, changed the chronology of certain events mentioned in his notes.
57. Jones Papers, Archives of the British Psycho-Analytical Society.
58. Freud (1912), 115–16.
59. Freud (1915a), 166.
60. Freud (1915a), 166.
61. Binswanger (1957), 7–8; Binswanger's emphasis.
62. Freud (1937b), 259–60.

63. Freud (1905c), 37. We know that Ida Bauer terminated the treatment after Freud had tried once again to convince her of her love for Mr K.
64. Freud (1905c), 61; our emphasis.
65. An example pointed out by Scharnberg (1993), vol. 1, 27.
66. On this subject, see Makari's interesting article (1998b), which reconstructs this theory strangely ignored by the majority of Freud's commentators.
67. Freud (1905c), 79–80; our emphasis.
68. *Ibid.*, 80; our emphasis.
69. *Ibid.*, 76.
70. *Ibid.*, 57.
71. Freud (1918), 36.
72. One will note that Freud, according to Pankejeff's account, had asked him exactly the same thing at the beginning of the treatment. 'When he had explained everything to me, I said to him, "All right then, I agree, but I am going to check whether it is correct." And he said: "Don't start that. Because the moment you try to view things critically, your treatment will get nowhere." So I naturally gave up the idea of any further criticism' (Obholzer 1982, 31).
73. Freud (1918), 38–9.
74. *Ibid.*, 39.
75. *Ibid.*, 39.
76. *Ibid.*, 41.
77. *Ibid.*, 70.
78. *Ibid.*, 45.
79. *Ibid.*, 88.
80. For the highly conjectural character of this second 'scene' constructed from one of Pankejeff's vague memories, see Viderman (1970), 109–11; Jacobsen and Steele (1979), 357–8; Spence (1982), 117–20; Esterson (1993), ch. 5.
81. Freud (1918), 92.
82. *Ibid.*, 12.
83. Obholzer (1982), 35–6.
84. Hamburger (1973), 83: 'Epic fiction is the sole epistemological instance where the I-originarity (or subjectivity) of a third-person *qua* third person can be portrayed' (quoted in Cohn 1978, 7).
85. Freud (1908a), 153.
86. 'With her spasmodic cough, which, as is usual, was referred for its exciting stimulus to a tickling in her throat, she pictured to herself a scene of sexual gratification *per os* between the two people whose love-affair occupied her mind so incessantly. Her cough vanished a very short time after this *tacitly accepted explanation* – which fitted in very well with my view' (Freud 1905c, 48; our emphasis). The preceding lines established on the contrary that Ida Bauer, far from having accepted Freud's interpretation, had explicitly rejected it: 'she would not hear of going so far as this in recognizing her own thoughts' (*ibid.*).

87. On free indirect style, first discussed by Bally (1912), see Lips (1926) and Pascal (1977).

88. Spitzer (1928).

89. Cohn (1978), 99–140.

90. Genette (1972), 194.

91. Cohn (1978), 105. Pascal (1977) speaks in this regard of 'dual voice'.

92. Concerning Ida Bauer's hypothetical 'primal scene', Scharnberg thus writes: 'the spying event . . . has been transmuted into *an observed datum*. Dora herself had *recounted her recollection* of having spied' (Scharnberg 1993, vol. 1, 27; Scharnberg's emphasis). But Freud, as we have seen, at no point says that it concerns a memory that Ida Bauer would have told to him.

93. Esterson: 'The Wolf Man himself confirmed that he had not recalled the supposed event [the "primal scene"]. Yet on two occasions Freud reports alleged statements made by his patient in which he describes specific details of the primal scene. Since the Wolf Man is hardly likely to have given descriptions of an occurrence he did not remember, it would seem that Freud misleadingly embellished his account in order to give more credence to his vital interpretation of the wolf-dream' (1993, 69). Here again, Freud's formulations turn out to be much more ambiguous when we examine these passages closely: Pankejeff at most had vague 'auto-perceptions' and it was the 'analysis' – or the analyst? – that made him 'make an assertion' about the primal scene.

94. Lerch (1930), 132–3; Jauss (1970), 203–6 (quoted in Cohn 1978, 106–7).

95. We do not know how these notes escaped destruction, unlike all the others (see Strachey's 'Editorial note', in volume 10 of the *Standard Edition*).

96. As Billig remarks, 'it only takes five minutes to read aloud the longest of Freud's reports of these fifty-minute sessions. Thus, the bulk of the dialogue must be treated as being lost' (1999, 58).

97. Reprinted in Nunberg and Federn (1962), 227–37.

98. Jones (1955), 230.

99. Freud (1907–8b), 76.

100. In the quotations that follow, the italicised and bold-face passages are emphasised by Freud. In Hawelka's edition the italics correspond to passages underlined in ink in the manuscript and the bold characters to passages underlined in crayon. Hawelka explains that 'one can suppose that the author underlined in ink at the moment when he wrote these notes. The lines traced in crayon were added to mark what interested Freud when he read them with a view to editing for publication' (Freud 1907–8b, 14). We have added Hawelka's italics and bold characters whenever we cite from Strachey's editions of the notes. Those that are underlined indicate our emphasis.

101. *Ibid.*, 178 and 180.

102. Freud (1909b), 195–9.

103. The chronological distortion is pointed out by Mahony (1986), 72–4, and the transformation of the patient's refusal into acceptation by Kanzer: 'In the supplementary notes, however, we find no evidence that the patient was really overwhelmed or even influenced by the interpretation' (1952, 234).

104. Freud's interpretation is in fact based on his theory of symbolic equivalence: money–excrement (Freud 1908b, 172–4; 1917b), which theory itself goes back to a series of associations elicited during the treatment of Oscar Fellner ('Mr E'), in January 1897: 'I read one day that the gold the devil gives his victims regularly turns into excrement; and the next day Mr E, who reports that his nurse had money deliria, suddenly told me (by way of Cagliostro – alchemist – *Dukatenscheißer* [one who defecates ducats]) that Louise's money always was excrement' (Freud 1985, 227). Here again, it's unclear if these associations are Freud's or Fellner's.

105. Lacan (2005), 177 and 178, and more generally 176–85.

106. *Ibid.*, 178–80.

107. On the interpretation of psychoanalysis in terms of self-reflection, see Habermas (1971), ch. 10.

108. Freud (1907–8b), 50. One will note that the idea of the torture of the father only comes to Lanzer when he meets Lieutenant David, and not when Captain Nemeczek tells him about the rat torture, as Freud asserts in the case history. Freud's chronological revision can be explained by his desire to attribute the 'rat idea' to a revolt against the father who is represented by the 'cruel captain' (see Freud 1909b, 217–18). Lieutenant David, on the other hand, had no reason to awaken Lanzer's 'paternal complex', nor to elicit the obsessive idea.

109. Freud (1907–8b), 54–6.

110. *Ibid.*, 60: 'The next morning they [Lanzer and his friend Galatzer] go together to the post office to send the 3.80 crowns to the post office in Galicia.'

111. Freud (1909b), 172.

112. *Ibid.*, 211.

113. In this scenario, the young woman at the post office obviously corresponds to the poor girl, and the innkeeper's daughter to the rich girl. Compare the version proposed by Lacan, for whom the object of the Rat Man's fantasy is to 'repay the debt to the poor girl': 'the true object of the subject's tantalizing desire to return to the place where the woman at the post office is, it's not at all this woman; it's a character who, in recent history, *stands in for the character of the poor woman. She is a servant from the inn* whom he met during maneuvers, in the atmosphere of heroic ardor characteristic of historical fraternity, and with whom he indulged in the hanky-panky characteristic of this generous fraternity. It's a question, in some way, of repaying the debt to the poor girl' (Lacan 1953, 19; our emphasis). We see that Lacan's structural interpretation takes no fewer liberties with Freud's case history than Freud does with Lanzer's account. In the end, we are left to wonder what exactly we are talking about.

114. Freud (1907–8a), 290.
115. As we saw above (note 100), the underlining in pencil was subsequent to the underlining in ink.
116. In the margins of the manuscript, Freud wrote in ink (and thus, presumably, the same day): 'paternal transference'.
117. On this lecture of which we have no trace, see Jones (1955), 42, as well as Rank's decidedly uninformative 'report' (1910). According to a letter from Freud to Édouard Claparède, dated 24 May 1908, which is deposited in the collections of the Claparède Archive in Geneva (and we thank Anthony Stadlen for alerting us to its existence), Franz Riklin had made a rather long report of Freud's lecture, destined, it seems, for Claparède's *Archives de psychologie*. We were, unfortunately, unable to locate this document.
118. Freud and Jung (1974), 131.
119. *Ibid.*, 135.
120. *Ibid.*, 136.
121. Janet (1903), vol. 1, 454, 621 and 641–2.
122. Nunberg and Federn (1962), 370–1.
123. This would tend to support Patrick Mahony's hypothesis, according to which Freud would have seen Lanzer only sporadically after 20 January 1908, the date on which the analysis notes end: 'My suspicion is that after January 20 [1908], Freud saw the Rat Man irregularly until April, and after that most irregularly, hence accounting for the absence of any more reference to the patient at meetings of the Vienna Psychoanalytic Society' (Mahony 1986, 81). If we accept this, Lanzer's treatment, which Freud tells us in the case history lasted 'for about a year' (Freud 1909b, 155), would have in fact lasted less than four months, followed by a few individual sessions. This hypothesis would provide an opportune explanation of why the published case, as Hawelka notes, 'adds very little data to that which already appears in the manuscript' (Freud 1907–8b, 12). Mahony's hypothesis, nevertheless, seems to be contradicted by Freud's letter to Édouard Claparède on 24 May 1908, in which Freud declines Claparède's invitation to publish his Salzburg lecture in the *Archives de psychologie*: 'Another reason standing in the way is that the patient in question will not finish his treatment until July, meaning that a definitive report of the case would, at present, be impossible' (Archives Claparède, Geneva).
124. Freud (1909b), 210–11.
125. *Ibid.*, 213–14.
126. Lacan (2005), 249.
127. Once again, we observe that Lacan's narrative revisions are no less blatant than Freud's: where exactly does Lacan find it that Lanzer's father had been dismissed from the Army and that this was the reason for his marriage?
128. Lacan (2005), 293. Also see Lacan (1953); on Lacan's rereading of the 'Rat Man' in terms of 'symbolic debt', see Forrester (1997b).

129. Ellenberger (1972).
130. Ellenberger (1977); Andersson (1979).
131. Gay (1988), 72.
132. Swales (1986).
133. Swales (1988).
134. Swales (1996).
135. Decker (1991), 14.
136. Anna Freud, in Gardiner (1972), xi.
137. Interview with Karin Obholzer, Vienna, 15 March 1994.
138. Five thousand Austrian shillings per month, which were delivered by Kurt Eissler (interview with Karin Obholzer, Vienna, 15 March 1994). Muriel Gardiner, for her part, would occasionally send him much higher sums (up to 12,000 shillings) as 'advances' on the royalties from his 'Memoirs', in exchange for receipts signed by him (Muriel Gardiner to Sergius Pankejeff, 1 November 1976, Muriel Gardiner Collection, Manuscript Division, Library of Congress, Washington, DC). She also paid his taxes. Wilhelm Solms, President of the Psychoanalytic Society of Vienna, provided free analysis that was in fact paid for by the Freud Archives.
139. Gardiner, for example, wouldn't forward him the mail from readers of his 'Memoirs', which he bitterly complained about (Obholzer 1982, 46). This epistolary embargo didn't apply, however, to the letters from analysts like Richard Sterba, Frederick S. Weil, Alfred Lubin or Leo Rangell (Sergius Pankejeff Collection, Manuscript Division, Library of Congress, Washington, DC).
140. See Obholzer's introductory account (1982). Also see Sergius Pankejeff's letter of 18 July 1974 to Muriel Gardiner, in which he mentions Obholzer's proposal: 'Dr. Eissler is of the opinion, as is Dr. Solms, that I should decline this proposition' (Muriel Gardiner Collection, Manuscript Division, Library of Congress, Washington, DC).
141. Freud (1918), 122.
142. Freud (1937a), 218.
143. Gardiner (1972), 263–4. Passage written after Pankejeff's breakdown following his wife's suicide in 1938, which had necessitated a new period of analysis with Mack Brunswick in Paris, then in London.
144. Gardiner (1972), 366.
145. Gardiner sent him psychotropic drugs (Dexamyl) from the United States; see Obholzer (1982), 209–10; see also letter from Kurt Eissler to Muriel Gardiner on 7 March 1965, Muriel Gardiner Collection, Manuscript Division, Library of Congress, Washington, DC. After meeting Pankejeff in Paris, Marie Bonaparte wrote to Jones on 18 June 1954: 'He seems a very sick man' (Jones Papers, Archives of the British Psycho-Analytical Society). According to recently declassified documents at the Library of Congress in Washington, DC, Kraepelin, with whom Pankejeff had been in treatment before going to see Freud, had diagnosed

him as suffering from a manic-depressive state which was hereditary in nature: 'We went to see Kraepelin, who knew my father very well since my father was often at his office ... As far as the diagnosis is concerned, he was of the opinion that like my father I was suffering from states of manic-depression. Exactly like him, I had depression, which was also of a cyclical nature' (typed interview with Kurt Eissler from 29 July 1952, IV, 13–14, Sigmund Freud Collection, Manuscript Division, Library of Congress, Washington, DC). Pankejeff, after decades of analysis, came to the conclusion that it was Kraepelin and not Freud who correctly saw his case for what it was: 'Ah, Kraepelin, he's the only one who understood something about it!' (typed interview with Kurt Eissler from 30 July 1954, 19, *ibid.*).

146. Letter from Pankejeff to Eissler on 3 December 1955 (Sergius Pankejeff Collection, Manuscript Division, Library of Congress, Washington, DC).

147. Gardiner (1983), 872.

148. Gardiner (1972), 363.

149. Obholzer (1982), 171–2.

150. *Ibid.*, 112–13.

151. *Ibid.*, 35.

152. Interview with Karin Obholzer, Vienna, 15 March 1994.

153. Obholzer (1982), 40.

154. Freud (1918), 93.

155. *Ibid.*

156. Obholzer (1982), 134.

157. *Ibid.*, 47.

158. Freud (1918), 122.

159. On Freud's constipation, which he called his 'Konrad', and for which he often sought treatment, see Jones (1955), 59–60 and 83.

160. Gardiner (1972), 266.

161. At the beginning of the analysis, Odessa was still under English control. This was not the only time that Freud put the analysis before Pankejeff's personal wishes and plans: 'But I remember, one time I wanted to go to Budapest for one or two days, but Freud didn't let me go ... "There are many beautiful women in Budapest; you could fall in love with one of them while you're there!" ... Eissler: Why didn't the Professor want you to fall in love? Pankejeff: I believe he thought that the treatment wouldn't progress any further' (typed interview with Kurt Eissler of 30 July 1952, V, 9–10; Sigmund Freud Collection, Manuscript Division, Library of Congress, Washington, DC). Freud had also forbidden Pankejeff from getting married and having children: 'Freud hadn't let P. get married, had forbidden him from having children' (Kurt Eissler, commentary on two interviews with Pankejeff, 30 July 1952, 12, *ibid.*).

162. Gardiner (1972), 111.

163. *Ibid.*, 142, n. 2.

164. Interview with Karin Obholzer, Vienna, 15 March 1994.
165. Obholzer (1982), 47–8.
166. Freud (1910d), 134.
167. Freud (1920b), 263.
168. Freud (1960), 339.
169. Remarks quoted in Trilling (1950), 34.
170. Freud (1907b), 8–9.
171. Nunberg and Federn (1967), 189. See Shamdasani (2003b).
172. For an early and penetrating critique of the reductive confusion Freud imple-
    mented between hermeneutical understanding and the causal explanation
    proper to the natural sciences, see Jaspers (1973). For the reuse of this critique
    in a hermeneutical defence of psychoanalysis, see Habermas (1971), chs. 10
    and 11; Ricoeur (1970; 1981). In brief, for Habermas and Ricoeur, psycho-
    analysis can be saved as a hermeneutics if it lets go of its 'scientific self-
    misunderstanding'; for Jaspers this self-misunderstanding irremediably stamped
    psychoanalysis as a *bad* hermeneutics.
173. Cocteau (1953), 39–42.

4 POLICING THE PAST

1. Anna Freud Collection, Manuscript Division, Library of Congress,
   Washington, DC.
2. It is notably true of Pankejeff, who presented two very different versions of his
   analysis in his *Memoirs* and in his interviews with Obholzer. One example shows
   that his memory wasn't always reliable: to Obholzer, he indicated that he had
   never corresponded with Jones, contrary to what the latter had written in his
   Freud biography (Obholzer 1982, 154–5, 167–9; Jones 1955, 273); however,
   there are two letters sent by Pankejeff to Jones in September 1953 and June 1954
   in which he asks Jones to help him publish one of his articles in English (Jones
   Papers, Archives of the British Psycho-Analytical Society).
3. Wilkinson (1985), 27. On the editing of Freud's correspondences, see Falzeder
   (1997). On the editing of the Freud–Jung letters, see Shamdasani (1997).
4. See above, pp. 33f.
5. Cited by Jeffrey Masson in Freud (1985), 9.
6. See his letter of 17 December 1928 to Ida Fliess in *ibid.*, 5.
7. Marie Bonaparte to Freud, 7 January 1937, *ibid.*, 7.
8. Anna Freud to Ernst Kris, 10 May 1946, cited in Young-Bruehl (1989), 283.
9. Ernst Kris to Siegfried Bernfeld, 5 December 1946, Ernst Kris Collection,
   Manuscript Division, Library of Congress, Washington, DC.
10. Fliess (1897).
11. *Ibid.*, iii.

12. Interview with Frank Sulloway, Cambridge, MA, 19 November 1994.

13. 'I noticed that on certain dates, which clearly recur every 28 days, I have no sexual desire and am impotent – which otherwise is not yet the case, after all' (Freud 1985, 217).

14. 'My father always maintained that he was born on the same day as Bismark – April 1, 1815. In view of the need to convert the date from the Jewish calendar, I never gave much credence to this assertion. So he died after what is probably a typical long life, on October 23/24, 1896; B. on July 30, 1898. B. survived him by 645 days = 23 × 28 + 1. The "1" is no doubt due to my father's error. Therefore the life difference is 23 × 28. You undoubtedly know what that must mean' (Freud 1985, 322). The example is reproduced in Fliess (1906b), 154. For other confirmations provided by Freud, see Fliess (1906b), 51 and 60.

15. The references to cocaine in the correspondence run from 30 May 1893 to 26 October 1896.

16. Freud (1985), 106.

17. Ibid., 320.

18. Ibid., 448.

19. Ibid., 461.

20. See above, p. 323, note 313.

21. Weininger (1903).

22. See above, p. 321, note 188.

23. Freud (1954), 8, n. 2.

24. Ibid., 40, n. 1. The thesis of Fliess' paranoia appears to have been accepted by most of the members of the Freudian circle – see for example the letter of Suzanne Bernfeld to Ernest Jones of 18 November 1953: 'Of course I think that a correct description of this relationship [between Freud and Fliess] would have to include something which it might not be feasible to say at this time when the son and the niece of Fliess are still alive and active psychoanalysts. I think there can be no doubt that Fliess wound up in a real paranoid delusion' (Jones Papers, Archives of the British Psycho-Analytical Society).

25. Freud (1954), 8, n. 1.

26. Ibid., 40.

27. Robert Fliess to Siegfried Bernfeld, 28 August 1944, apropos the 'strongly emotional character' of the relations between Freud and Fliess: 'I have heard a good deal about this from both of them – over a long stretch of years, of course, from my father, and in a long conversation with Freud in 1929, in which he spoke with a frankness apparently not too customary to him in personal matters' (Siegfried Bernfeld Collection, Manuscript Division, Library of Congress, Washington, DC; cited by Masson in Freud 1985, 3).

28. Ernst Kris Collection, Manuscript Division, Library of Congress, Washington, DC.

29. Ibid.

30. *Ibid.*
31. *Ibid.*
32. Anna Freud to Ernst Kris, 29 October 1946, *ibid.*
33. Ernst Kris to Anna Freud, 29 April 1947, *ibid.*
34. James Strachey to Max Schur, 22 December 1966, Sigmund Freud Copyrights, Wivenhoe. Strachey was the only member of the Freudian circle who disapproved of Anna Freud's and Kris' cuts: 'I've just got hold of the Procter-Gregg translation [of the Fliess letters into English] in typescript. It contains a certain amount that was evidently cut out of the German edition subsequently. I confess that I'm *shocked* by some of the omissions' (James Strachey to Ernest Jones, 1 October 1951, Jones Papers, Archives of the British Psycho-Analytical Society; Strachey's emphasis); 'I was much interested by your account of the suppressed passages in the Fliess letters … I do hope that if they come out in English the censorship may be lifted a bit. Unless Anna [Freud] proposes to burn the originals, they're bound to come out in the end; and surely it's better that they should while people are alive who can correct their effect' (James Strachey to Ernest Jones, 24 October 1951, *ibid.*). By contrast Jones was unperturbed by the cuts: 'I am more than half way through the cuts from the Anfänge, most of which, I think, were fully justified' (Ernest Jones to Anna Freud, 16 October 1951, Anna Freud Collection, Manuscript Division, Library of Congress, Washington, DC).
35. Freud (1954), ix.
36. Jones (1953), 288–9.
37. On this edifying episode, revealed for the first time by Max Schur, see Schur (1966; 1972); Masson (1992).
38. Ernst Kris Collection, Manuscript Division, Library of Congress, Washington, DC.
39. Anna Freud Collection, Manuscript Division, Library of Congress, Washington, DC.
40. Freud (1954), 179. Kris simply omitted to signal that this passage was preceded in the original by two pages of calculations designed to align the 'psychological epochs' corresponding to the psychoneuroses with the sexual periods of 23 and 28 days postulated by Fliess.
41. Freud (1910a), 39.
42. Ernst Kris Collection, Manuscript Division, Library of Congress, Washington, DC.
43. On all this, see Sulloway (1992a), ch. 6.
44. Freud (1954), 192; (1985), 230.
45. Freud (1954), 240. Here, without being mentioned, a censored passage ends with 'enough of my smut' (1985), 289.
46. On how Freud's conjectures and hypotheses preceded his clinical observations, see 'Neurotica: Freud and the seduction theory', in Borch-Jacobsen (2009).

47. See the passages cited above, chapter 2, p. 147.
48. See the passages cited above, chapter 2, p. 148.
49. Freud (1985), 213.
50. *Ibid.*, 218.
51. *Ibid.*, 220.
52. *Ibid.*, 223–4.
53. *Ibid.*, 230. In a letter to Strachey of 27 October 1951, Jones noted that Freud arrived at Oedipus through accusing his father of incest: 'And it is odd that he believes his own father seduced only his brother and some younger sisters, thus accounting for their hysteria, at a time when he was suffering from it badly himself' (Jones Papers, Archives of the British Psycho-Analytical Society).
54. Ernst Kris Collection, Manuscript Division, Library of Congress, Washington, DC.
55. *Ibid.*
56. See the letter to Fliess of 28 April 1897: 'Add to this, first, that you were unable to take any pleasure at all in the Middle Ages' (Freud 1985, 237).
57. Freud (1954), 187–8; (1985), 225, for the censured passage. The 'blood' is an allusion to Emma Eckstein's haemorrhages following the disastrous nasal operations performed on her by Fliess.
58. Freud (1985), 189; *ibid.*, 227, for the censured passage.
59. Ernst Kris Collection, Manuscript Division, Library of Congress, Washington, DC.
60. Anna Freud Collection, Manuscript Division, Library of Congress, Washington, DC; cited in Young-Bruehl (1989), 296.
61. Anna Freud Collection, Manuscript Division, Library of Congress, Washington, DC.
62. Jones Papers, Archives of the British Psycho-Analytical Society.
63. *Ibid.*
64. Freud and Ferenczi (1993), 221.
65. See above, chapter 1, 'The politics of self-analysis'.
66. Kris (1947), 4.
67. Freud (1954), 30.
68. *Ibid.*, 33
69. *Ibid.*, 34.
70. See the letters of 12 December 1897 and 27 April 1898.
71. This is why Kris and others in the Freudian circle were very irritated by an otherwise orthodox article of Buxbaum (1951), who had suggested that Fliess had played the role of an analyst to Freud. Suzanne Bernfeld immediately published a critique (Cassirer Bernfeld 1952). As for Jones, he confided to Anna Freud that his 'first thought on reading the Buxbaum article was one of gratitude that the Puner woman [Helen Puner, the author of an unauthorised biography of Freud] had written her book before the *Anfänge* appeared' (Ernest

Jones to Anna Freud, 15 December 1951, Anna Freud Collection, Manuscript Division, Library of Congress, Washington, DC).

72. This is the title of the fourth and last part of Kris' introduction: 'Psychoanalysis as an independent science. (End of the relationship with Fliess).'

73. On this question, see Borch-Jacobsen and Shamdasani (2008).

74. Ernst Kris Collection, Manuscript Division, Library of Congress, Washington, DC.

75. Freud (1954), 32.

76. Anna Freud Collection, Manuscript Division, Library of Congress, Washington, DC.

77. Marie Bonaparte, cited by Ernst Kris in his letter to her of 6 November 1947, Ernst Kris Collection, Manuscript Division, Library of Congress, Washington, DC.

78. Anna Freud to Ernst Kris, 12 October 1947, cited by Kris in his response of 22 October 1947; Ernst Kris Collection, Manuscript Division, Library of Congress, Washington, DC.

79. Ernst Kris Collection, Manuscript Division, Library of Congress, Washington, DC (cf. Freud 1954, 43).

80. Thornton (1983).

81. See for example the letter of 30 May 1893 (Freud 1985, 49). The cardiac symptoms appeared for the first time in the autumn of the same year and became alarming in the spring of 1894.

82. Thornton has compared Freud's symptoms to those described by others who took cocaine nasally at the same time in a convincing manner (Thornton 1983, chs. 10 and 11, 192–5). Freud did not experience the same symptoms between 1884 and 1887, when he first started using cocaine, as he took it orally, which had less powerful pharmacological effects.

83. One notes that Kris silently passed over Fliess' 'nasal diagnosis' which is referred to in Freud's letter of 12 June 1895: 'I am feeling I to IIa [an allusion to Fliessian "periods"]. I need a lot of cocaine. Also, I have started smoking again, moderately, in the last two weeks, since the nasal conviction has become evident to me' (Freud 1985, 132). In the expurgated edition, this passage simply became: 'I have started smoking again, because I still missed it' (Freud 1954, 121).

84. Cited in Kris' letter to Marie Bonaparte of 6 November 1947, Ernst Kris Collection, Manuscript Division, Library of Congress, Washington, DC. There is an undated text in English in the Kris Collection which seems to be a part of the section of his introduction dealing with the self-analysis in which Kris conscientiously cited all the passages in which Freud referred to his own 'neurosis' and 'hysteria'. 'In 1894, when his relation to Breuer went through a crisis, he described cardiac symptoms, which he himself evaluated as psychogenic. While we do not know how far this diagnosis was justified, the "Interpretation of Dreams" and the letters familiarize us with other symptoms, with a fear of

premature death and with a railway phobia, symptoms that disappeared after his self-analysis.'

85. Ernst Kris Collection, Manuscript Division, Library of Congress, Washington, DC.

86. The reference is the letter of 19 April 1894, in Freud (1985), 67–9.

87. Ernst Kris to Marie Bonaparte, 6 November 1947, Ernst Kris Collection, Manuscript Division, Library of Congress, Washington, DC. Max Schur later changed his mind, returning to his diagnosis of coronary thrombosis (Schur 1972, ch. 2), whilst remaining silent on the pharmacological effects of cocaine.

88. Ernst Kris Collection, Manuscript Division, Library of Congress, Washington, DC.

89. Schur (1966) and (1972). Immediately after the publication of his article, Schur tried to convince the Freud family to publish an unexpurgated edition of the letters and he seems to have had a favourable response from Anna Freud (Max Schur to James Strachey, 10 April 1967, Archives of the British Psycho-Analytical Society; Max Schur to Ernst Freud, 5 June 1968, Sigmund Freud Copyrights, Wivenhoe). However, the idea got nowhere.

90. Freud (1985) for the English edition; Freud (1986) for the German edition.

91. Ernst Kris Collection, Manuscript Division, Library of Congress, Washington, DC.

92. *Ibid.*

93. See above, pp. 33f.

94. Despite everything, this appeared in 1971 (Stone 1971).

95. Anna Freud Collection, Manuscript Division, Library of Congress, Washington, DC.

96. Ludwig (1946). Emil Ludwig, who was known for his novelistic biographies and whose works were burned by the Nazis along with those of Freud, had been critiqued by the later in his *New Introductory Lectures on Psychoanalysis*, because he had the misfortune of interpreting the personality of Emperor William II with Adler's theories (Freud 1933, 66). Ludwig conceived of his book on Freud as a response to Freud's critique.

97. Puner (1947).

98. Anna Freud to Ernest Jones, 2 June 1954, Jones Papers, Archives of the British Psycho-Analytical Society.

99. Anna Freud to Ernest Jones, 23 March 1953, *ibid.* Oliver Freud, Anna Freud's brother, thought that Puner's book wasn't that bad and that the errors which it contained were attributable to the fact that she cited accounts by Jung, Stekel and Wittels (Oliver Freud to Ernest Jones, 4 December 1952, *ibid.*).

100. Anna Freud to Ernest Jones, 25 November 1952, *ibid.* See Erikson (1954).

101. Adams (1954).

102. Anna Freud to Ernest Jones, 15 January 1954, Jones Papers, Archives of the British Psycho-Analytical Society.

103. See Eissler's response to Anna Freud's question as to how to respond to Wortis' publication (1954): 'I think Wortis perpetrated almost a crime, and since at least one letter by Prof. Freud was published in facsimile, The Sigmund Freud Copyrights, Ltd. may have a legal angle . . . it is my feeling that the President of the New York Society, or of the American [Psychoanalytic Association], or of the International [Psychoanalytic Association] should do something . . . I think it is the duty of the psychoanalytic organizations to take a very strong stand . . . P.S. Of course, people who understand such matters should decide here, in the United States, whether such a stand against the book may not give it additional publicity, and thus increase the harm' (Kurt Eissler to Anna Freud, 7 February 1955, Anna Freud Collection, Manuscript Division, Library of Congress, Washington, DC).

104. Anna Freud Collection, Manuscript Division, Library of Congress, Washington, DC; cited in Young-Bruehl (1989), 296.

105. Jones (1953), xi.

106. Ernest Jones to Anna Freud, 10 October 1946, Anna Freud Collection, Manuscript Division, Library of Congress, Washington, DC.

107. See Young-Bruehl (1989), 169ff. Jones had accused Anna Freud of having been badly analysed, which led to a rebuff from her analyst, Freud. On 23 September 1927, Freud wrote to Eitingon: 'I got personal and told him that Anna certainly was analyzed for a longer time and more profoundly than he' (cited in Young-Bruehl 1989, 171).

108. On the small group in the 1920s formed by Anna Freud, Siegfried Bernfeld, Willi Hoffer and August Aichhorn, see Young-Bruehl (1989), 99–102.

109. These researches initially appeared in journals in English, and have been collected together in German by Ilse Grubrich-Simitis in Bernfeld and Cassirer Bernfeld (1981).

110. Ernst Kris Collection, Manuscript Division, Library of Congress, Washington, DC.

111. Anna Freud Collection, Manuscript Division, Library of Congress, Washington, DC.

112. The Bernfeld Collection in the Library of Congress contains the sketch of a preface, as well as a plan of fourteen chapters which cover the same period as the first volume of Jones' biography: 'Introduction; 1. Freiberg; 2. Before the Gymnasium; 3. Gymnasium; 4. Three chaotic years; 5. Brücke's Institute; 6. The turn; 7. The General Hospital; 8. Cocaine I; 9. Paris; 10. The first year of practice; 11. Cocaine II; 12. Hypnotism; 13. Free association; 14. (Back to Freiberg)'.

113. Anna Freud Collection, Manuscript Division, Library of Congress, Washington, DC.

114. *Ibid.*

115. Anna Freud to Ernst Kris, 16 May 1947, Anna Freud Collection, Manuscript Division, Library of Congress, Washington, DC.

116. Ernst Kris to Anna Freud, 22 May 1947, Ernst Kris Collection, Manuscript Division, Library of Congress, Washington, DC.

117. Anna Freud to Leon Shimkin, 23 June 1947, Anna Freud Collection, Manuscript Division, Library of Congress, Washington, DC.

118. Ernest Jones to Anna Freud, 3 September 1947, Anna Freud Collection, Manuscript Division, Library of Congress, Washington, DC.

119. Ernest Jones to Siegfried Bernfeld, 23 March 1950, Jones Papers, Archives of the British Psycho-Analytical Society.

120. Jones Papers, Archives of the British Psycho-Analytical Society.

121. Jones (1953), xiv.

122. Interviews with Peter Swales, London, 20 August 1993, to New York, 27 January 1995. This point is also made by Ilse Grubrich-Simitis, who notes that the first volume of Jones' biography is largely a rewriting of Bernfeld's articles. She noted passages which Jones copied without attribution, and Bernfeld's two letters of 1952 expresssing his irritation in this regard (see Bernfeld and Cassirer Bernfeld 1981, 43–6). See Trosman and Wolf (1973).

123. Bernfeld had established the autobiographical nature of this article in Bernfeld (1946).

124. Jones Papers, Archives of the British Psycho-Analytical Society.

125. Ernest Jones to Siegfried Bernfeld, 15 April 1952, Jones Papers, Archives of the British Psycho-Analytical Society.

126. Anna Freud to Ernst Kris, 3 January 1947, Ernst Kris Collection, Manuscript Division, Library of Congress, Washington, DC.

127. Anna Freud to Ernst Kris, 12 October 1949, *ibid*.

128. Anna Freud Collection, Manuscript Division, Library of Congress, Washington, DC.

129. Anna Freud to Kurt Eissler, 27 January 1951, Anna Freud Collection, Manuscript Division, Library of Congress, Washington, DC.

130. Kurt Eissler to Anna Freud, 28 March 1951, *ibid*.

131. Freud (1885b), 51.

132. Erlenmayer (1886), 483.

133. Freud (1900), 111 and 115: 'The misuse abuse of that drug [cocaine] had hastened the death of a dear friend of mine … These injections reminded me once more of my unfortunate friend who had poisoned himself with cocaine. I had advised him to use the drug internally [i.e., orally] only, while morphia was being withdrawn; but he had at once given himself cocaine injections.'

134. Freud (1925a), 62–3. After Jones had qualified this account as 'somewhat disingenuous' in the first volume of his Freud biography (Jones 1953, 79), Albert Hirst, a nephew of Emma Eckstein, wrote to Anna Freud to report that during his analysis with Freud between 1909 and 1910, the latter had affirmed that he had clearly anticipated Koller's discovery and pointed to a passage at the end of his 1884 article where he 'announced' it (Albert Hirst to

Anna Freud, 19 October 1953, Archives of the British Psycho-Analytical Society).

135. In two letters to Jones of 14 May and 18 October 1952, Bernfeld traced the relation between Fleischl's cocaine addiction and his death in 1891 (Jones Papers, Archives of the British Psycho-Analytical Society).

136. Ernest Jones to Siegfried Bernfeld, 28 April 1952, Jones Papers, Archives of the British Psycho-Analytical Society.

137. *Ibid.*

138. Jones Papers, Archives of the British Psycho-Analytical Society.

139. Anna Freud Collection, Manuscript Division, Library of Congress, Washington, DC.

140. For further details on the content of these letters, see Israëls (1999) and Borch-Jacobsen (2000).

141. Sigmund Freud to Martha Bernays, 23 May 1884; cited in Israëls (1999), 97–8.

142. Sigmund Freud to Martha Bernays, 12 July 1884; cited in Israëls (1999), 100.

143. Bernfeld (1975 [1953]).

144. *Ibid.*, 342.

145. *Ibid.*, 348; our emphasis.

146. *Ibid.*, 352. Bernfeld did not ignore Freud's enthusiasm for Fliess' nasal therapy. See Bernfeld to Jones, 14 May 1952, Jones Papers, Archives of the British Psycho-Analytical Society.

147. James Strachey to Ernest Jones, 23 September 1952, Jones Papers, Archives of the British Psycho-Analytical Society.

148. Jones Papers, Archives of the British Psycho-Analytical Society.

149. *Ibid.*

150. Anna Freud Collection, Manuscript Division, Library of Congress, Washington, DC.

151. *Ibid.*

152. Jones (1953), 90.

153. *Ibid.*, 91.

154. *Ibid.*, 93.

155. *Ibid.*, 96.

156. *Ibid.*, 95.

157. Siegfried Bernfeld Collection, Manuscript Division, Library of Congress, Washington, DC.

158. *Ibid.*

159. In a letter to Kurt Eissler of 11 May 1953, Anna Freud was concerned about the control of Bernfeld's papers, which were now in his wife's keeping: 'I don't know how far her judgment can be trusted and how we can prevent her from putting the material to a wrong use, if she should want to do so . . . Does Suse Bernfeld really have the right, for example, to publish my father's correspondence with Wagner-Jauregg?' On 18 May Eissler replied: 'I obtained the

impression that Mrs. Bernfeld is in a particularly labile condition and any counter-measure against her publication of that paper [on Freud and Wagner-Jauregg] may precipitate a serious reaction ... I have the feeling that Otto Maenchen would be a very good person to discuss the matter with her and possibly could do it without mentioning at all that this was requested from him by London' (Anna Freud Collection, Manuscript Division, Library of Congress, Washington, DC). Anna Freud's fears were baseless, as Suzanne Bernfeld continued to respond to Jones' requests for information.

160. Anna Freud to Ernest Jones, 18 March 1954, Jones Papers, Archives of the British Psycho-Analytical Society.

161. Anna Freud to Ernest Jones, 5 and 25 November 1952, *ibid.*; Ernest Jones to Anna Freud, 10 and 18 November 1952, Anna Freud Collection, Manuscript Division, Library of Congress, Washington, DC.

162. Anna Freud to Ernest Jones, 4 April 1954, Jones Papers, Archives of the British Psycho-Analytical Society.

163. Anna Freud to Ernest Jones, 16 June 1954, *ibid.*

164. Anna Freud to Ernest Jones, 16 June 1954, *ibid.* Anna Freud continued: 'Personally, I wish that the letters concerning him had been destroyed.'

165. Ernest Jones to Anna Freud, 28 November 1951, Anna Freud Collection, Manuscript Division, Library of Congress, Washington, DC.

166. Ernst Kris to Anna Freud, 29 April 1947, Ernst Kris Collection, Manuscript Division, Library of Congress, Washington, DC.

167. Jones (1953), 304.

168. *Ibid.*, 287, n. 1.

169. *Ibid.*, 306.

170. *Ibid.*, 305. Contrary to what Jones implies, *Reisefieber* in German signifies nothing other than a banal travel nerves.

171. Jones (1955), 19.

172. Jones (1953), 311.

173. *Ibid.*, 304–5.

174. *Ibid.*, 309.

175. *Ibid.*, 291.

176. *Ibid.*, 316.

177. *Ibid.*, 300.

178. *Ibid.*, 303.

179. *Ibid.*, 324.

180. *Ibid.*, 307.

181. In private, however, Jones didn't fail to criticize the 'Kris atrocities' (Ernest Jones to James Strachey, 6 November 1951, Jones Papers, Archives of the British Psycho-Analytical Society). On 24 October 1951, Strachey had sent him a detailed critique of Kris' argument, according to which the discovery of infantile sexuality was to have coincided with the self-analysis and the

abandonment of the seduction theory: 'My point is that the recognition of infantile sexuality as a normal activity – as distinct from the mere occurrence of abnormal sexual experiences – was only accepted by Freud *gradually* – over the years between 1897 and 1899' (Jones Papers, Archives of the British Psycho-Analytical Society). Response to Jones, 27 October 1951: 'I have been too complacent about Kris's pre-vision of the future, although it is a fascinating topic. Many of them [*sic*] are very *nachträglich*' (*ibid.*).

182. Jones (1953), 3–4.
183. *Ibid.*, 254.
184. *Ibid.*, 255. This description was sharply contested by Breuer's daughter-in-law; see Borch-Jacobsen (1996), Appendix 2.
185. Jones (1953), 225.
186. See above, p. 170, where we reproduce the letter in question.
187. Jones (1953), 225.
188. Jones Papers, Archives of the British Psycho-Analytical Society. Cf. Freud (1925a), 20 and 25.
189. See above, pp. 168f.
190. Jones Papers, Archives of the British Psycho-Analytical Society.
191. Freud (1953–74), vol. 2, 40–1.
192. Jones (1953), 255.
193. *Ibid.*, 252.
194. *Ibid.*, 360.
195. Jones (1955), 12–13.
196. Jones (1953), 271. We will compare with the document entitled 'Freud in Paris' which Marie Bonaparte sent to Jones and in which she reported what Freud had said to her on 8 April 1928 about his 1885–6 stay in Paris: 'Then Freud went, with his friend, into a café, and there, the friend invited five or six "respectable" women to their table. One, who had a suspicious efflorescence on her nose, prided herself on undressing in just seconds.' Freud had added, it is true: 'Everything with these ladies was limited to a few drinks' (Jones Papers, Archives of the British Psycho-Analytical Society).
197. Jones (1953), 139.
198. Jones (1955), 421; see also 386: 'His wife was assuredly the only woman in Freud's love life, and she came first before all other mortals.' Here, however, is what Helen Puner, who gained this information from dissidents like Jung and Stekel, had to say: 'Early in their marriage he came to regard his wife with the same analytic detachment he regarded a neurotic symptom' (Puner 1947, 136). Max Schur, likewise, expressed his disbelief about Jones' description in a letter to him on 30 September 1955: 'As to Martha – here I have my doubts whether at the time I knew them she still was the "one and only". As far as I could see it, he spent less and less time with her . . . there was so little left of the great love that I was quite surprised by Volume I [the account of the engagement]' (Anna

Freud Collection, Manuscript Division, Library of Congress, Washington, DC).

199. Jones (1955), 386.

200. To Ferenczi, who had developed the habit of exchanging kisses with his patients, he wrote: 'Now I am assuredly not one of those who from prudishness or from consideration of bourgeois convention would condemn little erotic gratification of this kind' (Freud and Ferenczi 2000, 479). To James Jackson Putnam, Freud wrote: 'I stand for a much freer sexual life. However, I have made little use of such freedom, except in so far as I was convinced of what was permissible for me in this area' (Hale 1971, 189). This issue is taken by Peter Swales in 'Did Freud always carry an umbrella – or – did he ever take a cab?' (Swales 1994).

201. Jones (1955), 5.

202. Bettelheim (1957), 419. Rumours had circulated in Vienna about a liaison between Freud and Minna Bernays, which Jung later corroborated. 'Jung: This is a fact: the youngest sister made a giant transference and Freud *was not insensible* [in English in the text], – Eissler: You mean, there was a liaison with the youngest sister? – Jung: Oh, a liaison!? I don't know to what extent!? But, my God, we know very well how it is, don't we!?' (typewritten interview of 29 August 1953, 11; also see Billinsky 1969 and Swales 1982b). The testimony of Max Graf, father of 'Little Hans', is just as ambiguous: 'Graf: I had the impression that there was something strange in the relationship with the sister-in-law . . . But as things weren't very clear, I didn't want to speak publicly about it . . . – Eissler: Did he have sexual relations with her? – Graf: I don't believe so' (Graf 1995–6, 155). These are the rumours that Jones surreptitiously evoked when he wrote: 'Freud no doubt appreciated [Minna Bernays'] conversation, but to say that she in any way replaced her sister in his affection is sheer nonsense' (Jones 1955, 387).

203. *Ibid.*, 3.

204. Jones (1953), 255.

205. Jones (1955), 137; Jones quoting Freud.

206. *Ibid.*, 7.

207. *Ibid.*, 33.

208. *Ibid.*, 62.

209. *Ibid.*, 82.

210. *Ibid.*, 130.

211. *Ibid.*, 160.

212. *Ibid.*, 112 and 118.

213. *Ibid.*, 114: Jones quoting Freud.

214. *Ibid.*, 115.

215. *Ibid.*, 114.

216. *Ibid.*, 117.

217. *Ibid.*, 40.
218. *Ibid.*, 256.
219. *Ibid.*, 114.
220. *Ibid.*, 117.
221. Jones (1953), 361.
222. Jones (1955), 115.
223. *Ibid.*, 108–9.
224. Lilla Veszy-Wagner to Ernest Jones, 29 January 1954, Jones Papers, Archives of the British Psycho-Analytical Society.
225. These abstracts can be consulted in the Jones Archive collection of the Institute of Psycho-Analysis in London. Insofar as certain abstracts are reproduced word for word in Jones' biography, we are led to conclude that he hadn't read for himself some of the articles he was ridiculing.
226. Jones (1955), 111; quoted by Lilla Veszy-Wagner in her abstract of Spielmeyer (1905).
227. Jones (1955), 116; this supposed quotation from Hoche (1910) was in fact an adaptation of the *abstract* by Lilla Veszy-Wagner.
228. Jones (1955), 111; quoted by Lilla Veszy-Wagner in her abstract of Rieger (1896); 'simply' was added by Jones.
229. 'Notes on Defamatory Passages by J. E. C. Macfarlane, 27.1.55', Hogarth Press Archives, University of Reading.
230. Veszy-Wagner (1966), 119.
231. 'Notes on Defamatory Passages by J. E. C. Macfarlane, 27.1.55', 5, Hogarth Press Archives, University of Reading.
232. Hogarth Press Archives, University of Reading.
233. *Ibid.*
234. *Ibid.*
235. Jung (1975), 144. Jones referred to Freud's fainting at Bremen in Jones (1955), 61.
236. Bennet (1985), 114. In the unpublished version of Bennet's notebooks, Jung told Bennet on 16 September 1959 that Jones never had any original ideas and never liked him. On 19 September, he noted that Jones was mistaken to claim that it was Freud and Ferenczi who had persuaded him to break his vow of abstinence from alcohol (required of all physicians at the Burghölzli) to drink wine in August 1909 (Jones 1955, 61), as he had already left the Burghölzli, and celebrated by going drinking (Bennet Papers, Swiss Federal Institute of Technology, Zurich). Alphonse Maeder recalled that on occasion, at a meeting of the Swiss Society of Psychiatry, 'Bleuler made a violent storm of abuse . . . against the assistants who let themselves abandon abstinence (Jung after his trip with Freud in the USA, and myself later); and went so far as to say that if he had seen this in advance, he would not have introduced psychoanalysis into the Burghölzli' (Maeder to Ellenberger, 1 March 1967, Centre Henri Ellenberger, Hôpital Sainte-Anne, Paris).

237. Jones (1957), 45.
238. Freud and Ferenczi (2000), 15.
239. On this edifying episode, see Lieberman (1985).
240. Freud and Ferenczi (2000), 215.
241. Quoted in Jones (1957), 76.
242. Wortis (1954), 121. In 1926, the American psychiatrist Martin Peck had abandoned the idea of being analysed by Rank after hearing that Jones considered him to be 'hypomanic' (Lieberman 1985, 268).
243. Jones (1957), 12–13.
244. *Ibid.*, 47.
245. *Ibid.*, 58.
246. *Ibid.*, 74.
247. *Ibid.*, 77.
248. *Ibid.*
249. Sigmund Freud to Marie Bonaparte, 11 September 1932; quoted in *ibid.*, 174.
250. Sigmund Freud to Max Eitingon, 3 April 1933; quoted in Gay (1988), 585.
251. Freud and Jones (1993), 721; our emphasis.
252. Jones (1957), 176.
253. *Ibid.*, 178.
254. Jones Papers, Archives of the British Psycho-Analytical Society.
255. *Ibid.*
256. *Ibid.* Publicly, Balint expressed his disagreement with Jones much more mutedly and prudently in a letter that was published in the *International Journal of Psychoanalysis* with a response from Jones (Balint 1958). Commenting on this exchange, Erich Fromm remarked that 'if such a tortuous and submissive letter had been written by a personality of less stature than Balint or else to avoid serious consequences relating to life or liberty in a dictatorial system, that would be understandable. But ... this only shows the intensity of the pressure that forbids any criticism, if not extremely mild, from a member of the organisation' (Fromm 1970, 22).
257. Jones Papers, Archives of the British Psycho-Analytical Society.
258. Quoted in Falzeder (1998), 133.
259. *The Observer* (Sydney), 9 January 1960.
260. Jones (1955), 421.
261. See Freud and Ferenczi (2000). Also see the letter from Jones to Anna Freud of 29 July 1952: 'Balint makes life as complicated as he can. Now he has discovered a promise to Gisella Fer. [Gizella Ferenczi, ex-Pálos] that no one is to use the allusions to her for 50 years (as if I wanted to, or as if I didn't know all about their problems!)' (Anna Freud Collection, Manuscript Division, Library of Congress, Washington, DC).
262. See Young-Bruehl (1989), ch. 3; Mahony (1992a).
263. On Tausk, see Roazen (1969); on Silberer, see Roazen (1975).

264. Jones Papers, Archives of the British Psycho-Analytical Society.
265. Storfer's doubts concerning the *Diary*'s authenticity were mentioned by Anna Freud in a *Rundbrief* of 17 February 1927 (Jones Papers, Archives of the British Psycho-Analytical Society).
266. Jones Papers, Archives of the British Psycho-Analytical Society. In fact, the *Diary*'s inauthenticity was definitively established by Josef Krug in 1926, based on anachronisms and chronological contradictions. The following year, the *Internationaler Psychoanalytischer Verlag* printed an advertisement in the newsletter of German bookstores with the aim of retrieving all the copies of the work that were still for sale (about this, see Israëls 2006, 139–43). It is difficult to believe that Jones hadn't been aware of this.
267. Jones (1957), 49.
268. In fact, *The Origins of Psychoanalysis* only appeared in 1954.
269. Jones Papers, Archives of the British Psycho-Analytical Society.
270. Ernest Jones to James Strachey, 3 November 1953, Jones Papers, Archives of the British Psycho-Analytical Society.
271. Inscription written by Kurt Eissler on an envelope he deposited in the Library of Congress and which contained newspaper articles relating to the trial of Freud's uncle for trafficking counterfeit coins: 'Top secret microfilm of newspaper article. – *Not* to be opened, except by Dr K. R. Eissler.' The contents of the present section reproduce elements developed more fully in Borch-Jacobsen and Shamdasani (2002). The first to reconstruct and document the history of the Freud archives and its systematic obstruction of research was Peter Swales, in his landmark presentation, 'Freud and the unconscionable: the obstruction of Freud studies, 1946–2113' (Swales 1991).
272. Bettelheim (1957), 418.
273. Jones Papers, Archives of the British Psycho-Analytical Society.
274. *Ibid.*
275. Anna Freud Collection, Manuscript Division, Library of Congress, Washington, DC.
276. *Ibid.*
277. Siegfried Bernfeld to Kurt Eissler, 4 January 1951, Anna Freud Collection, Manuscript Division, Library of Congress, Washington, DC.
278. The philosopher Richard Avenarius was, along with Ernst Mach, one of the originators of empirico-criticism (empirical criticism).
279. Anna Freud Collection, Manuscript Division, Library of Congress, Washington, DC.
280. *Ibid.*
281. *Ibid.*
282. *Ibid.*
283. *Ibid.*
284. *Ibid.*

285. *Ibid.*
286. For an example of a particularly lucrative appraisal, see Borch-Jacobsen and Shamdasani (2002), 294.
287. 1994 Interview; the situation has changed in part since Eissler's death in 1999.
288. Interview with Paul Roazen, Toronto, 20 November 1994.
289. 'Agreement between The Library of Congress and The Sigmund Freud Archives, Inc.', 5 July 1951. We thank the Library of Congress for allowing us to consult this internal document pursuant to article 1917–3 of the Library of Congress Regulations.
290. Swales (1991). Swales was the first, in this debate, to reconstruct the history of the creation of the Freud Archives.
291. Kurt R. Eissler, transcript of an interview with E. A. Bennet, July 1972, Sigmund Freud Collection, Manuscript Division, Library of Congress, Washington, DC; our emphasis. These two letters, for which Bennet had not demanded any restrictions on access, were only made available to researchers in the year 2000.
292. Interview with Marvin W. Kranz, Manuscript Historian, Library of Congress, Washington, DC, 15 June 2000.
293. 'Erstes Treffen mit Dr. P. nach der Vorbesprechung 10 A. M. im Hotel', Sigmund Freud Collection, Manuscript Division, Library of Congress, Washington, DC; could not be photocopied until 2010.
294. Pfister Archives, Zentralbibliothek, Zurich.
295. Typewritten interview, 1, Sigmund Freud Collection, Manuscript Division, Library of Congress, Washington, DC; cannot be photocopied until 2013.
296. Marie Bonaparte Collection, Manuscript Division, Library of Congress, Washington, DC.
297. Eissler interviewed her three times – twice in 1952 and once in 1953. The respective derestriction dates are 2010, 2017 and 2057.
298. Pointed out by Swales (1991).
299. Interview with Frank J. Sulloway, Cambridge, MA, 19 November 1994.
300. Interview with Paul Roazen, Toronto, 20 November 1994. Roazen is the first researcher to have openly criticised the restrictions imposed by the Freud Archives.
301. Roazen (1990), 96.
302. Private correspondence.
303. Declaration by James H. Billington, Librarian of Congress, during the bicentennial celebration of the Library of Congress, 24 April 2000.
304. See for example Malcolm's anecdotal description (1984).

CODA: WHAT WAS PSYCHOANALYSIS?

1. Wittenberger and Teugel (1999), 118. Given the constantly moving goalposts, Jones himself was not always clear on this point – on 8 December 1915, he wrote to Freud: 'In my article on repression and memory ... I criticised Jung for a statement which I now find in your recent article on repression. This is very sad, isn't it?' (Freud and Jones 1993, 314).
2. Burnham (1967), 214.
3. Hacking (1998).
4. Lévi-Strauss (1973), xliv–l.
5. Lawrence (1986 [1923]), 201.
6. Cioffi (2005), 316–17.
7. See Borch-Jacobsen (2009), ch. 9.
8. Wallerstein (1995), 510.
9. Wallerstein (1988), 17.
10. See Crews (1995; 1998) and Skues (1998).
11. See Borch-Jacobsen, 'Foreword', in Dufresne (2000).
12. For an anthropological study of (now rapidly declining) psychoanalytic institutes in the USA, see Kirschner (2000).

Bibliography

Abraham, Hilda (1976), *Karl Abraham. Sein Leben für die Psychoanalyse*, Munich, Kindler.

Abraham, Karl (1954 [1919]), 'A particular form of neurotic resistance against the psycho-analytic method', in *Selected Papers of Karl Abraham*, with an introductory essay by Ernest Jones, trans. Douglas Bryan and Alix Strachey, New York, Basic Books, 303–11.

Adam, Émile (1923), *Le freudisme. Étude historique et critique de méthodologie psychothérapique*, Colmar, Alsatia.

Adams, Leslie (1954), 'Sigmund Freud's correct birthdate: misunderstanding and solution', *Psychoanalytic Review*, **41**, 359–62.

Adler, Alfred (1972 [1912]), *Über den nervösen Charakter*, Frankfurt, Fischer.

Alexander, Franz and Selesnick, Sheldon T. (1965), 'Freud–Bleuler correspondence', *Archives of General Psychiatry*, **12**, 1–9.

Alt, Konrad (1908) in Gerard van Weyenburg (ed.), *Comptes rendus du Congrès international de psychiatrie et de neurologie*, Amsterdam, G. H. De Bussy, 293.

Andersson, Ola (1962), *Studies in the Prehistory of Psychoanalysis. The Etiology of Psychoneuroses and Some Related Themes in Sigmund Freud's Scientific Writings and Lectures, 1888–1896*, Stockholm, Svenska Bokförlaget.

(1979), 'A supplement to Freud's case history of "Frau Emmy v. N."', in *Studies on Hysteria 1895*, *Scandinavian Psychoanalytic Review*, **2**, no. 5, 5–16.

Anzieu, Didier (1986), *Freud's Self-Analysis*, trans. P. Graham, London, Hogarth Press.

Arduin, Dr (1900), 'Die Frauenfrage und die sexuellen Zwischenstufen', *Jahrbuch für sexuelle Zwischenstufen*, **2**, 211–23.

Aschaffenburg, Gustav (1906), 'Die Beziehung des sexuellen Lebens zur Entstehung von Nerven- und Geistes Krankheiten', *Münchener medizinische Wochenschrift*, **53**, 11 September, 1793–8.

(1907), 'Internationaler Kongress für Psychiatrie, Neurologie, Psychologie und Kranksinnigen Verpflegung', *Monatsschrift für Psychologie und Neurologie*, **22**.

(1911), review of Freud (1910a), *Zeitschrift für die gesammte Strafrechtwissenschaft*, **30**, 754–5.

Assoun, Paul-Laurent (1981), *Introduction à l'épistémologie freudienne*, Paris, Payot.

Balint, Michael (1958), Letter to the Editor, *International Journal of Psycho-Analysis*, **34**, 68.

Bally, Charles (1912), 'Le style indirect libre en français moderne', *Germanisch-Romanische Monatsschrift*, **4**, 549–56 and 597–606.

Beard, George and Rockwell, Alphonso (1880 [1872]), *A Practical Treatise on the Medical and Surgical Uses of Electricity, Including Localized and General Electricization*, New York, William Wood.

Bell, Sanford (1902), 'A preliminary study of the emotions of love between the sexes', *American Journal of Psychology*, **13**, 325–54.

Bennet, Edward A. (1985), *Meetings with Jung. Conversations Recorded by E. A. Bennet during the Years 1946–1961*, Einselden, Daimon.

Bernfeld, Siegfried (1946), 'An unknown autobiographical fragment by Freud', *American Imago*, **4**, no. 1, 3–19.

(1975 [1953]), 'Freud's studies on cocaine', in Sigmund Freud, *Cocaine Papers*, ed. Robert Byck, New York and Scarborough, Ontario, New American Library, 321–52.

Bernfeld, Siegfried and Cassirer Bernfeld, Suzanne (1981), *Bausteine der Freud-Biographik*, ed. Ilse Grubrich-Simitis, Frankfurt am Main, Suhrkamp.

Bernheim, Hippolyte (1892 [1891]), *Neue Studien über Hypnotismus, Suggestion und Psychotherapie*, trans. into German by Sigmund Freud, Leipzig and Vienna, Deuticke.

(1980 [1891]), *New Studies in Hypnotism*, trans. Richard S. Sandor, New York, International Universities Press.

Bettelheim, Bruno (1957), review of Ernest Jones, *The Life and Work of Sigmund Freud*, vols. 1 and 2, *American Journal of Sociology*, **62**, January.

Bezzola, Dumeng (1908), 'Zur Analyse psychotraumatischer Symptome', *Journal für Psychologie und Neurologie*, **8**, 204–19.

Billig, Michael (1999), *Freudian Repression. Conversation Creating the Unconscious*, Cambridge, Cambridge University Press.

Billinsky, John M. (1969), 'Jung and Freud (the end of a romance)', *Andover Newton Quarterly*, **10**, 39–43.

Binet, Alfred and Simon, Théodore (1910), 'Hystérie', *L'Année Psychologique*, **16**, 67–122.

Binswanger, Ludwig (1957), *Sigmund Freud. Reminiscences of a Friendship*, New York and London, Grune & Stratton.

Bjerre, Poul (1920 [1916]), *The History and Practice of Psychoanalysis*, trans. Elizabeth N. Barrow, Boston, R. G. Badger.

Bleuler, Eugen (1892), review of Hippolyte Bernheim, *Neue Studien über Hypnotismus, Suggestion und Psychotherapie*, *Münchener medizinische Wochenschrift*, **39**, 431.

(1896), review of Breuer and Freud (1895), *Münchener medizinische Wochenschrift*, **43**, 524–5.

(1904), review of Leopold Löwenfeld, *Die psychischen Zwangserscheinungen*, *Münchener medizinische Wochenschrift*, **51**, 718.

(1910), 'Die Psychanalyse Freuds: Verteidigung und kritische Bemerkungen', *Jahrbuch für psychoanalytische und psychopathologische Forschungen*, **2**, 623–730.

(1913), 'Kritik der Freudschen Theorien', *Zeitschrift für Psychiatrie*, **70**, 665–718.

(1928), review of Sigmund Freud, *Gesammelte Schriften*, **11**, *Münchener medizinische Wochenschrift*, **75**, 1728.

Bleuler, Manfred (ed.) (1979), *Beiträge zur Schizophrenielehre der Zürcher Psychiatrischen Universitätsklinik Burghölzli (1902–1971)*, Darmstadt, Wissenschaftliche Buchgesellschaft.

Bloor, David (1976), *Knowledge and Social Imagery*, London, Routledge and Kegan Paul.

Blum, Harold and Pacella, Bernard L. (1995), 'Exchange', in Frederick Crews (ed.), *The Memory Wars. Freud's Legacy in Dispute*, New York, A New York Review Book, 104–6.

Borch-Jacobsen, Mikkel (1987), 'L'hypnose dans la psychanalyse', followed by 'Dispute', in Léon Chertok (ed.), Hypnose et psychanalyse,
Paris, Bordas, 29–54, 194–215.
——— (1988 [1982]), The Freudian Subject, trans. Catherine Porter, Stanford,
CA, Stanford University Press.
——— (1992 [1991]), The Emotional Tie. Psychoanalysis, Mimesis, and Affect,
trans. Douglas Brick and others, Stanford, CA, Stanford University
Press.
——— (1996), Remembering Anna O. A Century of Mystification, trans.
Kirby Olson in collaboration with Xavier Callahan and the author,
New York, Routledge.
——— (1997), Anna O. zum Gedächtnis. Eine hundertjährige Irreführung,
revised and augmented edition, trans. into German by
Martin Stingelin, Munich, Wilhelm Fink Verlag.
——— (2000), 'How a fabrication differs from a lie', London Review of Books,
April 13, 3–7.
——— (2002), Folies à plusieurs. De l'hystérie à la dépression, Paris, Les
Empêcheurs de Penser en Rond/Seuil.
——— (2009), Making Minds and Madness. From Hysteria to Depression, trans.
Douglas Brick et al. in collaboration with the author, Cambridge,
Cambridge University Press.
Borch-Jacobsen, Mikkel and Shamdasani, Sonu (2002), 'Une visite aux
Archives Freud', in Borch-Jacobsen (2002), 253–300.
——— (2006), Le dossier Freud. Enquête sur l'histoire de la psychanalyse, Paris,
Les Empêcheurs de Penser en Rond/Seuil.
——— (2008), 'Interprefactions: Freud's legendary science', History of the
Human Sciences, 21, 1–25.
Boring, Edwin G. (1929), A History of Experimental Psychology, New York
and London, D. Appleton-Century Company.
Brentano, Franz (1874), Psychology from an Empirical Standpoint, trans.
A. Rancurello, D. Terrell and L. McAlister, London, Routledge, 1973.
Breton, André (1990 [1924]), Les pas perdus, Paris, Gallimard.
Breuer, Josef (1895), review of the intervention of 4 November 1895 of
Josef Breuer at the Vienna Medical College on the subject of the
lecture of Sigmund Freud 'On hysteria', Wiener medizinische Presse,
36, 1717–18.

Breuer, Josef and Freud, Sigmund (1895), *Studies on Hysteria*, SE 2.

Brill, Abraham Arden (1944), *Freud's Contribution to Psychiatry*, London, Chapman & Hall.

(1948), *Lectures on Psychoanalytic Psychiatry*, London, John Lehmann.

Brome, Vincent (1984), *Freud and his Disciples. The Struggle for Supremacy*, London, Caliban.

Bry, Ilse and Rifkin, Alfred H. (1962), 'Freud and the history of ideas: primary sources, 1888–1910', Jules H. Masserman (ed.), *Science and Psychoanalysis*, **5**, 6–36.

Burnham John (1960), 'Sigmund Freud and G. Stanley Hall: exchange of letters', *Psychoanalytic Quarterly*, **29**, 307–16.

(1967), *Psychoanalysis and American Medicine, 1894–1918. Medicine, Science and Culture*, New York, International Universities Press.

(1983), *Jelliffe. American Psychoanalyst and Physician and His Correspondence with Sigmund Freud and C. G. Jung*, ed. William Mcguire, Chicago, IL, University of Chicago Press.

Buxbaum, Edith (1951), 'Freud's dream interpretation in the light of his letters to Fliess', *Bulletin of the Menninger Clinic*, **15**, no. 6, 197–212.

Callon, Michel and Latour, Bruno (eds.) (1990), *La science telle qu'elle se fait. Anthologie de la sociologie des sciences de langue anglaise*, Paris, La Découverte.

Campbell, Joseph (1968 [1949]), *The Hero with a Thousand Faces*, Princeton, NJ, Princeton University Press.

Carlyle, Thomas (1959 [1841]), *On Heroes, Hero-Worship and the Heroic in History*, in *Sartor Resartus*, London, J. M. Dent & Sons, 239–467.

Cassirer Bernfeld, Suzanne (1952), 'Discussion of Buxbaum, Freud's dream interpretation in the light of his letters to Fliess', *Bulletin of the Menninger Clinic*, **16**, no. 2, 70–2.

Charteris, Hugo (1960), 'Dr Jung looks back and on', *Daily Telegraph*, 21 January.

Chesterton, Gilbert K. (1923), 'The game of psychoanalysis', *The Century*, **106**, 34–5.

Chevalier, Julien (1893), *Une maladie de la personnalité. L'inversion sexuelle; psycho-physiologie, sociologie, tératologie, aliénation mentale, psychologie morbide, anthropologie, médecine judiciaire*, Lyon and Paris, A. Storck.

Chodoff, Paul (1966), 'A critique of Freud's theory of infantile sexuality', *American Journal of Psychiatry*, **123**, no. 5, 507–18.

Cioffi, Frank (1973), 'The myth of Freud's hostile reception', in Frank Cioffi (ed.), *Modern Judgements. Freud*, London, Macmillan. Also in Cioffi (1998a), 161–81.

——(1974), 'Was Freud a liar?', *The Listener*, 7 February. Also in Cioffi (1998a), 199–204.

——(1984), 'The cradle of neurosis', *Times Literary Supplement*, 6 July. Also in Cioffi (1998a), 205–10.

——(1988), '"Exegetical myth-making" in Grünbaum's indictment of Popper and exoneration of Freud', in Crispin Wright and Peter Clark (eds.), *Psychoanalysis and Theories of the Mind*, Oxford, Blackwell. Also in Cioffi (1998a), 240–64.

——(1998a), *Freud and the Question of Pseudoscience*, Chicago and La Salle, IL, Open Court.

——(1998b), 'The Freud controversy: what is at issue', in Michael S. Roth (ed.), *Freud. Conflict and Culture*, New York, Knopf, 171–82.

——(2005), 'Épistémologie et mauvaise foi: le cas freudien', in Catherine Meyer (ed.), *Le livre noir de la psychanalyse*, Paris, Les Arènes, 306–27.

Clarke, Adele E. and Fujimura, Joan H. (eds.) (1992), *The Right Tools for the Job. At Work in the Twentieth-Century Life Sciences*, Princeton, NJ, Princeton University Press.

Clarke, John Michell (1896), review of Breuer and Freud (1895), *Brain*, **19**, 401–14.

Cocteau, Jean (1953), *Journal d'un inconnu*, Paris, Grasset.

Cohen, I. Bernard (1976), 'The eighteenth-century origins of the concept of scientific revolution', *Journal of the History of Ideas*, **27**, 257–88.

Cohn, Dorrit (1978), *Transparent Minds. Narrative Modes for Presenting Consciousness in Fiction*, Princeton, NJ, Princeton University Press.

Collins, Harry M. (1985), *Changing Order. Replication and Induction in Scientific Practice*, London, Sage.

Comte, Auguste (1830–42), *Cours de philosophie positive*, 6 vols., Paris, Bachelier.

Cranefield, Paul F. (1958), 'Josef Breuer's evaluation of his contribution to psycho-analysis', *International Journal of Psychoanalysis*, **39**, no. 5, 319–22.

Crews, Frederick (ed.) (1995), *The Memory Wars. Freud's Legacy in Dispute*, New York, A New York Review Book.

Danto, Arthur (1965), *Analytical Philosophy of History*, Cambridge, MA, Cambridge University Press.

Danziger, Kurt (1991), *Constructing the Subject. Historical Origins of Psychological Research*, Cambridge, Cambridge University Press.

Decker, Hannah S. (1971), 'The medical reception of psychoanalysis in Germany, 1894–1907: three brief studies', *Bulletin of the History of Medicine*, **45**, 461–81.

(1975), '*The Interpretation of Dreams*: early reception by the educated German public', *Journal of the History of the Behavioral Sciences*, **11**, 129–41.

(1977), *Freud in Germany. Revolution and Reaction in Science, 1893–1907*, *Psychological Issues*, **11**, no. 1 (Monograph 41).

(1991), *Freud, Dora, and Vienna 1900*, New York, Free Press.

Delbœuf, Joseph (1886), 'De l'influence de l'éducation et de l'imitation dans le somnambulisme provoqué', *Revue philosophique*, **22**, 146–71.

(1993a [1890]), *Le magnétisme animal. À propos d'une visite à l'École de Nancy*, in *Le sommeil et les rêves, et autres textes*, ed. Jacqueline Carroy and François Duyckaerts, Paris, Fayard.

(1993b [1885]), *Le sommeil et les rêves, et autres textes*, ed. Jacqueline Carroy and François Duyckaerts, Paris, Fayard.

Derrida, Jacques (1987), *The Post Card. From Socrates to Freud and Beyond*, trans. Alan Bass, Chicago, IL, University of Chicago Press.

Derrida, Jacques and Roudinesco, Élisabeth (2004), *For What Tomorrow... A Dialogue*, Stanford, CA, Stanford University Press.

Dessoir, Max (1889), *Das Doppel-Ich*, Berlin, W. Karl Sigismund.

Devereux, Georges (1967), *From Anxiety to Method in the Behavioral Sciences*, The Hague, Mouton.

Donkin, H. B. (1892), 'Hysteria', in Daniel Hack Tuke (ed.), *A Dictionary of Psychological Medicine, Giving the Definition, Etymology and Synonyms of the Terms Used in Medical Psychology with the Symptoms, Treatment, and Pathology of Insanity and the Law of Lunacy in Great Britain and Ireland*, Philadelphia, PA, Blakiston.

Du Bois-Reymond, Emil (1883), 'Darwin und Kopernicus', 25 January 1883, Friedrichs-Sitzung der Akademie der Wissenschaften, in *Reden*, Leipzig, 1886, 2, 496–502.

Dufresne, Todd (2000), *Tales from the Freudian Crypt. The Death Drive in Text and Context*, Stanford, CA, Stanford University Press.

—— (2007), *Against Freud: Critics Talk Back*, Stanford, CA, Stanford University Press.

Duyckaerts, François (1993), 'Les références de Freud à Delbœuf', *Revue internationale d'histoire de la la psychanalyse*, 6, 231–50.

Eder, David (1913), 'The present position of psycho-analysis', *British Medical Journal*, 8 November, 1213–15.

Edmunds, Lavinia (1988), 'His master's choice', *The Johns Hopkins Magazine*, April, 40–9.

Eissler, Kurt Robert (1965), *Medical Orthodoxy and the Future of Psychoanalysis*, New York, International Universities Press.

—— (1971), *Talent and Genius. The Fictitious Case of Tausk Contra Freud*, New York, Quadrangle Books.

—— (2001), *Freud and the Seduction Theory. A Brief Love Affair*, Madison, CT, International Universities Press.

Eitingon, Max (1998), 'Anna O. (Breuer) in psychoanalytischer Betrachtung', *Jahrbuch der Psychoanalyse*, 40, 14–30.

Ellenberger, Henri Frédéric (1961), 'La psychiatrie et son histoire inconnue', *L'Union médicale du Canada*, 90, no. 3, 281–9.

—— (1970a), *The Discovery of the Unconscious. The History and Evolution of Dynamic Psychiatry*, New York, Basic Books.

—— (1970b), 'Methodology in writing the history of dynamic psychiatry', in George Mora and Jeanne L. Brand (eds.), *Psychiatry and Its History. Methodological Problems in Research*, Springfield, IL, Charles C. Thomas, 26–40.

—— (1972), 'The story of "Anna O.": a critical review with new data', *Journal of the History of the Behavioral Sciences*, 8, no. 3, 267–79.

—— (1973), 'Freud in perspective: a conversation with Henri F. Ellenberger', interview with Jacques Mousseau, *Psychology Today*, March, 50–60.

—— (1977), 'L'histoire d'"Emmy von N.": étude critique avec documents nouveaux', *L'évolution psychiatrique*, 42, no. 3 519–40.

(1995), *Médecines de l'âme. Essais d'histoire de la folie et des guérisons psychiques*, Paris, Fayard.

Ellis, Havelock (1898a), 'Auto-erotism: a psychological study', *Alienist and Neurologist*, **19**, no. 2, 260–99.

(1898b), 'Hysteria in relation to the sexual emotions', *Alienist and Neurologist*, **19**, no. 4, 599–615.

(1939), *My Life. Autobiography of Havelock Ellis*, Boston, MA, Houghton Mifflin.

Elms, Alan (1994), *Uncovering Lives. The Uneasy Alliance of Biography and Psychology*, New York, Oxford University Press.

Eng, Erling (1984), 'Coleridge's "psycho-analytical understanding" and Freud's psychoanalysis', *International Review of Psycho-analysis*, **11**, 463–6.

Erikson, Erik H. (1954), 'The dream specimen of psychoanalysis', *Journal of the American Psychoanalytic Association*, **2**, 5–56.

Erlenmeyer, Albrecht (1886), 'Über Cocainsucht: Vorläufige Mitteilung', *Deutsche Medizinal-Zeitung*, **7**, 438–84.

Esterson, Allen (1993), *Seductive Mirage*, Chicago and La Salle, IL, Open Court.

Falzeder, Ernst (1994a), 'My grand-patient, my chief tormentor: a hitherto unnoticed case of Freud's and the consequences', *Psychoanalytic Quarterly*, **63**, 297–331.

(1994b), 'The threads of psychoanalytic filiations or psychoanalysis taking effect', in André Haynal and Ernst Falzeder (eds.), *100 Years of Psychoanalysis. Contributions to the History of Psychoanalysis*, London, Karnac Books, 169–94.

(1997), 'Whose Freud is it? Some reflections on editing Freud's correspondence', in *Behind the Scenes. Freud in Correspondence*, ed. Patrick Mahony, Carlo Bonomi and Jan Stensson, Oslo, Scandinavian University Press, 335–56.

(1998), 'Family tree matters', *Journal of Analytical Psychology*, **43**, no. 1, 127–54.

(2000), 'Profession – psychoanalyst: a historical view', *Psychoanalysis and History*, **2**, 37–60.

(2004), 'Sigmund Freud und Eugen Bleuler: die Geschichte einer ambivalenten Beziehung', *Luzifer-Amor, Zeitschrift zur Geschichte der Psychoanalyse*, **17**, no. 34, 85–104.

Falzeder, Ernst and Burnham, John (2007), 'A perfectly staged "concerted action" against psychoanalysis: the 1913 congress of German psychiatrists', *International Journal of Psycho-Analysis*, 88, no. 5, 1223–44.

Ferenczi, Sándor (1911), 'On the organization of the psychoanalytic movement', in *Final Contributions to the Problems and Methods of Psycho-Analysis*, ed. Michael Balint, trans. E. Mosbacher, London, Hogarth Press, 1955, 299–307.

— (1914), review of Eugen Bleuler, 'Kritik der Freudschen Theorien', *Internationale Zeitschrift für ärztliche Psychoanalyse*, 2, 62–6.

— (1988), *The Clinical Diary of Sándor Ferenczi*, ed. Judith Dupont, trans. Michael Balint and Nicola Zarday Jackson, Cambridge, MA, Harvard University Press.

Fichtner, Gerhard (1988), 'Freuds Briefe als historische Quelle', conference held at the second congress of the International paper presented to the Association for the History of Psychoanalysis, Vienna, 21–23 July.

Fliess, Wilhelm (1897), *Die Beziehung zwischen Nase und weiblichen Geschlechtsorganen. In ihrer biologischen Bedeutungeng dargestellt*, Leipzig and Vienna, Franz Deuticke.

— (1906a), *In eigener Sache. Gegen Otto Weininger und Hermann Swoboda*, Berlin, Emil Goldschmidt.

— (1906b), *Der Ablauf des Lebens. Grundlegung zur exakten Biologie*, Leipzig and Vienna, Franz Deutike.

Flournoy, Théodore (1896), *Notice sur le laboratoire de psychologie de l'université de Genèva*, Geneva, Eggiman.

— (1903a), review of Sigmund Freud, *Die Traumdeutung*, Archives de psychologie, 2, 72–3.

— (1903b), 'F. W. H. Myers et son œuvre posthume', *Archives de psychologie*, 2, 269–96.

— (1911), *Esprits et médiums. Mélanges de métapsychique et de psychologie*, Geneva, Kündig.

Forel, August (1889), *Der Hypnotismus. Seine Bedeutung und seine Handhabung*, Stuttgart, Ferdinand Enke.

— (1891), *Der Hypnotismus, seine psycho-physiologische, medicinische, strafrechtliche Bedeutung und seine Handhabung*, Stuttgart, Ferdinand Enke (2nd revised edn of Forel 1889).

(1899), 'Hypnotism and cerebral activity', in *Clark University 1889–1899. Decennial Celebration*, Worcester, MA, printed for the University.

(1905), *Die sexuelle Frage. Eine naturwissenschaftliche, psychologische, hygienische und soziologische Studie für Gebildete*, Munich, E. Reinhardt.

(1907 [1903]), *Hygiene of Nerves & Mind in Health and Disease*, trans. Austin Aikins, London, John Murray.

(1906a), *L'âme et le système nerveux. Hygiène et pathologie*, Paris, G. Steinheil.

(1906b), *Hypnotism or, Suggestion and psychotherapy*, trans. H. Armit (based on the 5th, revised edn of Forel 1889), London, Rebman.

(1908), 'Zum heutigen Stand der Psychotherapie: ein Vorschlag', *Journal für Psychologie und Neurologie*, 11, 266–9.

(1909), *Ethische und rechtliche Konflikte im Sexualleben in- und ausserhalb der Ehen*, Munich, Ernst Reinhardt.

(1910a), 'Fondation de la Société Internationale de Psychologie Médicale et de Psychothérapie', *Informateur des aliénistes et des neurologistes* (supplement to *L'Encéphale*), 5, 25 February, 42–5.

(1910b), 'La psychologie et la psychothérapie à l'université', *Journal für Psychologie und Neurologie*, 17, Ergänzungsheft, 307–17.

(1910c), *Gehirn und Seele. Elfte, vollständig neu bearbeitete Auflage*, Leipzig, Alfred Kröner.

(1919), *Der Hypnotismus oder die Suggestion und die Psychologie*, Stuttgart, Ferdinand Enke (8–9th edn of Forel 1889).

(1935), *Rückblick auf mein Leben*, Zurich, Europa-Verlag.

(1968), *August Forel. Briefe/Correspondance 1864–1927*, ed. Hans H. Walser, Berne and Stuttgart, Hans Huber.

Forel, August and Bezzola, Dumeng (1989), 'August Forel und Dumeng Bezzola – ein Briefwechsel', ed. Christian Müller, *Gesnerus*, 46, 55–79.

Forrester, John (1980), *Language and the Origins of Psychoanalysis*, London, Macmillan.

(1997a), *Dispatches from the Freud Wars*, Cambridge, MA, Harvard University Press.

(1997b), 'Lacan's debt to Freud: how the Ratman paid off his debt', in Todd Dufresne (ed.), *Freud, Lacan, and Beyond*, New York, Routledge, 67–89.

Forrester, John and Cameron, Laura (1999), '"A cure with a defect": a previously unpublished letter by Freud concerning "Anna O."', *International Journal of Psycho-Analysis*, 80, 929–41.

Frank, Jerome (1961), *Persuasion and Healing. A Comparative Study of Psychotherapy*, Baltimore, MD, Johns Hopkins University Press.

Frank, Ludwig (1908), 'Zur Psychanalyse', *Journal für Psychologie und Neurologie*, 13, Festschrift Forel, 126–35.

(1910), *Die Psychanalyse*, Munich, Ernst Reinhardt.

Frank, Ludwig and Bezzola, Dumeng (1907), 'Über die Analyse psycho-traumatischer Symptome', *Zentralblatt für Nervenheilkunde*, 30 (new series, 18), 179–86.

Freud Sigmund (1885a), 'Beitrag zur Kenntnis der Cocawirkung', *Wiener Medizinische Wochenschrift*, 35, no. 5, 129–33.

(1885b), 'Ueber die Allgemeinwirkung des Cocains', *Zeitschrift für Therapie*, 3, no. 7, 1 April, 49–51.

(1889), review of August Forel's *Hypnotism*, SE 1, 89–102.

(1892–3), 'A case of successful treatment by hypnotism', SE 1, 115–28.

(1893), 'Quelques considérations pour une étude comparative des paralysies motrices organiques et hystériques', *Archives neurologiques*, 93, no. 77, 29–43.

(1895), 'Project for a scientific psychology', SE 1, 281–397.

(1896a), 'Heredity and the aetiology of the neuroses', SE 3, 141–56.

(1896b), 'The aetiology of hysteria', SE 3, 189–221.

(1896c), 'Further remarks on the neuro-psychoses of defence', SE 3, 157–85.

(1899), 'Screen memories', SE 3, 301–22.

(1900), *The Interpretation of Dreams*, SE 4–5.

(1901), *The Psychopathology of Everyday Life*, SE 6.

(1904), 'Freud's psycho-analytic procedure', SE 7, 249–54.

(1905a), 'Three essays on the theory of sexuality', SE 7, 121–245.

(1905b), 'On psychotherapy', SE 7, 257–68.

(1905c), 'Fragment of an analysis of a case of hysteria', SE 7, 3–122.

(1906), 'My views on the part played by sexuality in the aetiology of the neuroses', SE 7, 269–79.

(1907b), *Delusions and Dreams in Jensen's Gradiva*, SE 9, 3–95.

(1907–8a), *Original Record of the* ['Ratman'] *Case*, SE **10**, 253–318.

(1907–8b [1994]), *L'homme aux rats. Journal d'une analyse*, trans. into French by Elza Ribeiro Hawelka in collaboration with Pierre Hawelka, Paris, Presses Universitaires de France (4th edn).

(1907–8c [1987]), *Originalnotizen zu einem Fall von Zwangsneurose* (*'Rattenmann'*), ed. Angela Richards and Ilse Grubrich-Simitis, in *Gesammelte Werke – Nachtragsband*, Frankfurt am Main, S. Fischer Verlag, 1987, 501–69.

(1908a), 'Creative writers and day-dreaming', SE **9**, 141–53.

(1908b), 'Character and anal erotism', SE **9**, 167–75.

(1909a), 'Analysis of a phobia in a five-year-old boy', SE **10**, 3–149.

(1909b), 'Notes upon a case of obsessional neurosis', SE **10**, 153–249.

(1910a), 'Five lectures on Psycho-Analysis', SE **11**, 1–56.

(1910b), 'The future prospects of psycho-analytic therapy', SE **11**, 139–51.

(1910c), '"Wild" psycho-analysis', SE **11**, 219–27.

(1910d), 'Leonardo da Vinci and a memory of his childhood', SE **11**, 59–137.

(1912), 'Recommendations to physicians practising psycho-analysis', SE **12**, 109–20.

(1913a), 'The claims of psycho-analysis to scientific interest', SE **13**, 165–90.

(1913b), 'On beginning the treatment. (Further recommendations on the technique of psycho-analysis I)', SE **12**, 121–44.

(1914a), 'On the history of the psycho-analytic movement', SE **14**, 7–66.

(1914b), 'Remembering, repeating and working-through. (Further recommendations on the technique of psycho-analysis II)', SE **12**, 145–56.

(1914c), 'On narcissism: an introduction', SE **14**, 67–102.

(1915a), 'The unconscious', SE **14**, 159–215.

(1915b), 'Instincts and their vicissitudes', SE **14**, 109–40.

(1916–17), *Introductory Lectures on Psycho-Analysis*, SE **15–16**.

(1917a), 'A difficulty on the path of psycho-analysis', SE **17**, 135–44.

(1917b), 'On transformations of instinct as exemplified in anal erotism', SE **17**, 125–33.

(1918), 'From the history of an infantile neurosis', SE **18**, 3–122.

(1920a), 'Beyond the pleasure principle', SE 18, 3–64.

(1920b), 'A note on the prehistory of the technique of analysis', SE 18, 263–5.

(1921), 'Psycho-analysis and telepathy', SE 18, 175–93.

(1923), 'Two encyclopedia articles', SE 18, 231–59.

(1925a), 'An autobiographical study', SE 20, 1–74.

(1925b), 'The resistances to psycho-analysis', SE 19, 213–22.

(1925c), 'Josef Breuer', SE 19, 277–80.

(1926a), 'The question of lay-analysis: conversations with an impartial person', SE 20, 179–258.

(1926b), 'Psycho-analysis', SE 20, 259–70.

(1933), 'Introductory lectures to psycho-analysis', SE 22, 1–182.

(1937a), 'Analysis terminable and interminable', SE 23, 209–53.

(1937b), 'Constructions in analysis', SE 23, 255–69.

(1939), 'Moses and monotheism: three essays', SE 23, 3–137.

(1953–74), *The Standard Edition of the Complete Psychological Works of Sigmund Freud*, 24 vols., ed. James Strachey, Anna Freud, Alix Strachey, Alan Tyson and Angela Richards, London, Hogarth Press and the Institute of Psycho-Analysis. (Hereafter, SE.)

(1954), *The Origins of Psycho-Analysis. Letters to Wilhelm Fliess, Drafts and Notes, 1887–1902*, ed. Marie Bonaparte, Anna Freud and Ernst Kris, trans. Eric Mosbacher and James Strachey, intro. Ernst Kris, New York, Basic Books.

(1960), *Letters of Sigmund Freud*, ed. Ernst L. Freud, trans. Tania and James Stern, New York, Basic Books.

(1985), *The Complete Letters of Sigmund Freud to Wilhelm Fliess 1887–1904*, ed. Jeffrey Moussaief Masson, Cambridge, MA, and London, The Belknap Press of Harvard University Press.

(1986), *Briefe an Wilhelm Fließ*, ed. Jeffrey Moussaief Masson, Frankfurt am Main, Fischer Verlag.

Freud, Sigmund and Abraham, Karl (2002), *The Complete Correspondence of Sigmund Freud and Karl Abraham, 1907–1925, Completed Edition*, ed. Ernst Falzeder, London, Karnac.

Freud, Sigmund and Andreas-Salomé, Lou (1966), *Sigmund Freud/Lou Andreas-Salomé. Briefwechsel*, ed. Ernst Pfeiffer, Frankfurt am Main, S. Fischer.

Freud, Sigmund and Binswanger, Ludwig (2003), *The Sigmund Freud – Ludwig Binswanger Correspondence 1908–1938*, ed. Gerhard Fichtner, London, Open Gate Press.

Freud, Sigmund and Eitingon, Max (2004), *Sigmund Freud Max Eitingon Briefwechsel 1906–1939*, vol. 1, ed. Michael Schröter, Tübingen, Edition Diskord.

Freud, Sigmund and Ferenczi, Sándor (1993), *The Correspondence of Sigmund Freud and Sándor Ferenczi*, vol. 1: 1908–1914, ed. Eva Brabant, Ernst Falzeder and Patrizia Giampieri-Deutsch, introd. André Haynal, trans. Peter Hoffer, Cambridge, MA, Harvard University Press.

(2000), *The Correspondence of Sigmund Freud and Sándor Ferenczi*, vol. 3: 1920–1933, ed. Ernst Falzeder and Eva Brabant, trans. Peter Hoffer, Cambridge, MA, Harvard University Press.

Freud, Sigmund and Jones, Ernest (1993), *The Complete Correspondence of Sigmund Freud and Ernest Jones 1908–1939*, ed. R. Andrews Paskauskas, Cambridge, MA, Harvard University Press.

Freud, Sigmund and Jung, Carl Gustav (1974), *The Freud/Jung Letters. The Correspondence between Sigmund Freud and C. G. Jung*, ed. William McGuire, trans. Ralph Manheim and R. F. C. Hull, Bollingen Series, Princeton, NJ, Princeton University Press.

Freud, Sigmund and Pfister, Oskar (1963), *Psycho-Analysis and Faith. The Letters of Sigmund Freud and Oskar Pfister*, ed. Ernst L. Freud and Heinrich Meng, trans. Eric Mosbacher, London, Hogarth Press.

Freund, C. S. (1895), 'Über psychische Lähmungen', *Neurologisches Zentralblatt*, 14, 938–46.

Friedländer, A. A. (1907), 'Über Hysterie und die Freudsche psycho-analytische Behandlung derselben', *Monatschrift für Psychiatrie und Neurologie*, 22, 45–54.

(1911), 'Hysteria and modern psychoanalysis', *Journal of Abnormal Psychology*, 5, 297–319.

Fromm, Erich (1970), *The Crisis of Psychoanalysis. Essays on Freud, Marx and Social Psychology*, Harmondsworth, Penguin.

Furtmüller, Carl (1912), *Psychoanalyse und Ethik. Eine vorläufige Untersuchung*, Schriften des Vereins für freie psychoanalytischen Forschung, 1, Munich, Reinhardt Verlag.

Gardiner, Muriel (1983), 'The wolf-man's last years', *Journal of the American Psychoanalytic Association*, **31**, 867–97.

Gardiner, Muriel (ed.) (1972), *The Wolf-Man and Sigmund Freud*, London, Hogarth Press and the Institute of Psycho-Analysis.

Gasché, Rodolphe (1997), 'The witch metapsychology', in Todd Dufresne (ed.), *Returns of the 'French Freud'. Freud, Lacan, and Beyond*, New York, Routledge, 169–208.

Gattel, Felix (1898), *Ueber die sexuellen Ursachen der Neurasthenie und Angstneurose*, Berlin, August Hirschwald.

Gaupp, Robert (1900), review of Sigmund Freud (1899), *Zeitschrift für Psychologie und Physiologie der Sinnesorgane*, **23**, 233–4.

Gay, Peter (1988), *Freud. A Life for Our Time*, New York, Norton.

Genette, Gérard (1972), *Figures III*, Paris, Seuil.

Gesell, Arnold and Gesell, Beatrice (1912), *The Normal Child and Primary Education*, London, Ginn.

Gicklhorn, Josef and Gicklhorn, Renée (1960), *Sigmund Freud's akademische Laufbahn im Lichte der Dokumente*, Vienna and Innsbruck, Urban & Schwarzenberg.

Giddens, Anthony (1990), *Consequences of Modernity*, Stanford, CA, Stanford University Press.

Gley, E. (1884), 'Les aberrations de l'instinct sexuel d'après des travaux récents', *Revue philosophique*, **17**, 66–92.

Golinski, Jan (1998), *Making Natural Knowledge. Constructivism and the History of Science*, Cambridge, Cambridge University Press.

Gould, Stephen Jay (1989), *Wonderful Life. The Burgess Shale and the Nature of History*, New York, W. W. Norton & Company.

Graf, Max (1995–6), 'Entretien du père du Petit Hans, Max Graf, avec Kurt Eissler, 16 décembre 1952', *Bloc-notes de la psychanalyse*, **14**, 123–59.

Green, André (1995), 'Mythes et mystifications psychanalytiques', *Le Monde*, 28 December.

Grünbaum, Adolf (1985), *The Foundations of Psychoanalysis. A Philosophical Critique*, Berkeley, Los Angeles and London, University of California Press.

Gubrich-Simitis, Ilse (1997), *Early Freud and Late Freud. Reading anew Studies on Hysteria and Moses and Monotheism*, trans. Philip Slotkin, London, Routledge.

Gundlach, Horst (2002), 'Psychoanalysis and the story of "O": an embarrassment', *Semiotic Review of Books*, **13**, no. 1, 4–5.

Haberman, J. Victor (1914–15), 'A criticism of psychoanalysis', *Journal of Abnormal Psychology*, **9**, 265–82.

Habermas, Jürgen (1971), *Knowledge and Human Interests*, trans. Jeremy J. Shapiro, Boston, Beacon Press.

Hacking, Ian (1983), *Representing and Intervening. Introductory Topics in the Philosophy of Natural Science*, Cambridge, Cambridge University Press.

(1998), *Mad Travelers. Reflections on the Reality of Transient Mental Illnesses*, Charlottesville and London, University Press of Virginia.

Haeckel, Ernst (1876 [1868]), *The History of Creation, Or the Development of the Earth and its Inhabitants by the Action of Natural Causes*, 2 vols., trans. E. Ray Lankester, London, Henry S. King & Co.

(1902 [1899]), *Les énigmes de l'univers*, trans. into French by Camille Bos, Paris, Schleicher Frères.

(1920 [1892]), *Monisme, profession de foi d'un naturaliste*, trans. into French by Vacher de Lapouge, Paris, Schleicher Frères.

Hale, Nathan G., Jr (1971), *Freud and America*, vol. 1: *Freud and the Americans. The Beginnings of Psychoanalysis in the United States, 1876–1917*, New York, Oxford University Press.

(ed.) (1971), *James Jackson Putnam and Psychoanalysis. Letters between Putnam and Sigmund Freud, Ernest Jones, William James, Sandor Ferenczi, and Morton Prince, 1877–1917*, Cambridge, MA, Harvard University Press.

(1999), 'Freud's critics: a critical review', *Partisan Review*, **66**, 235–54.

Hall, Stanley (1909), 'Evolution and psychology', in *Fifty Years of Darwinism. Modern Aspects of Evolution. Centennial Addresses in Honor of Charles Darwin before the AAAS*, New York, Henry Holt, 251–67.

(1923), *Life and Confessions of a Psychologist*, New York, D. Appleton & Co.

Hamburger, Käte (1973 [1957]), *The Logic of Literature*, trans. Marilynn J. Rose, Bloomington, Indiana University Press.

Hart, Bernard (1929), *Psychopathology. Its Development and Its Place in Medicine*, Cambridge, Cambridge University Press.

Hemecker, Wilhelm (1987), 'Sigmund Freud und die Herbartianische Psychologie des 19. Jahrhunderts', *Conceptus*, 21, 217–31.

Henry, Michel (1993), *The Genealogy of Psychoanalysis*, trans. Douglas Brick, Stanford, CA, Stanford University Press.

Herman, G. (1903), *'Genesis'. Das Gesetz der Zeugung*, vol. 5: *Libido und Manie*, Leipzig, Arwed Strauch.

Hesnard, Angelo (1925), review of Maurice Blondel, *La psychanalyse*, *L'évolution psychiatrique*, 1, no. 1, 277–8.

Hildebrandt, F. W. (1881), *Der Traum und seine Verwertung für's Leben. Eine psychologische Studie*, Leipzig, Feodor Reinboth (2nd edn).

Hirschfeld, Magnus (1899), 'Die objektive Diagnose der Homosexualität', *Jahrbuch für sexuelle Zwischenstufen*, 1, 4–35.

Hirschmüller, Albrecht (1989), *The Life and Work of Josef Breuer. Physiology and Psychoanalysis*, New York, International Universities Press.

(1998), 'Max Eitingon über Anna O.', *Jahrbuch der Psychoanalyse*, 40, 9–13.

Hitschmann, Eduard (1911), *Freuds Neurosenlehre*, Leipzig and Vienna, Deuticke.

Hobbes, Thomas (1968 [1651]), *Leviathan*, ed. C. M. Macpherson, Harmondsworth, Penguin.

Hoche, Alfred (1908), 'Vereinsbericht, Sammlung südwestdeutscher Irrenärzte in Tübigen am 3 und 4 November 1906', *Zentralblatt für Nervenheilkunde und Psychiatrie*, 31, 184–5.

(1910), 'Eine psychische Epidemie unter Aerzten', *Medizinische Klinik*, 6, no. 26, 1007–10.

(1913), 'Ueber den Wert der "Psychoanalyse"', *Archiv für Psychiatrie*, 51, no. 3, 1054–79.

Hollingworth, H. L. (1930), *Abnormal Psychology, Its Concepts and Theories*, New York, The Ronald Press Company.

Homburger, Paul (1954), 'Letter to the Editor re: Bertha Pappenheim', *Aufbau*, 20, 7 June, 20.

Huxley, Aldous (1925), 'Our contemporary hocus-pocus', *The Forum*, 313–20.

(1926), *Lectures and Lay Sermons*, New York, E. P. Dutton.

Israëls, Han (1992), 'Freuds Phantasien über Leonardo da Vinci', *Luzifer-Amor, Zeitschrift zur Geschichte der Psychoanalyse*, 10, 8–41.

(1999 [1993]), *Der Fall Freud. Die Geburt der Psychoanalyse aus der Lüge*, trans. from Dutch by Gerd Busse, Hamburg, Europäische Verlaganstalt/Rotbuch Verlag.

(2006 [1999]), *Der Wiener Quacksalber. Kritische Betrachtungen über Sigmund Freud und die Psychoanalyse*, trans. from Dutch by Gerd Busse, Verlag Dr. Bussert & Stadeler, Jena-Quedlinburg.

Israëls, Han and Schatzman, Morton (1993), 'The seduction theory', *History of Psychiatry*, **4**, 23–59.

Isserlin, Max (1907), 'Ueber Jung's "Psychologie der Dementia Praecox" und die Anwendung Freud'scher Forschungsmaximen in der Psychopathologie', *Centralblat für Nervenheilkunde und Psychiatrie*, **29**, 330–43.

Jacobsen, Paul B. and Steele, Robert S. (1979), 'From present to past: Freudian archeology', *International Review of Psychoanalysis*, **6**, no. 3, 349–62.

James, William (1890), *The Principles of Psychology*, 2 vols., New York, Henry Holt and Company.

(1892), *Text-Book of Psychology*, London, Macmillan.

(1920), *The Letters of William James*, 2 vols., ed. Henry James, Boston, Altlantic Monthly Press.

(1929), *The Varieties of Religious Experience. A Study in Human Nature*, London, Longmans, Green and Co. (37th edn).

(1999), *The Correspondence of William James*, vol. 7, 1890–1894, ed. I. K. Skrupskelis and E. M. Berkeley, Charlottesville, University of Virginia Press.

Janet, Pierre (1894), *L'état mental des hystériques*, vol. 2, *Les accidents mentaux*, Paris, Rueff.

(1898), *Névroses et idées fixes*, 2 vols., Paris, Alcan.

(1903), *Les obsessions et la psychasthénie*, 2 vols. (vol. 2 in collaboration with Fulgence Raymond), Paris, Alcan.

(1908), Discussion, *Compte-rendu des travaux du Ier Congrès international de neurologie, de psychologie et de l'assistance des aliénés, du 2 au 7 Septembre 1907*, ed. G. Van Wayenburg, Amsterdam, J. H. de Bussy, 301–2.

(1913), 'Psycho-analysis', *XVIIth International Congress of Medicine*, London, Section XII, Psychiatry I, 1–52.

(1919), *Les médications psychologiques*, 3 vols., Paris, Alcan.

(1925), *Psychological Healing*, 2 vols., trans. E. and C. Paul, London, George Allen and Unwin.

Jaspers, Karl (1973 [1913]), *Allgemeine Psychopathologie*, Berlin, Springer.

Jastrow, Joseph (1932), *The House That Freud Built*, New York, Greenberg.

Jauss, Hans Robert (1970), *Literaturgeschichte als Provokation*, Frankfurt am Main, Suhrkamp.

Jones, Ernest (1913), *Papers on Psycho-Analysis*, London, Baillière, Tindall and Cox.

(1918), 'Why is the "unconscious" unconscious?', *British Journal of Psychology*, 9, 247–56.

(1953), *The Life and Work of Sigmund Freud*, vol. 1, New York, Basic Books.

(1955), *The Life and Work of Sigmund Freud*, vol. 2, New York, Basic Books.

(1956), 'Eulogy', in *Sigmund Freud. Four Centenary Addresses*, New York, Basic Books, 117–50.

(1957), *The Life and Work of Sigmund Freud*, vol. 3, New York, Basic Books.

Jung, Carl Gustav (1905), 'Psychoanalysis and associations experiment', *CW* 2, 288–317.

(1906), 'Freud's theory of hysteria: a reply to Aschaffenburg's criticism', in *The Collected Works of C. G. Jung* (hereafter, *CW*), vol. 4, ed. Gerhard Adler, Michael Fordham and Herbert Read; William Mcguire, executive editor; trans. R. F. C. Hull; Bollingen Series, New York and Princeton, NJ, and London, 1953–83, 3–9.

(1906–9), *Diagnostische Assoziationsstudien*, 2 vols., Leipzig, J. A. Barth.

(1907), 'On the psychology of dementia praecox', *CW* 3, 1–152.

(1908a), 'The Freudian theory of hysteria', *CW* 4, 10–24.

(1908b), presentation, *Compte-rendu des travaux du Ier Congrès international de neurologie, de psychologie et de l'assistance des aliénés, du 2 au 7 Septembre 1907*, ed. G. Van Wayenburg, Amsterdam, J. H. de Bussy, 272–84.

(1909), review of August Forel, *Ethische und rechtliche Konflikte im Sexualleben in- und ausserhalb der Ehe*, *CW* 18, 387.

(1912a), 'Zur Psychoanalyse', *Wissen und Leben*, 5, 711–14.

(1912b), 'The theory of psychoanalysis', CW 4, 83–226.

(1925), *Analytical Psychology. Notes of the Seminar Given in 1925*, ed. William Mcguire, Bollingen Series, Princeton, NJ, Princeton University Press, 1989.

(1956), *Mysterium Coniunctionis*, CW 14.

(1973), C. G. *Jung Letters 1: 1906–1950*, ed. Gerhard Adler in collaboration with Aniela Jaffé, trans. R. F. C. Hull, Bollingen Series, Princeton, NJ, Princeton University Press.

(1975), C. G. *Jung Letters 2: 1951–1961*, ed. Gerhard Adler in collaboration with Aniela Jaffé, trans. R. F. C. Hull, Bollingen Series, Princeton, NJ, Princeton University Press.

Jung, Carl Gustav and Jaffé, Aniela (1962), *Memories, Dreams, Reflections*, New York, Pantheon.

Kant, Immanuel (1996 [1787]), *Critique of Pure Reason. Unified Edition*, trans. Werner Pluhar, introd. Patricia Kitcher, Indianapolis, IN, Hackett.

(1985 [1786]), *Metaphysical Foundations of Natural Science*, in *Kant's Philosophy of Material Nature*, ed. James Ellington, trans. Paul Carus, Indianapolis, ID, Hackett.

Kanzer, Mark (1952), 'The transference neurosis of the Rat Man', *Psychoanalytic Quarterly*, 21, 181–9.

Kern, Stephen (1975), 'The prehistory of Freud's dream theory: Freud's masterpiece anticipated', *Medical History*, 6, no. 3–4, 83–92.

Kiell, Norman (1988), *Freud without Hindsight. Reviews of His Work (1893–1939)*, Madison, CT, International Universities Press.

Kiernan, James G. (1888), 'Sexual perversion, and the Whitechapel murders', *Medical Standard*, 4, 129–30 and 170–2.

King, A. F. A. (1891), 'Hysteria', *American Journal of Obstetrics and Diseases of Women and Children*, 24, no. 5, 513–32.

Kirschner, Douglas (2000), *Unfree Associations. Inside Psychoanalytic Institutes*, London, Process Press.

Kohler, Robert E. (1994), *Lords of the Fly. Drosophila Genetics and the Experimental Life*, Chicago, IL, University of Chicago Press.

Kohnstamm, O. (1913), Intervention in *Bericht über die Jahresversammlung des Deutschen Vereins für Psychiatrie zu Breslau am 13. und 14. Mai 1913, Allgemeine Zeitschrift für Psychiatrie*, 70, 789–93.

Kraepelin, Emil (1913a), *Psychiatrie. Ein Lehrbuch für Studierende und Ärzte, III. Band, Klinische Psychiatrie, II. Teil*, Leipzig, J. A. Barth.

(1913b), intervention in *Bericht über die Jahresversammlung des Deutschen Vereins für Psychiatrie zu Breslau am 13. und 14. Mai 1913, Allgemeine Zeitschrift für Psychiatrie*, 70, 787.

Krafft-Ebing, Richard von (1894), *Psychopathia sexualis, mit besonderer Berücksichtigung der conträren Sexualempfindung. Eine klinisch-forensische Studie*, Stuttgart, Ferdinand Enke (9th edn).

(1895), 'Zur Erklärung der conträren Sexualempfindung', *Jahrbücher für Psychiatrie und Nervenheilkunde*, 13, no. 1, 98–112.

Kris, Ernst (1947), 'The nature of psychoanalytic propositions and their validation', in Sidney Hook and Milton R. Konvitz (eds.), *Freedom and Experience. Esays in Honour of Horace Kallen*, Ithaca, NY, Cornell University Press, 239–59.

Kronfeld, Arthur (1912), 'Ueber die psychologischen Theorien Freuds und verwandte Anschauungen. Systematik und kritische Erörtung', *Archiv für die Gesamte Psychologie*, 22, 130–248.

Kuhn, Philip (1999), 'A Professor through the looking-glass: contending narratives of Freud's relationship with the sister Bernays', *International Journal of Psychoanalysis*, 80, 943–959.

Kuhn, Thomas (1970), *The Copernican Revolution*, Cambridge, MA, Harvard University Press.

Lacan, Jacques (1953), 'Le mythe individuel du névrosé ou "Poésie et Vérité" dans la névrose', Paris, Centre de Documentation Universitaire.

(1981 [1973]), *The Four Fundamental Concepts of Psycho-Analysis*, ed. Jacques-Alain Miller, trans. Alan Sheridan, New York and London, Norton.

(1988 [1975]), *Freud's Papers on Technique, 1953–1954*, ed. Jacques-Alain Miller, trans. John Forrester, New York, Norton.

(2005 [1966]), *Écrits*, trans. Bruce Fink, New York, and London, Norton.

Laplanche, Jean and Pontalis, Jean-Bertrand (1973), *The Language of Psycho-Analysis*, trans. Donald Nicholson-Smith, New York, Norton.

Latour, Bruno (1987), *Science in Action. How to Follow Scientists and Engineers through Society*, Cambridge, MA, Harvard University Press.

(1996), *Petite réflexion sur le culte moderne des dieux faitiches*, Paris, Synthélabo.

Latour, Bruno and Woolgar, Steve (1979), *Laboratory Life. The Social Construction of Scientific Facts*, introd. Jonas Salk, Beverley Hills, Sage Publications.

Lawrence, D. H. (1986 [1923]), *Fantasia of the Unconscious & Psychoanalysis and the Unconscious*, Harmondsworth, Penguin.

Lerch, Eugen (1930), *Hauptprobleme der französischen Sprache*, Braunschweig, G. Westermann.

Lévi-Strauss, Claude (1973), 'Introduction à l'œuvre de Marcel Mauss', in Marcel Mauss, *Sociologie et anthropologie*, Paris, Presses Universitaires de France, ix–lii.

Lieberman, James E. (1985), *Acts of Will. The Life and Work of Otto Rank*, New York, The Free Press.

Liebscher, Martin and Nicholls, Angus (eds.) (2010), *Thinking the Unconscious. Nineteenth-Century German Thought*, Cambridge, Cambridge University Press.

Lips, Marguerite (1926), *Le style indirect libre*, Paris, Payot.

Loch, Wolfgang (1977), 'Some comments on the subject of psycho-analysis and truth', in Joseph H. Smith (ed.), *Thought, Consciousness and Reality*, New Haven, CT, Yale University Press.

Lothane, Zvi (1989), 'Schreber, Freud, Flechsig, and Weber revisited: an inquiry into methods of interpretation', *Psychoanalytic Review*, **76**, no. 2, 203–62.

Löwenfeld, Leopold (1899), *Sexualleben und Nervenleiden. Die Nervöse Störungen sexuellen Ursprungs*, Wiesbaden, J. F. Bergmann (2nd edn).

(1904), *Die psychischen Zwangserscheinungen*, Wiesbaden, J. F. Bergmann.

Ludwig, Emil (1946 [1947]), *Doctor Freud. An Analysis and a Warning*, New York, Hellman, Williams.

Luhmann, Niklas (1979), *Trust and Power*, New York, John Wiley and Sons.

Lydston, Frank G. (1889), 'Sexual perversion, satyriasis and nympho-mania', *Medical and Surgical Reporter*, **61**, 253–8 and 281–5.

Lynn, David J. (1993), 'Freud's analysis of A.B., a psychotic man, 1925–1930', *Journal of the American Academy of Psychoanalysis*, **21**, 1, 63–78.

Lynn, D. and Vaillant, G. (1998), 'Anonymity, neutrality and confidentiality in the actual methods of Freud', *American Journal of Psychiatry*, **155**, 163–71.

MacCurdy, John Thompson (1923), *Problems in Dynamic Psychology. A Critique of Psychoanalysis and Suggested Formulations*, New York, Macmillan.

Mach, Ernst (1976), *Knowledge and Error. Sketches on the Psychology of Enquiry*, ed. Brian McGuinness, trans. Thomas J. McCormack and Paul Foulkes, Dordrecht and Boston, D. Reidel.

Maciejewski, Franz (2006), 'Freud, his wife, and his "wife"', *American Imago*, **63**, 497–506.

MacIntyre, Alasdair (1958), *The Unconscious. A Conceptual Analysis*, London, Routledge & Kegan Paul.

(1976), 'Psychoanalysis: the future of an illusion', in *Against the Self-Images of the Age*, London, Duckworth, 27–37.

(1997), *Freud Evaluated. The Completed Arc*, Cambridge, MA, MIT Press (2nd, revised edn).

Mahony, Patrick (1986), *Freud and the Rat Man*, New Haven and London, Yale University Press.

(1992a), 'Freud as family therapist: reflections', in Toby Gelfand and John Kerr (eds.), *Freud and the History of Psychoanalysis*, Hillsdale, NJ, Analytic Press, 307–17.

(1992b), 'A psychoanalytic translation of Freud', in Darius G. Ornston (ed.), *Translating Freud*, New Haven and London, Yale University Press, 24–47.

(1996), *Freud's Dora. A Psychoanalytic, Historical, and Textual Study*, New Haven and London, Yale University Press.

Major, René (1999), *Au commencement. La vie la mort*, Paris, Galilée.

Makari, George J. (1997), 'Towards defining the Freudian unconscious: seduction, sexology and the negative of perversion (1896–1905)', *History of Psychiatry*, 8, no. 32, 459–86.

(1998a), 'Between seduction and libido: Sigmund Freud's masturbation hypotheses and the realignment of his etiologic thinking, 1897–1905', *Bulletin of the History of Medicine*, **72**, 638–62.

(1998b), 'Dora's hysteria and the maturation of Sigmund Freud's transference theory: a new historical interpretation', *Journal of the American Psychoanalytic Association*, **45**, no. 4, 1061–96.

(2008), *Revolution in Mind. The Creation of Psychoanalysis*, New York, HarperCollins.

Malcolm, Janet (1984), *In the Freud Archives*, New York, Knopf.

Marcinowski, Jaroslav (1900), 'Selbstbeobachtungen in der Hypnose', *Zeischrift für Hypnotismus*, **9**, 5–46.

Marmor, Judd (1962), 'Psychoanalytic therapy as an educational process', in Jules Masserman (ed.), *Psychoanalytic Education*, New York, Grune and Stratton, vol. 5, 286–99.

Massey, Irving (1990), 'Freud before Freud: K. A. Scherner (1825–1889)', *Centenial Review*, **34**, no. 4, 567–76.

Masson, Jeffrey Moussaïeff (1992), *The Assault on Truth. Freud's Suppression of the Seduction Theory*, New York, HarperCollins (3rd edn).

Maury, Alfred (1861), *Le sommeil et les rêves. Etudes psychologiques sur ces phénomènes*, Paris, Didier.

Mayer, Andreas (2001), 'L'hypnotisme introspectif et l'auto-analyse de Freud. Les procédés d'auto-observation dans la pratique clinique', *Revue d'histoire des sciences humaines*, **5**, 171–96.

McDougall, William (1936), *Psycho-Analysis and Social Psychology*, London, Methuen.

McGrath, William (1967), 'Student radicalism in Vienna', *Journal of Contemporary History*, **2**, 183–201.

Merton, Robert K. (1976), 'The ambivalence of scientists', *Sociological Ambivalence and Other Essays*, New York, Free Press.

Meyer, Catherine (ed.) (2005), with Mikkel Borch-Jacobsen, Jean Cottraux, Didier Pleux and Jacques Van Rillaer, *Le livre noir de la psychanalyse. Vivre, penser et aller mieux sans Freud*, Paris, Les Arènes.

Micale, Mark S. (1990), 'Charcot and the idea of hysteria in the male: gender, mental science, and medical diagnosis in late nineteenth-century France', *Medical History*, **34**, 4, 363–411.

(2008), *Hysterical Men. The Hidden History of Male Nervous Illness*, Cambridge, MA, Harvard University Press.

Mijolla, Alain de (1993), 'Freud, la biographie, son autobiographie et ses biographes', *Revue internationale d'histoire de la psychanalyse*, 81–108.

Mink, Louis O. (1965), 'The autonomy of historical understanding', *History and Theory*, 5, no. 1, 24–47.

Moll, Albert (1913 [1909]), *The Sexual Life of the Child*, trans. Eden Paul, New York, Macmillan.

(1936), *Ein Leben als Arzt der Seele. Erinnerungen*, Dresden, Carl Reissner.

Murchison, Carl (ed.) (1961– [1930–]), *A History of Psychology in Autobiography*, 5 vols., London, Russell & Russell.

Muthmann, Arthur (1907), *Zur Psychologie und Therapie neurotischer Symptome. Eine Studie auf Grund der Neurosenlehre Freuds*, Halle a/S, Carl Marhold Verlag.

Nietzsche, Friedrich (1895–1904), *Nietzsches Werke*, 11 vols., Leipzig, C. G. Naumann.

Nunberg, Herman and Federn, Ernst (eds.) (1962), *Minutes of the Vienna Psychoanalytic Society*, vol. 1: 1906–1908, trans. M. Nunberg, New York, International Universities Press.

(1967), *Minutes of the Vienna Psychoanalytic Society*, vol. 2: 1908–1910, trans. M. Nunberg, New York, International Universities Press.

(1974), *Minutes of the Vienna Psychoanalytic Society*, vol. 3: 1910–1911, trans. M. Nunberg, New York, International Universities Press.

(1977), *Protokolle der Wiener Psychoanalytischen Vereinigung*, vol. 2: 1908–1910, Frankfurt am Main, S. Fischer Verlag.

Obholzer, Karin (1982), *The Wolf-Man. Conversations with Freud's Patient – Sixty Years Later*, trans. Michael Shaw, New York, Continuum.

Ohayon, Annick (1999), *L'impossible rencontre. Psychologie et psychanalyse en France 1919–1969*, Paris, La Découverte.

Onfray, Michel (2010), *Le crépuscule d'une idole. L'affabulation freudienne*, Paris, Grasset.

Pascal, Roy (1977), *The Dual Voice. Free Indirect Speech and Its Functionning in the Nineteenth-Century European Novel*, Manchester, Manchester University Press.

Pickering, Andrew (1995), *The Mangle of Practice. Time, Agency, and Science*, Chicago, IL, and London, University of Chicago Press.

Popper, Karl (1963), *Conjectures and Refutations. The Growth of Scientific Knowledge*, London, Routledge and Kegan Paul.

Popper [Lynkeus], Josef (1899), *Phantasien eines Realisten*, 2 vols., Dresden and Leipzig, Carl Reissner.

Porter, Roy (1986), 'The scientific revolution: a spoke in the wheel?', in Roy Porter and Mikuláš Teich (eds.), *Revolution in History*, Cambridge, Cambridge University Press, 290–316.

Prince, Morton (1911), 'The mechanism and interpretation of dreams: a reply to Dr. Jones', *Journal of Abnormal Psychology*, 5, 337–53.

(1929), *Clinical and Experimental Studies in Personality*, Cambridge, Sci-Art.

Puner, Helen Walker (1947), *Freud. His Life and his Mind. A Biography*, New York, Howell, Soskin.

Putnam, James Jackson (1906), 'Recent experiences in the study and treatment of hysteria at Massachusetts General Hospital', *Journal of Abnormal Psychology*, 1, 26–41.

(1911), 'What is psychoanalysis?' Putnam papers, Countway Library of Medicine, Boston.

Rank, Otto (1910), review of Freud's presentation on the case of the Rat-Man at the private psychoanalytic meeting held in Salzburg, 27 April 1908, *Zentralblatt für Psychoanalyse: Medizinische Monatschrift für Seelenkunde*, 1, 125–6.

(1996), *A Psychology of Difference. The American Lectures*, ed. Robert Kramer, Princeton, NJ, Princeton University Press.

Ricoeur, Jean-Paul (1970), *Freud and Philosophy. An Essay on Interpretation*, trans. Denis Savage, New Haven, CT, Yale University Press.

(1974), 'A philosophical interpretation of Freud', in *The Conflict of Interpretations*, Evanston, IL, Northwestern University Press, 160–76.

(1981), 'The question of proof in Freud's psychoanalytic writings', in *Hermeneutics and the Human Sciences. Essays on Language, Action, and Interpretation*, Cambridge, Cambridge University Press, 247–73.

Rieger, Konrad (1896), 'Über die Behandlung "Nervenkranker"', *Schmidt's Jahrbücher der in- und ausländischen gesammten Medicin*, 251, 193–8, 273–6.

Ritvo, Lucille B. (1990), *Darwin's Influence on Freud. A Tale of Two Sciences*, New Haven, CT, Yale University Press.

Roazen, Paul (1969), *Brother Animal. The Story of Freud and Tausk*, New York, New York University Press.

(1975), *Freud and his Followers*, New York, Knopf.

(1985), *Helene Deutsch. A Psychoanalyst's Life*, New York, Anchor Press.

(1990), *Encountering Freud. The Politics and Histories of Psychoanalysis*, New Brunswick, NJ, Transaction.

Rose, Steven (1993), *The Making of Memory*, New York, Anchor Books.

Rosenzweig, Saul (1986), *Freud and Experimental Psychology. The Emergence of Idiodynamics*, St Louis, Rana House.

Roustang, François (1986), *Dire Mastery. Discipleship from Freud to Lacan*, trans. Ned Lukacher, Washington, DC, American Psychiatric Press.

Sachs, Heinrich (1893), *Vorträge über Bau und Tätigkeit des Großhirns und die Lehre von der Aphasie und Seelenblindheit*, Breslau.

Sand, Rosemarie (1992), 'Pre-Freudian discovery of dream meaning: the achievements of Charcot, Janet, and Krafft-Ebing', in Toby Gelfand and John Kerr (eds.), *Freud and the History of Psychoanalysis*, Hillsdale, NJ, Analytic Press, 215–29.

Satzinger, Helga (1998), *Die Geschichte der genetisch orientieren Hirnforschung von Cécile und Oskar Vogt in der Zeit von 1895 bis ca. 1927*, Stuttgart, Deutscher Apotheker Verlag.

Saussure, Raymond de (1926), 'La psychologie du rêve dans la tradition française', in René Laforgue (ed.), *Le rêve et la psychanalyse*, Paris, Maloine, 18–59.

(1957), 'Sigmund Freud', *Schweizerische Zeitschrift für Psychologie und ihre Anwendungen/Revue suisse de psychologie pure et appliquée*, 16, 136–9.

Schafer, Roy (1980), 'Narration in the Psychoanalytic Dialogue', *Critical Inquiry*, 7, no. 1, 29–53.

Scharnberg, Max (1993), *The Non-Authentic Nature of Freud's Observations*, 2 vols., Acta Universitatis Upsaliensis, Uppsala, Studies in Education.

Scherner, Karl Albert (1861), *Das Leben des Traums*, Berlin, Heinrich Schindler.

Schimek, Jean G. (1987), 'Fact and fantasy in the seduction theory: a historical review', *Journal of the American Psychoanalytic Association*, **35**, 937–65.

Schreber, Daniel Paul (1955 [1903]), *Memoirs of My Nervous Illness*, ed. and trans. Ida Macalpine and Richard A. Hunt, London, W. Dawson.

Schröter, Michael and Hermanns, Ludger M. (1992), 'Felix Gattel (1870–1904): Freud's first pupil. Part 1', *International Review of Psychoanalysis*, **19**, 91–104.

Schur, Max (1966), 'Some additional "day residues" of the specimen dream of psychoanalysis', in Rudolp M. Löwenstein, Lottie M. Newman, Max Schur and Albert J. Solnit (eds.), *Psychoanalysis, a General Psychology. Essays in Honor of Heinz Hartmann*, New York, Intenational Universities Press, 45–85.

(1972), *Freud, Living and Dying*, London, Hogarth Press.

Schwartz, Joseph (1999), *Cassandra's Daughter. A History of Psychoanalysis in Europe and America*, London, Allen Lane.

Shakow, David and Rapaport, David (1968), *The Influence of Freud on American Psychology*, Cleveland, OH, Meridian Books.

Shamdasani, Sonu (1995), 'Memories, dreams, omissons', *Spring: A Journal of Archetype and Culture*, **57**, 115–37.

(1997), '"Should this remain?" Anna Freud's misgivings concerning the Freud–Jung letters', in Patrick Mahony, Carlo Bonomi and Jan Stensson (eds.), *Behind the Scenes. Freud in Correspondence*, Oslo, Scandinavian University Press, 357–68.

(1998), *Cult Fictions. C. G. Jung and the Founding of Analytical Psychology*, London, Routledge.

(2002), 'Psychoanalysis, Inc.', *Semiotic Review of Books*, **13**, no. 1, 6–11.

(2003a), *Jung and the Making of Modern History. The Dream of a Science*, Cambridge, Cambridge University Press.

(2003b), 'Psychoanalysis in the mirror of literature', in *Richard Strauss' Elektra*, London, Royal Opera House, 48–52.

(2004), 'Psychologies as ontology-making practices: William James and the pluralities of psychological experience', in Jeremy Carette (ed.), *William James and the Varieties of Religious Experience*, London, Routledge, 27–46.

(2005a), *Jung Stripped Bare by His Biographers, Even*, London and New York, Karnac Books.

(2005b), 'Psychotherapy: the invention of a word', *History of the Human Sciences*, 18, 1–22.

(2006), 'Auguste Forel', in W. F. and Helen Bynum (eds.), *Dictionary of Medical Biography*, vol. 2., Westport, CT, Greenwood Press, 508–9.

Shapin, Steven (1984), 'Pump and circumstances: Robert Boyle's literary theory', *Social Studies of Science*, 14, 481–520.

(1994), *A Social History of Truth. Civility and Science in Seventeenth-Century England*, Chicago, IL, University of Chicago Press.

Shapin, Steven and Schaffer, Simon (1986), *Leviathan and the Air-Pump. Hobbes, Boyle and the Politics of Experiment*, Princeton, NJ, Princeton University Press.

Sherwood, Michael (1969), *The Logic of Explanation in Psychoanalysis*, New York, Academic Press.

Skues, Richard A. (1998), 'The first casualty: the war over psychoanalysis and the poverty of historiography', *History of Psychiatry*, 9, no. 2, 151–77.

(2001), 'On the dating of Freud's *Aliquis slip*', *International Journal of Psychoanalysis*, 86, no. 6, 1185–204.

(2006), *Sigmund Freud and the History of Anna O. Reopening a Closed Case*, Basingstoke and New York, Palgrave Macmillan.

Smith, Dinitia (1995), 'Freud may be dead, but his critics still kick', *The New York Times*, 10 December 1995.

Spector, Jack (1972), *The Aesthetics of Freud. A Study in Psychoanalysis and Art*, New York, Praeger.

Spence, Donald P. (1982), *Narrative Truth and Historical Truth. Meaning and Interpretation in Psychoanalysis*, New York, Norton.

Spielmeyer, Walther (1905), review of Sigmund Freud, 'Fragment d'une analyse d'hystérie', *Centralblat für Nervenheilkunde und Psychiatrie*, 15 April, 322–4.

Spitzer, Leo (1928), 'Zur Entstehung der sog. "erlebten Rede"', *Germanisch-Romanische Monatsschrift*, 16, 327ff.

Stadlen, Anthony (1989), 'Was Dora "Ill"?', in Laurence Spurling (ed.), *Sigmund Freud. Critical Assessments*, London, Routledge, vol. 1, 196–203.

(2003), 'Just how interesting psychoanalysis really is', *Arc de Cercle. An International Journal of the History of the Mind-Sciences*, 1, no. 1, 143–75.

Stekel, Wilhelm (1911), 'Festgruss an den dritten psychoanalytischen Kongress in Weimar', *Zentralblatt für Psychoanalyse*, 1, 36.

(1925), 'Zur Geschichte der analytischen Bewegung', *Fortschritte der Sexualwissenschaft und Psychoanalyse*, 2, supplement, 539–75.

(1950), *The Autobiography of Wihelm Stekel. The Life Story of a Pioneer Psychoanalyst*, ed. Emil Gutheil, New York, Liveright.

Stengers, Isabelle (1992), *La volonté de faire science. À propos de la psychanalyse*, Paris, Les Empêcheurs de Penser en Rond, Synthélabo.

(2002), *L'hypnose entre magie et science*, Paris, Les Empêcheurs de Penser en Rond/Seuil.

Stepansky, Paul (1993), *In Freud's Shadow. Alfred Adler in Context*, Hillsdale, NJ, Analytic Press.

Stern, William (1900), 'Die psychologische Arbeit des neunzehnten Jahrhunderts, insbesondere in Deutschland', *Zeitschrift für pädagogische Psychologie und Pathologie*, 2, 413–36.

(1913), in *Bericht über die Jahresversammlung des Deutschen Vereins für Psychiatrie zu Breslau am 13. und 14. Mai 1913*, *Allgemeine Zeitschrift für Psychiatrie*, 70, 784–6.

Stone, Irving (1971), *The Passions of the Mind. A Novel of Sigmund Freud*, Garden City, NY, Doubleday.

Strachey, James (1958), 'Editor's introduction', *SE* 12, 85–8.

(1976), 'Sigmund Freud: a sketch of his life and ideas', in *Pelican Freud*, vol. 5: *The Psychopathology of Everyday Life*, Harmondsworth, Penguin, 11–24.

Stransky, Erwin (1913), in *Bericht über die Jahresversammlung des Deutschen Vereins für Psychiatrie zu Breslau am 13. und 14. Mai 1913*, *Allgemeine Zeitschrift für Psychiatrie*, 70, 786.

Sulloway, Frank J. (1992a), *Freud, Biologist of the Mind. Beyond the Psychoanalytic Legend*, Cambridge, MA, Harvard University Press (2nd revised edn).

(1992b), 'Reassessing Freud's case histories: the social construction of psychoanalysis', in Toby Gelfand and John Kerr (eds.), *Freud and the History of Psychoanalysis*, Hillsdale, NJ, Analytic Press, 153–92.

Swales Peter J. (1982a), *Freud, Johann Weier, and the Status of Seduction. The Role of the Witch in the Conception of Phantasy*, New York, privately published by the author.

(1982b), 'Freud, Minna Bernays, and the conquest of Rome: new light on the origins of psychoanalysis', *New American Review*, 1, no. 2–3, 1–23.

(1982c), *Freud, Fliess, and Fratricide. The Role of Fliess in* Freud's Conception of Paranoia', privately published by the author.

(1983), *Freud, Krafft-Ebing, and the Witches. The Role of Krafft-Ebing in Freud's Flight into Fantasy*, New York, privately published by the author.

(1986), 'Freud, his teacher and the birth of psychoanalysis', in Paul E. Stepansky (ed.), *Freud. Appraisals and Reappraisals*, vol. 1, Hillsdale, NJ, Analytic Press, 2–82.

(1988), 'Freud, Katharina, and the first "wild analysis"', in Paul Stepansky (ed.), *Freud. Appraisals and Reappraisals*, vol. 3, Hillsdale, NJ, Analytic Press, 81–164.

(1989), 'Freud, cocaine, and sexual chemistry: the role of cocaine in Freud's conception of the libido', in Laurence Spurling (ed.), *Sigmund Freud. Critical Assessments*, vol. 1, London, Routledge, 273–301.

(1991), 'Freud and the unconscionable: the obstruction of Freud studies, 1946–2113', lecture given at the Institute of Contemporary Arts, London.

(1994). 'Did Freud always carry an umbrella – or – did he ever take a cab?', lecture presented at the Institute of Contemporary Arts, London.

(1995), 'Freud's Immaculate Conception: passion plays, private theater and private religions in the prehistory of psychoanalysis', lecture given to the conference 'The Psychoanalytic Century: Psyche, Soma, Gender, Word', New York University, 4–6 May.

(1996), 'Freud, his Ur-patient, and their romance of Oedipus and their descent into pre-history: the role of 'Herr E.' in the conception of psychoanalysis', lecture given to the History of Psychiatry Section, Cornell Medical Center, New York Hospital, 4 December.

(2003), 'Freud, death and sexual pleasures: on the psychical mechanism of Dr. Sigmund Freud', *Arc-de-Cercle. An International Journal
of the History of the Mind-Sciences*, 1, no. 1, 6–74.

Szasz, Thomas (1989 [1963]), 'Freud as a leader', in Laurence Spurling
(ed.), *Sigmund Freud. Critical Assessments*, vol. 4, London,
Routledge, 146–155.

Talbot, Margaret (1998), 'The Museum show has an ego disorder', *The
New York Times Magazine*, 11 October, 56–60.

Tanner, Terence A. (2003), 'Sigmund Freud and the *Zeitschrift für
Hypnotismus*', *Arc de Cercle. An International Journal of the History
of the Mind-Sciences*, 1, no. 1, 75–142.

The Lancet (1938), 11 June, 1341.

Thornton, E. M. (1983), *Freud and Cocaine. The Freudian Fallacy*,
London, Blond & Briggs.

Tichy, Marina, and Zwetter-Otte, Sylvia (1999), *Freud in der Presse.
Rezeption Sigmunds Freuds und der Psychoanalyse in Österreich 1895–
1938*, Vienna, Sonderzahl.

Trilling, Lionel (1950), *The Liberal Imagination. Essays on Literature and
Society*, Garden City, NY, Doubleday.

Trosman, Harry and Wolf, Ernest S. (1973), 'The Bernfeld collaboration
in the Jones biography of Freud', *International Journal of
Psychoanalysis*, **54**, 227–33.

Veith, Ilza (1965), *Hysteria. The History of a Disease*, Chicago, IL, The
University of Chicago Press.

Veszy-Wagner, Lilla (1966), 'Ernest Jones (1879–1958), The Biography of
Freud', in Franz Alexander, Samuel Eisenstein and Martin Grotjahn
(eds.), *Psychoanalytic Pioneers*, New York, Basic Books.

Veyne, Paul (1971), *Comment on écrit l'histoire. Essai d'épistémologie*,
Paris, Seuil.

Vidal, Fernando (1994a), *Piaget before Piaget*, Cambridge, MA, Harvard
University Press.

Viderman, Serge (1970), *La construction de l'espace analytique*, Paris, Denoël.

Vogel, L. Z. (1986), 'The case of Elise Gomperz', *American Journal of
Psychoanalysis*, **46**, no. 3, 230–8.

Vogt, Oskar (1898), 'Zur Methodik der ätiologischen Erforschung der
Hysterie', *Zeitschrift für Hypnotismus*, 8, 65–83.

(1899), review of 'S. Freud, "Die Sexualität in der Aetiologie [der Neurosen]," *Wiener klinische Rundschau*, 12 Jahrg. 1898', *Zeitschrift für Hypnotismus*, 8, 366–7.

Wallerstein, Robert (1988), 'One psychoanalysis or many?', *International Journal of Psycho-Analysis*, **69**, 5–21.

(1995), *The Psychoanalyses and the Psychotherapies*, New Haven, CT, Yale University Press.

Warda, W. (1900), 'Ein Fall von Hysterie: dargestellt nach der kathartischen Methode von Breuer und Freud', *Monatschrift für Psychiatrie und Neurologie*, **7**, 301–18 and 471–89.

Webster, Richard (1995), *Why Freud Was Wrong. Sin, Science, and Psychoanalysis*, New York, Basic Books.

Weininger, Otto (1903), *Geschlecht und Charakter. Eine principielle Untersuchung*, Vienna, Braumüller.

Wells, Harry K. (1960), *Pavlov and Freud*, vol. 2: *Sigmund Freud. A Pavlovian Critique*, New York, International Publishers.

Weygandt, Wilhelm (1907), 'Kritische Bemerkungen zur Psychologie der Dementia Praecox', *Monatschrift für Psychiatrie und Neurologie*, **22**, 289–302.

(1913), in *Bericht über die Jahresversammlung des Deutschen Vereins für Psychiatrie zu Breslau am 13. und 14. Mai 1913*, *Allgemeine Zeitschrift für Psychiatrie*, **70**, 787–8.

Wilkinson, Ronald (1985), Section 'History of science/ Psychoanalytic collections', *Library of Congress Acquisitions, Manuscript Division*, 27–31.

Wittels, Fritz (1924), *Sigmund Freud. His Personality, His Teaching, & His School*, ed. C. Paul, London, George Allen & Unwin.

Wittenberger, Gerhard and Teugel, Christopher (1999), *Die Rundbriefe des 'Geheime Komitees'*, vol. 1: *1913–1920*, Tübingen, Edition Diskord.

Wittgenstein, Ludwig (1966), *Lectures and Conversations on Aesthetics, Psychology and Religious Belief*, ed. Cyril Barrett, Oxford, Blackwell.

Wohlgemuth, Adolf (1923), *A Critical Examination of Psycho-Analysis*, New York, Macmillan.

(1924), 'The refutation of psychoanalysis', *Journal of Mental Science*, July.

Woodworth, Robert Sessions (1917), 'Some criticisms of the Freudian psychology', *Journal of Abnormal Psychology*, **12**, 174–94.

Wortis, Joseph (1954), *Fragments of an Analysis with Freud*, New York, Simon & Schuster.

Wundt, Wilhelm (1921), *Erlebtes und Erkanntes*, Stuttgart, Alfred Kröner Verlag.

Wyss, Dieter (1961), *Die tiefenpsychologischen Schulen von den Anfängen bis zur Gegenwart*, Göttingen, Vandenhoeck & Ruprecht.

Yerushalmi, Yosef Hayim (1996), 'Série Z. Une fantaisie archivistique', *Le Débat*, **92**, 141–52.

Young-Bruehl, Elisabeth (1989), *Anna Freud*, London, Macmillan.

Zilboorg, Gregory (1941), *History of Medical Psychology*, New York, Norton.

Index of names